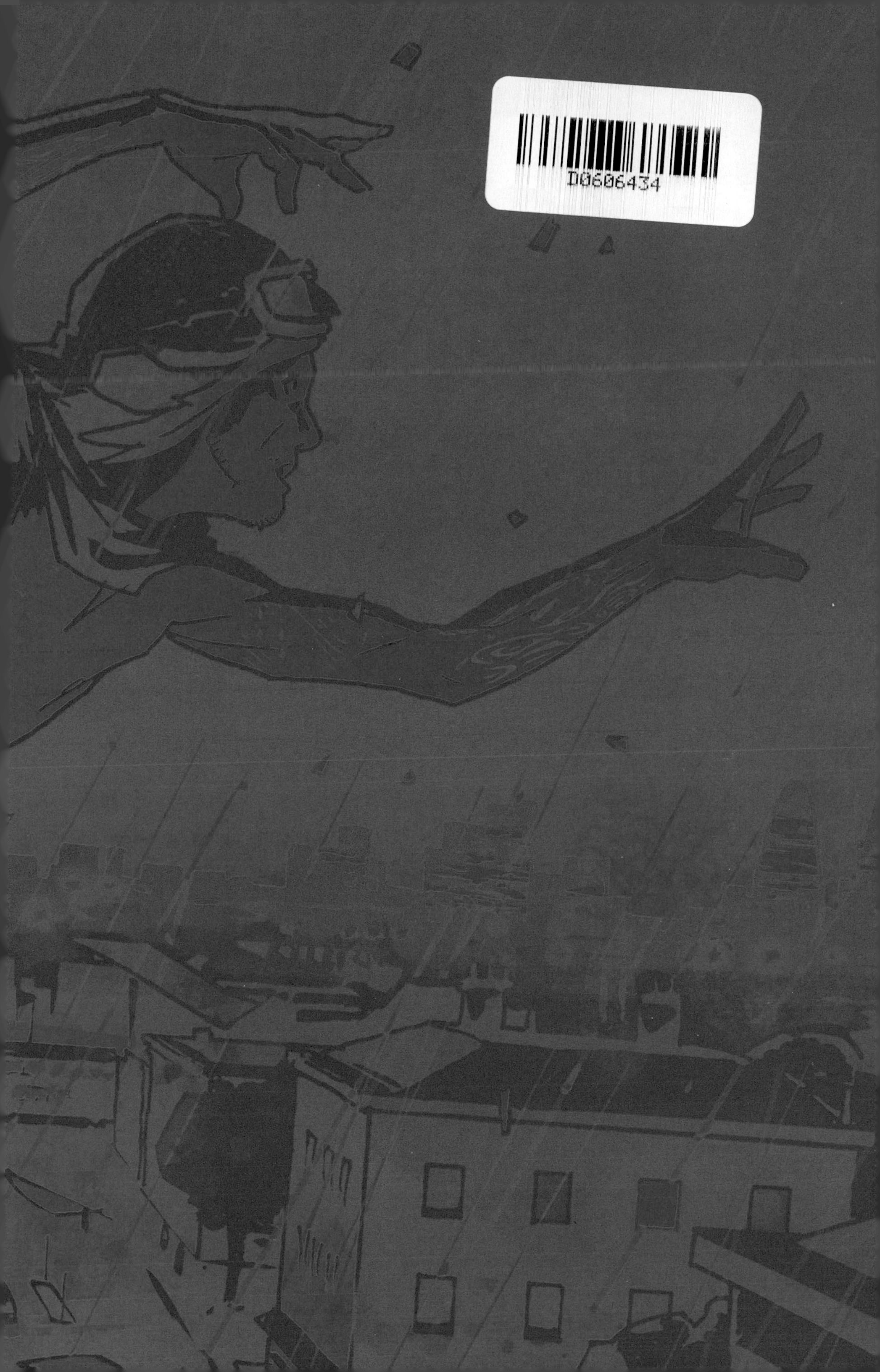

DEATH SENTENCE

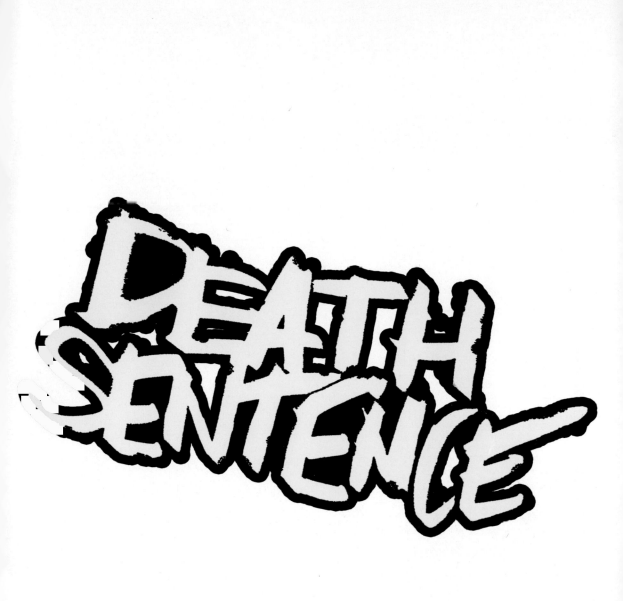

TITAN COMICS

Montynero

Andrew James

Dan Bura

Russ Seal, Dan Bura, Rob Farmer, Siobhan Gallagher

Steve White

Gabriela Houston

Obi Onoura

Jackie Flook, Maria Pearson

Peter James

Selina Juneja

Steve Tothill

Ricky Claydon

Owen Johnson

Darryl Tothill

Chris Teather

Leigh Baulch

Vivian Cheung

Nick Landau

Montynero
Props to everyone who offered kind words of encouragement and advice, especially David Lloyd, Eddie Deighton, Jon Sloan, Andy Diggle, Kieron Gillen, John Freeman, Rob Williams, Al Ewing, Nick Landau, Chris Teather, Ned Hartley, Andrew James, Klaus Janson, Diamond UK, Dave Gibbons, Mark Millar and my Dad. And the biggest thanks of all to Mike, for drawing this so well - and the readers who supported us all the way.

Mike Dowling
Big thanks to Monty for having faith that I could draw the book. Thanks also to Mark Millar and everyone at Titan for getting it out there.

ISBN: 9781782760085
Published by Titan Comics, a division of Titan Publishing Group Ltd. 144 Southwark St. London, SE1 0UP

A CIP catalogue record for this title is available from the British Library. First edition: August 2014.

10 9 8 7 6 5 4 3 2 1

Printed in China.
Titan Comics. TC019

Page 07 quote from The Language of the Genes, written by Steve Jones and originally published in 2000 by Flamingo, an imprint of HarperCollins Publishers.

readercomments@titanemail.com

To receive news, competitions, and exclusive offers online, please sign up for the Titan Comics newsletter on our website:

www.titan-comics.com

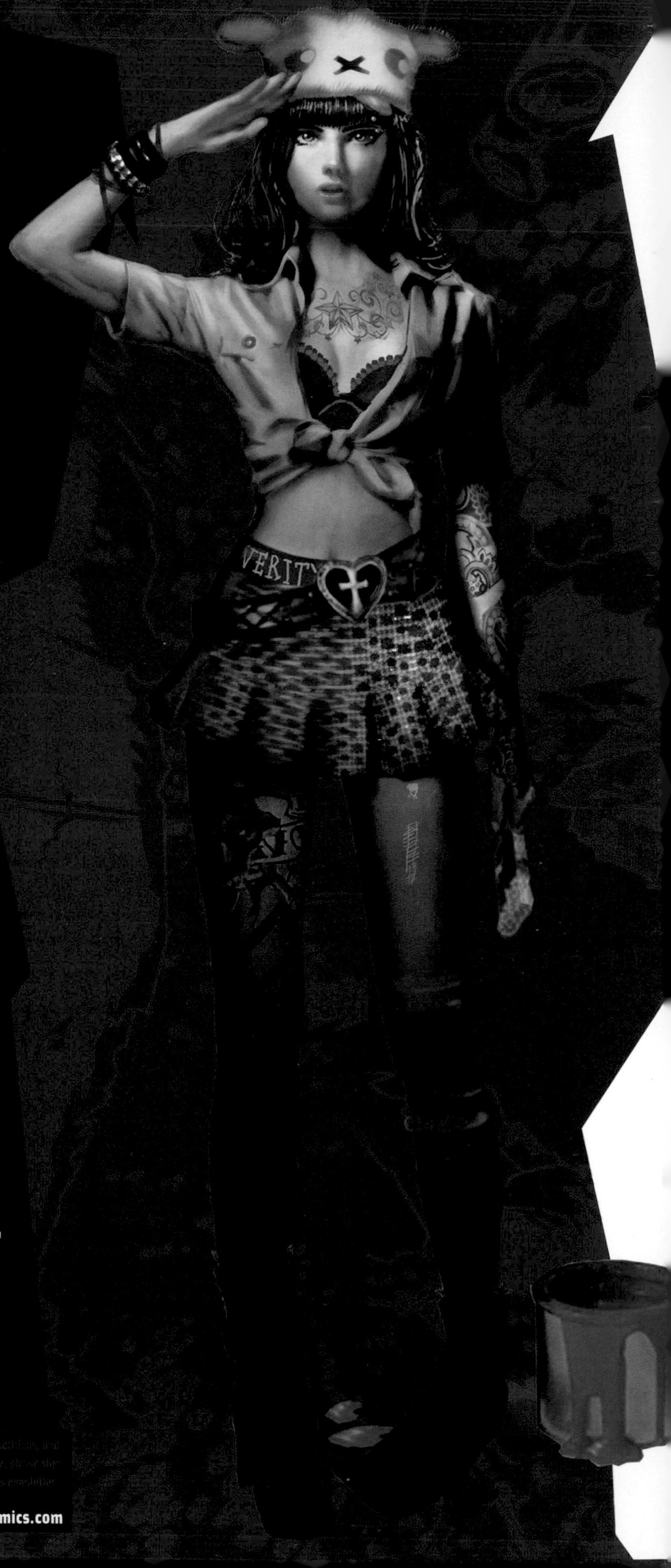

COVERS & SCRIPT
MONTYNERO

ART & COLORS
MIKE DOWLING

LETTERING
COMICRAFT'S JIMMY BETANCOURT

Titan
COMICS

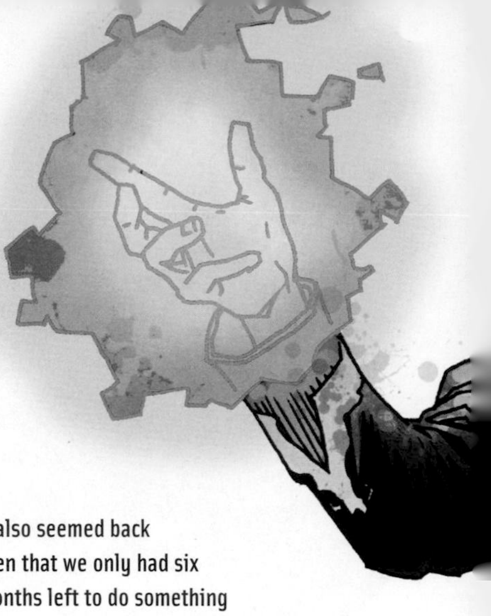

INTRODUCTION

It all started at the Hi-Ex comic convention, nestled in the Scottish highlands on the banks of the river Ness. It was a wonderful event: relaxed but exciting; informal and unpretentious. Lovely people, warmed by the spring sun, creators and fans mingling as one, families and children soaking it all in without cynicism. It's still my favorite ever comic con.

It was just what I needed - because I was frustrated. I love comics with an irrational passion and I'd come to the con to try and reconnect to the things that brought me joy and satisfaction, rather than the things that made me money. I was so creatively frustrated, in fact, that I was willing to do more or less anything it took to make myself content. There was a restless ache within me to create a comic book, to create something personal, to create something I owned. I felt I wouldn't die happy unless I did it, and the thought of spending the next forty years wondering 'what if' and dying bitter and frustrated, and then haunting my descendants with pained and incoherent groaning about sequential storytelling was too much to bear.

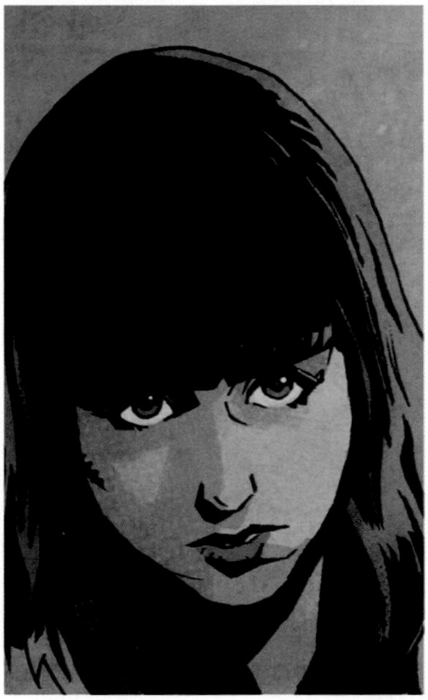

In the spirit of full disclosure you should know that my wife was with child, which was truly joyous news! It was the kind of news that left you in a grinning stupor – that made you want to buy a top hat just so you could throw it in the air and dance like a loon. But it also seemed back then that we only had six months left to do something recklessly creative before beginning a new life of sober responsibility and financial prudence. Absolute bollocks, as it turned out, but a very powerful feeling at the time. And from that turbulent well of emotions sprang the G+ virus, the catalyst for our story.

I didn't care if no-one read the comic (though I'd rather they did) and I didn't care if it was financially and emotionally disastrous (though I'd prefer it wasn't). I was going to do this thing and to hell with the consequences.

I'd probably still be toiling away at it if I hadn't met the inestimable Mike Dowling who is a) a lovely bloke, and b) a much better comic artist than I am. Recognising your limitations and working with people more talented than yourself is the key to success, trust me.

So we made this comic together, and we put our heart and soul into it. For my own part I put everything I knew about life, creativity, sex, humour, art and music into a vast pot and stirred it around until it tasted like a great story.

I really hope you enjoy *Death Sentence*, but I don't mind if you don't. Because we did it, and I can die happy now.

Cheers,
Monty, Dundee, 2014

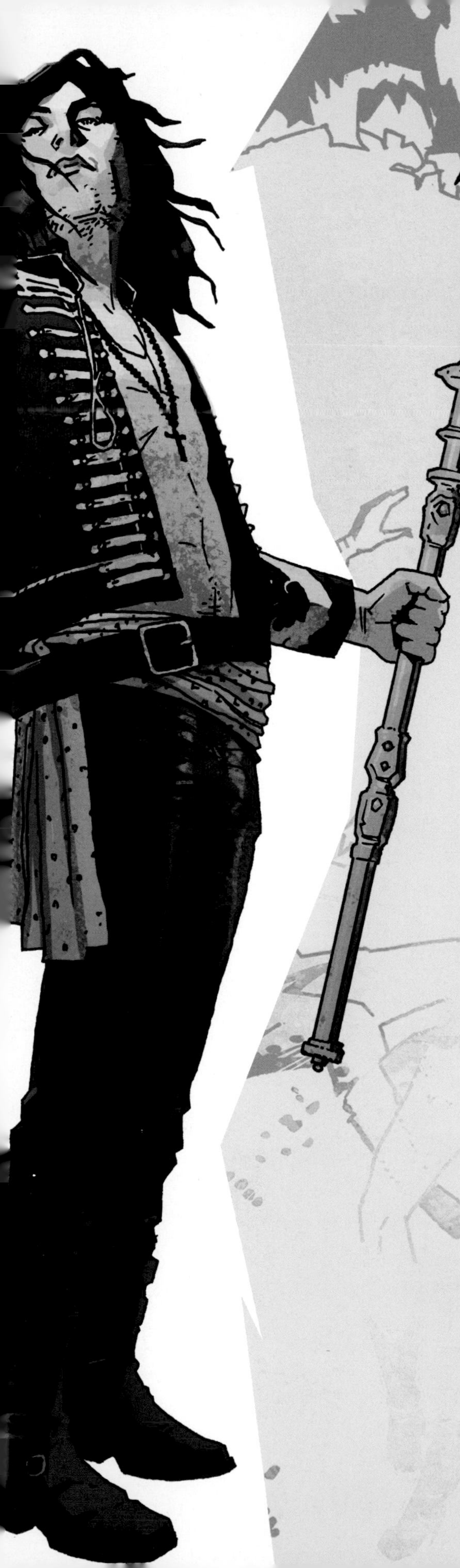

When you're making a comic, it's the easiest thing in the world to have someone fly, explode, or be superfast. Superpowers are the common language of the medium. Just as Eskimos have fifty words for snow, so the stories that can be written with this vocabulary are many and varied. But the extraordinary doesn't stand out on the comic page unless you make it do something else, something *other*. Something with a dynamic, resonant hook.

For *Death Sentence,* that hook is adding superpowers to sex, drugs, and rock'n'roll. Possibly in that order. And who among us doesn't love sex, drugs and rock'n'roll – as Mary Whitehouse may well not have said...? There's celebrity here, too – a deconstruction of the tabloid's love of excess, in a narrative with a loud, satirical punk edge.

Death Sentence's G+ Virus, that provides its contractee with superpowers, is a sexually-transmitted disease. Sex is in the very inception of the book (and it fills a great deal of the panels, too). It's a sharp, 21st Century idea. And the virus also gives the sufferer six months to live – now that's what writers call an 'elevator pitch'! Would you have superpowers if it meant you'd die in six months?

There's plainly a sharp mind behind the often surprisingly lyrical script. Montynero is that credited mind (the insane and egotistical bad guy's called Monty too; hmmm...) and *Death Sentence* is brilliantly depicted by Mike Dowling, whose accessible storytelling pleasingly never loses the characters amidst the debauchery and ultra-violence.

Lastly – any story only goes as far as its characters. *Death Sentence*'s cast can be largely obnoxious, but they have heart and soul, too.

Enjoy!

ROB WILLIAMS, March 2014

Rob Williams is the celebrated writer of such titles as *The Royals: Masters of War, Ordinary, 2000AD,* and Marvel's *Revolutionary War*.

CHAPTER LIST

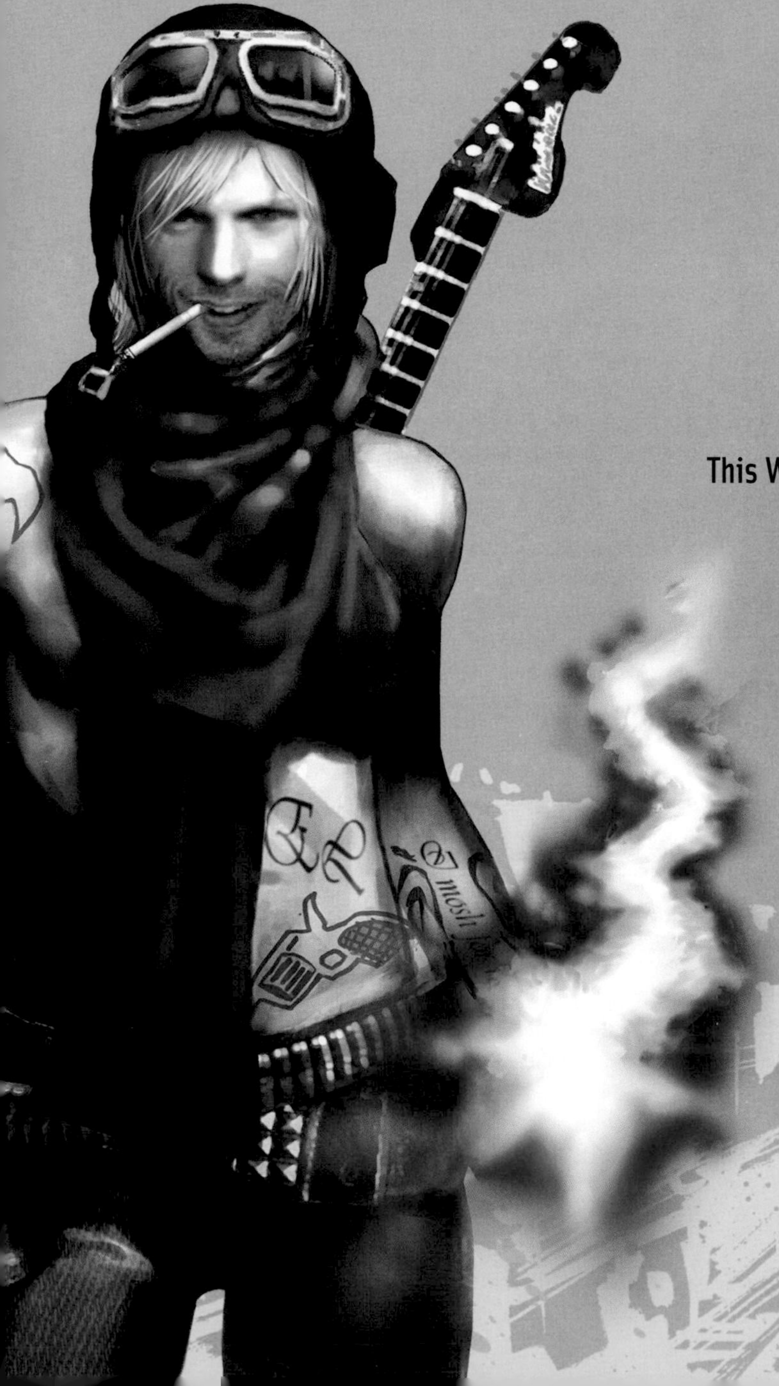

"SEX RESHUFFLES LIFE'S CARDS: IT MAKES BEAUTIFUL GENIUSES WHO SURVIVE AND UGLY FOOLS WHO DO NOT. IT IS A CONVENIENT WAY TO BRING TOGETHER THE BEST AND PURGE THE WORST AND TO SEPARATE THE FATE OF GENES FROM THAT OF THOSE WHO CARRY THEM.

RECOMBINATION IS A REDEMPTION, WHICH, EACH GENERATION, REVERSES BIOLOGICAL DECAY. IN SOME WAYS, IT IS THE KEY TO IMMORTALITY; A FOUNTAIN OF ETERNAL YOUTH – NOT FOR THOSE WHO INDULGE IN IT, BUT FOR THE GENES THEY CARRY."

STEVE JONES, THE LANGUAGE OF THE GENES

DEATH SENTENCE

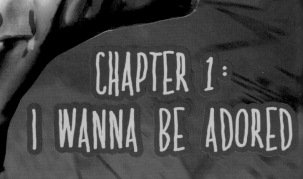

CHAPTER 1:
I WANNA BE ADORED

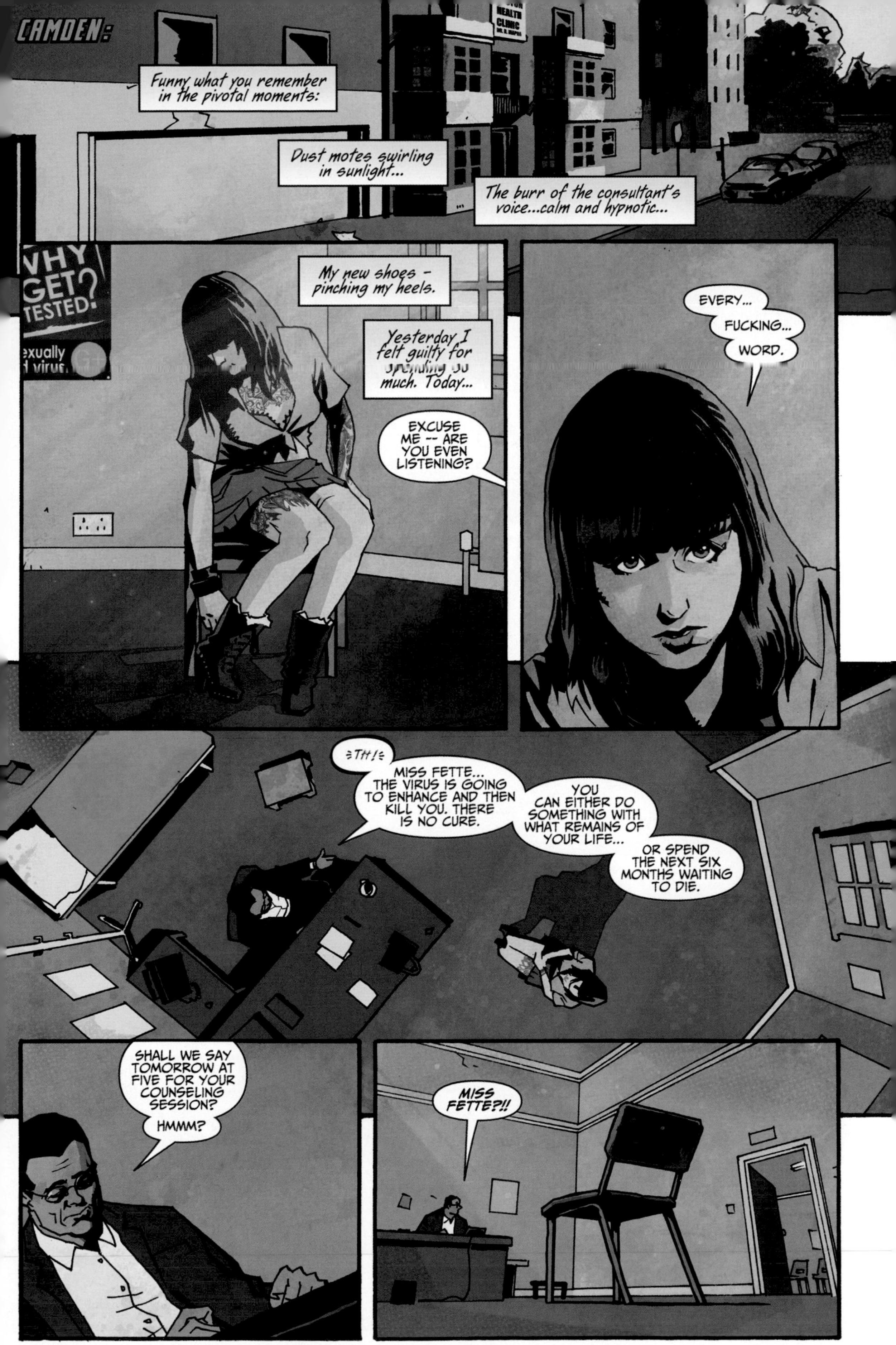

CAMDEN:
HEALTH CLINIC
Funny what you remember in the pivotal moments:
Dust motes swirling in sunlight...
The burr of the consultant's voice...calm and hypnotic...
My new shoes - pinching my heels.
Yesterday I felt guilty for
much. Today...
EXCUSE ME -- ARE YOU EVEN LISTENING?
EVERY...
FUCKING...
WORD.
MISS FETTE... THE VIRUS IS GOING TO ENHANCE AND THEN KILL YOU. THERE IS NO CURE.
YOU CAN EITHER DO SOMETHING WITH WHAT REMAINS OF YOUR LIFE...
OR SPEND THE NEXT SIX MONTHS WAITING TO DIE.
SHALL WE SAY TOMORROW AT FIVE FOR YOUR COUNSELING SESSION?
HMMM?
MISS FETTE?!!

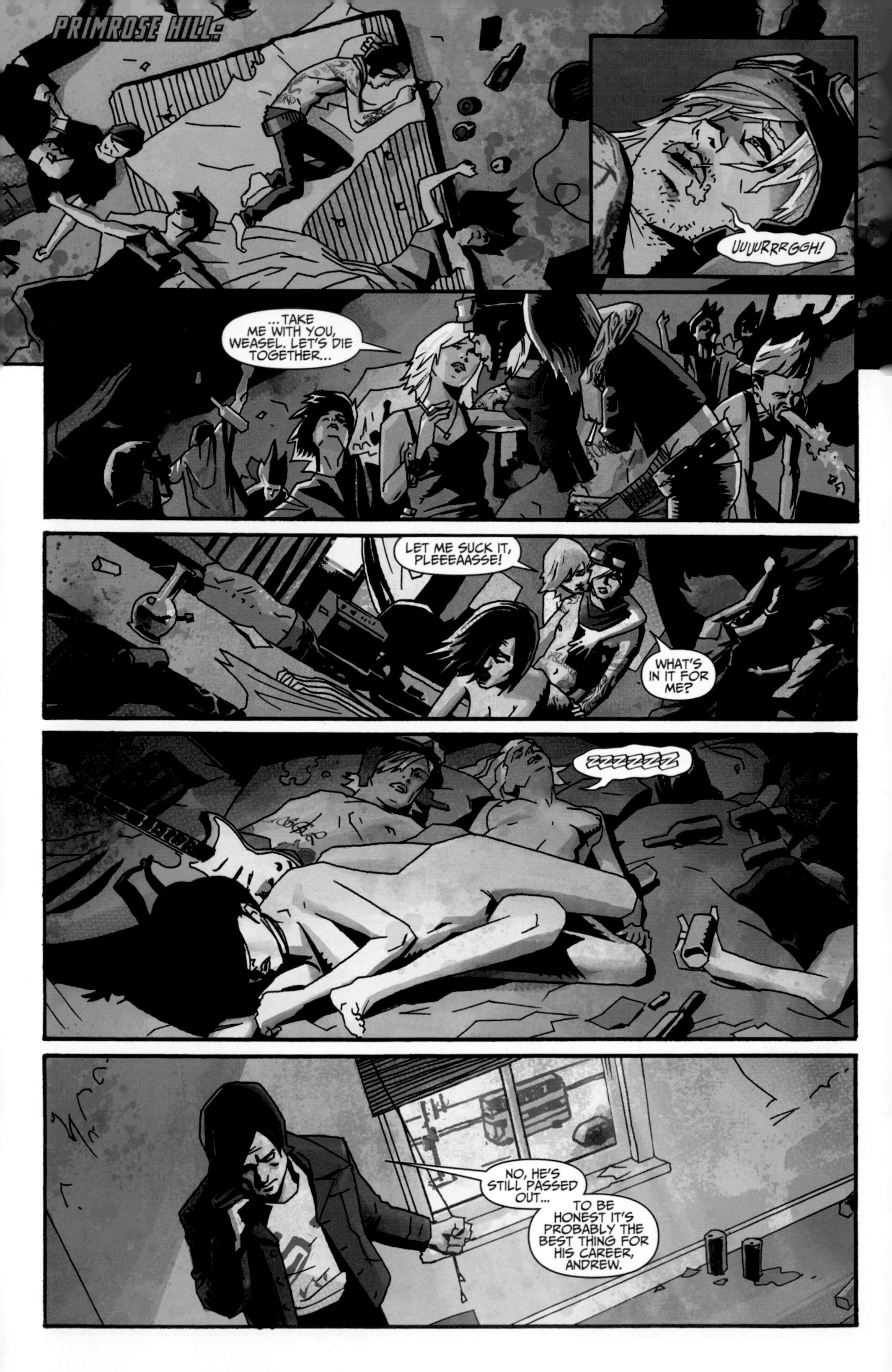
PRIMROSE HILL:
UUUURRRGGH!
...TAKE ME WITH YOU, WEASEL. LET'S DIE TOGETHER...
LET ME SUCK IT, PLEEEAASSE!
WHAT'S IN IT FOR ME?
ZZZZZZZ
NO, HE'S STILL PASSED OUT...
TO BE HONEST IT'S PROBABLY THE BEST THING FOR HIS CAREER, ANDREW.

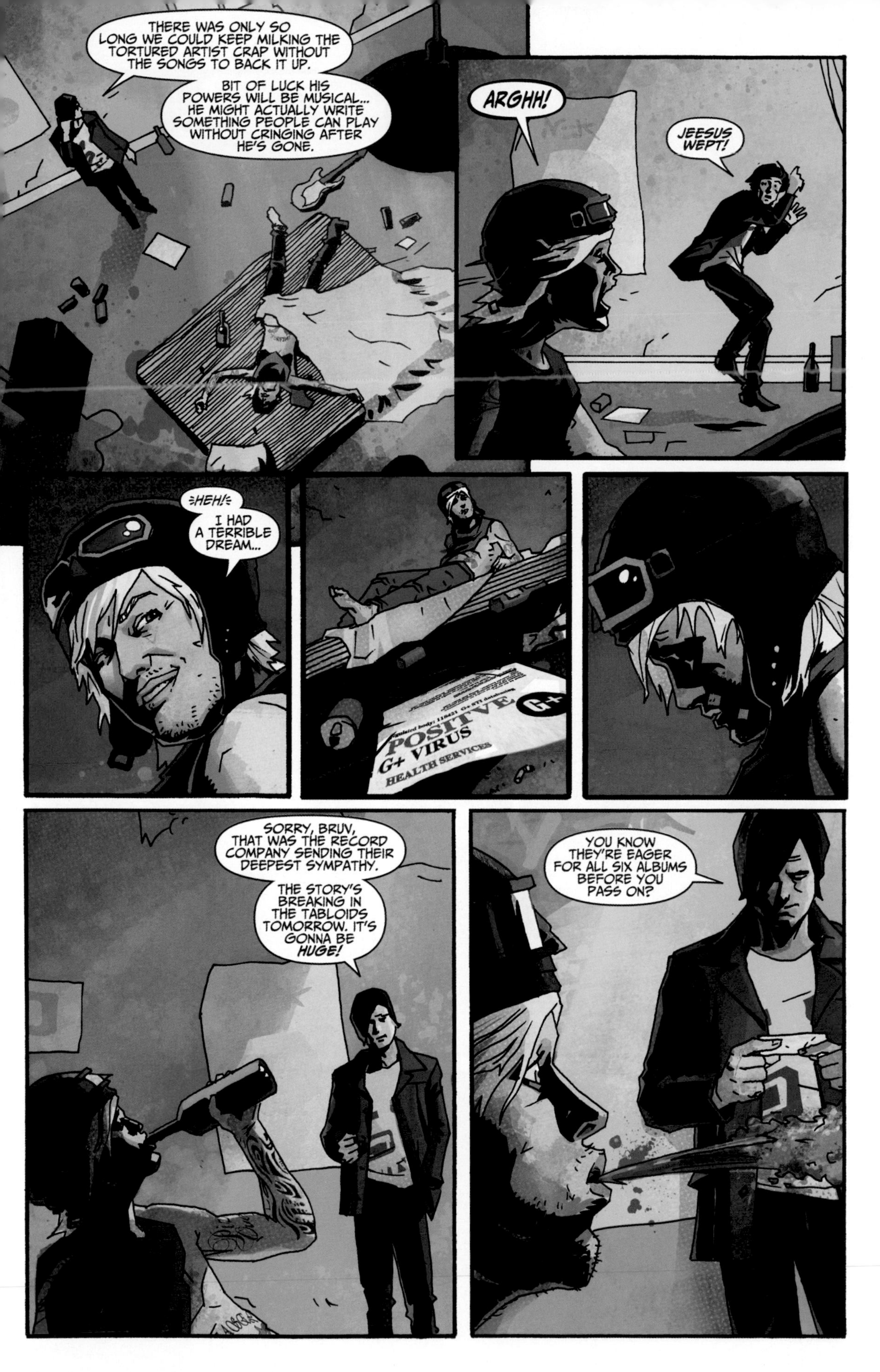
THERE WAS ONLY SO LONG WE COULD KEEP MILKING THE TORTURED ARTIST CRAP WITHOUT THE SONGS TO BACK IT UP.
BIT OF LUCK HIS POWERS WILL BE MUSICAL... HE MIGHT ACTUALLY WRITE SOMETHING PEOPLE CAN PLAY WITHOUT CRINGING AFTER HE'S GONE.
ARGHH!
JEESUS WEPT!
HEH!
I HAD A TERRIBLE DREAM...
POSITVE
G+
G+ VIRUS
HEALTH SERVICES
SORRY, BRUV, THAT WAS THE RECORD COMPANY SENDING THEIR DEEPEST SYMPATHY.
THE STORY'S BREAKING IN THE TABLOIDS TOMORROW. IT'S GONNA BE HUGE!
YOU KNOW THEY'RE EAGER FOR ALL SIX ALBUMS BEFORE YOU PASS ON?

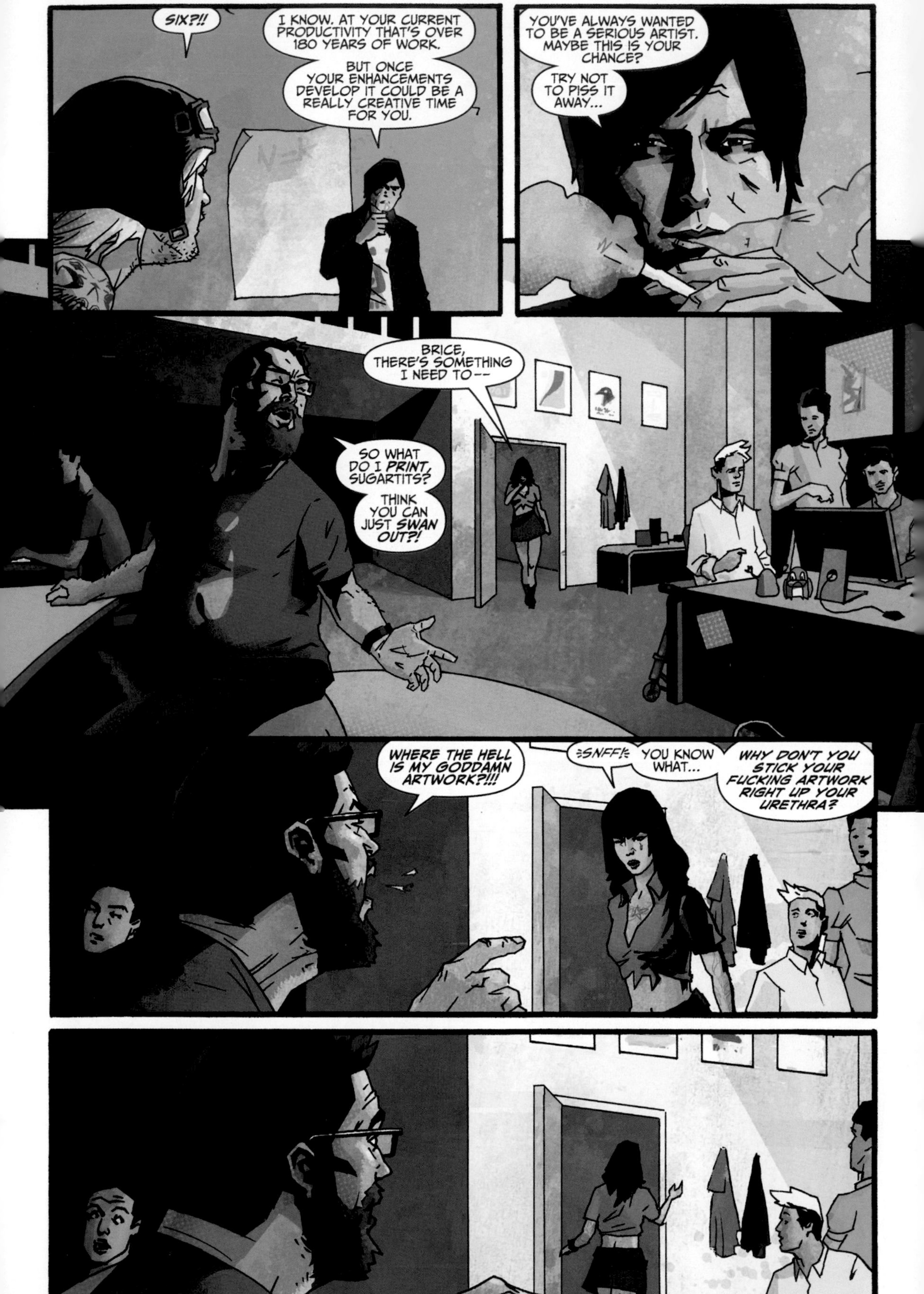
SIX?!!
I KNOW. AT YOUR CURRENT PRODUCTIVITY THAT'S OVER 180 YEARS OF WORK.
BUT ONCE YOUR ENHANCEMENTS DEVELOP IT COULD BE A REALLY CREATIVE TIME FOR YOU.
YOU'VE ALWAYS WANTED TO BE A SERIOUS ARTIST. MAYBE THIS IS YOUR CHANCE?
TRY NOT TO PISS IT AWAY...
BRICE, THERE'S SOMETHING I NEED TO--
SO WHAT DO I PRINT, SUGARTITS?
THINK YOU CAN JUST SWAN OUT?!
WHERE THE HELL IS MY GODDAMN ARTWORK?!!!
≈SNFF!≈
YOU KNOW WHAT...
WHY DON'T YOU STICK YOUR FUCKING ARTWORK RIGHT UP YOUR URETHRA?

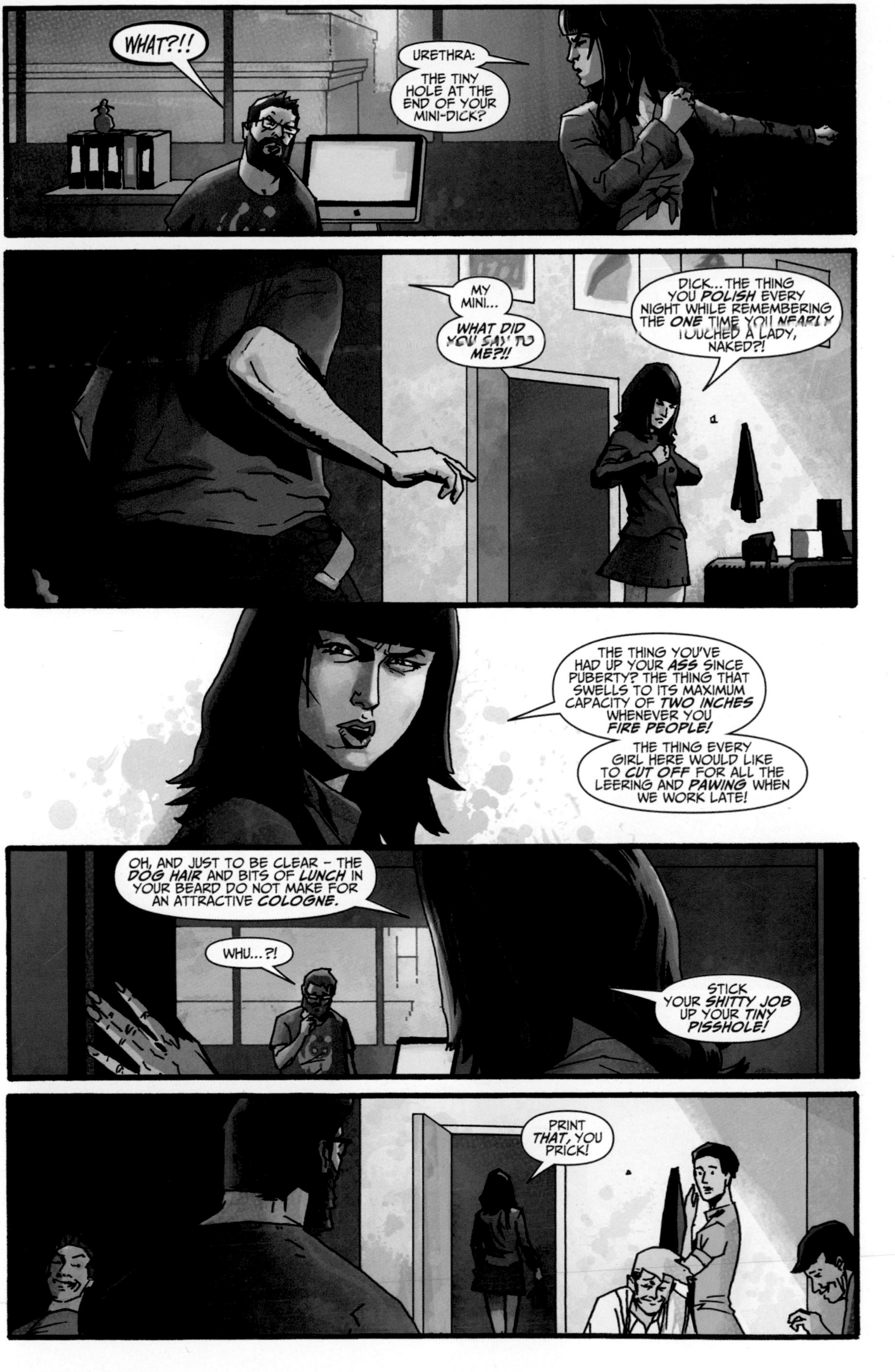
WHAT?!!
URETHRA:
THE TINY HOLE AT THE END OF YOUR MINI-DICK?
MY MINI...
WHAT DID YOU SAY TO ME?!!
DICK...THE THING YOU POLISH EVERY NIGHT WHILE REMEMBERING THE ONE TIME YOU NEARLY TOUCHED A LADY, NAKED?!
THE THING YOU'VE HAD UP YOUR ASS SINCE PUBERTY? THE THING THAT SWELLS TO ITS MAXIMUM CAPACITY OF TWO INCHES WHENEVER YOU FIRE PEOPLE!
THE THING EVERY GIRL HERE WOULD LIKE TO CUT OFF FOR ALL THE LEERING AND PAWING WHEN WE WORK LATE!
OH, AND JUST TO BE CLEAR – THE DOG HAIR AND BITS OF LUNCH IN YOUR BEARD DO NOT MAKE FOR AN ATTRACTIVE COLOGNE.
WHU...?!
STICK YOUR SHITTY JOB UP YOUR TINY PISSHOLE!
PRINT THAT, YOU PRICK!

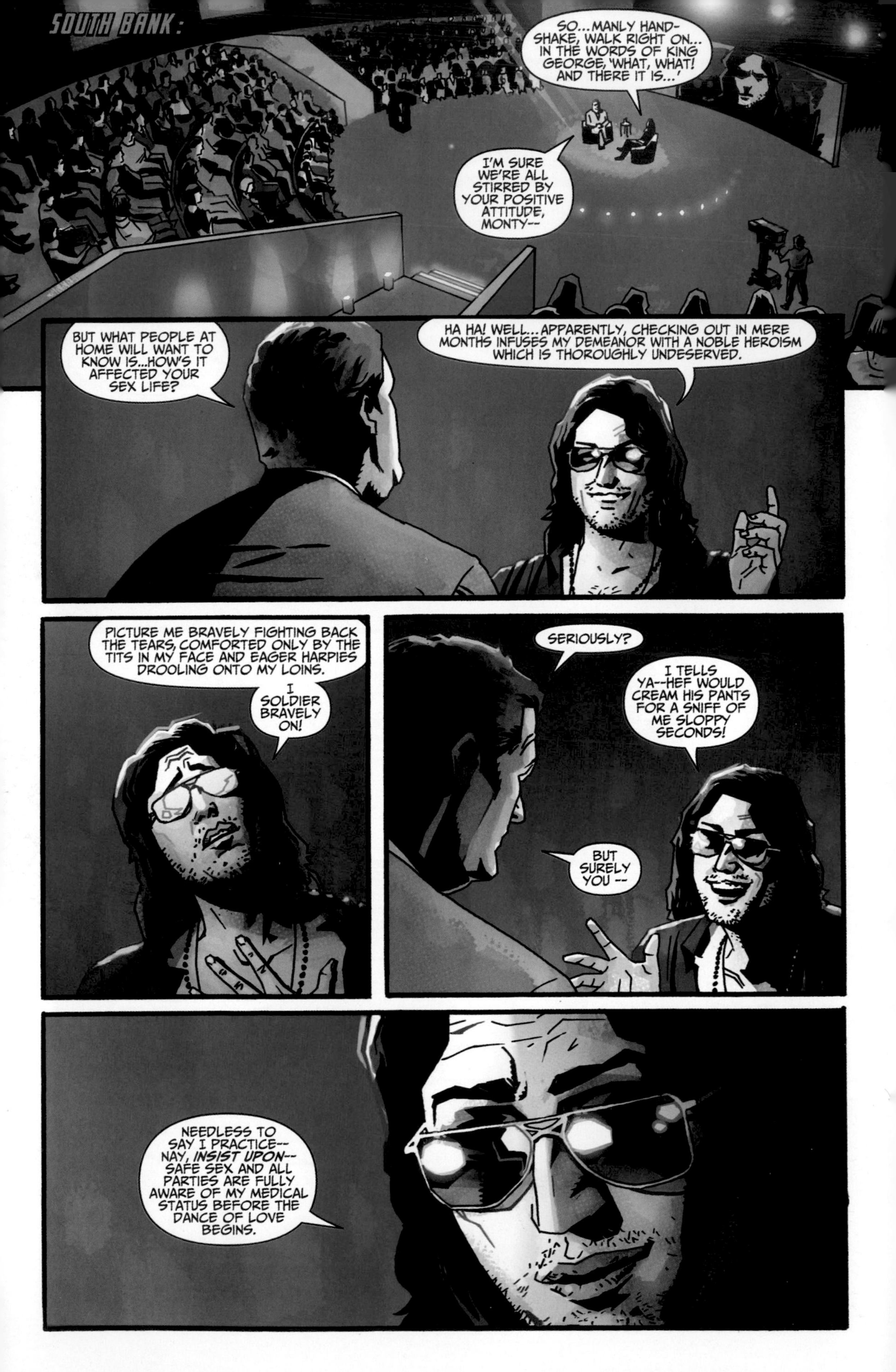
SOUTH BANK:
SO...MANLY HAND-SHAKE, WALK RIGHT ON... IN THE WORDS OF KING GEORGE, 'WHAT, WHAT! AND THERE IT IS...'
I'M SURE WE'RE ALL STIRRED BY YOUR POSITIVE ATTITUDE, MONTY--
BUT WHAT PEOPLE AT HOME WILL WANT TO KNOW IS...HOW'S IT AFFECTED YOUR SEX LIFE?
HA HA! WELL...APPARENTLY, CHECKING OUT IN MERE MONTHS INFUSES MY DEMEANOR WITH A NOBLE HEROISM WHICH IS THOROUGHLY UNDESERVED.
PICTURE ME BRAVELY FIGHTING BACK THE TEARS, COMFORTED ONLY BY THE TITS IN MY FACE AND EAGER HARPIES DROOLING ONTO MY LOINS.
I SOLDIER BRAVELY ON!
SERIOUSLY?
I TELLS YA--HEF WOULD CREAM HIS PANTS FOR A SNIFF OF ME SLOPPY SECONDS!
BUT SURELY YOU --
NEEDLESS TO SAY I PRACTICE--NAY, INSIST UPON--SAFE SEX AND ALL PARTIES ARE FULLY AWARE OF MY MEDICAL STATUS BEFORE THE DANCE OF LOVE BEGINS.

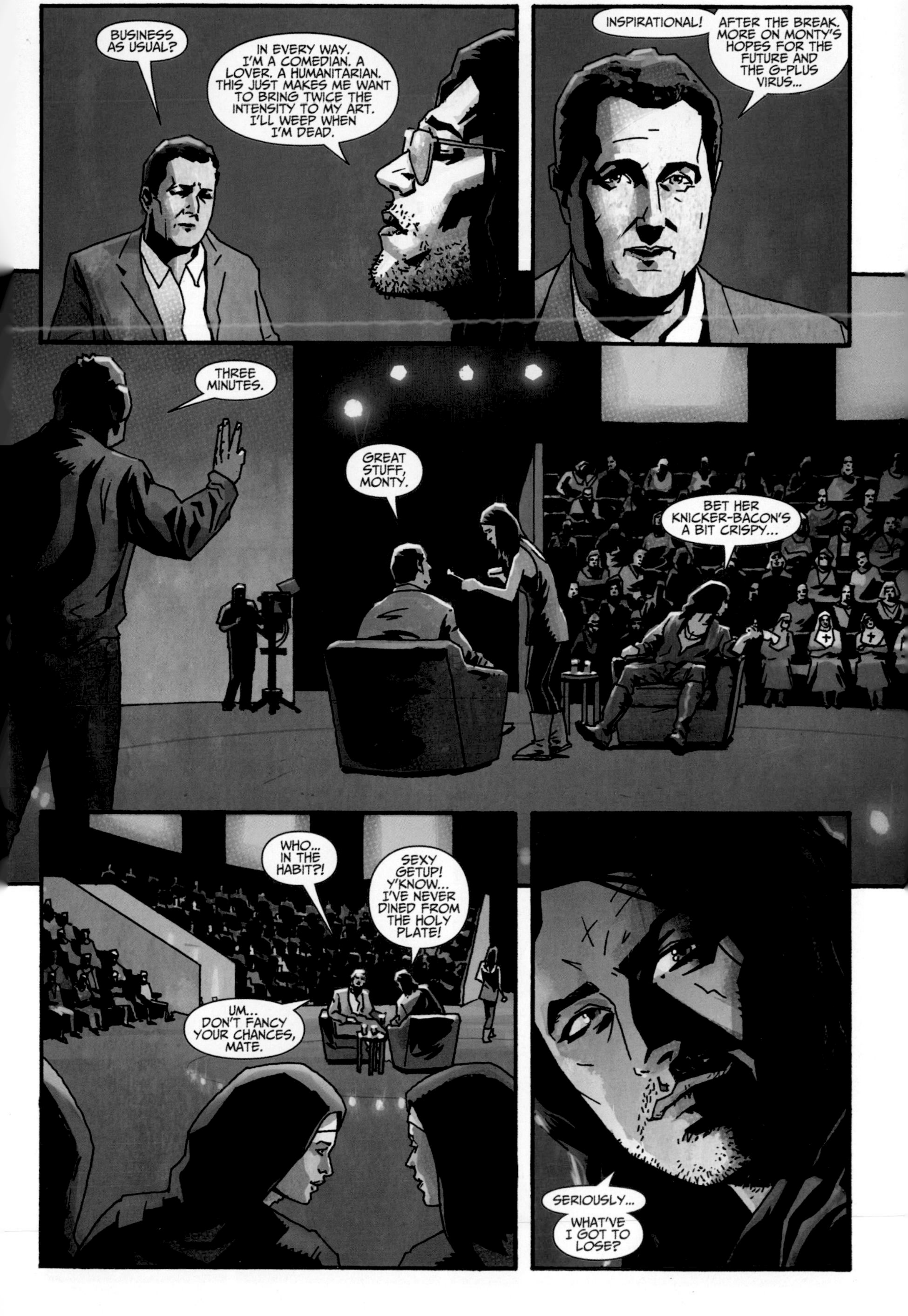
BUSINESS AS USUAL?
IN EVERY WAY. I'M A COMEDIAN. A LOVER. A HUMANITARIAN. THIS JUST MAKES ME WANT TO BRING TWICE THE INTENSITY TO MY ART. I'LL WEEP WHEN I'M DEAD.
INSPIRATIONAL!
AFTER THE BREAK. MORE ON MONTY'S HOPES FOR THE FUTURE AND THE G-PLUS VIRUS...
THREE MINUTES.
GREAT STUFF, MONTY.
BET HER KNICKER-BACON'S A BIT CRISPY...
WHO... IN THE HABIT?!
SEXY GETUP! Y'KNOW... I'VE NEVER DINED FROM THE HOLY PLATE!
UM... DON'T FANCY YOUR CHANCES, MATE.
SERIOUSLY...
WHAT'VE I GOT TO LOSE?

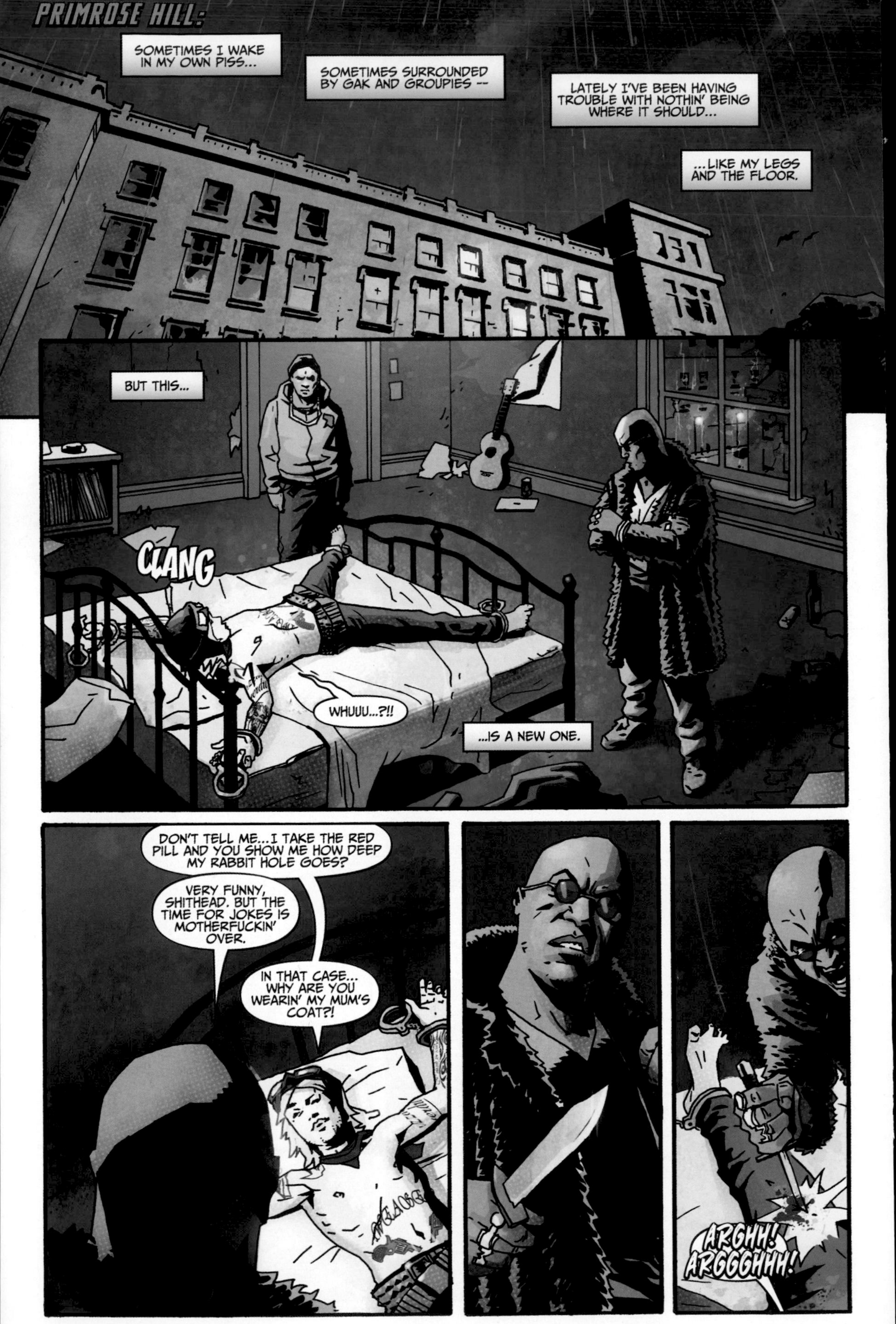
PRIMROSE HILL:
SOMETIMES I WAKE IN MY OWN PISS...
SOMETIMES SURROUNDED BY GAK AND GROUPIES --
LATELY I'VE BEEN HAVING TROUBLE WITH NOTHIN' BEING WHERE IT SHOULD...
...LIKE MY LEGS AND THE FLOOR.
BUT THIS...
CLANG
WHUUU...?!!
...IS A NEW ONE.
DON'T TELL ME...I TAKE THE RED PILL AND YOU SHOW ME HOW DEEP MY RABBIT HOLE GOES?
VERY FUNNY, SHITHEAD. BUT THE TIME FOR JOKES IS MOTHERFUCKIN' OVER.
IN THAT CASE... WHY ARE YOU WEARIN' MY MUM'S COAT?!
ARGHH! ARGGGHHH!

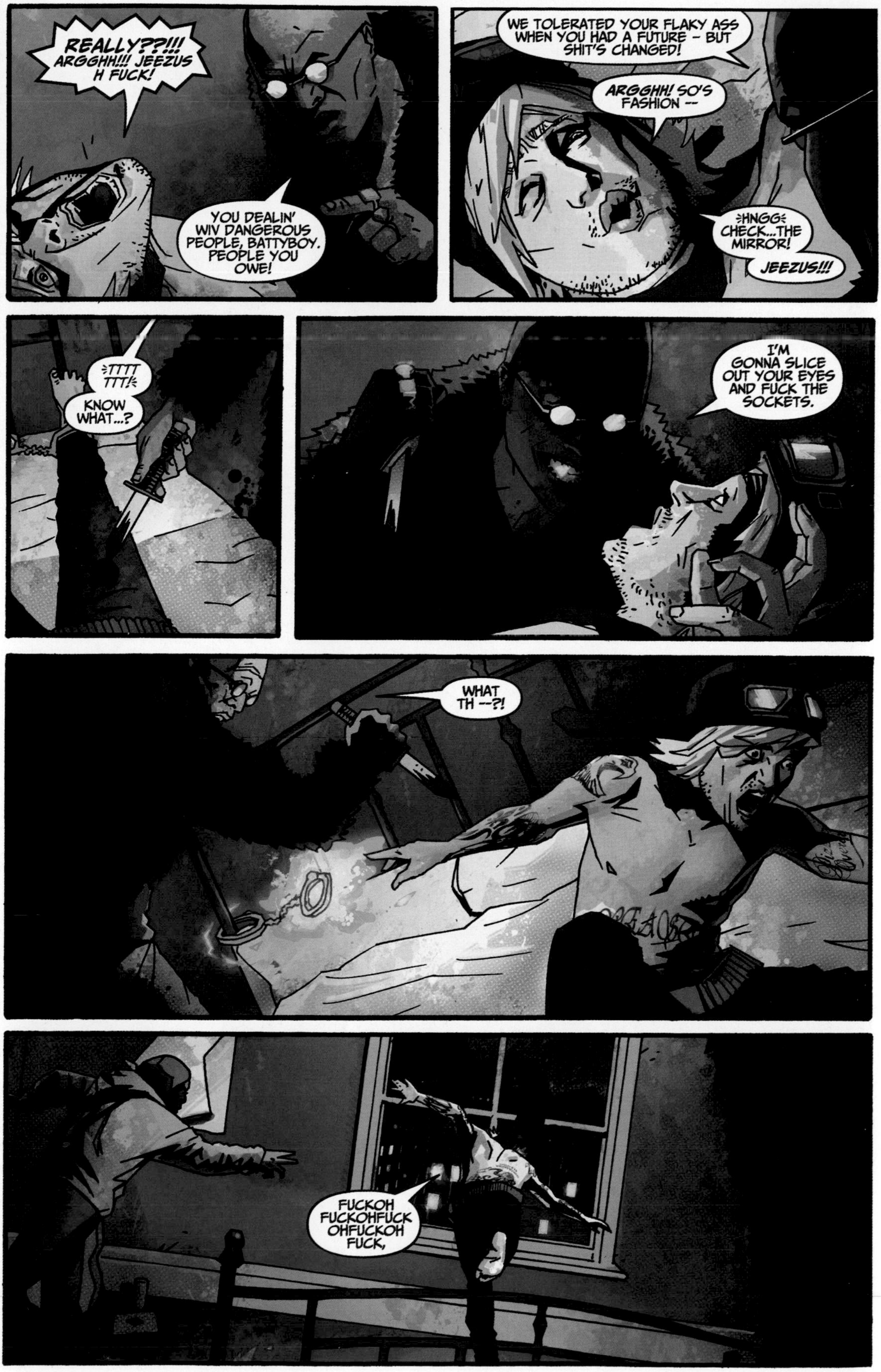
REALLY??!!! ARGGHH!!! JEEZUS H FUCK!
YOU DEALIN' WIV DANGEROUS PEOPLE, BATTYBOY. PEOPLE YOU OWE!
WE TOLERATED YOUR FLAKY ASS WHEN YOU HAD A FUTURE - BUT SHIT'S CHANGED!
ARGGHH! SO'S FASHION --
HNGG CHECK...THE MIRROR!
JEEZUS!!!
TTTT TTT!
KNOW WHAT...?
I'M GONNA SLICE OUT YOUR EYES AND FUCK THE SOCKETS.
WHAT TH --?!
FUCKOH FUCKOHFUCK OHFUCKOH FUCK,

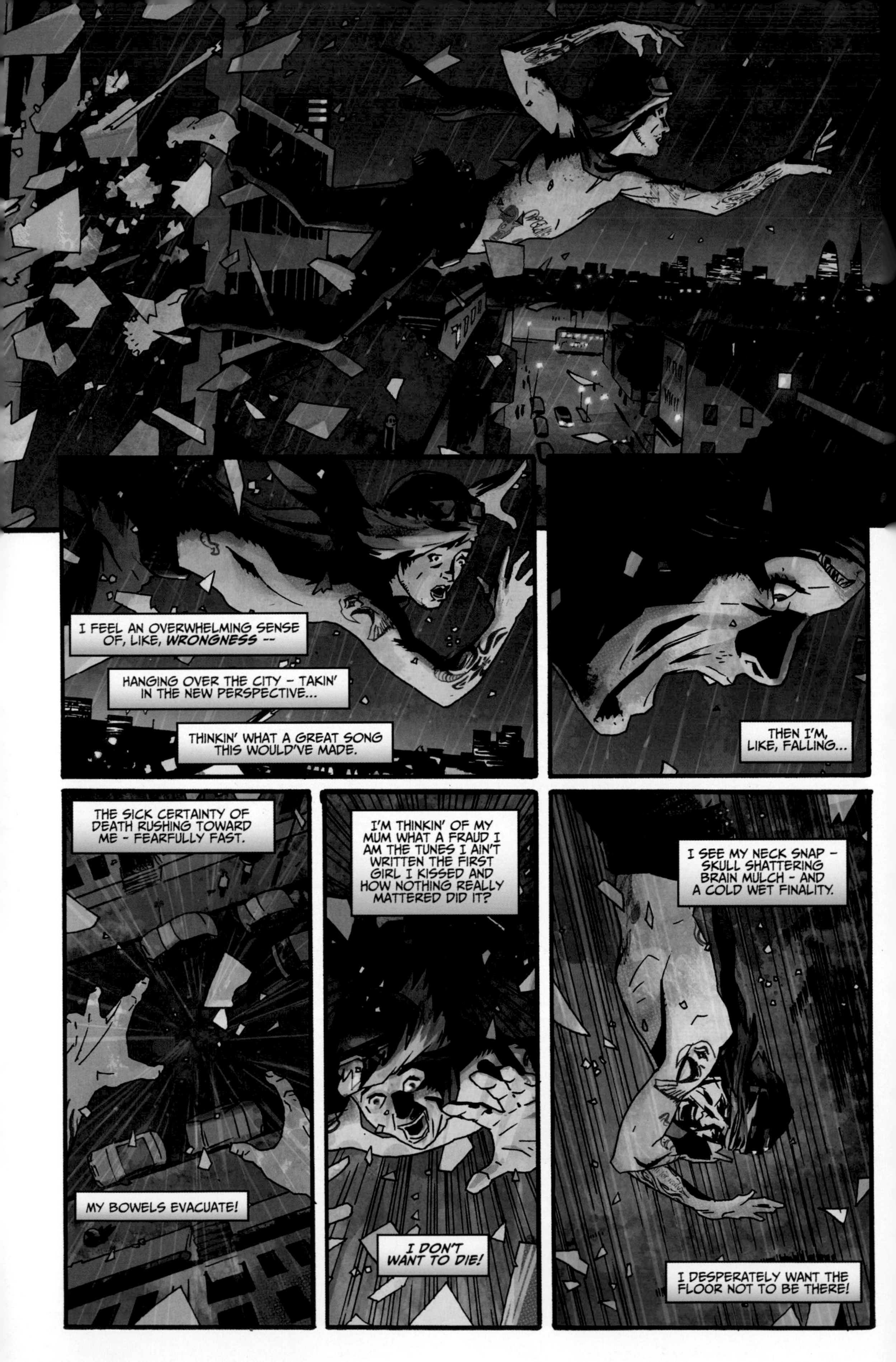
I FEEL AN OVERWHELMING SENSE OF, LIKE, *WRONGNESS* --
HANGING OVER THE CITY - TAKIN' IN THE NEW PERSPECTIVE...
THINKIN' WHAT A GREAT SONG THIS WOULD'VE MADE.
THEN I'M, LIKE, FALLING...
THE SICK CERTAINTY OF DEATH RUSHING TOWARD ME - FEARFULLY FAST.
MY BOWELS EVACUATE!
I'M THINKIN' OF MY MUM WHAT A FRAUD I AM THE TUNES I AIN'T WRITTEN THE FIRST GIRL I KISSED AND HOW NOTHING REALLY MATTERED DID IT?
I DON'T WANT TO DIE!
I SEE MY NECK SNAP - SKULL SHATTERING BRAIN MULCH - AND A COLD WET FINALITY.
I DESPERATELY WANT THE FLOOR NOT TO BE THERE!

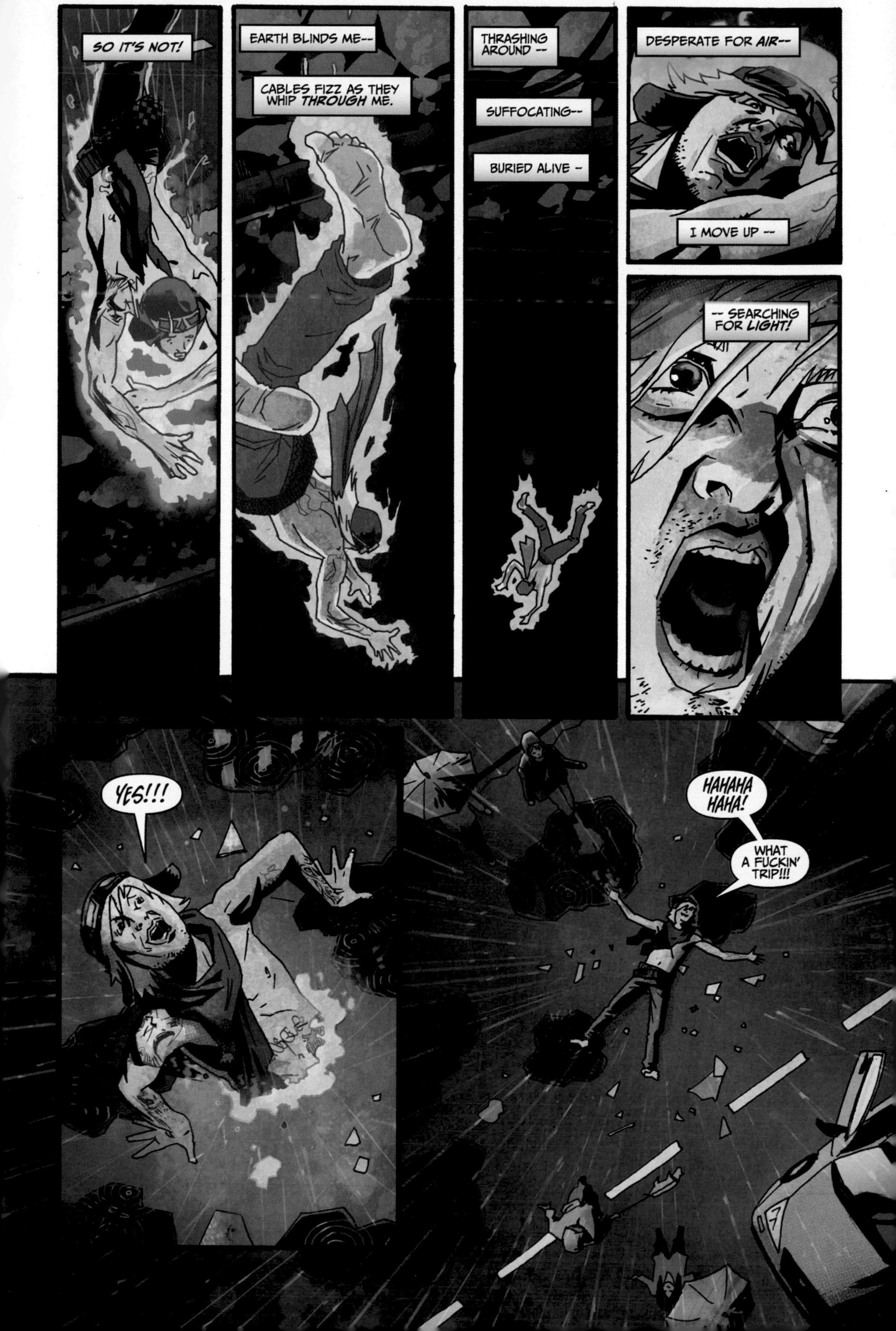
SO IT'S NOT!
EARTH BLINDS ME--
CABLES FIZZ AS THEY WHIP THROUGH ME.
THRASHING AROUND --
SUFFOCATING--
BURIED ALIVE -
DESPERATE FOR AIR--
I MOVE UP --
-- SEARCHING FOR LIGHT!
YES!!!
HAHAHA HAHA!
WHAT A FUCKIN' TRIP!!!

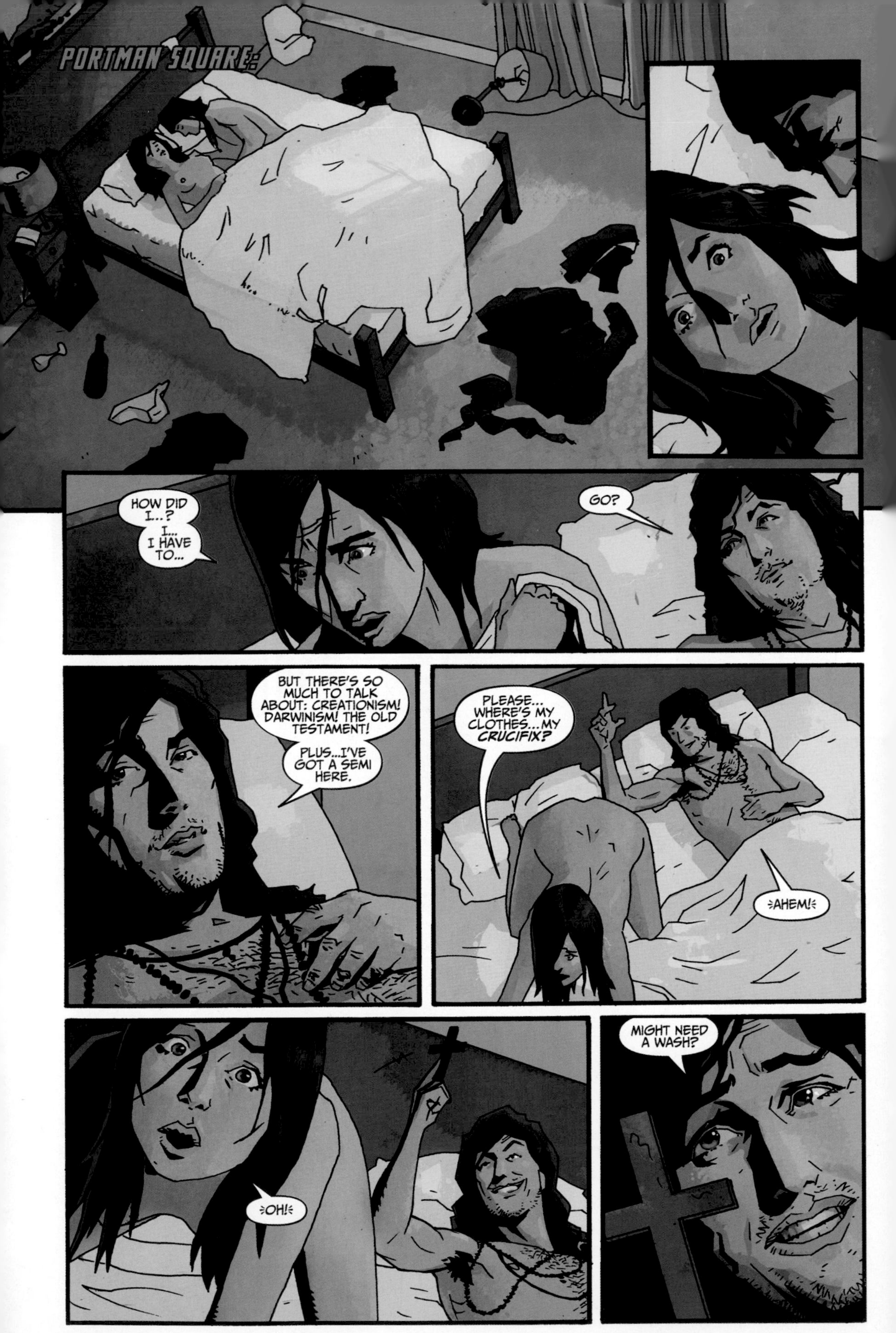
PORTMAN SQUARE:
HOW DID I...? I... I HAVE TO...
GO?
BUT THERE'S SO MUCH TO TALK ABOUT: CREATIONISM! DARWINISM! THE OLD TESTAMENT!
PLUS...I'VE GOT A SEMI HERE.
PLEASE... WHERE'S MY CLOTHES...MY CRUCIFIX?
AHEM!
OH!
MIGHT NEED A WASH?

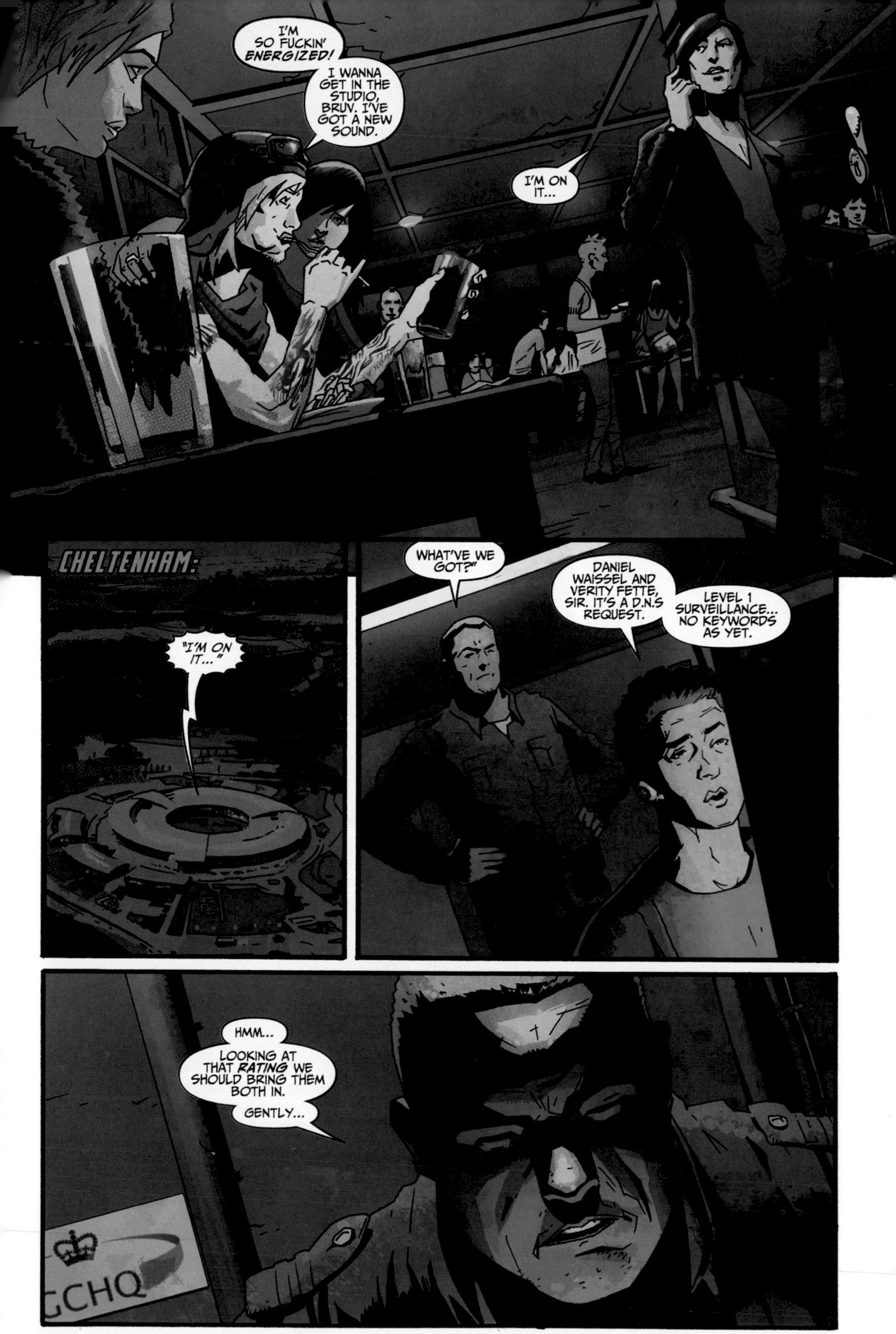
I'M SO FUCKIN' *ENERGIZED!*
I WANNA GET IN THE STUDIO, BRUV. I'VE GOT A NEW SOUND.
I'M ON IT...
CHELTENHAM:
"I'M ON IT..."
WHAT'VE WE GOT?"
DANIEL WAISSEL AND VERITY FETTE, SIR. IT'S A D.N.S REQUEST.
LEVEL 1 SURVEILLANCE... NO KEYWORDS AS YET.
HMM...
LOOKING AT THAT *RATING* WE SHOULD BRING THEM BOTH IN.
GENTLY...
GCHQ

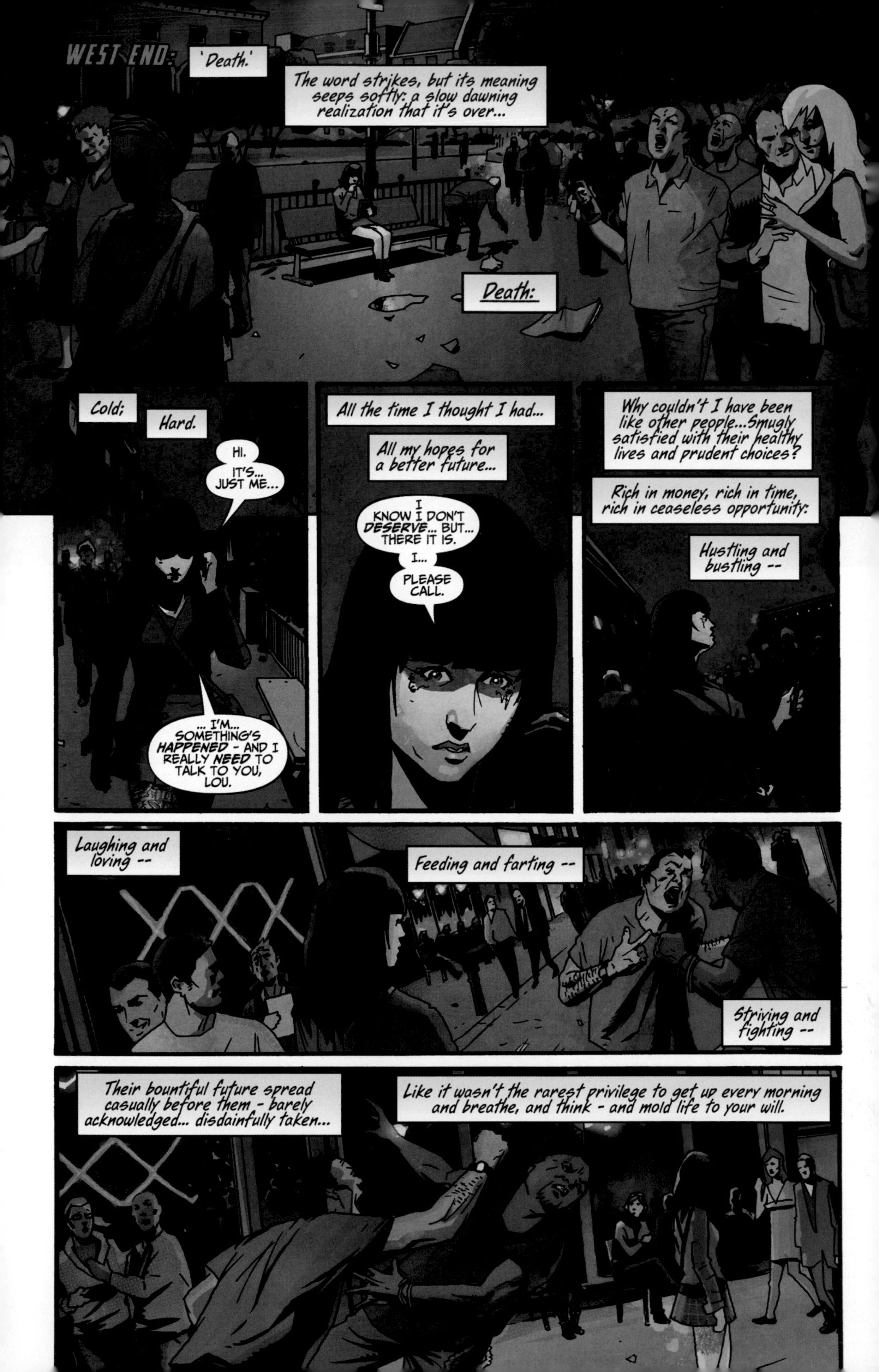
WEST END:
'Death.'
The word strikes, but its meaning seeps softly: a slow dawning realization that it's over...
Death:
Cold;
Hard.
HI. IT'S... JUST ME...
... I'M... SOMETHING'S HAPPENED - AND I REALLY NEED TO TALK TO YOU, LOU.
All the time I thought I had...
All my hopes for a better future...
I KNOW I DON'T DESERVE... BUT... THERE IT IS.
I...
PLEASE CALL.
Why couldn't I have been like other people...Smugly satisfied with their healthy lives and prudent choices?
Rich in money, rich in time, rich in ceaseless opportunity:
Hustling and bustling --
Laughing and loving --
Feeding and farting --
Striving and fighting --
Their bountiful future spread casually before them - barely acknowledged... disdainfully taken...
Like it wasn't the rarest privilege to get up every morning and breathe, and think - and mold life to your will.

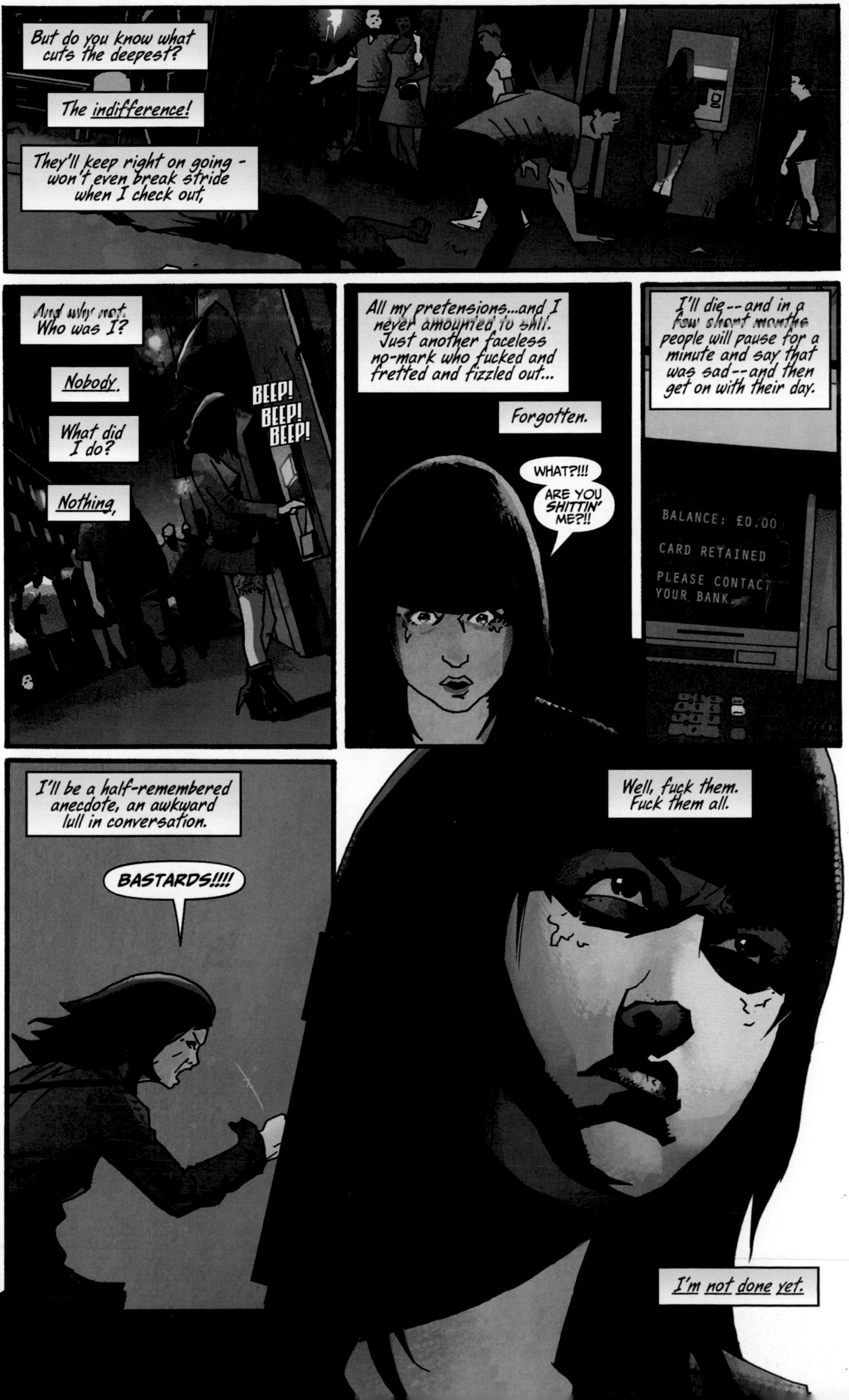

But do you know what cuts the deepest?
The indifference!
They'll keep right on going - won't even break stride when I check out,
And why not. Who was I?
Nobody.
What did I do?
Nothing,
BEEP! BEEP! BEEP!
All my pretensions...and I never amounted to shit. Just another faceless no-mark who fucked and fretted and fizzled out...
Forgotten.
WHAT?!!! ARE YOU SHITTIN' ME?!!
I'll die--and in a few short months people will pause for a minute and say that was sad--and then get on with their day.
BALANCE: £0.00
CARD RETAINED
PLEASE CONTACT YOUR BANK.
I'll be a half-remembered anecdote, an awkward lull in conversation.
BASTARDS!!!!
Well, fuck them. Fuck them all.
I'm not done yet.

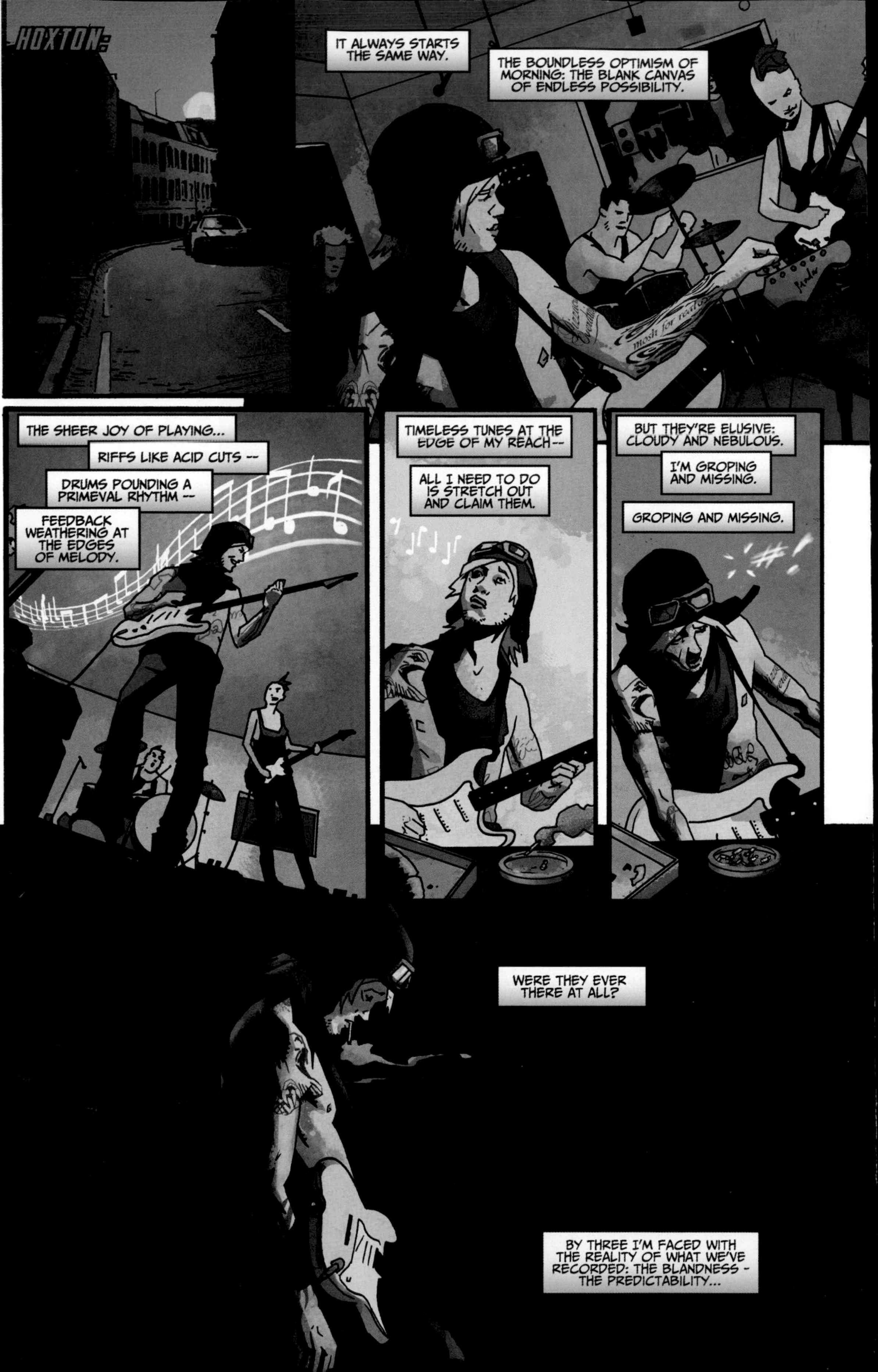
HOXTON:
IT ALWAYS STARTS THE SAME WAY.
THE BOUNDLESS OPTIMISM OF MORNING: THE BLANK CANVAS OF ENDLESS POSSIBILITY.
THE SHEER JOY OF PLAYING...
RIFFS LIKE ACID CUTS --
DRUMS POUNDING A PRIMEVAL RHYTHM --
FEEDBACK WEATHERING AT THE EDGES OF MELODY.
TIMELESS TUNES AT THE EDGE OF MY REACH--
ALL I NEED TO DO IS STRETCH OUT AND CLAIM THEM.
BUT THEY'RE ELUSIVE: CLOUDY AND NEBULOUS.
I'M GROPING AND MISSING.
GROPING AND MISSING.
WERE THEY EVER THERE AT ALL?
BY THREE I'M FACED WITH THE REALITY OF WHAT WE'VE RECORDED: THE BLANDNESS - THE PREDICTABILITY...

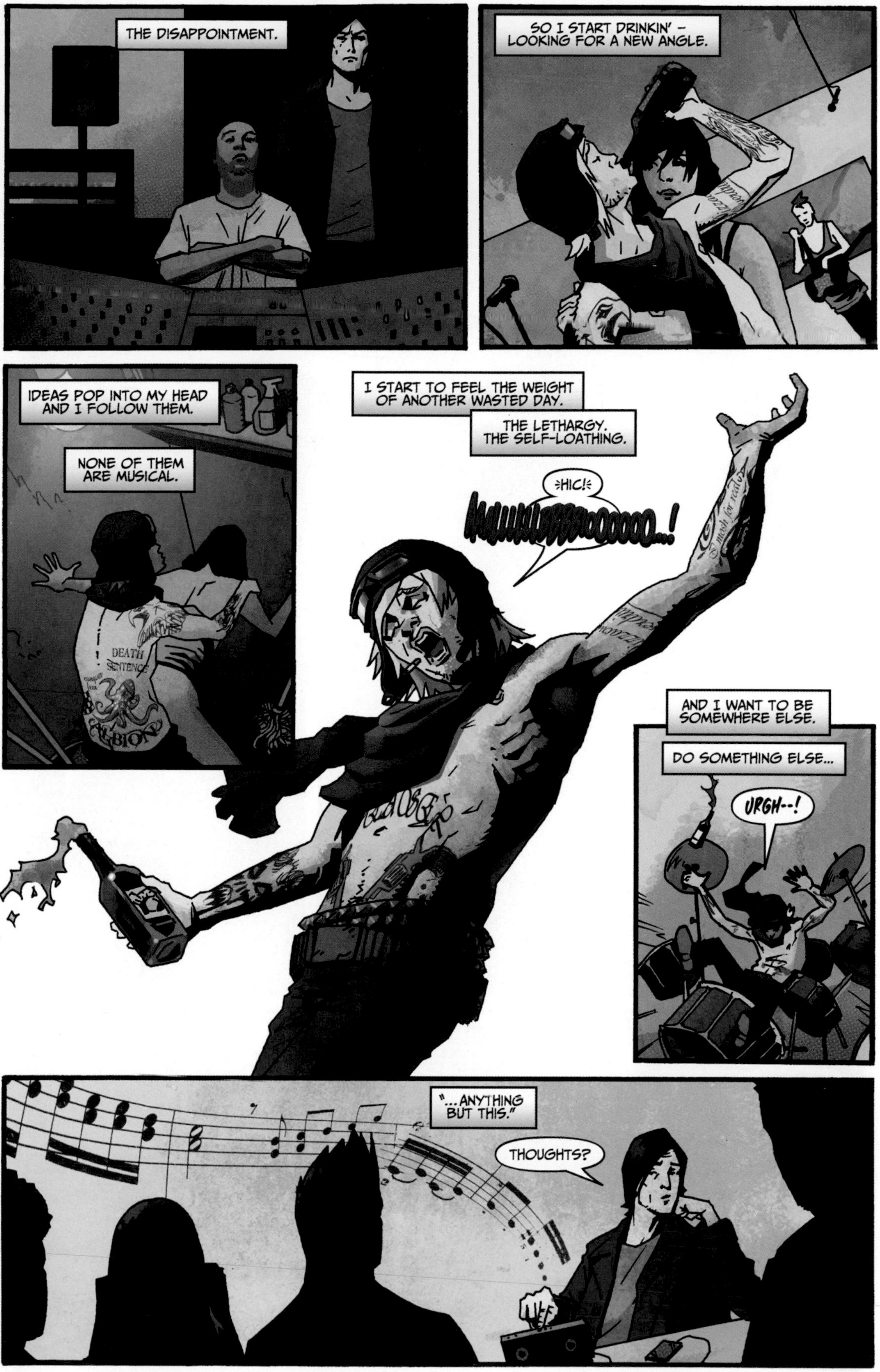
THE DISAPPOINTMENT.
SO I START DRINKIN' – LOOKING FOR A NEW ANGLE.
IDEAS POP INTO MY HEAD AND I FOLLOW THEM.
NONE OF THEM ARE MUSICAL.
DEATH SENTENCE
ALBION
I START TO FEEL THE WEIGHT OF ANOTHER WASTED DAY.
THE LETHARGY. THE SELF-LOATHING.
HIC!
AND I WANT TO BE SOMEWHERE ELSE.
DO SOMETHING ELSE...
URGH--!
"...ANYTHING BUT THIS."
THOUGHTS?

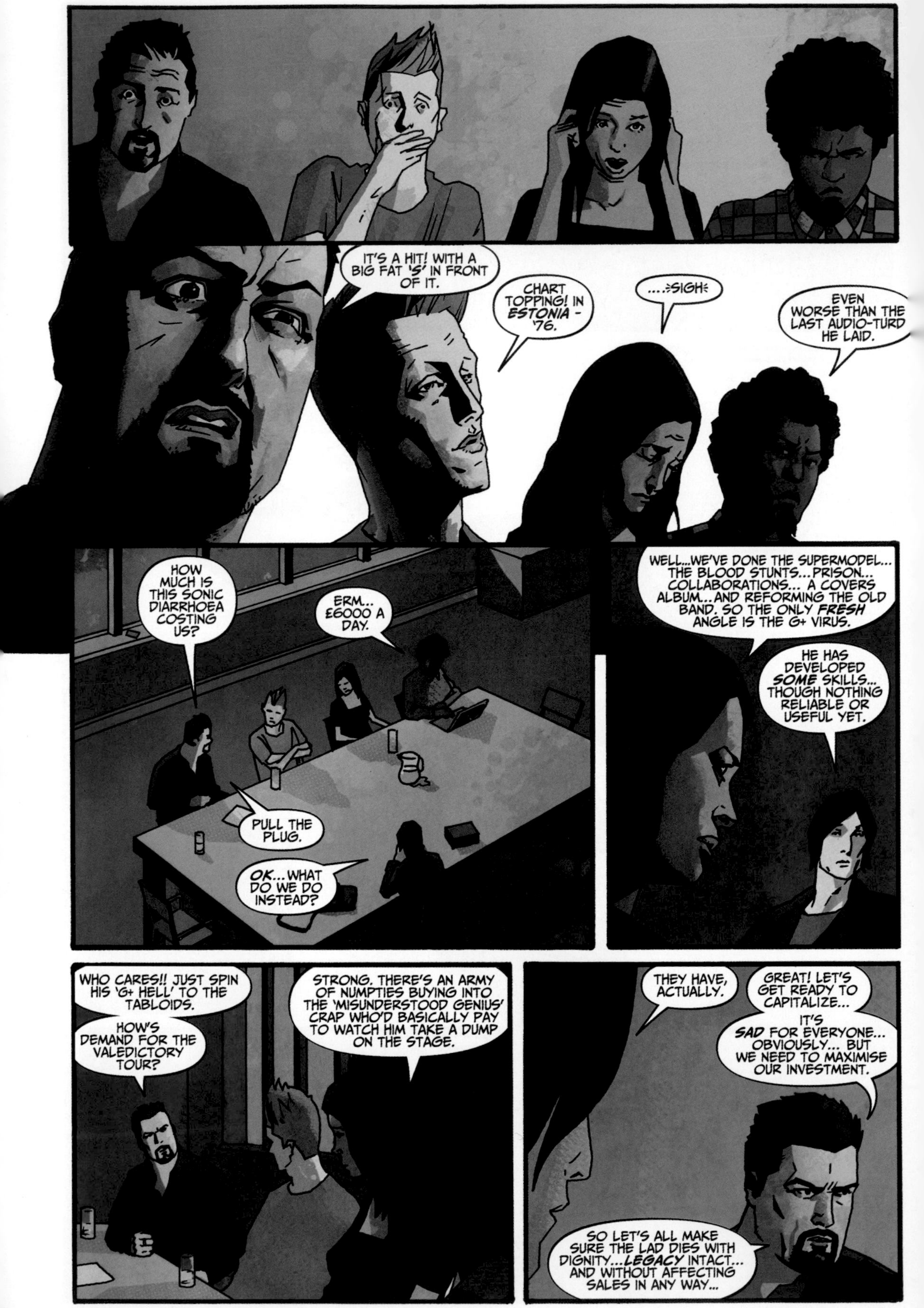
IT'S A HIT! WITH A BIG FAT 'S' IN FRONT OF IT.
CHART TOPPING! IN ESTONIA - '76.
...SIGH
EVEN WORSE THAN THE LAST AUDIO-TURD HE LAID.
HOW MUCH IS THIS SONIC DIARRHOEA COSTING US?
ERM... £6000 A DAY.
PULL THE PLUG.
OK...WHAT DO WE DO INSTEAD?
WELL...WE'VE DONE THE SUPERMODEL... THE BLOOD STUNTS...PRISON... COLLABORATIONS... A COVERS ALBUM...AND REFORMING THE OLD BAND. SO THE ONLY FRESH ANGLE IS THE G+ VIRUS.
HE HAS DEVELOPED SOME SKILLS... THOUGH NOTHING RELIABLE OR USEFUL YET.
WHO CARES!! JUST SPIN HIS 'G+ HELL' TO THE TABLOIDS.
HOW'S DEMAND FOR THE VALEDICTORY TOUR?
STRONG. THERE'S AN ARMY OF NUMPTIES BUYING INTO THE 'MISUNDERSTOOD GENIUS' CRAP WHO'D BASICALLY PAY TO WATCH HIM TAKE A DUMP ON THE STAGE.
THEY HAVE, ACTUALLY.
GREAT! LET'S GET READY TO CAPITALIZE...
IT'S SAD FOR EVERYONE... OBVIOUSLY... BUT WE NEED TO MAXIMISE OUR INVESTMENT.
SO LET'S ALL MAKE SURE THE LAD DIES WITH DIGNITY...LEGACY INTACT... AND WITHOUT AFFECTING SALES IN ANY WAY...

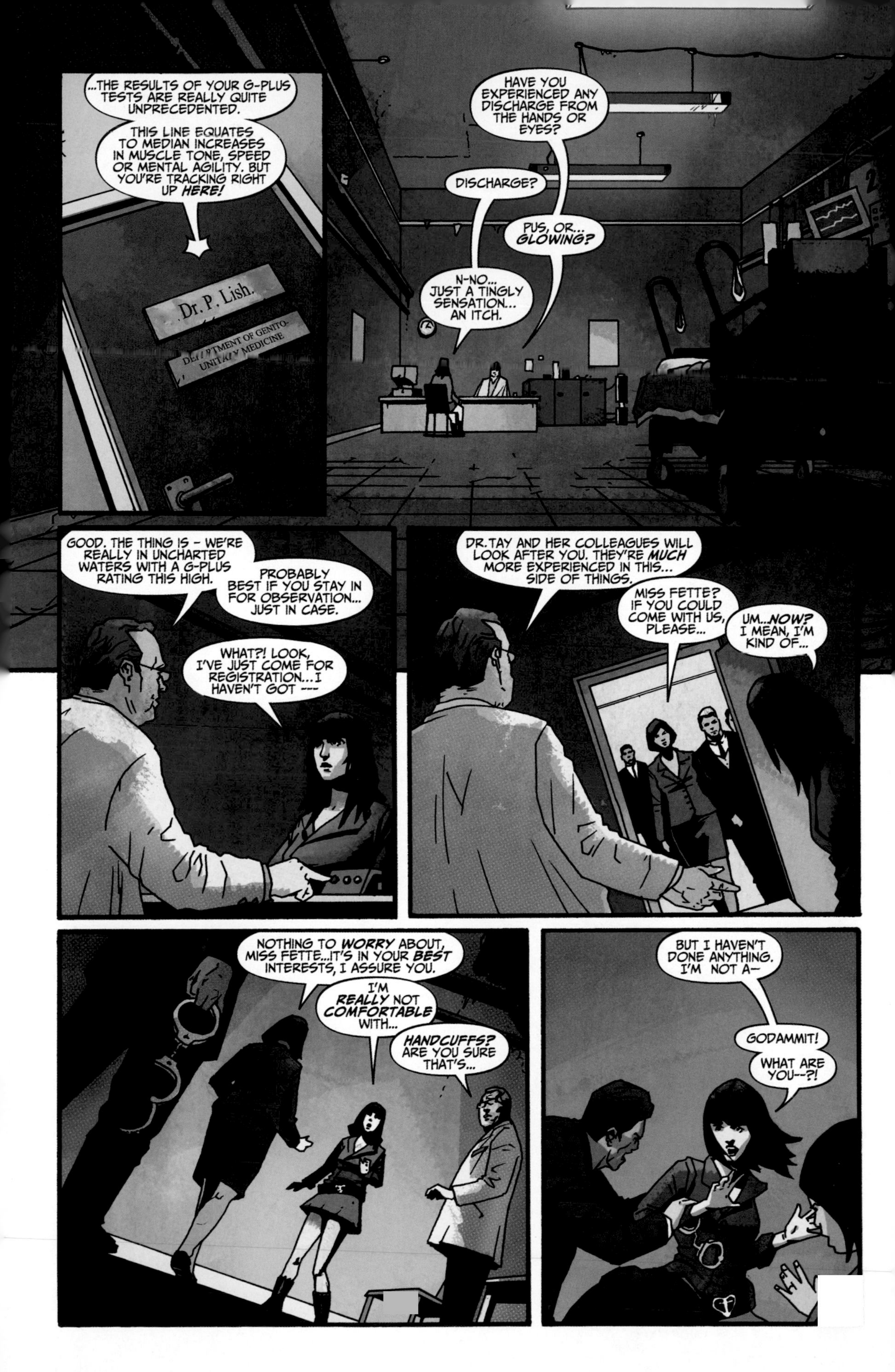

...THE RESULTS OF YOUR G-PLUS TESTS ARE REALLY QUITE UNPRECEDENTED.
THIS LINE EQUATES TO MEDIAN INCREASES IN MUSCLE TONE, SPEED OR MENTAL AGILITY. BUT YOU'RE TRACKING RIGHT UP *HERE!*
Dr. P. Lish.
DEPARTMENT OF GENITO-UNITARY MEDICINE
HAVE YOU EXPERIENCED ANY DISCHARGE FROM THE HANDS OR EYES?
DISCHARGE?
PUS, OR... *GLOWING?*
N-NO... JUST A TINGLY SENSATION... AN ITCH.
GOOD. THE THING IS - WE'RE REALLY IN UNCHARTED WATERS WITH A G-PLUS RATING THIS HIGH.
PROBABLY BEST IF YOU STAY IN FOR OBSERVATION... JUST IN CASE.
WHAT?! LOOK, I'VE JUST COME FOR REGISTRATION...I HAVEN'T GOT ---
DR.TAY AND HER COLLEAGUES WILL LOOK AFTER YOU. THEY'RE *MUCH* MORE EXPERIENCED IN THIS... SIDE OF THINGS.
MISS FETTE? IF YOU COULD COME WITH US, PLEASE...
UM...*NOW?* I MEAN, I'M KIND OF...
NOTHING TO *WORRY* ABOUT, MISS FETTE...IT'S IN YOUR *BEST* INTERESTS, I ASSURE YOU.
I'M *REALLY* NOT *COMFORTABLE* WITH...
HANDCUFFS? ARE YOU SURE THAT'S...
BUT I HAVEN'T DONE ANYTHING. I'M NOT A–
GODAMMIT!
WHAT ARE YOU--?!

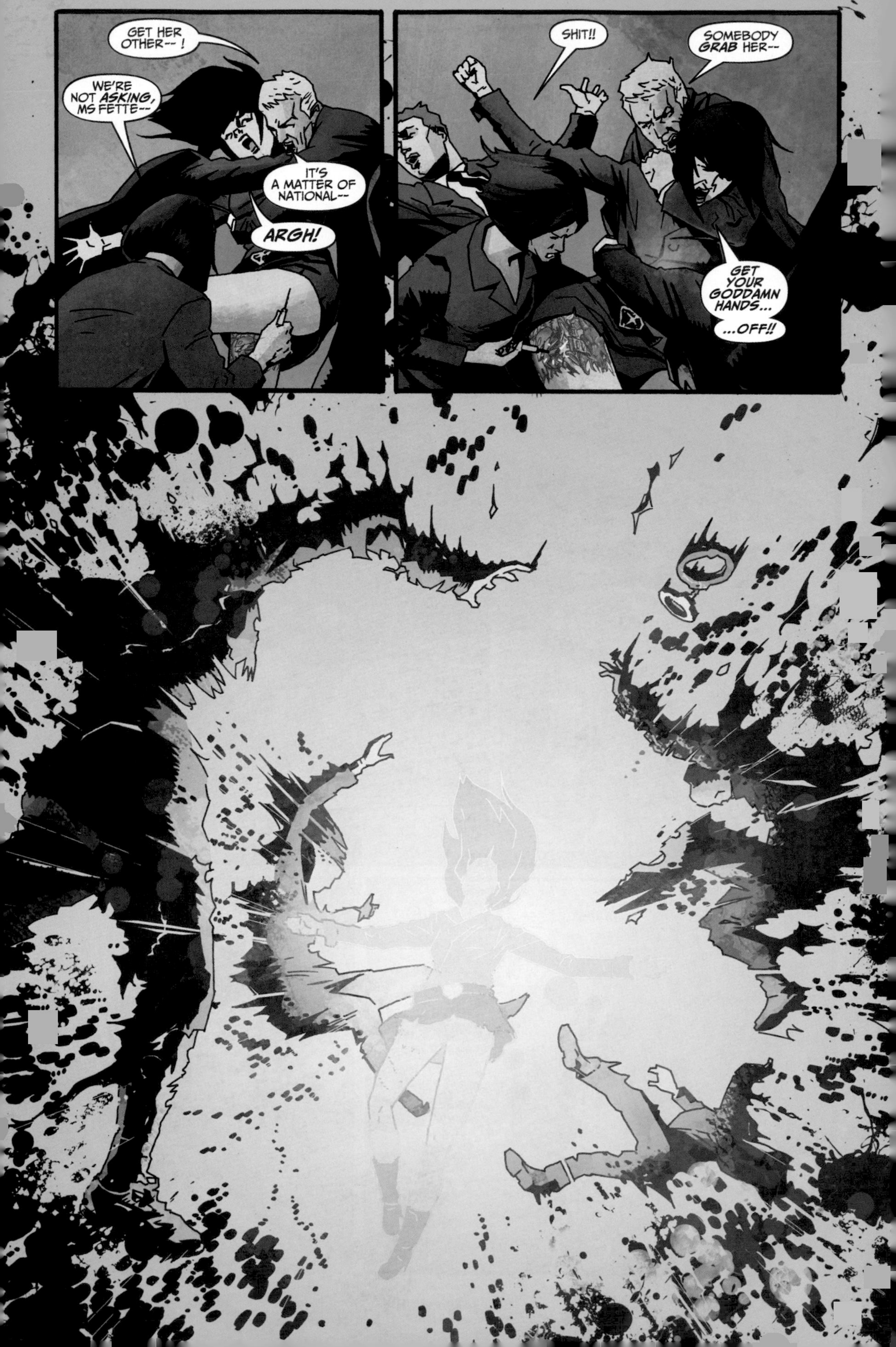
GET HER OTHER-- !
WE'RE NOT ASKING, MS FETTE--
IT'S A MATTER OF NATIONAL--
ARGH!
SHIT!!
SOMEBODY GRAB HER--
GET YOUR GODDAMN HANDS...
...OFF!!

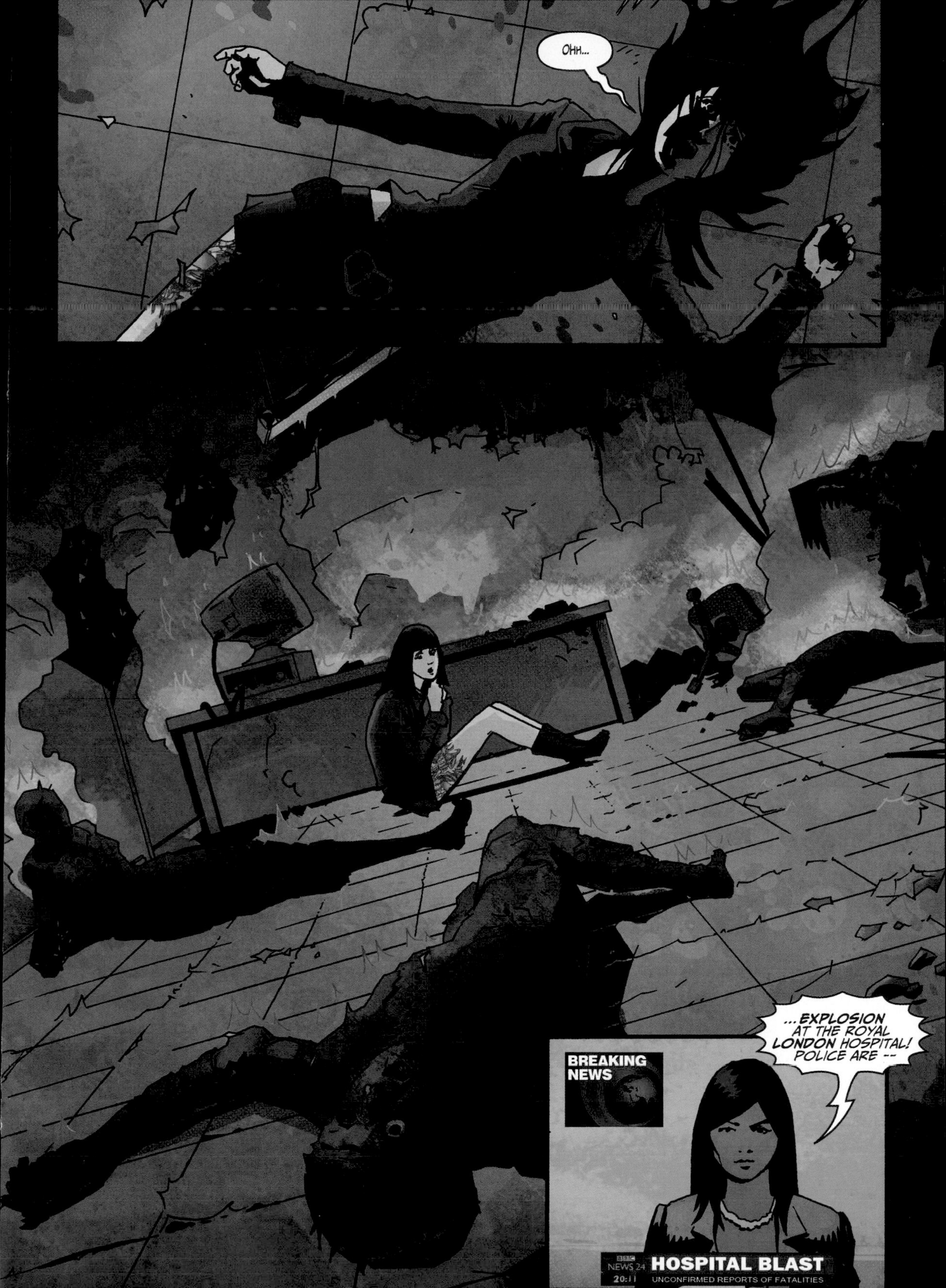
OHH...
...EXPLOSION AT THE ROYAL LONDON HOSPITAL! POLICE ARE --
BREAKING NEWS
BBC NEWS 24
20:11
HOSPITAL BLAST
UNCONFIRMED REPORTS OF FATALITIES

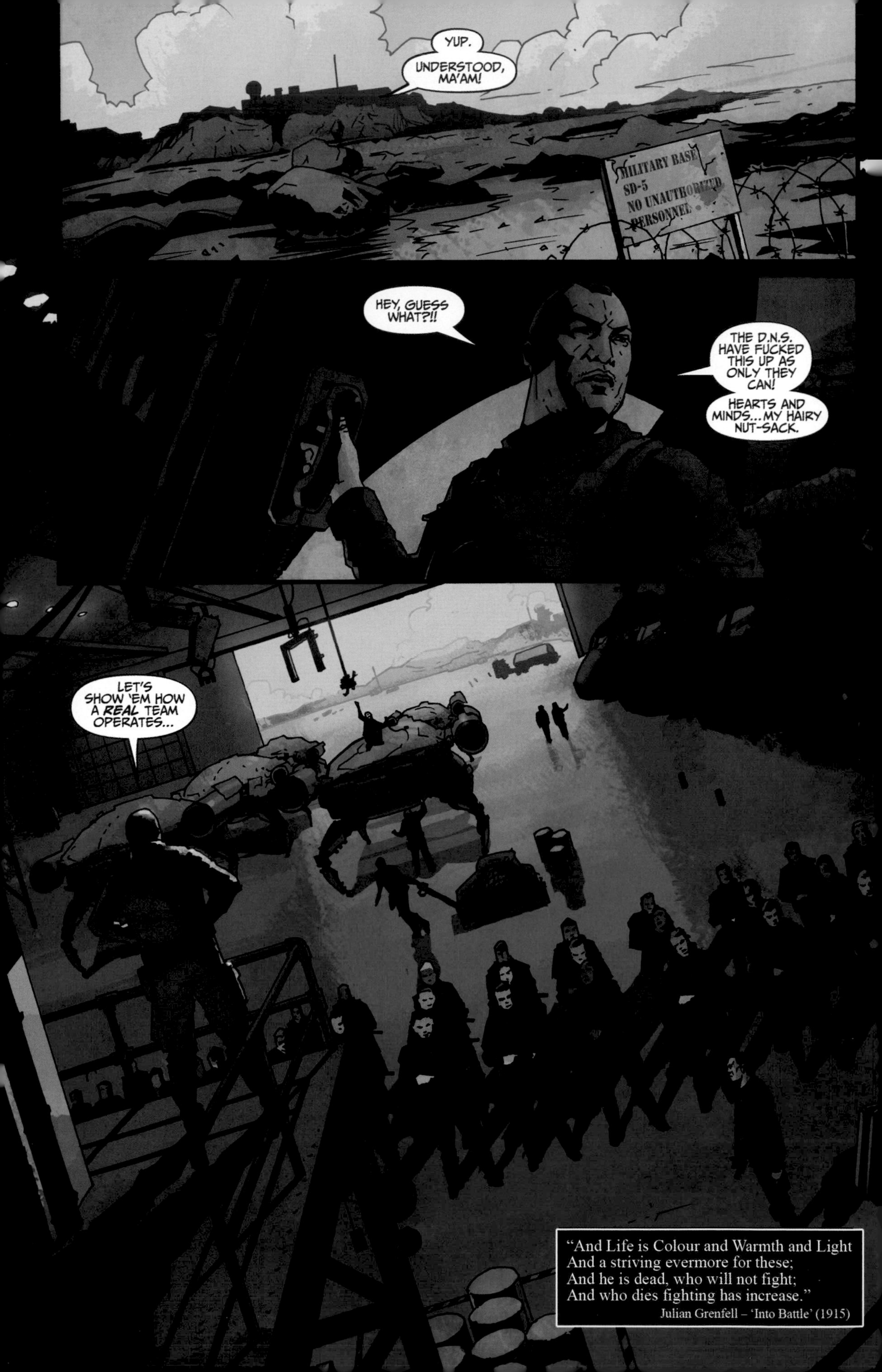
YUP.
UNDERSTOOD, MA'AM!
MILITARY BASE SD-5 NO UNAUTHORIZED PERSONNEL
HEY, GUESS WHAT?!!
THE D.N.S. HAVE FUCKED THIS UP AS ONLY THEY CAN!
HEARTS AND MINDS... MY HAIRY NUT-SACK.
LET'S SHOW 'EM HOW A *REAL* TEAM OPERATES...
"And Life is Colour and Warmth and Light
And a striving evermore for these;
And he is dead, who will not fight;
And who dies fighting has increase."
Julian Grenfell – 'Into Battle' (1915)

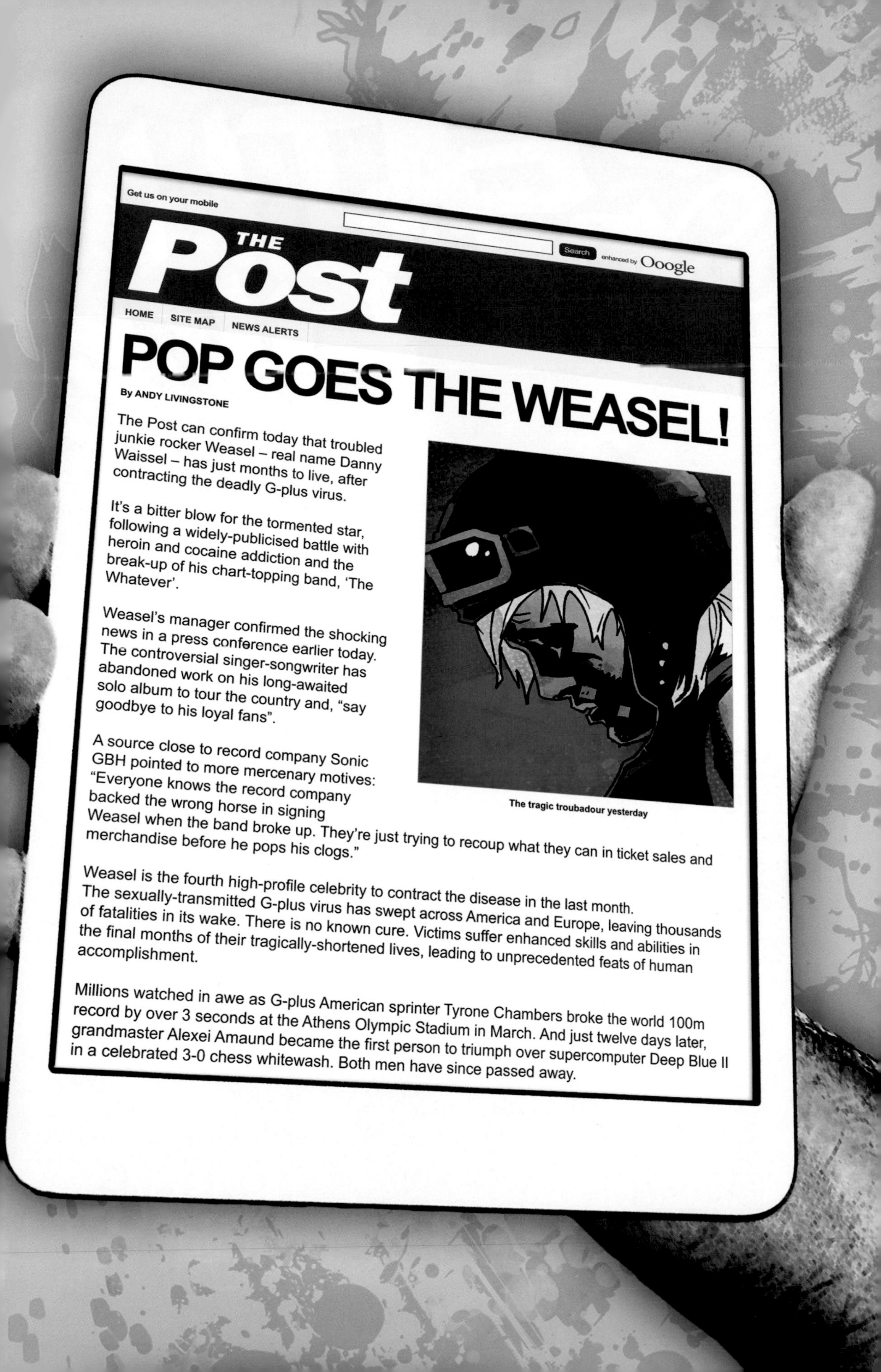

Get us on your mobile

Search enhanced by Ooogle

THE Post

HOME | SITE MAP | NEWS ALERTS

POP GOES THE WEASEL!

By ANDY LIVINGSTONE

The Post can confirm today that troubled junkie rocker Weasel – real name Danny Waissel – has just months to live, after contracting the deadly G-plus virus.

It's a bitter blow for the tormented star, following a widely-publicised battle with heroin and cocaine addiction and the break-up of his chart-topping band, 'The Whatever'.

Weasel's manager confirmed the shocking news in a press conference earlier today. The controversial singer-songwriter has abandoned work on his long-awaited solo album to tour the country and, "say goodbye to his loyal fans".

A source close to record company Sonic GBH pointed to more mercenary motives: "Everyone knows the record company backed the wrong horse in signing Weasel when the band broke up. They're just trying to recoup what they can in ticket sales and merchandise before he pops his clogs."

The tragic troubadour yesterday

Weasel is the fourth high-profile celebrity to contract the disease in the last month. The sexually-transmitted G-plus virus has swept across America and Europe, leaving thousands of fatalities in its wake. There is no known cure. Victims suffer enhanced skills and abilities in the final months of their tragically-shortened lives, leading to unprecedented feats of human accomplishment.

Millions watched in awe as G-plus American sprinter Tyrone Chambers broke the world 100m record by over 3 seconds at the Athens Olympic Stadium in March. And just twelve days later, grandmaster Alexei Amaund became the first person to triumph over supercomputer Deep Blue II in a celebrated 3-0 chess whitewash. Both men have since passed away.

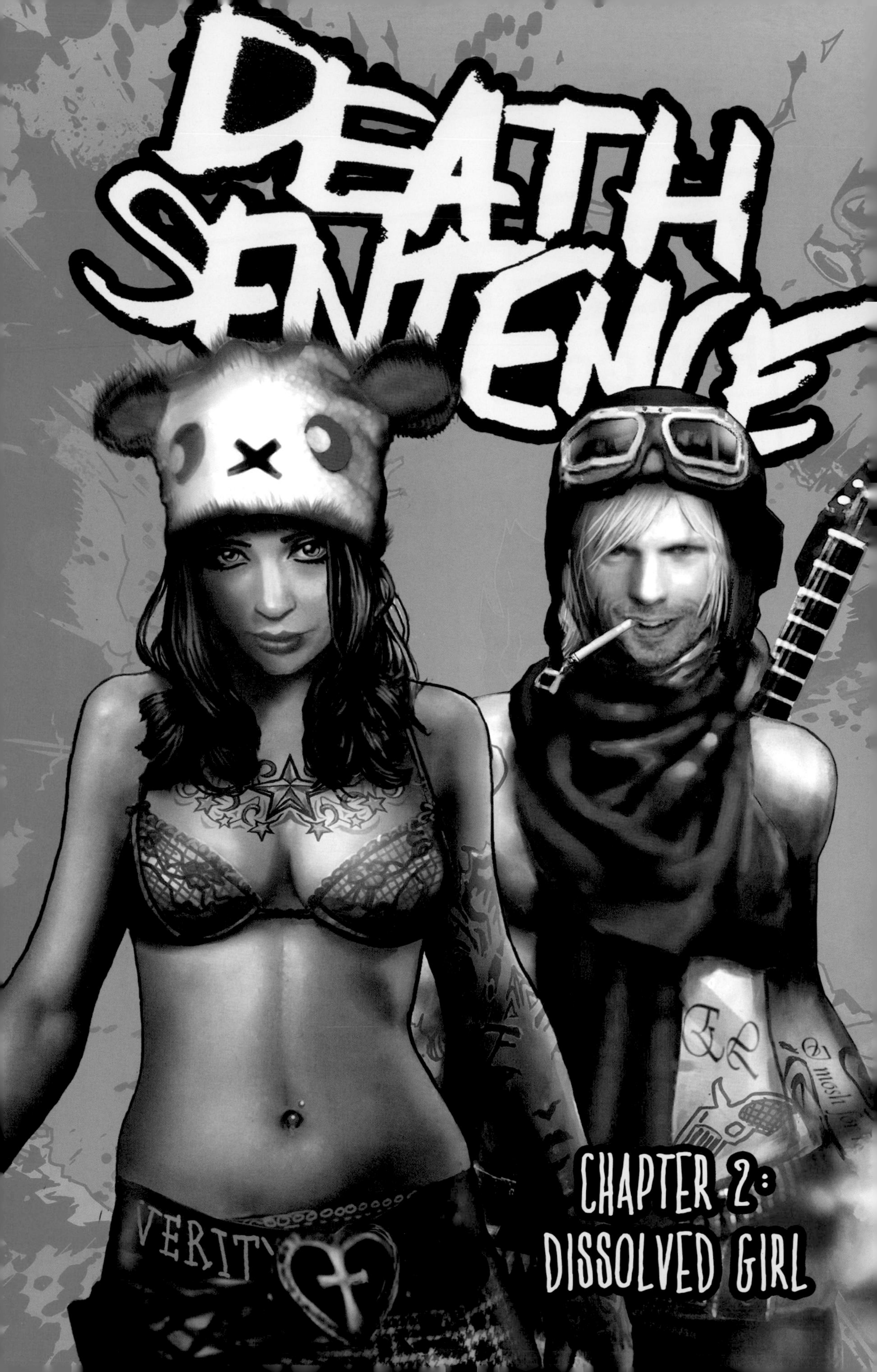
DEATH SENTENCE
CHAPTER 2:
DISSOLVED GIRL

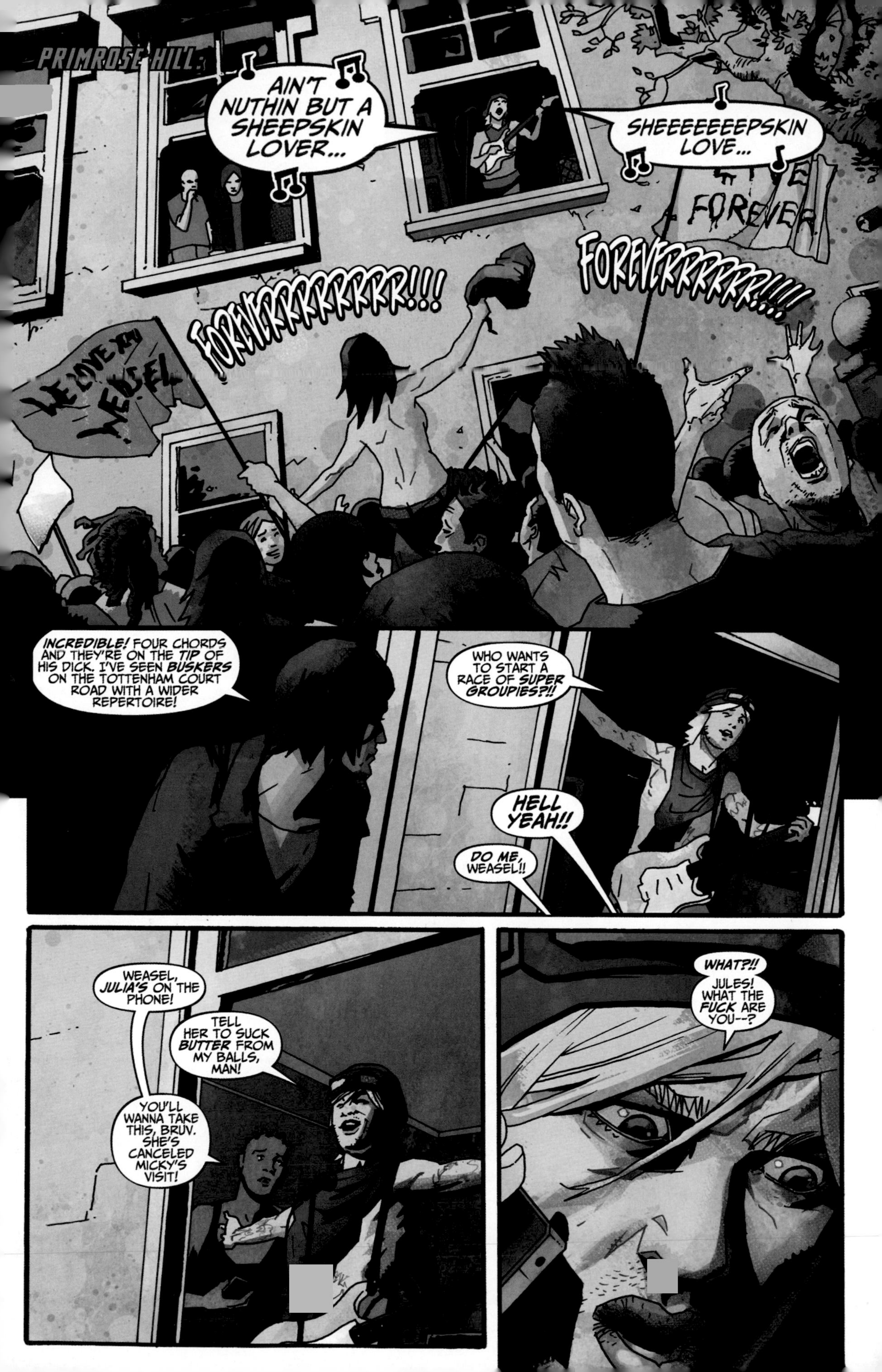
PRIMROSE HILL.
AIN'T NUTHIN BUT A SHEEPSKIN LOVER...
SHEEEEEEEEPSKIN LOVE...
FOREVERRRRRRRRR!!!
FOREVERRRRRRR!!!!
INCREDIBLE! FOUR CHORDS AND THEY'RE ON THE TIP OF HIS DICK. I'VE SEEN BUSKERS ON THE TOTTENHAM COURT ROAD WITH A WIDER REPERTOIRE!
WHO WANTS TO START A RACE OF SUPER GROUPIES?!!
HELL YEAH!!
DO ME, WEASEL!!
WEASEL, JULIA'S ON THE PHONE!
TELL HER TO SUCK BUTTER FROM MY BALLS, MAN!
YOU'LL WANNA TAKE THIS, BRUV. SHE'S CANCELED MICKY'S VISIT!
WHAT?!!
JULES! WHAT THE FUCK ARE YOU--?

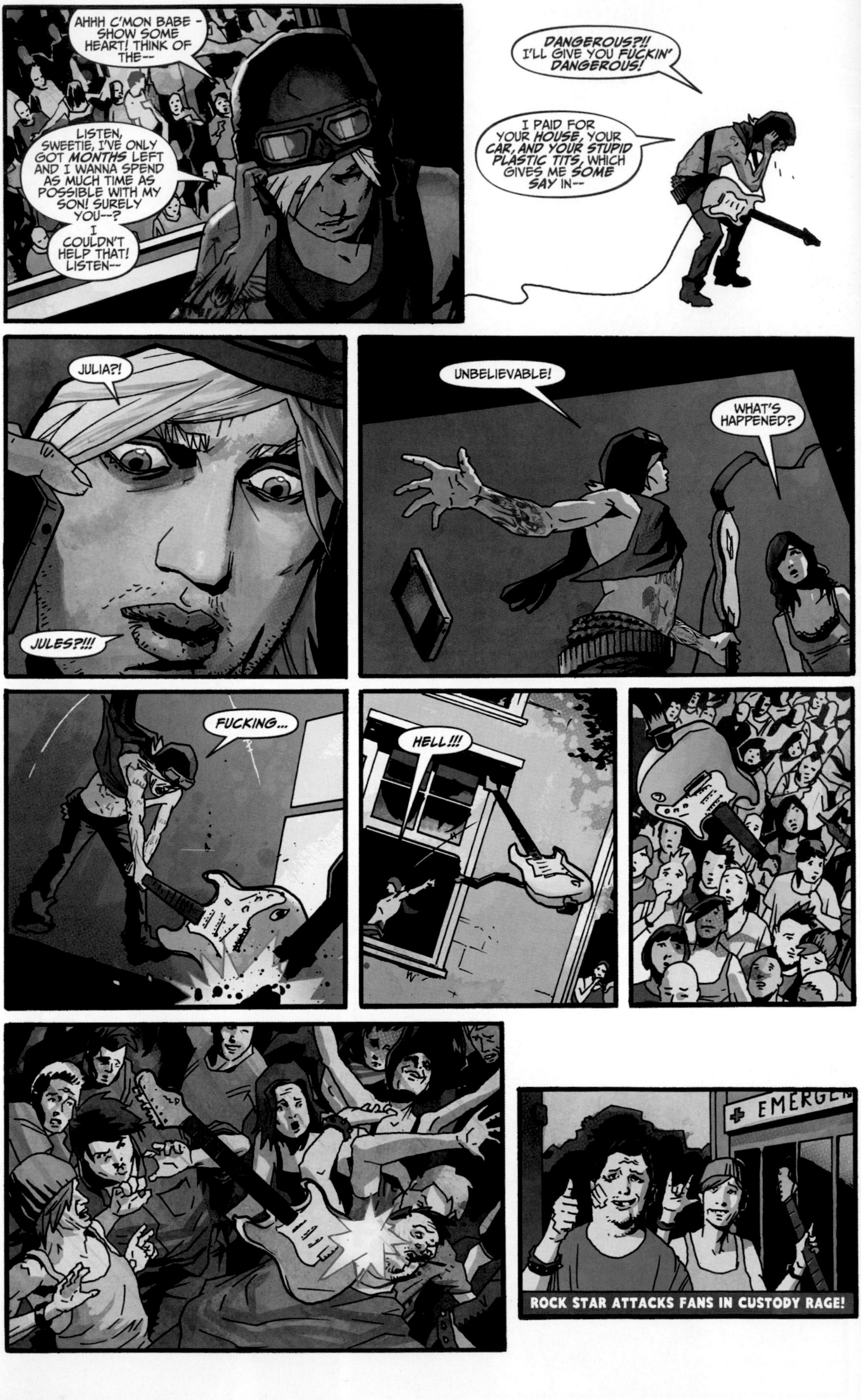
AHHH C'MON BABE - SHOW SOME HEART! THINK OF THE--
LISTEN, SWEETIE, I'VE ONLY GOT MONTHS LEFT AND I WANNA SPEND AS MUCH TIME AS POSSIBLE WITH MY SON! SURELY YOU--?
I COULDN'T HELP THAT! LISTEN--
DANGEROUS?!! I'LL GIVE YOU FUCKIN' DANGEROUS!
I PAID FOR YOUR HOUSE, YOUR CAR, AND YOUR STUPID PLASTIC TITS, WHICH GIVES ME SOME SAY IN--
JULIA?!
JULES?!!!
UNBELIEVABLE!
WHAT'S HAPPENED?
FUCKING...
HELL!!!
EMERGE
ROCK STAR ATTACKS FANS IN CUSTODY RAGE!

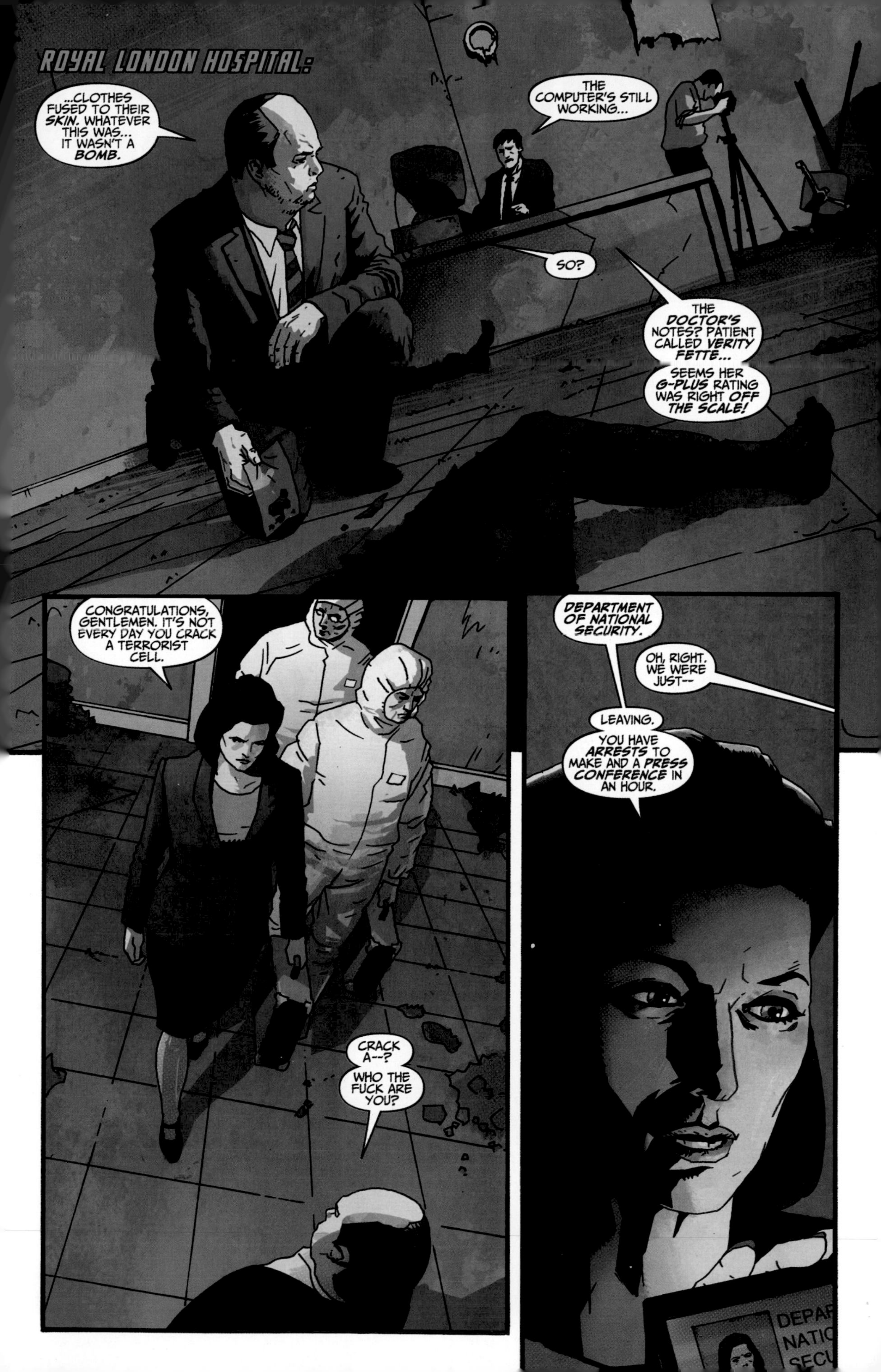
ROYAL LONDON HOSPITAL:
...CLOTHES FUSED TO THEIR SKIN. WHATEVER THIS WAS... IT WASN'T A BOMB.
THE COMPUTER'S STILL WORKING...
SO?
THE DOCTOR'S NOTES? PATIENT CALLED VERITY FETTE...
SEEMS HER G-PLUS RATING WAS RIGHT OFF THE SCALE!
CONGRATULATIONS, GENTLEMEN. IT'S NOT EVERY DAY YOU CRACK A TERRORIST CELL.
CRACK A--?
WHO THE FUCK ARE YOU?
DEPARTMENT OF NATIONAL SECURITY.
OH, RIGHT. WE WERE JUST--
LEAVING.
YOU HAVE ARRESTS TO MAKE AND A PRESS CONFERENCE IN AN HOUR.

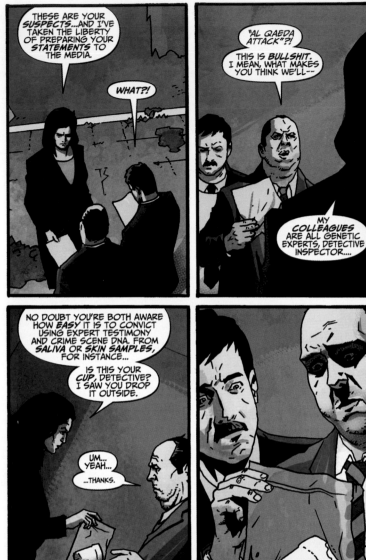

THESE ARE YOUR *SUSPECTS*...AND I'VE TAKEN THE LIBERTY OF PREPARING YOUR *STATEMENTS* TO THE MEDIA.

WHAT?!

"AL QAEDA ATTACK"?! THIS IS *BULLSHIT*. I MEAN, WHAT MAKES YOU THINK WE'LL--

MY COLLEAGUES ARE ALL GENETIC EXPERTS, DETECTIVE INSPECTOR....

THEY ARE CURRENTLY DISTRIBUTING THE *DNA* OF THE THREE PEOPLE NAMED ON THAT LIST *FREELY* ABOUT THE CRIME SCENE: SKIN CELLS. FABRIC. HAIR.

YOU'RE DISTRIBUTING--

WHAT?!

DOES YOUR COLLEAGUE HAVE *LEARNING DIFFICULTIES?*

NO DOUBT YOU'RE BOTH AWARE HOW *EASY* IT IS TO CONVICT USING EXPERT TESTIMONY AND CRIME SCENE DNA. FROM *SALIVA* OR *SKIN* SAMPLES, FOR INSTANCE...

IS THIS YOUR *CUP*, DETECTIVE? I SAW YOU DROP IT OUTSIDE.

UM... YEAH... ...THANKS.

≶AHEM≷

...SO...LIKE I WAS *SAYING*... IT LOOKS PRETTY MUCH LIKE ANOTHER *AL QAEDA* ATTACK. MY PARTNER AND I ARE FOLLOWING SOME LEADS IN THE...UH...

...LUTON AREA.

QUITE.

LISTEN... WHAT ABOUT THE *GIRL?* THIS VERITY *FETTE?*

I THINK YOU'LL FIND, WHEN YOU LOOK MORE *CAREFULLY*, DETECTIVE...

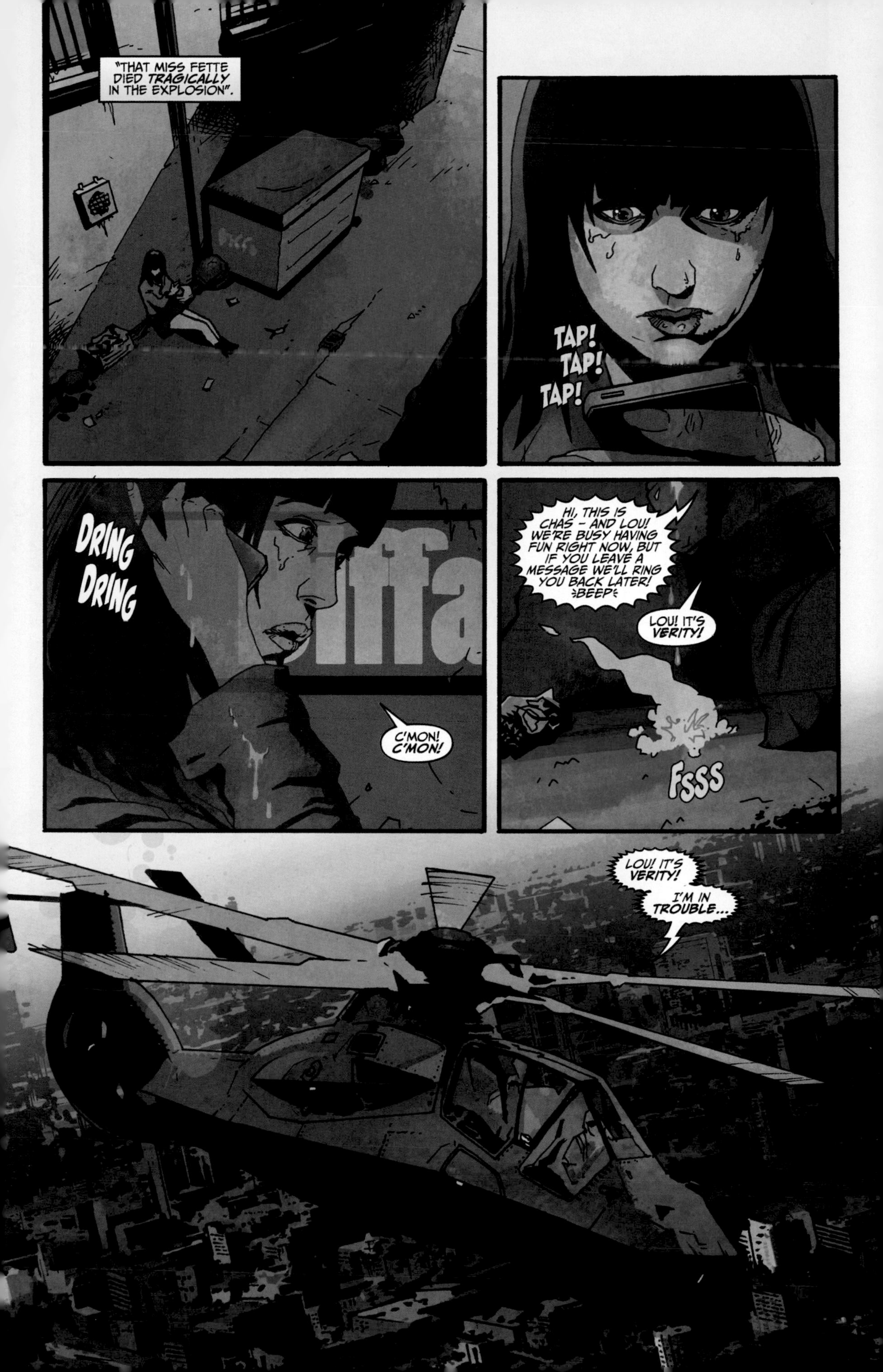
"THAT MISS FETTE DIED TRAGICALLY IN THE EXPLOSION".
TAP! TAP! TAP!
DRING DRING
C'MON! C'MON!
HI, THIS IS CHAS - AND LOU! WE'RE BUSY HAVING FUN RIGHT NOW, BUT IF YOU LEAVE A MESSAGE WE'LL RING YOU BACK LATER! *BEEP*
LOU! IT'S VERITY!
FSSS
LOU! IT'S VERITY!
I'M IN TROUBLE...

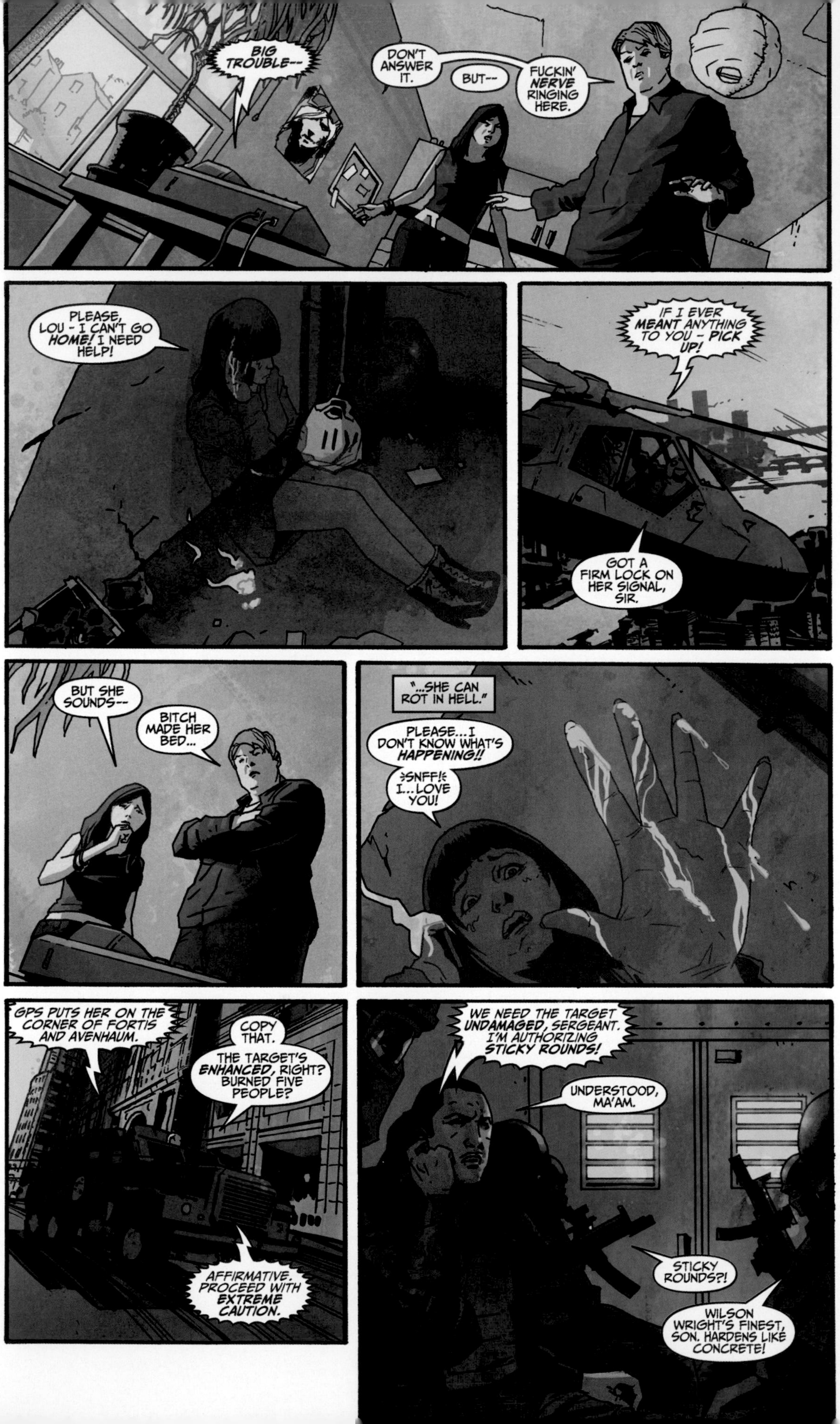
BIG TROUBLE--
DON'T ANSWER IT.
BUT--
FUCKIN' NERVE RINGING HERE.
PLEASE, LOU - I CAN'T GO HOME! I NEED HELP!
IF I EVER MEANT ANYTHING TO YOU - PICK UP!
GOT A FIRM LOCK ON HER SIGNAL, SIR.
BUT SHE SOUNDS--
BITCH MADE HER BED...
"...SHE CAN ROT IN HELL."
PLEASE...I DON'T KNOW WHAT'S HAPPENING!!
SNFF! I...LOVE YOU!
GPS PUTS HER ON THE CORNER OF FORTIS AND AVENHAUM.
COPY THAT.
THE TARGET'S ENHANCED, RIGHT? BURNED FIVE PEOPLE?
AFFIRMATIVE. PROCEED WITH EXTREME CAUTION.
WE NEED THE TARGET UNDAMAGED, SERGEANT. I'M AUTHORIZING STICKY ROUNDS!
UNDERSTOOD, MA'AM.
STICKY ROUNDS?!
WILSON WRIGHT'S FINEST, SON. HARDENS LIKE CONCRETE!

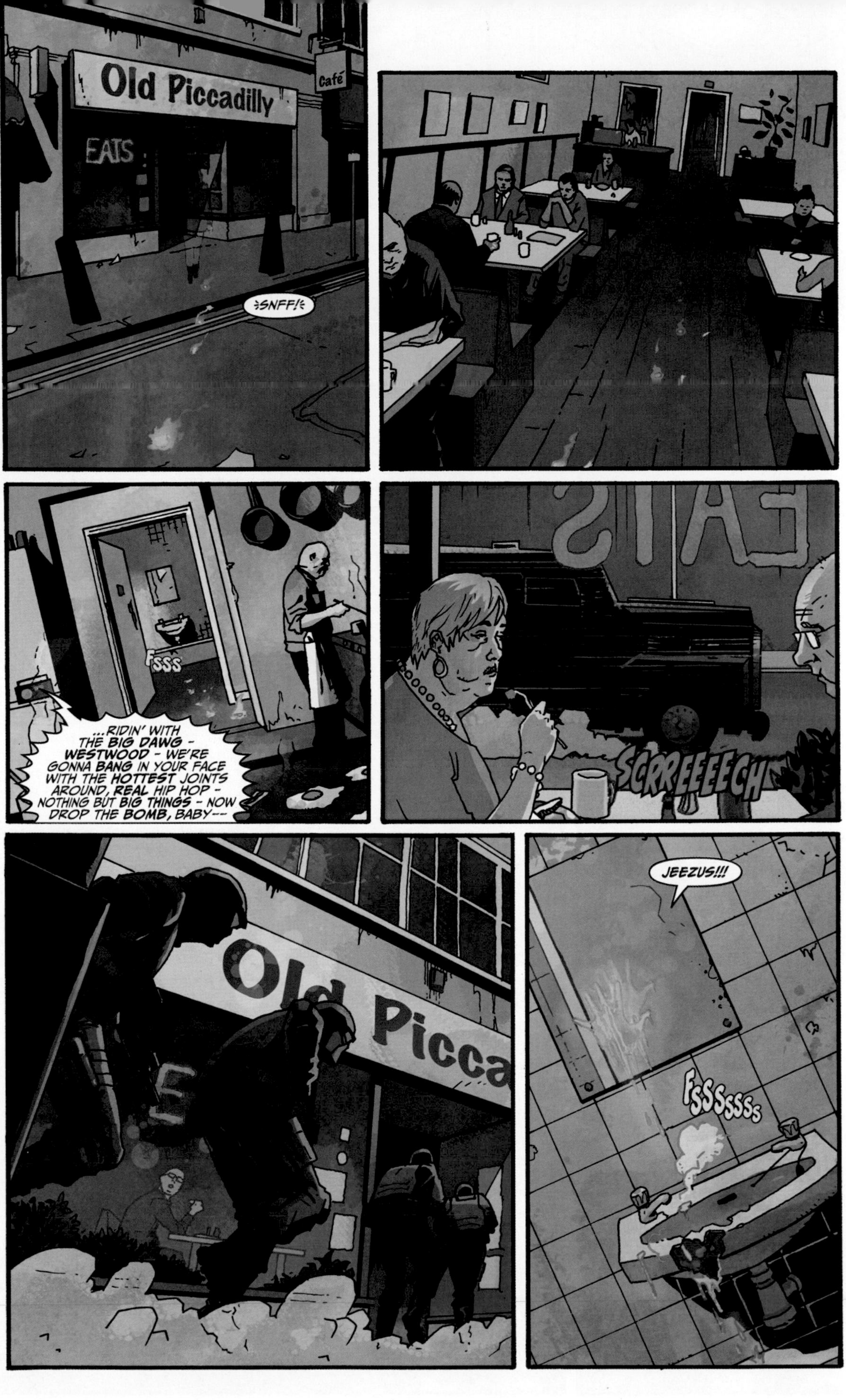
Old Piccadilly
Café
EATS
SNFF!
FSSS
...RIDIN' WITH THE BIG DAWG - WESTWOOD - WE'RE GONNA BANG IN YOUR FACE WITH THE HOTTEST JOINTS AROUND, REAL HIP HOP - NOTHING BUT BIG THINGS - NOW DROP THE BOMB, BABY---
SCRREEEEECH
Old Picca
JEEZUS!!!
FSSSSSSS

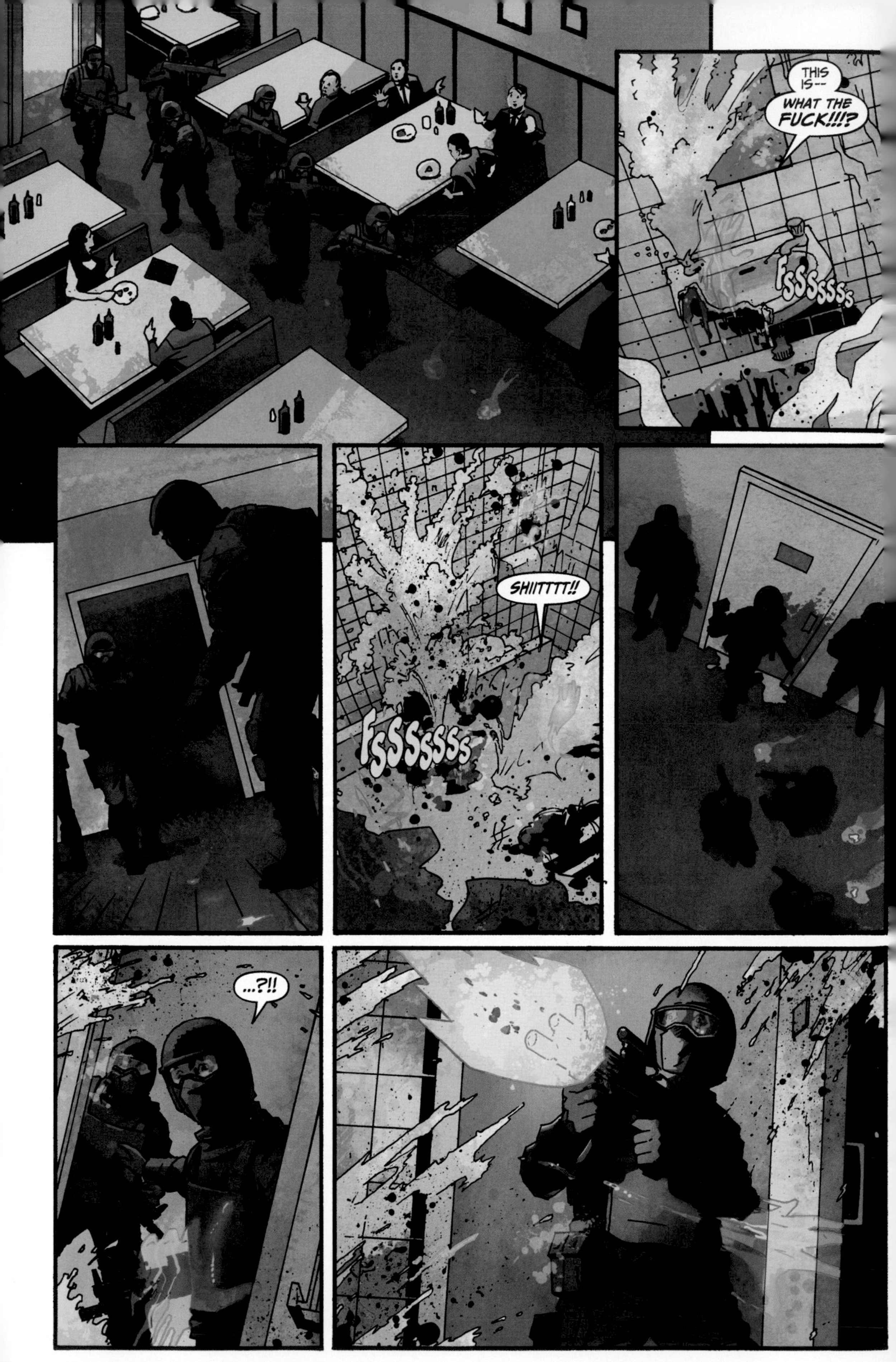
THIS IS--
WHAT THE FUCK!!!?
FSSSSSSS
SHIITTTT!!
FSSSSSSS
...?!!

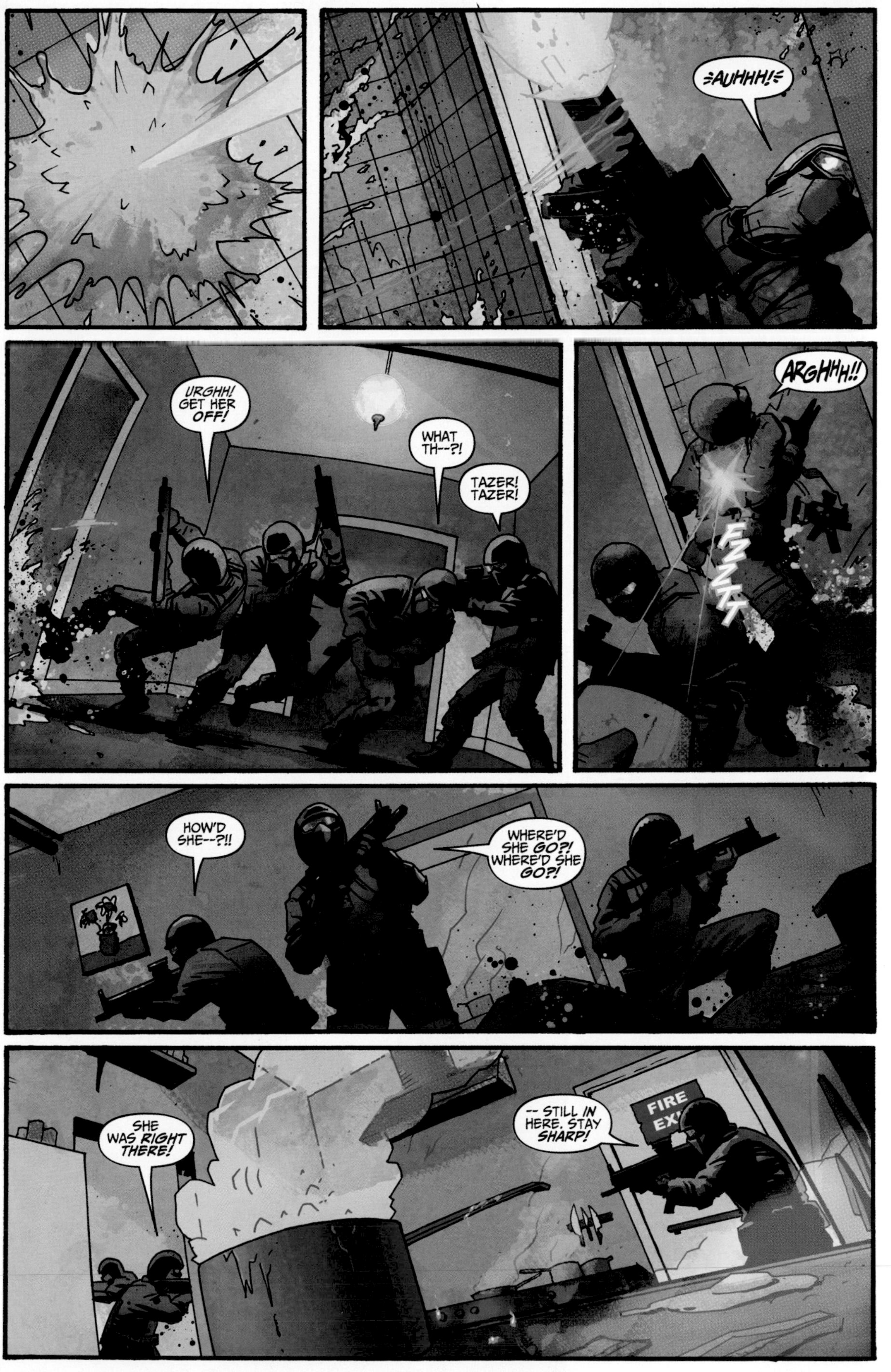
AUHHH!
URGHH! GET HER OFF!
WHAT TH--?!
TAZER! TAZER!
ARGHHH!!
FZZZKT
HOW'D SHE--?!!
WHERE'D SHE GO?! WHERE'D SHE GO?!
SHE WAS RIGHT THERE!
-- STILL IN HERE. STAY SHARP!
FIRE EXI

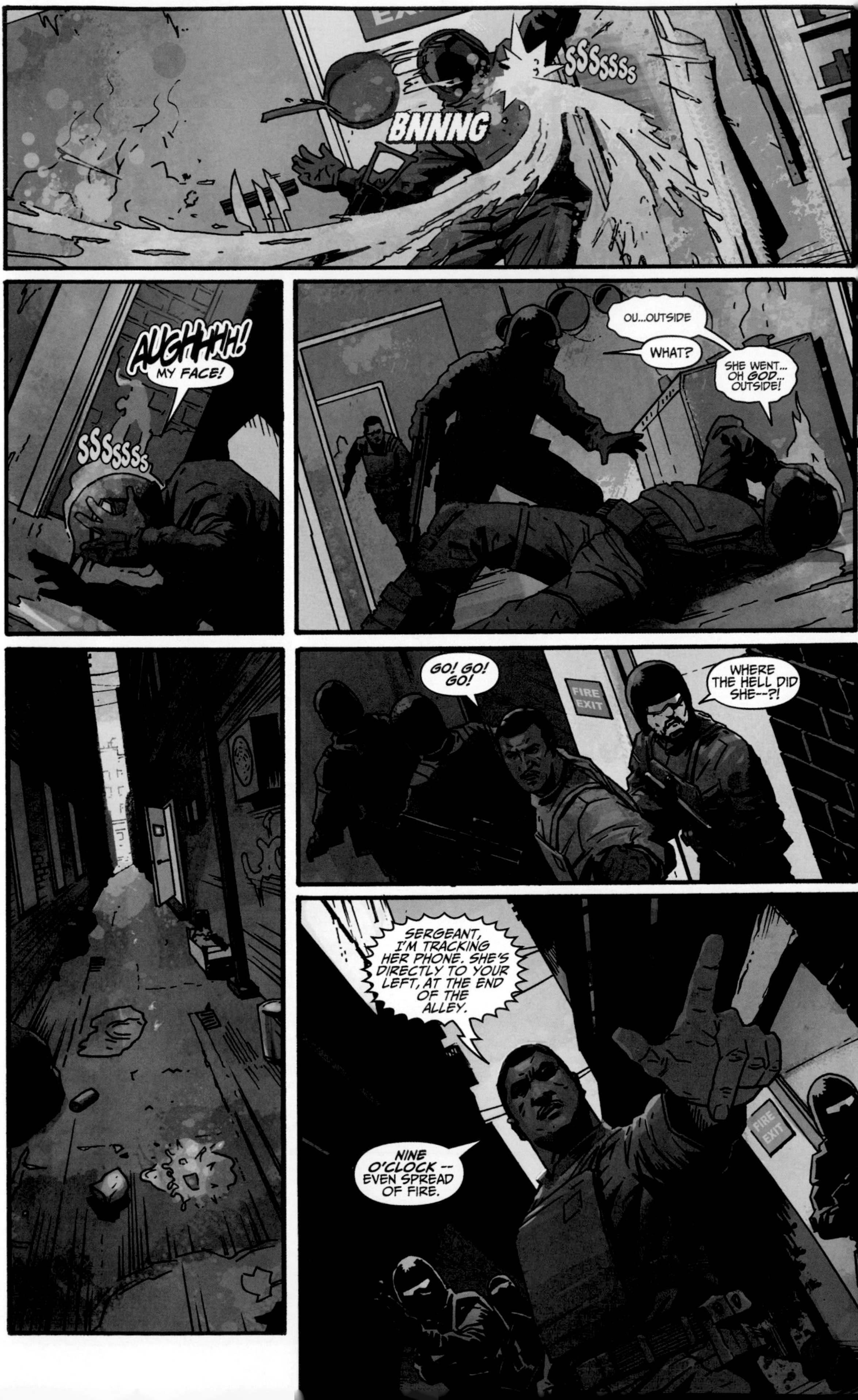
SSSssss
BNNNG
AUGHHH!
MY FACE!
SSSssss
OU...OUTSIDE
WHAT?
SHE WENT... OH GOD... OUTSIDE!
GO! GO! GO!
FIRE EXIT
WHERE THE HELL DID SHE--?!
SERGEANT, I'M TRACKING HER PHONE. SHE'S DIRECTLY TO YOUR LEFT, AT THE END OF THE ALLEY.
NINE O'CLOCK -- EVEN SPREAD OF FIRE.
FIRE EXIT

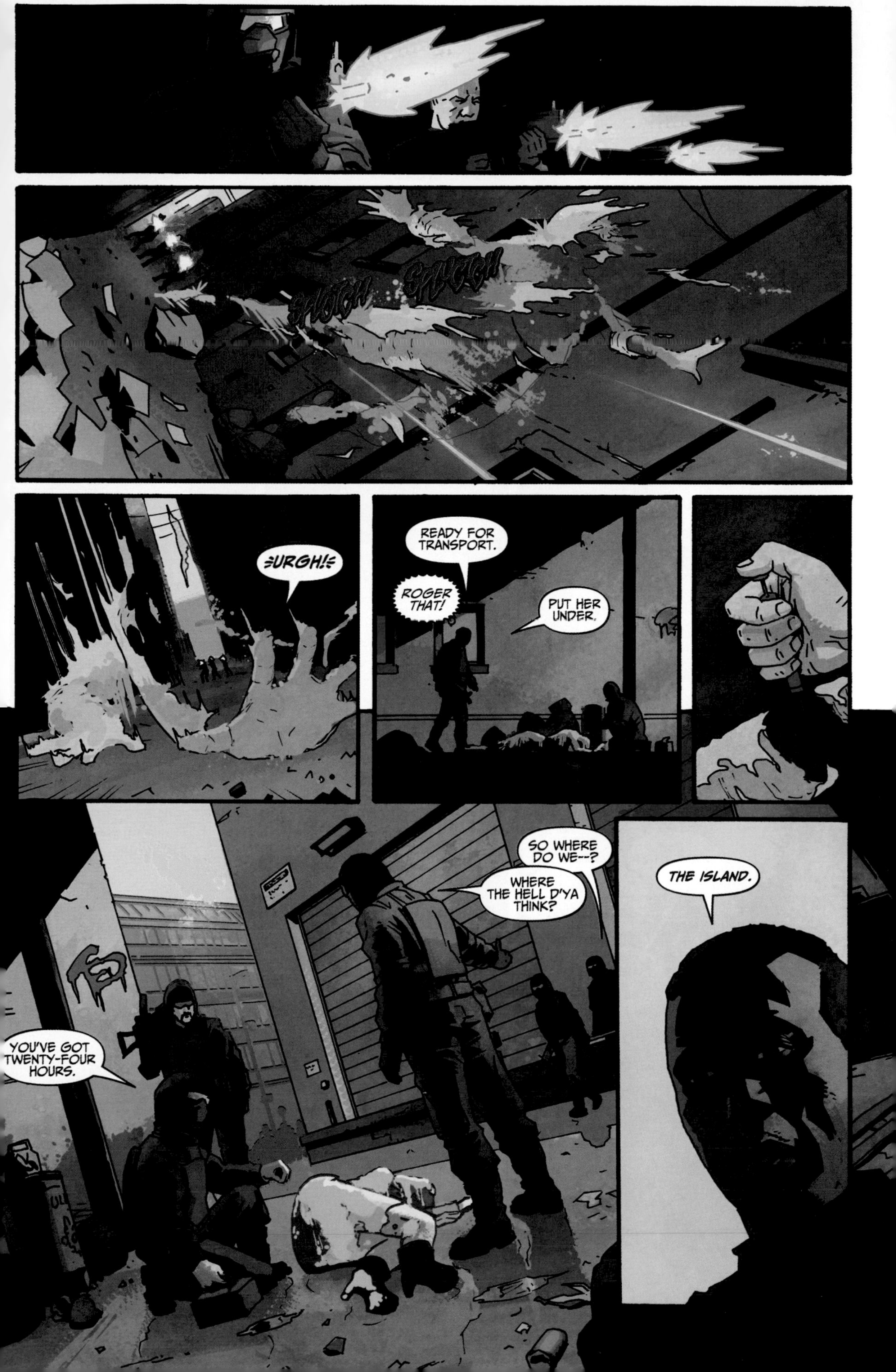
SPLOTCH
SPLATCH
URGH!
READY FOR TRANSPORT.
ROGER THAT!
PUT HER UNDER.
YOU'VE GOT TWENTY-FOUR HOURS.
SO WHERE DO WE--?
WHERE THE HELL D'YA THINK?
THE ISLAND.

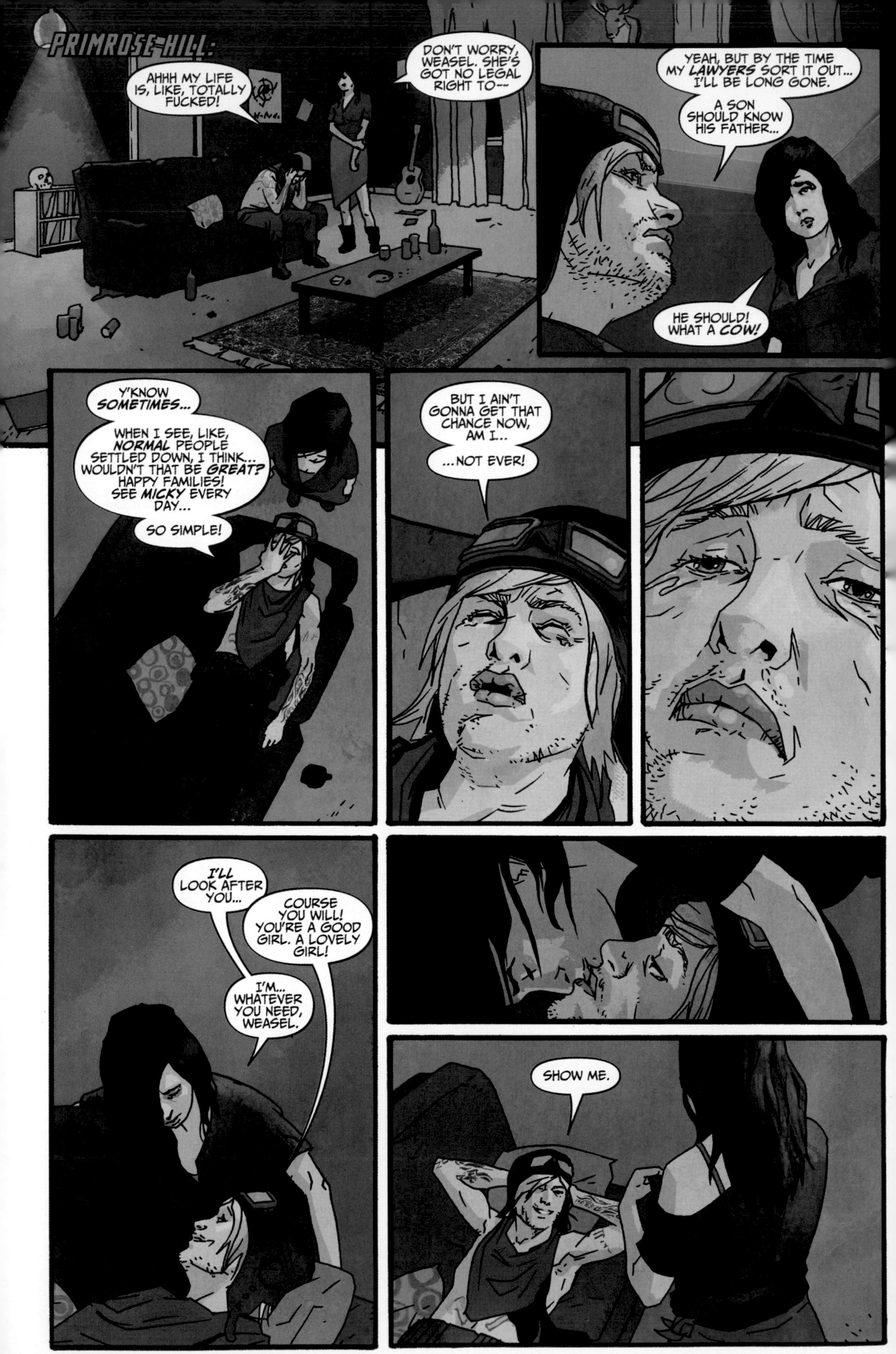
PRIMROSE HILL:
AHHH MY LIFE IS, LIKE, TOTALLY FUCKED!
DON'T WORRY, WEASEL. SHE'S GOT NO LEGAL RIGHT TO--
YEAH, BUT BY THE TIME MY LAWYERS SORT IT OUT... I'LL BE LONG GONE.
A SON SHOULD KNOW HIS FATHER...
HE SHOULD! WHAT A COW!
Y'KNOW SOMETIMES...
WHEN I SEE, LIKE, NORMAL PEOPLE SETTLED DOWN, I THINK... WOULDN'T THAT BE GREAT? HAPPY FAMILIES! SEE MICKY EVERY DAY...
SO SIMPLE!
BUT I AIN'T GONNA GET THAT CHANCE NOW, AM I...
...NOT EVER!
I'LL LOOK AFTER YOU...
COURSE YOU WILL! YOU'RE A GOOD GIRL. A LOVELY GIRL!
I'M... WHATEVER YOU NEED, WEASEL.
SHOW ME.

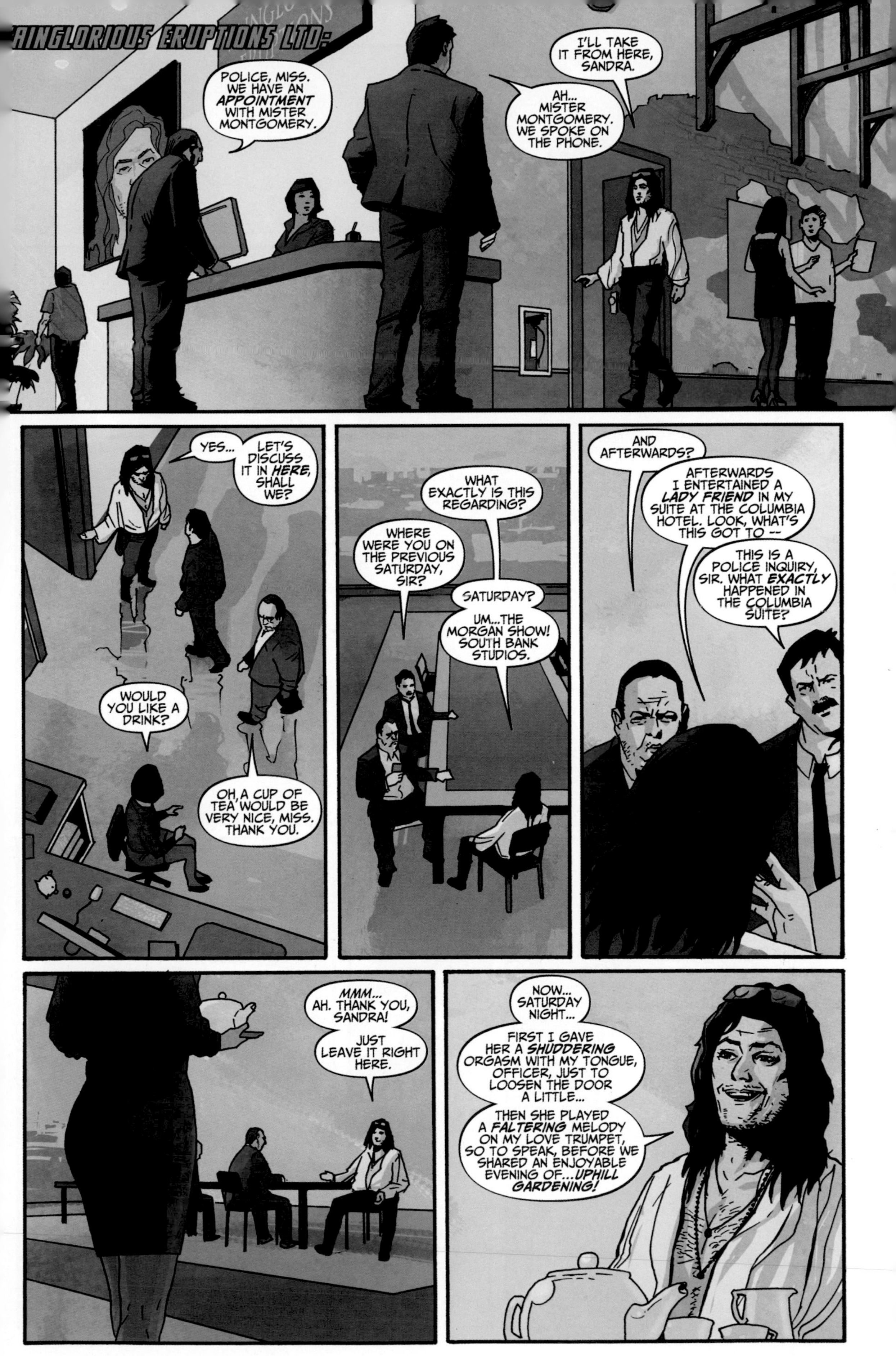

INGLORIOUS ERUPTIONS LTD:
POLICE, MISS. WE HAVE AN APPOINTMENT WITH MISTER MONTGOMERY.
AH... MISTER MONTGOMERY. WE SPOKE ON THE PHONE.
I'LL TAKE IT FROM HERE, SANDRA.
YES... LET'S DISCUSS IT IN HERE, SHALL WE?
WOULD YOU LIKE A DRINK?
OH, A CUP OF TEA WOULD BE VERY NICE, MISS. THANK YOU.
WHAT EXACTLY IS THIS REGARDING?
WHERE WERE YOU ON THE PREVIOUS SATURDAY, SIR?
SATURDAY?
UM...THE MORGAN SHOW! SOUTH BANK STUDIOS.
AND AFTERWARDS?
AFTERWARDS I ENTERTAINED A LADY FRIEND IN MY SUITE AT THE COLUMBIA HOTEL. LOOK, WHAT'S THIS GOT TO --
THIS IS A POLICE INQUIRY, SIR. WHAT EXACTLY HAPPENED IN THE COLUMBIA SUITE?
MMM... AH. THANK YOU, SANDRA!
JUST LEAVE IT RIGHT HERE.
NOW... SATURDAY NIGHT...
FIRST I GAVE HER A SHUDDERING ORGASM WITH MY TONGUE, OFFICER, JUST TO LOOSEN THE DOOR A LITTLE...
THEN SHE PLAYED A FALTERING MELODY ON MY LOVE TRUMPET, SO TO SPEAK, BEFORE WE SHARED AN ENJOYABLE EVENING OF...UPHILL GARDENING!

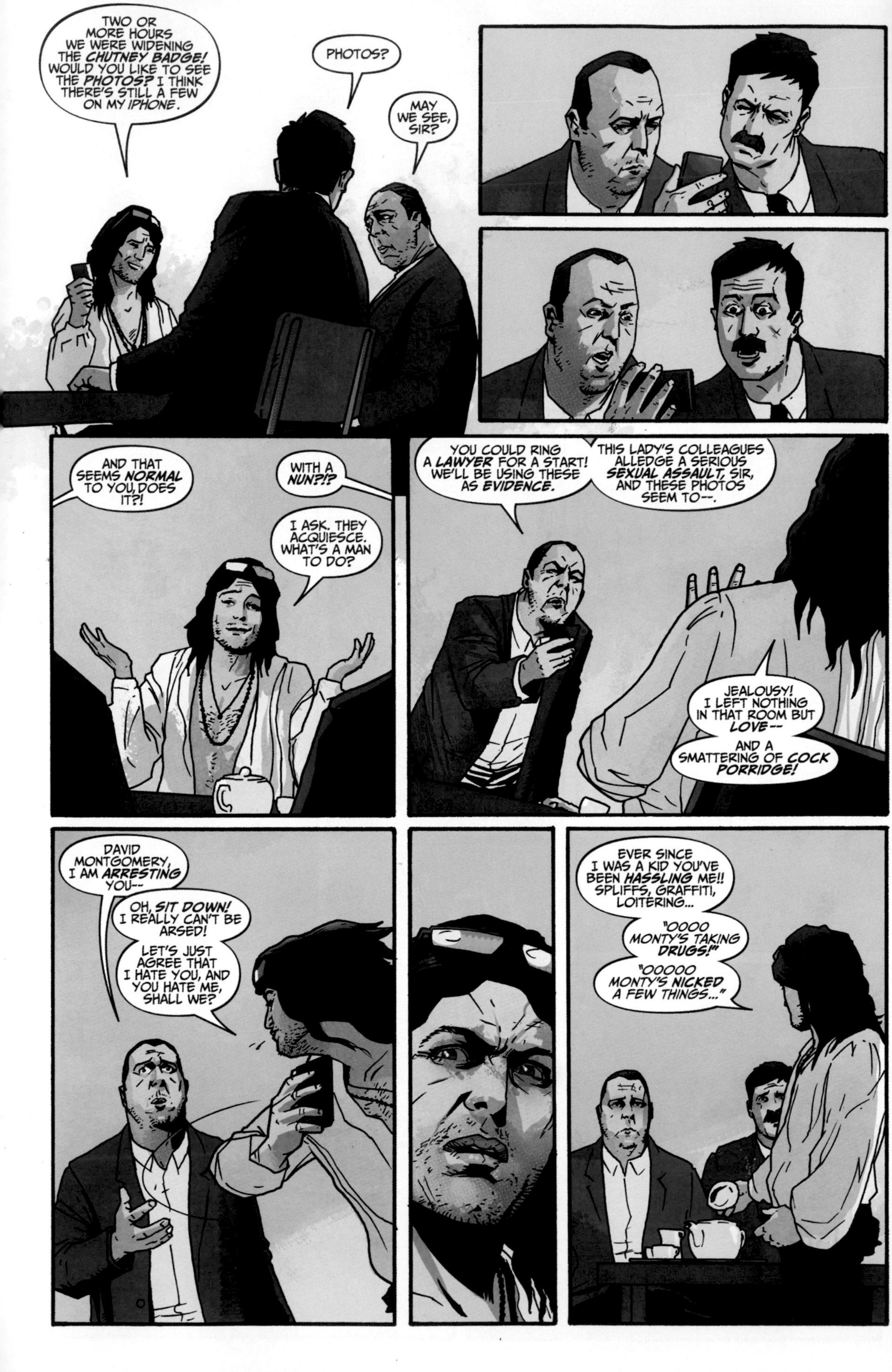
TWO OR MORE HOURS WE WERE WIDENING THE CHUTNEY BADGE! WOULD YOU LIKE TO SEE THE PHOTOS? I THINK THERE'S STILL A FEW ON MY IPHONE.
PHOTOS?
MAY WE SEE, SIR?
AND THAT SEEMS NORMAL TO YOU, DOES IT?!
WITH A NUN?!?
I ASK. THEY ACQUIESCE. WHAT'S A MAN TO DO?
YOU COULD RING A LAWYER FOR A START! WE'LL BE USING THESE AS EVIDENCE.
THIS LADY'S COLLEAGUES ALLEDGE A SERIOUS SEXUAL ASSAULT, SIR, AND THESE PHOTOS SEEM TO--.
JEALOUSY! I LEFT NOTHING IN THAT ROOM BUT LOVE--
AND A SMATTERING OF COCK PORRIDGE!
DAVID MONTGOMERY, I AM ARRESTING YOU--
OH, SIT DOWN! I REALLY CAN'T BE ARSED!
LET'S JUST AGREE THAT I HATE YOU, AND YOU HATE ME, SHALL WE?
EVER SINCE I WAS A KID YOU'VE BEEN HASSLING ME!! SPLIFFS, GRAFFITI, LOITERING...
"OOOO MONTY'S TAKING DRUGS!"
"OOOOO MONTY'S NICKED A FEW THINGS..."

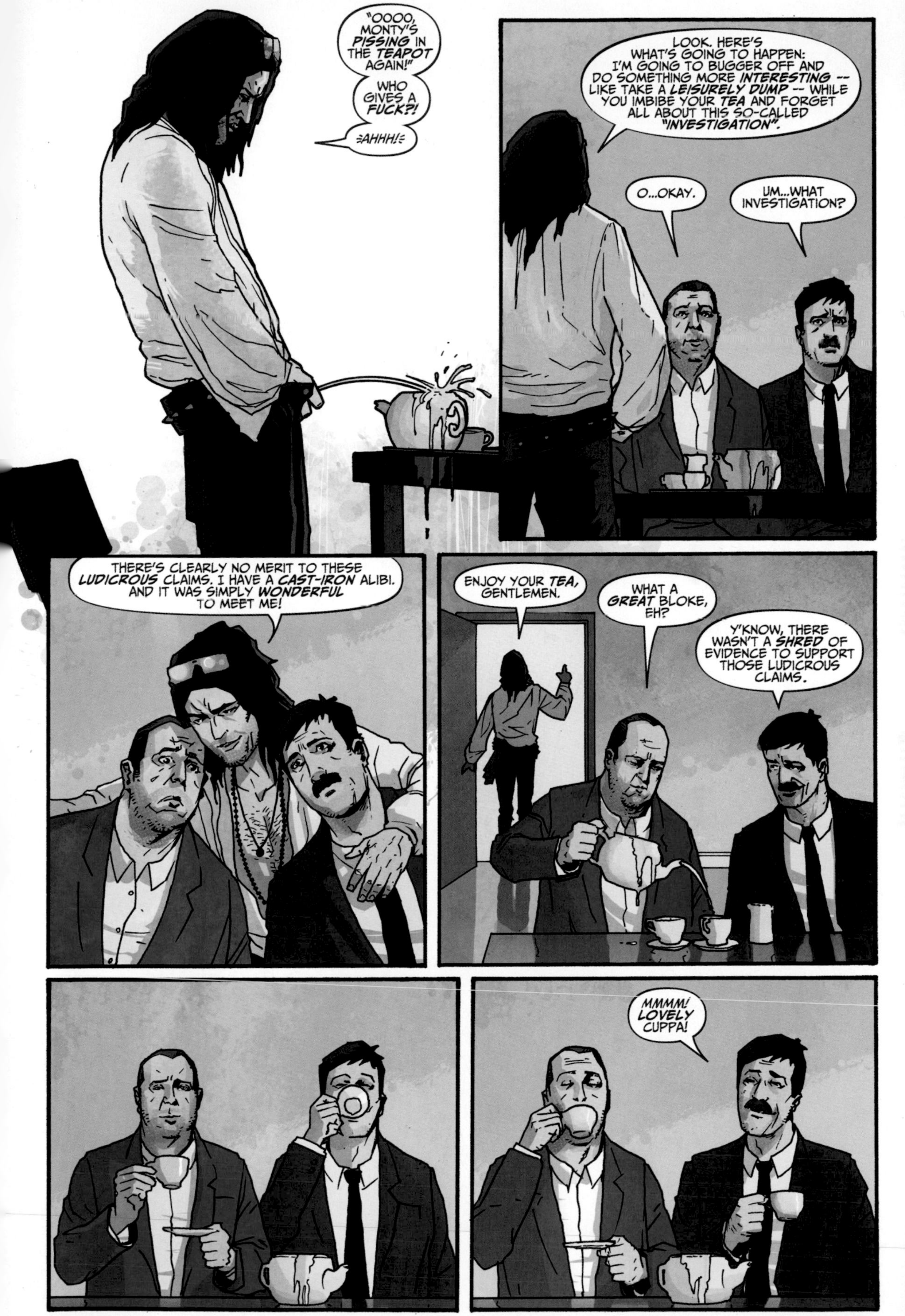
"OOOO, MONTY'S PISSING IN THE TEAPOT AGAIN!"
WHO GIVES A FUCK?!
AHHH!
LOOK. HERE'S WHAT'S GOING TO HAPPEN: I'M GOING TO BUGGER OFF AND DO SOMETHING MORE INTERESTING -- LIKE TAKE A LEISURELY DUMP -- WHILE YOU IMBIBE YOUR TEA AND FORGET ALL ABOUT THIS SO-CALLED "INVESTIGATION".
O...OKAY.
UM...WHAT INVESTIGATION?
THERE'S CLEARLY NO MERIT TO THESE LUDICROUS CLAIMS. I HAVE A CAST-IRON ALIBI. AND IT WAS SIMPLY WONDERFUL TO MEET ME!
ENJOY YOUR TEA, GENTLEMEN.
WHAT A GREAT BLOKE, EH?
Y'KNOW, THERE WASN'T A SHRED OF EVIDENCE TO SUPPORT THOSE LUDICROUS CLAIMS.
MMMM! LOVELY CUPPA!

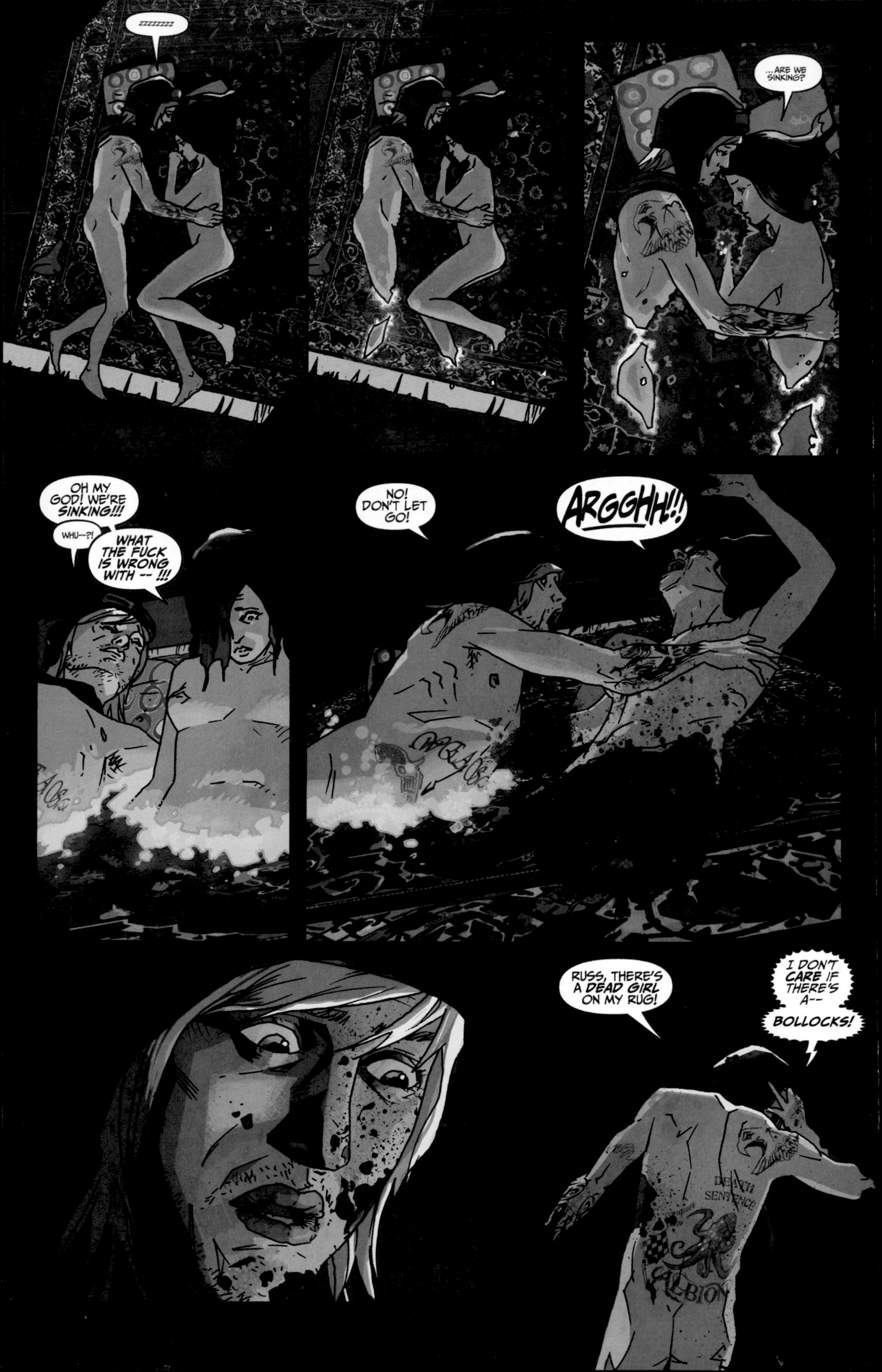
ZZZZZZZZ
...ARE WE SINKING?
OH MY GOD! WE'RE SINKING!!!
WHU--?!
WHAT THE FUCK IS WRONG WITH -- !!!
NO! DON'T LET GO!
ARGGHH!!!
RUSS, THERE'S A DEAD GIRL ON MY RUG!
I DON'T CARE IF THERE'S A--
BOLLOCKS!
DEATH SENTENCE
ALBION

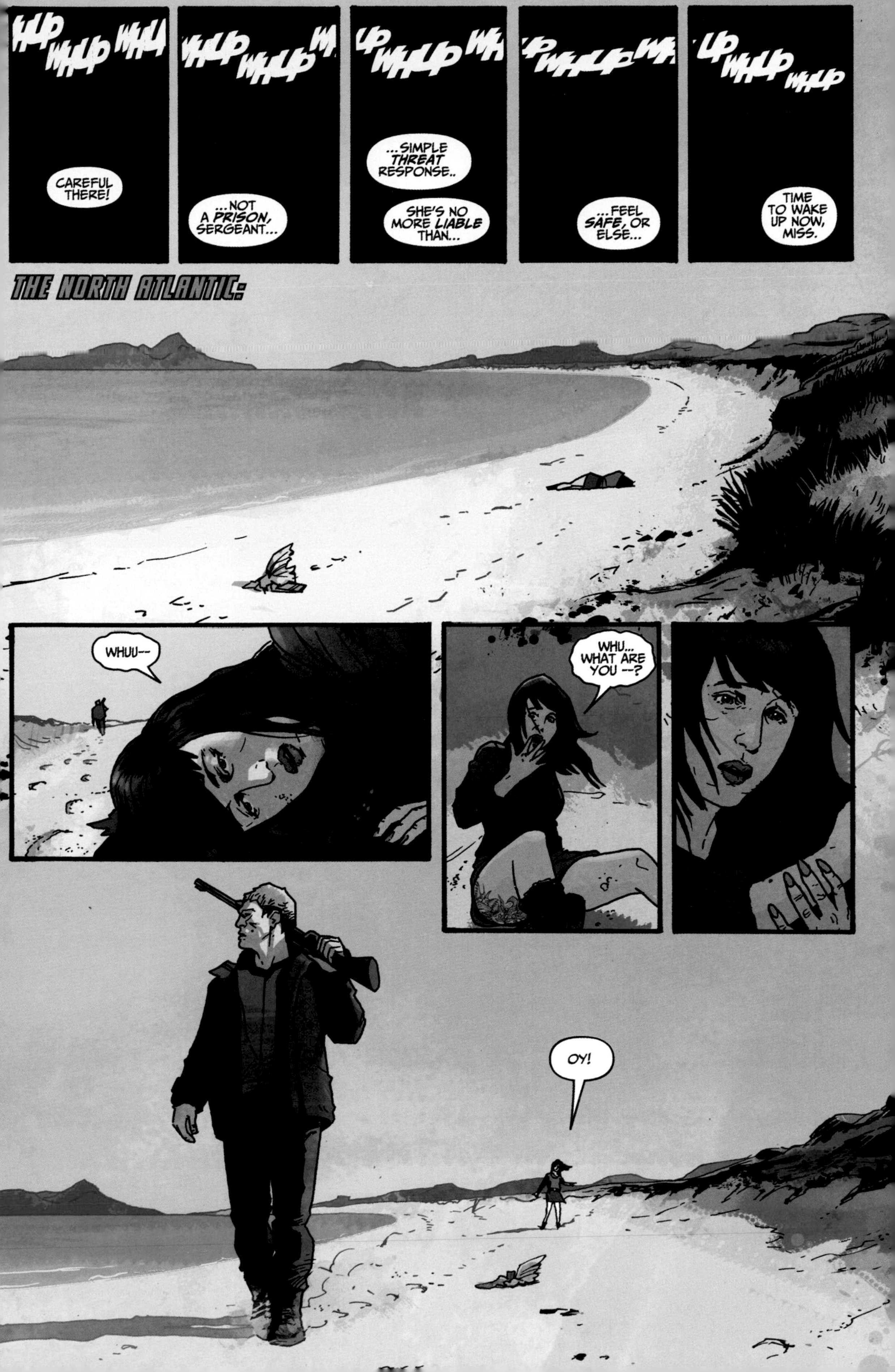

WHUP WHUP WHU
CAREFUL THERE!
WHUP WHUP WH
...NOT A PRISON, SERGEANT...
UP WHUP WH
...SIMPLE THREAT RESPONSE..
SHE'S NO MORE LIABLE THAN...
UP WHUP WH
...FEEL SAFE, OR ELSE...
UP WHUP WHUP
TIME TO WAKE UP NOW, MISS.
THE NORTH ATLANTIC:
WHUU--
WHU... WHAT ARE YOU --?
OY!

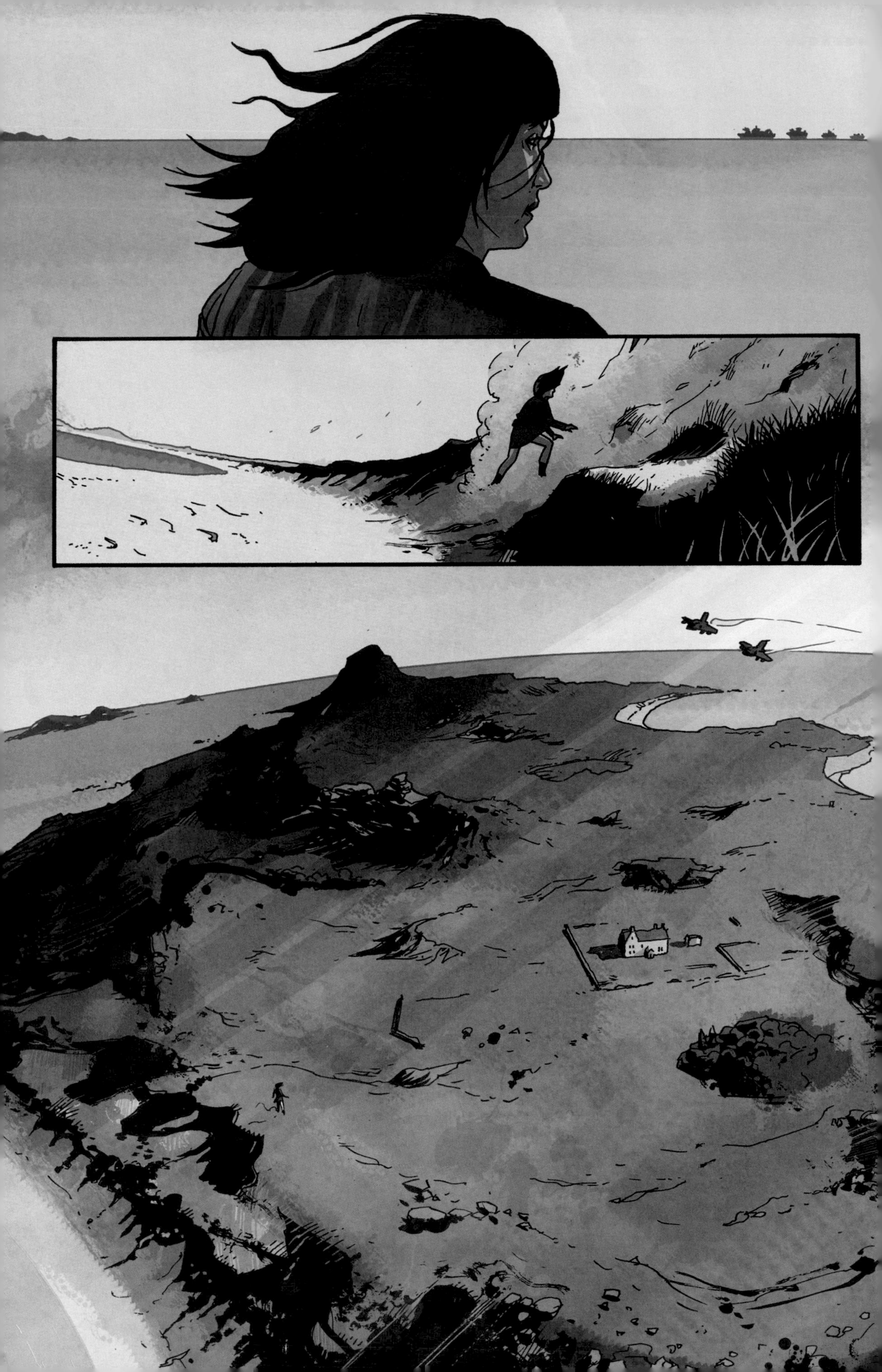

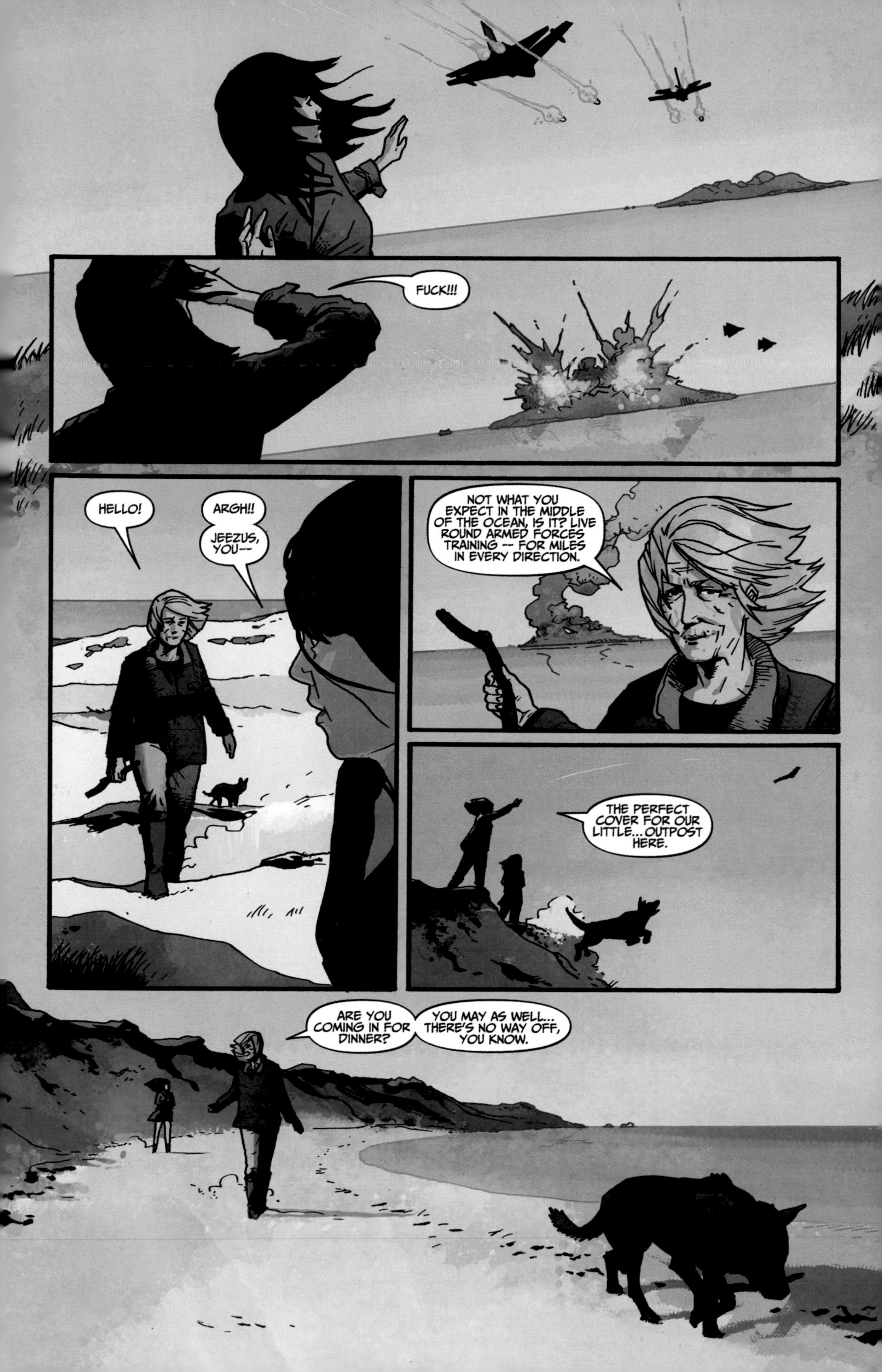
FUCK!!!
HELLO!
ARGH!!
JEEZUS, YOU--
NOT WHAT YOU EXPECT IN THE MIDDLE OF THE OCEAN, IS IT? LIVE ROUND ARMED FORCES TRAINING -- FOR MILES IN EVERY DIRECTION.
THE PERFECT COVER FOR OUR LITTLE...OUTPOST HERE.
ARE YOU COMING IN FOR DINNER?
YOU MAY AS WELL... THERE'S NO WAY OFF, YOU KNOW.

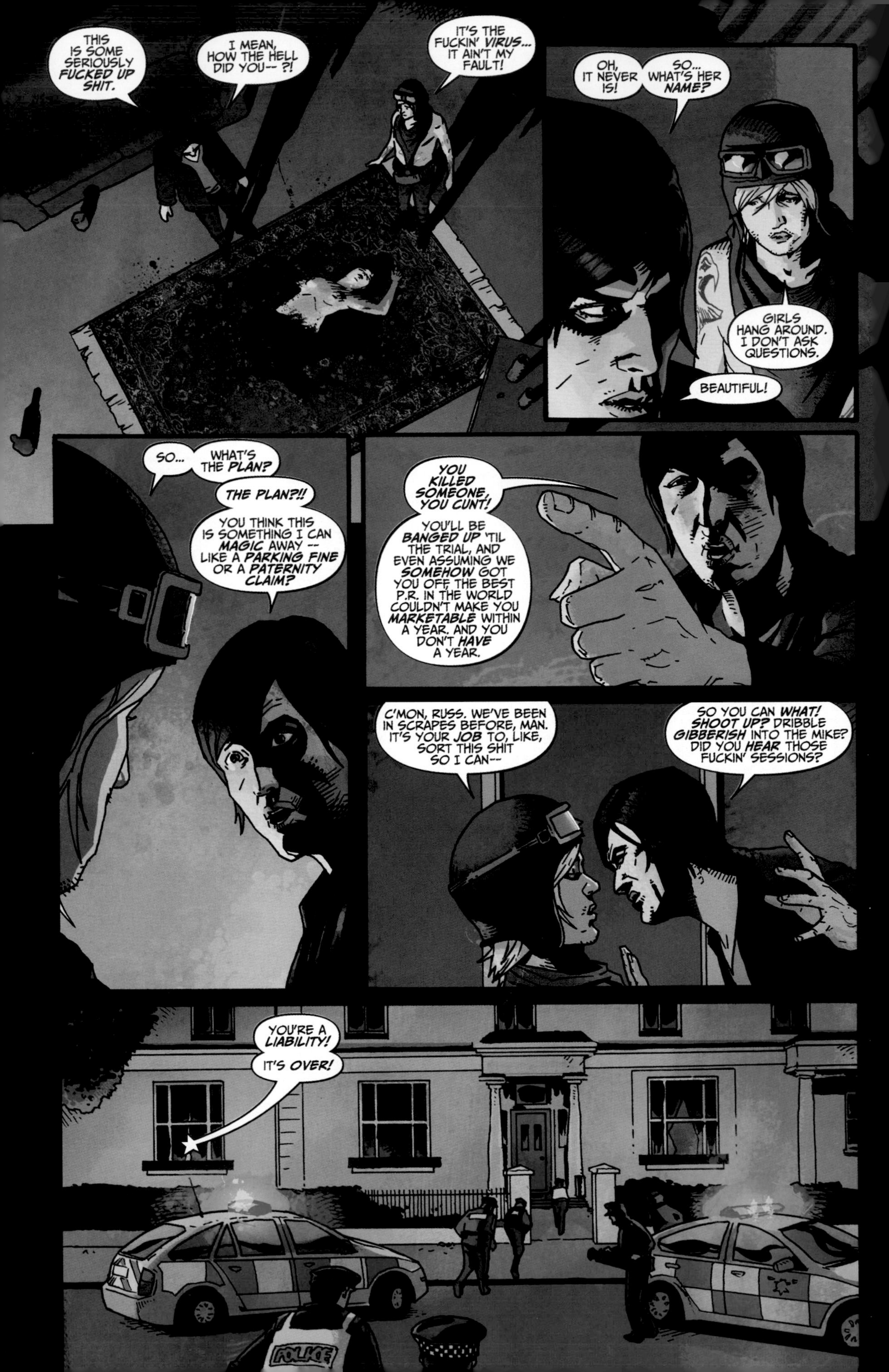

THIS IS SOME SERIOUSLY FUCKED UP SHIT.
I MEAN, HOW THE HELL DID YOU-- ?!
IT'S THE FUCKIN' VIRUS... IT AIN'T MY FAULT!
OH, IT NEVER IS!
SO... WHAT'S HER NAME?
GIRLS HANG AROUND. I DON'T ASK QUESTIONS.
BEAUTIFUL!
SO... WHAT'S THE PLAN?
THE PLAN?!!
YOU THINK THIS IS SOMETHING I CAN MAGIC AWAY -- LIKE A PARKING FINE OR A PATERNITY CLAIM?
YOU KILLED SOMEONE, YOU CUNT!
YOU'LL BE BANGED UP 'TIL THE TRIAL, AND EVEN ASSUMING WE SOMEHOW GOT YOU OFF THE BEST P.R. IN THE WORLD COULDN'T MAKE YOU MARKETABLE WITHIN A YEAR. AND YOU DON'T HAVE A YEAR.
C'MON, RUSS. WE'VE BEEN IN SCRAPES BEFORE, MAN. IT'S YOUR JOB TO, LIKE, SORT THIS SHIT SO I CAN--
SO YOU CAN WHAT! SHOOT UP? DRIBBLE GIBBERISH INTO THE MIKE? DID YOU HEAR THOSE FUCKIN' SESSIONS?
YOU'RE A LIABILITY!
IT'S OVER!
POLICE

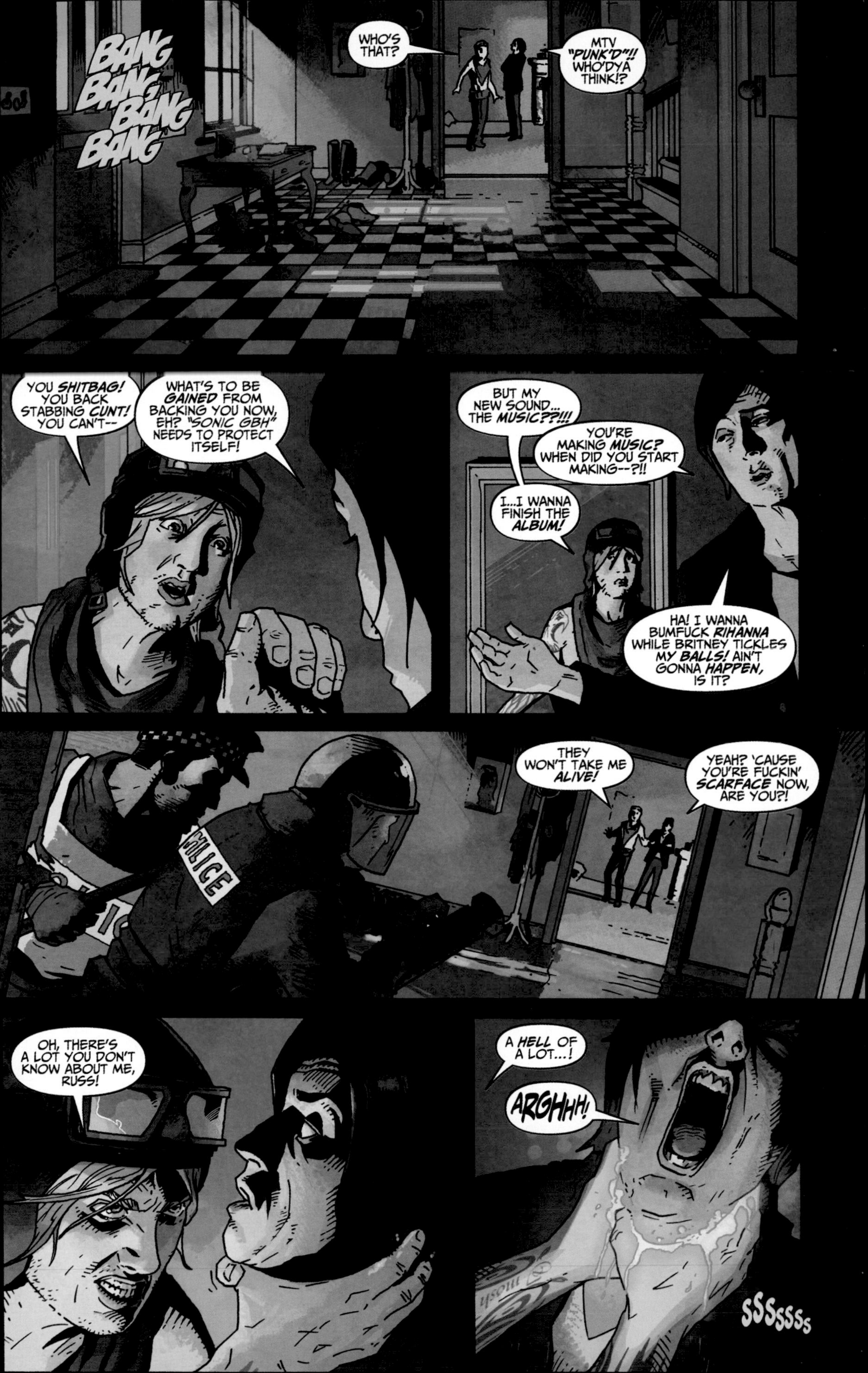
BANG BANG, BANG BANG
WHO'S THAT?
MTV "PUNK'D"!! WHO'D'YA THINK!?
YOU SHITBAG! YOU BACK STABBING CUNT! YOU CAN'T--
WHAT'S TO BE GAINED FROM BACKING YOU NOW, EH? "SONIC GBH" NEEDS TO PROTECT ITSELF!
BUT MY NEW SOUND... THE MUSIC??!!!
YOU'RE MAKING MUSIC? WHEN DID YOU START MAKING--?!!
I...I WANNA FINISH THE ALBUM!
HA! I WANNA BUMFUCK RIHANNA WHILE BRITNEY TICKLES MY BALLS! AIN'T GONNA HAPPEN, IS IT?
POLICE
THEY WON'T TAKE ME ALIVE!
YEAH? 'CAUSE YOU'RE FUCKIN' SCARFACE NOW, ARE YOU?!
OH, THERE'S A LOT YOU DON'T KNOW ABOUT ME, RUSS!
A HELL OF A LOT...!
ARGHHH!
SSSSSSS

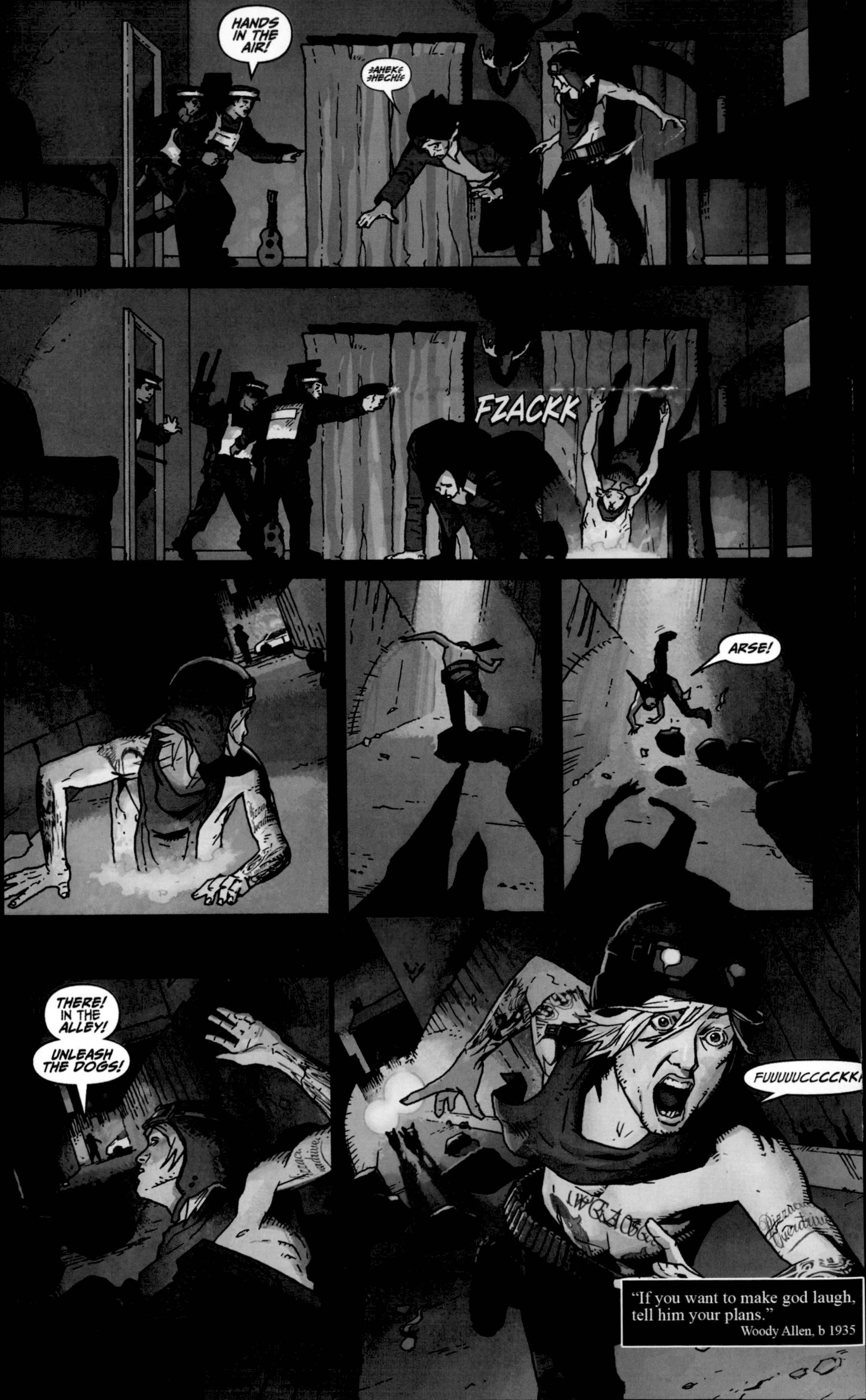
HANDS IN THE AIR!
AHEK HECH!
FZACKK
ARSE!
THERE! IN THE ALLEY!
UNLEASH THE DOGS!
FUUUUUCCCCKK
"If you want to make god laugh, tell him your plans."
Woody Allen, b 1935

MUSIC NEWS EXTRA

WEASEL INTERVIEW: 'Forever Fucked?'

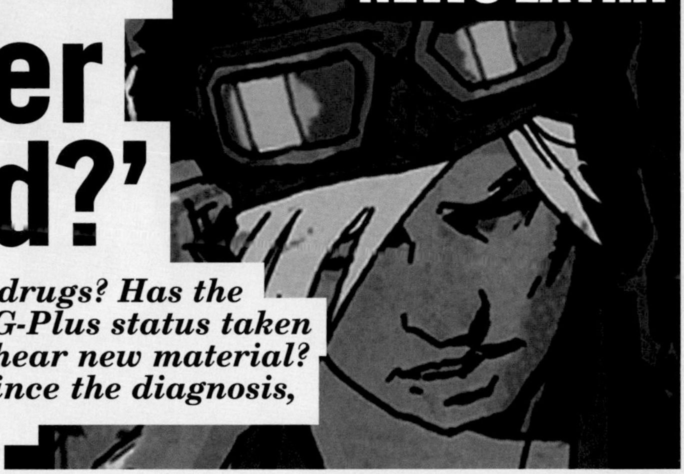

Has he really kicked drugs? Has the tabloid hell over his G-Plus status taken its toll? Will we ever hear new material? In his 1st interview since the diagnosis, Weasel comes clean.

By Steve Maconie

Danny Waissel's trapped inside one of the most iconic faces of his generation. And there's no way out.

Once he seemed on the brink of rock immortality. Aged just 21 years old, and just a few weeks off the release of The Whatever's debut single 'Burnished Bits', he held in his chaotic mind the blueprint to shambolic poet-cum-rockstar 'Weasel' – iconic frontman of the biggest band in the country and hero to a pilled-up generation intent on partying themselves senseless.

Over the next three years the mainstream media convulsed with indignation as The Whatever pissed their outrageous sound into the ears of a nation's youth – a journey of such lunatic cloud-scraping ambition that it seems, in retrospect, to have been beamed in from a far more glorious reality. And at the centre of this decadent success stood one man, mouthing poetic verses soon to be on everyone's lips – that charismatic, throaty Lou Reed burr echoed by 300,000 disciples at Knebworth, soundtracking two summers on seminal album 'Bertram's Bakery' and its era-defining successor 'Bang the Tins' – bewitching millions with his bohemian swagger and androgynous sexual potency.

Then came the reckoning: the band broke up in bitter acrimony – co-writer and guitarist Axel Faff staking claim to the creative heart of the band, while Weasel languished in gaol after a succession of drugs offences. The model girlfriend left him; solo gigs descended into fights or tuneless chaos; accusations of plagiarism and creative bankruptcy loomed large from the shadows. An army of loyal fans kept the faith – but then came the cruelest of blows: a G-Plus diagnosis that leaves the brightest star of his generation with just six months to live. Is there any way back to past glories – or is Weasel now 'Forever Fucked'?

It's clear from the days **MNE** spent recording this interview that illness hasn't jolted Weasel into curing his addictions. On one memorable night he casually jizzed into a groupie's tits while snorting cocaine and swigging vodka from the bottle, barely pausing to formulate an answer to MNE's probing inquisition. The minstrel of mayhem has lost none of his decadence. And yet it's clear that this is not the drug-addled loon of last summer, refusing to censor the barely coherent rants and impassioned asides that bewildered his increasingly polarised audience. When we meet in The Good Mixer Weasel looks lean and healthy, bantering wittily with the old men, tourists and hipsters crowding into the bar as word of his charismatic presence spreads. Beneath the battered flying helmet and red shemagh there's hope in those eyes, hope of salvation from the truest love of his life. The very thing that made us fall in love with him in the first place. Music.

It was John Lennon's birthday yesterday. Did you mark the day?

"'Course, man. I pulled an arty Japanese bird and we stayed in bed all day. She had a minge like a bear trapper's hat, so John would've felt right at home."

How do you feel about Axel's success since the band split? Three U.S. no. 1s, 2 Grammys, 4 Brits. And he wasn't exactly complimentary about you on 'Turtle's Head'.

"Couldn't care less, bruv. It's all sellout shit... sucking the man's cock. I ain't tongue buttering balls to get airplay, y'know? My shit is real shit. But Axel and me, we're like brothers, yeah? We have good times and bad times, but our shit runs deep. And I don't think he was singing about me there, y'know? Why would he?"

Well, you famously dissed him on your last single...

"Nah! The media misinterpreted that. I weave subtle layers, metaphors and allegories. My lyrics are like tone poems, open to many interpretations."

Even on 'Asshat Faff"?

"I'm talkin' about doors within doors, man. Transcending the obvious! Read between the lines, yeah? The message is there if you want to find it."

You're saying that we shouldn't take your work at face value?

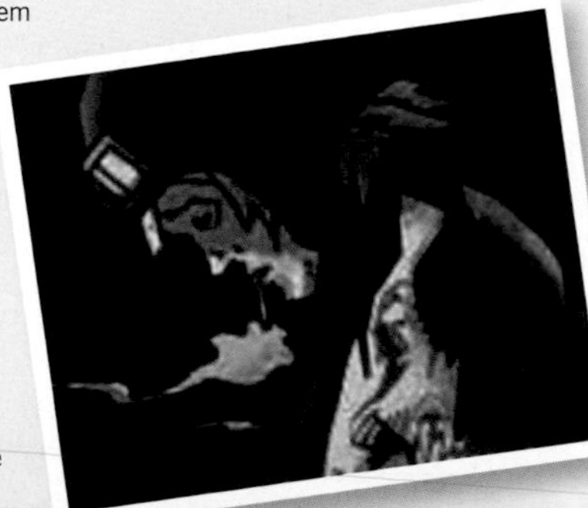

"That's the beauty of my lyrics. The ambiguities are myriad. It's deep and open – just like his ass for Radio 1."

Have you changed your plans since the diagnosis?

"Yeah, I'm working on a lot more solo work. I'm buzzin' with ideas. It's now or never."

continued on page 48

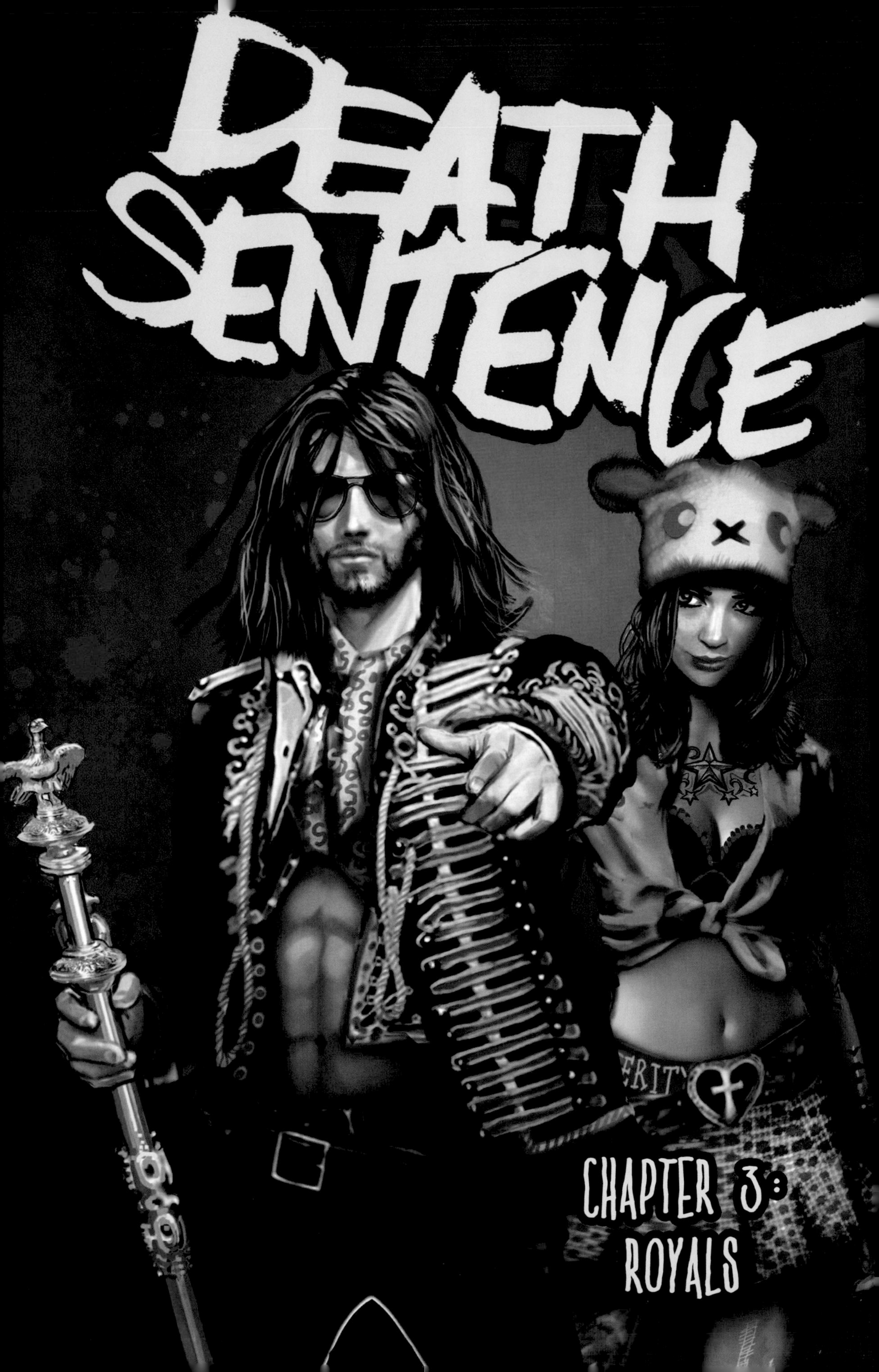
DEATH SENTENCE
CHAPTER 3:
ROYALS

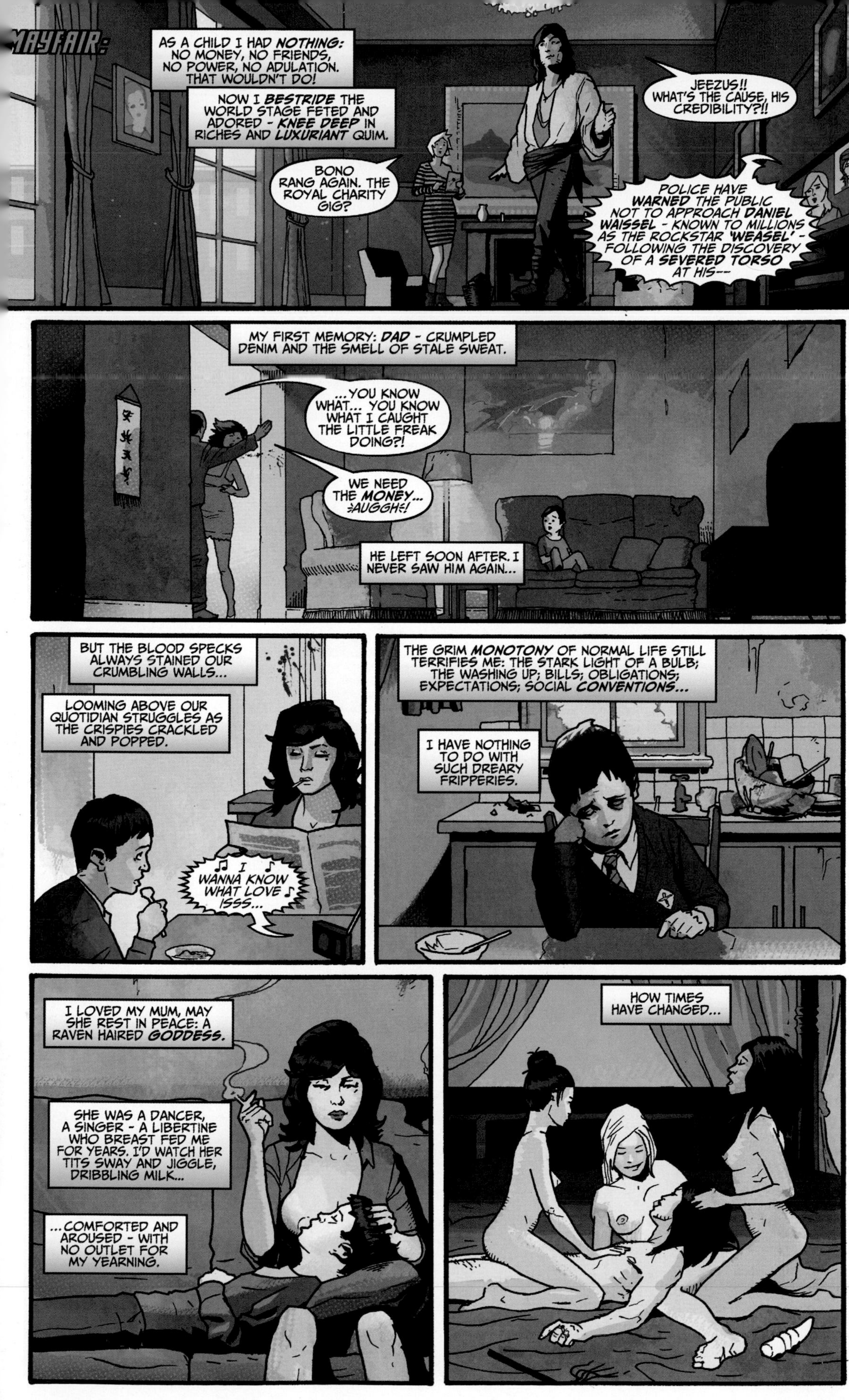
MAYFAIR:
AS A CHILD I HAD NOTHING: NO MONEY, NO FRIENDS, NO POWER, NO ADULATION. THAT WOULDN'T DO!
NOW I BESTRIDE THE WORLD STAGE FETED AND ADORED - KNEE DEEP IN RICHES AND LUXURIANT QUIM.
BONO RANG AGAIN. THE ROYAL CHARITY GIG?
JEEZUS!! WHAT'S THE CAUSE, HIS CREDIBILITY?!!
POLICE HAVE WARNED THE PUBLIC NOT TO APPROACH DANIEL WAISSEL - KNOWN TO MILLIONS AS THE ROCKSTAR 'WEASEL' - FOLLOWING THE DISCOVERY OF A SEVERED TORSO AT HIS--
MY FIRST MEMORY: DAD - CRUMPLED DENIM AND THE SMELL OF STALE SWEAT.
...YOU KNOW WHAT... YOU KNOW WHAT I CAUGHT THE LITTLE FREAK DOING?!
WE NEED THE MONEY... AUGGH!
HE LEFT SOON AFTER. I NEVER SAW HIM AGAIN...
BUT THE BLOOD SPECKS ALWAYS STAINED OUR CRUMBLING WALLS...
LOOMING ABOVE OUR QUOTIDIAN STRUGGLES AS THE CRISPIES CRACKLED AND POPPED.
♫ I ♪ WANNA KNOW WHAT LOVE ♪ ISSS...
THE GRIM MONOTONY OF NORMAL LIFE STILL TERRIFIES ME: THE STARK LIGHT OF A BULB; THE WASHING UP; BILLS; OBLIGATIONS; EXPECTATIONS; SOCIAL CONVENTIONS...
I HAVE NOTHING TO DO WITH SUCH DREARY FRIPPERIES.
I LOVED MY MUM, MAY SHE REST IN PEACE: A RAVEN HAIRED GODDESS.
SHE WAS A DANCER, A SINGER - A LIBERTINE WHO BREAST FED ME FOR YEARS. I'D WATCH HER TITS SWAY AND JIGGLE, DRIBBLING MILK...
...COMFORTED AND AROUSED - WITH NO OUTLET FOR MY YEARNING.
HOW TIMES HAVE CHANGED...

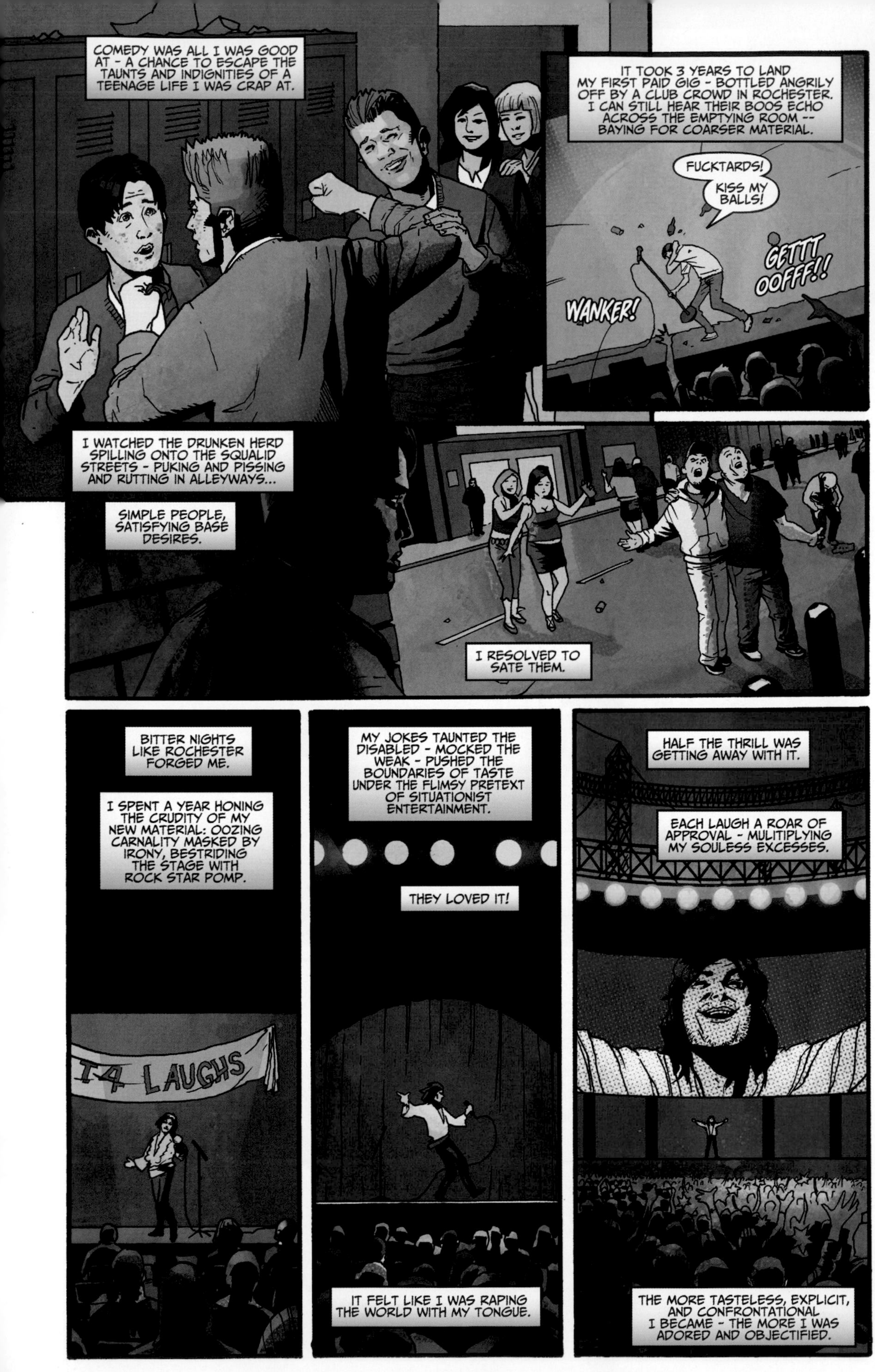
COMEDY WAS ALL I WAS GOOD AT - A CHANCE TO ESCAPE THE TAUNTS AND INDIGNITIES OF A TEENAGE LIFE I WAS CRAP AT.
IT TOOK 3 YEARS TO LAND MY FIRST PAID GIG - BOTTLED ANGRILY OFF BY A CLUB CROWD IN ROCHESTER. I CAN STILL HEAR THEIR BOOS ECHO ACROSS THE EMPTYING ROOM -- BAYING FOR COARSER MATERIAL.
FUCKTARDS!
KISS MY BALLS!
GETTT OOFFF!!
WANKER!
I WATCHED THE DRUNKEN HERD SPILLING ONTO THE SQUALID STREETS - PUKING AND PISSING AND RUTTING IN ALLEYWAYS...
SIMPLE PEOPLE, SATISFYING BASE DESIRES.
I RESOLVED TO SATE THEM.
BITTER NIGHTS LIKE ROCHESTER FORGED ME.
I SPENT A YEAR HONING THE CRUDITY OF MY NEW MATERIAL: OOZING CARNALITY MASKED BY IRONY, BESTRIDING THE STAGE WITH ROCK STAR POMP.
I 4 LAUGHS
MY JOKES TAUNTED THE DISABLED - MOCKED THE WEAK - PUSHED THE BOUNDARIES OF TASTE UNDER THE FLIMSY PRETEXT OF SITUATIONIST ENTERTAINMENT.
THEY LOVED IT!
IT FELT LIKE I WAS RAPING THE WORLD WITH MY TONGUE.
HALF THE THRILL WAS GETTING AWAY WITH IT.
EACH LAUGH A ROAR OF APPROVAL - MULITIPLYING MY SOULESS EXCESSES.
THE MORE TASTELESS, EXPLICIT, AND CONFRONTATIONAL I BECAME - THE MORE I WAS ADORED AND OBJECTIFIED.

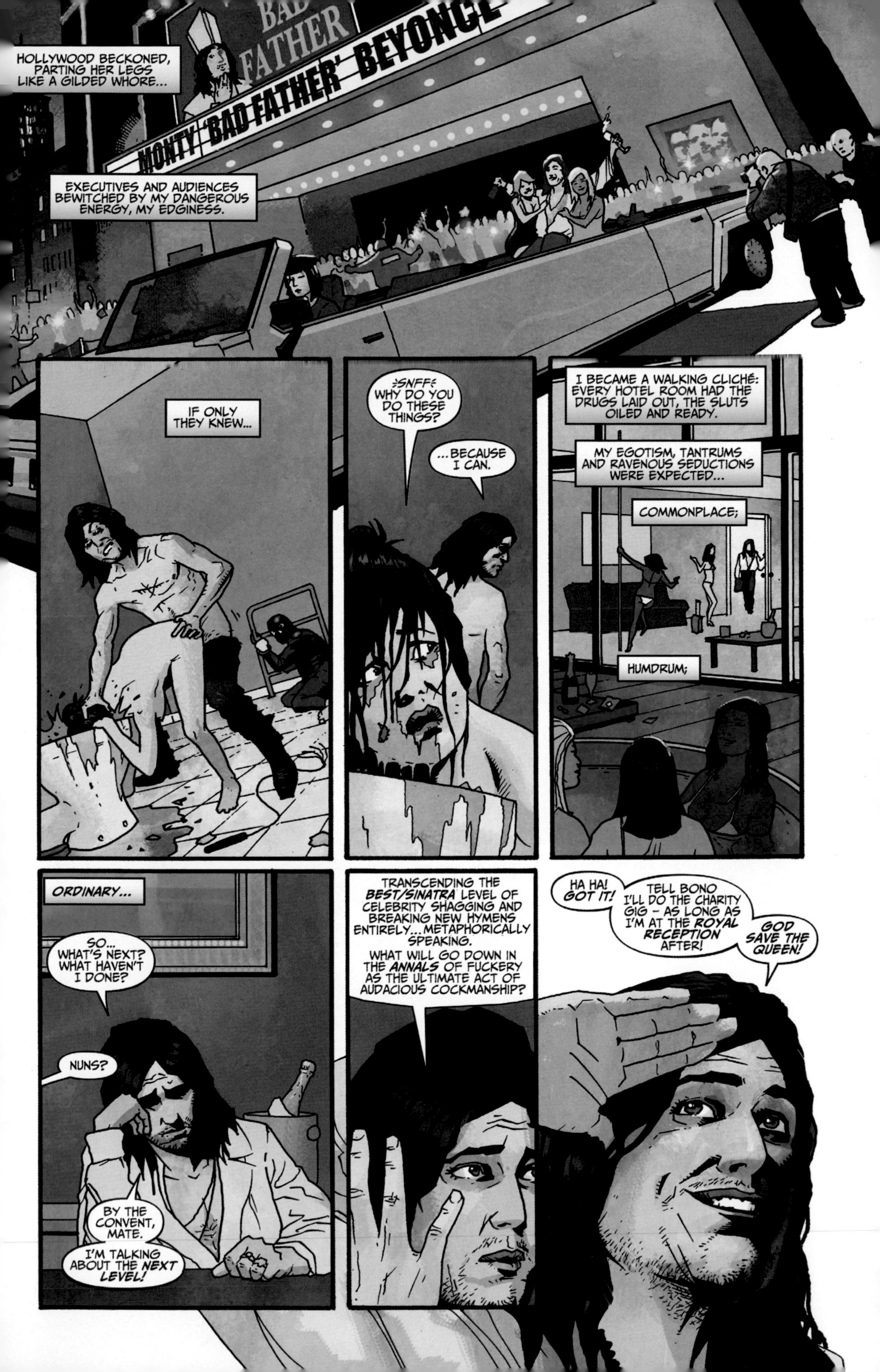
BAD FATHER
MONTY 'BAD FATHER' BEYONCE
HOLLYWOOD BECKONED, PARTING HER LEGS LIKE A GILDED WHORE...
EXECUTIVES AND AUDIENCES BEWITCHED BY MY DANGEROUS ENERGY, MY EDGINESS.
IF ONLY THEY KNEW...
SNFF WHY DO YOU DO THESE THINGS?
...BECAUSE I CAN.
I BECAME A WALKING CLICHÉ: EVERY HOTEL ROOM HAD THE DRUGS LAID OUT, THE SLUTS OILED AND READY.
MY EGOTISM, TANTRUMS AND RAVENOUS SEDUCTIONS WERE EXPECTED...
COMMONPLACE;
HUMDRUM;
ORDINARY...
SO... WHAT'S NEXT? WHAT HAVEN'T I DONE?
NUNS?
BY THE CONVENT, MATE.
I'M TALKING ABOUT THE NEXT LEVEL!
TRANSCENDING THE BEST/SINATRA LEVEL OF CELEBRITY SHAGGING AND BREAKING NEW HYMENS ENTIRELY... METAPHORICALLY SPEAKING.
WHAT WILL GO DOWN IN THE ANNALS OF FUCKERY AS THE ULTIMATE ACT OF AUDACIOUS COCKMANSHIP?
HA HA! GOT IT!
TELL BONO I'LL DO THE CHARITY GIG – AS LONG AS I'M AT THE ROYAL RECEPTION AFTER!
GOD SAVE THE QUEEN!

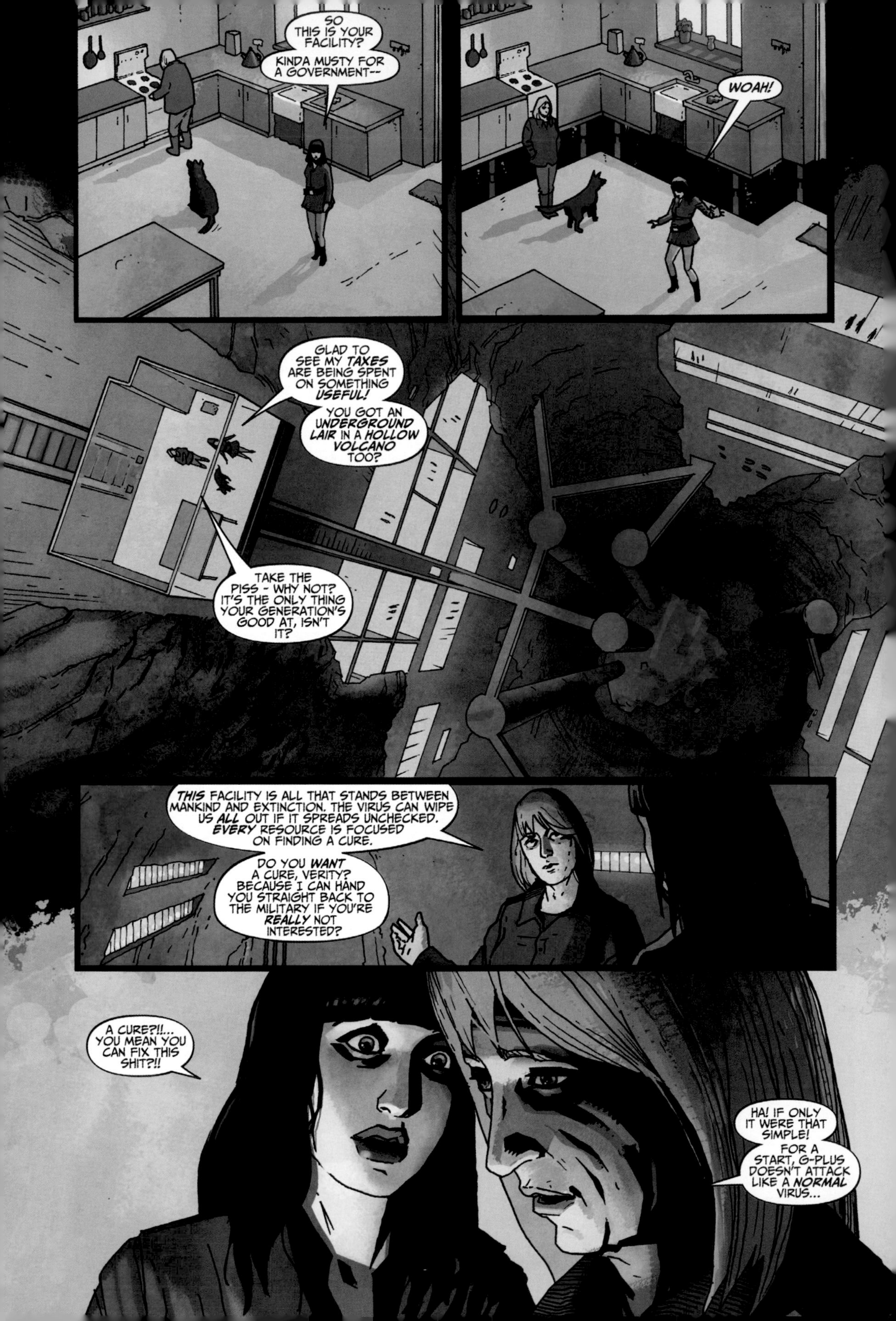

SO THIS IS YOUR FACILITY?
KINDA MUSTY FOR A GOVERNMENT--
WOAH!
GLAD TO SEE MY TAXES ARE BEING SPENT ON SOMETHING USEFUL!
YOU GOT AN UNDERGROUND LAIR IN A HOLLOW VOLCANO TOO?
TAKE THE PISS - WHY NOT? IT'S THE ONLY THING YOUR GENERATION'S GOOD AT, ISN'T IT?
THIS FACILITY IS ALL THAT STANDS BETWEEN MANKIND AND EXTINCTION. THE VIRUS CAN WIPE US ALL OUT IF IT SPREADS UNCHECKED. EVERY RESOURCE IS FOCUSED ON FINDING A CURE.
DO YOU WANT A CURE, VERITY? BECAUSE I CAN HAND YOU STRAIGHT BACK TO THE MILITARY IF YOU'RE REALLY NOT INTERESTED?
A CURE?!!... YOU MEAN YOU CAN FIX THIS SHIT?!!
HA! IF ONLY IT WERE THAT SIMPLE!
FOR A START, G-PLUS DOESN'T ATTACK LIKE A NORMAL VIRUS...

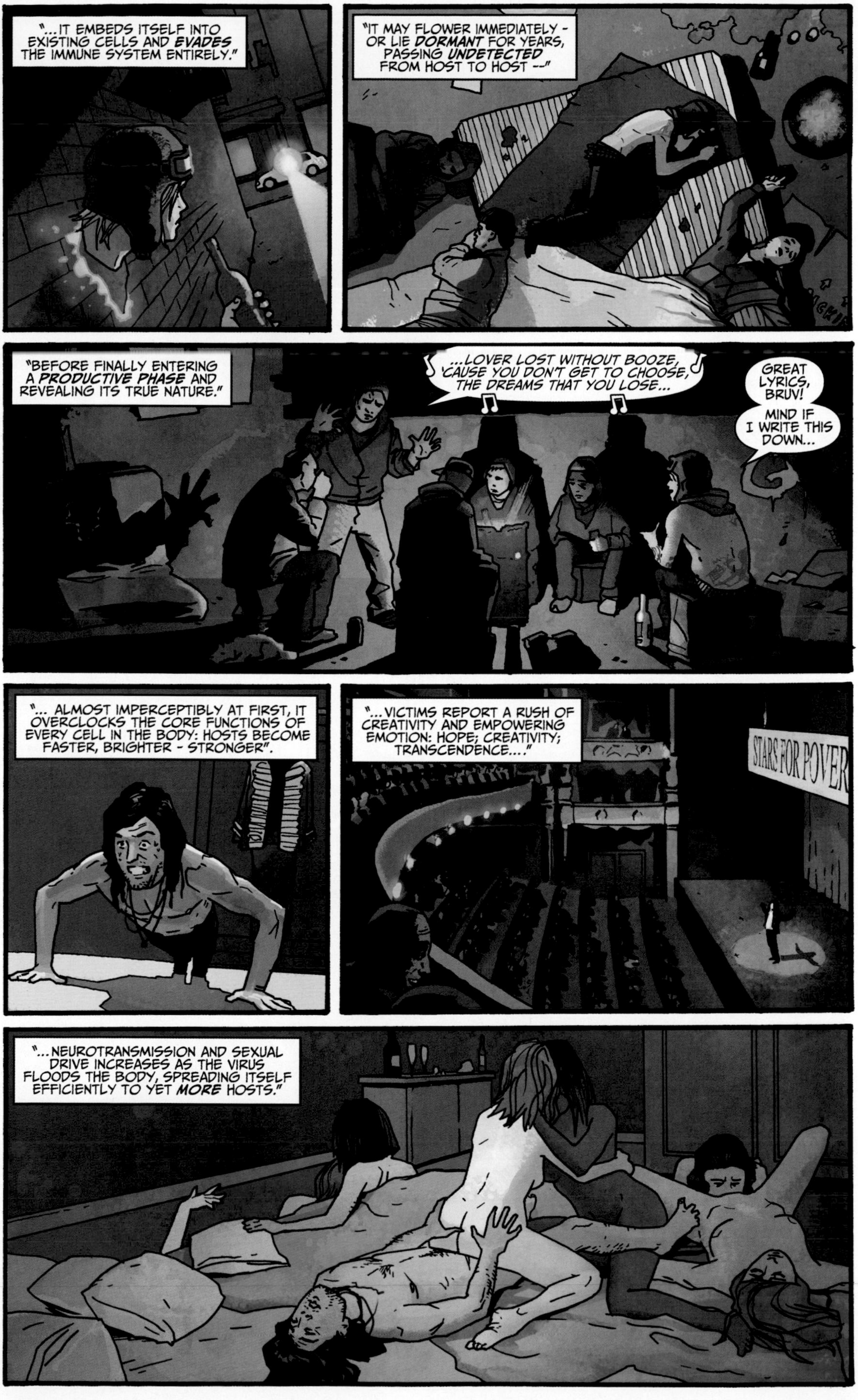
"...IT EMBEDS ITSELF INTO EXISTING CELLS AND EVADES THE IMMUNE SYSTEM ENTIRELY."
"IT MAY FLOWER IMMEDIATELY - OR LIE DORMANT FOR YEARS, PASSING UNDETECTED FROM HOST TO HOST --"
"BEFORE FINALLY ENTERING A PRODUCTIVE PHASE AND REVEALING ITS TRUE NATURE."
...LOVER LOST WITHOUT BOOZE, 'CAUSE YOU DON'T GET TO CHOOSE, THE DREAMS THAT YOU LOSE...
GREAT LYRICS, BRUV!
MIND IF I WRITE THIS DOWN...
"... ALMOST IMPERCEPTIBLY AT FIRST, IT OVERCLOCKS THE CORE FUNCTIONS OF EVERY CELL IN THE BODY: HOSTS BECOME FASTER, BRIGHTER - STRONGER".
"...VICTIMS REPORT A RUSH OF CREATIVITY AND EMPOWERING EMOTION: HOPE; CREATIVITY; TRANSCENDENCE..."
STARS FOR POVER
"...NEUROTRANSMISSION AND SEXUAL DRIVE INCREASES AS THE VIRUS FLOODS THE BODY, SPREADING ITSELF EFFICIENTLY TO YET MORE HOSTS."

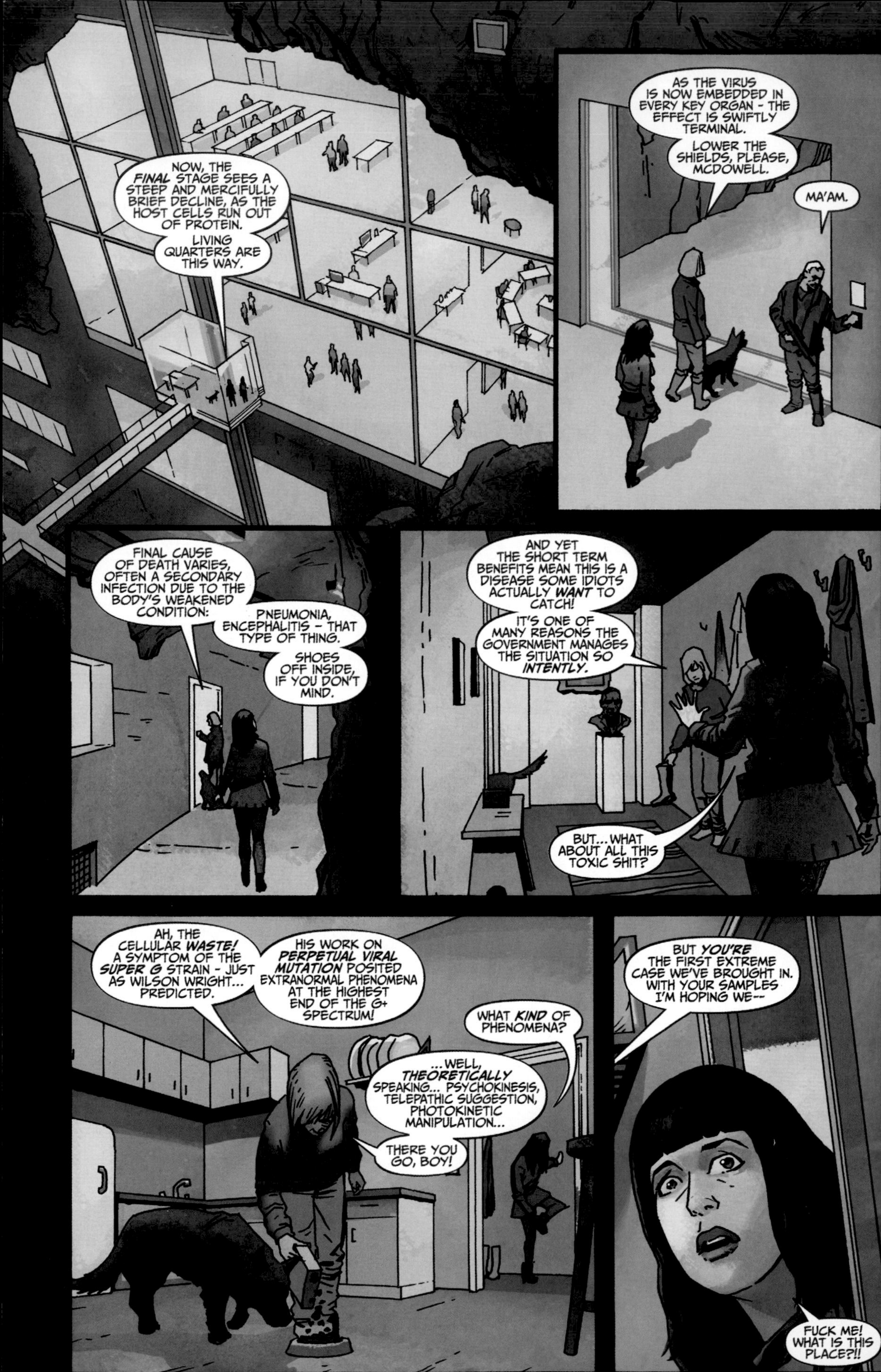
NOW, THE *FINAL* STAGE SEES A STEEP AND MERCIFULLY BRIEF DECLINE, AS THE HOST CELLS RUN OUT OF PROTEIN.
LIVING QUARTERS ARE THIS WAY.
AS THE VIRUS IS NOW EMBEDDED IN EVERY KEY ORGAN - THE EFFECT IS SWIFTLY TERMINAL.
LOWER THE SHIELDS, PLEASE, MCDOWELL.
MA'AM.
FINAL CAUSE OF DEATH VARIES, OFTEN A SECONDARY INFECTION DUE TO THE BODY'S WEAKENED CONDITION:
PNEUMONIA, ENCEPHALITIS - THAT TYPE OF THING.
SHOES OFF INSIDE, IF YOU DON'T MIND.
AND YET THE SHORT TERM BENEFITS MEAN THIS IS A DISEASE SOME IDIOTS ACTUALLY *WANT* TO CATCH!
IT'S ONE OF MANY REASONS THE GOVERNMENT MANAGES THE SITUATION SO *INTENTLY*.
BUT... WHAT ABOUT ALL THIS TOXIC SHIT?
AH, THE CELLULAR *WASTE!* A SYMPTOM OF THE *SUPER G* STRAIN - JUST AS WILSON WRIGHT... PREDICTED.
HIS WORK ON *PERPETUAL VIRAL MUTATION* POSITED EXTRANORMAL PHENOMENA AT THE HIGHEST END OF THE G+ SPECTRUM!
WHAT *KIND* OF PHENOMENA?
...WELL, *THEORETICALLY* SPEAKING... PSYCHOKINESIS, TELEPATHIC SUGGESTION, PHOTOKINETIC MANIPULATION...
THERE YOU GO, BOY!
BUT *YOU'RE* THE FIRST EXTREME CASE WE'VE BROUGHT IN. WITH YOUR SAMPLES I'M HOPING WE--
FUCK ME! WHAT IS THIS PLACE?!!

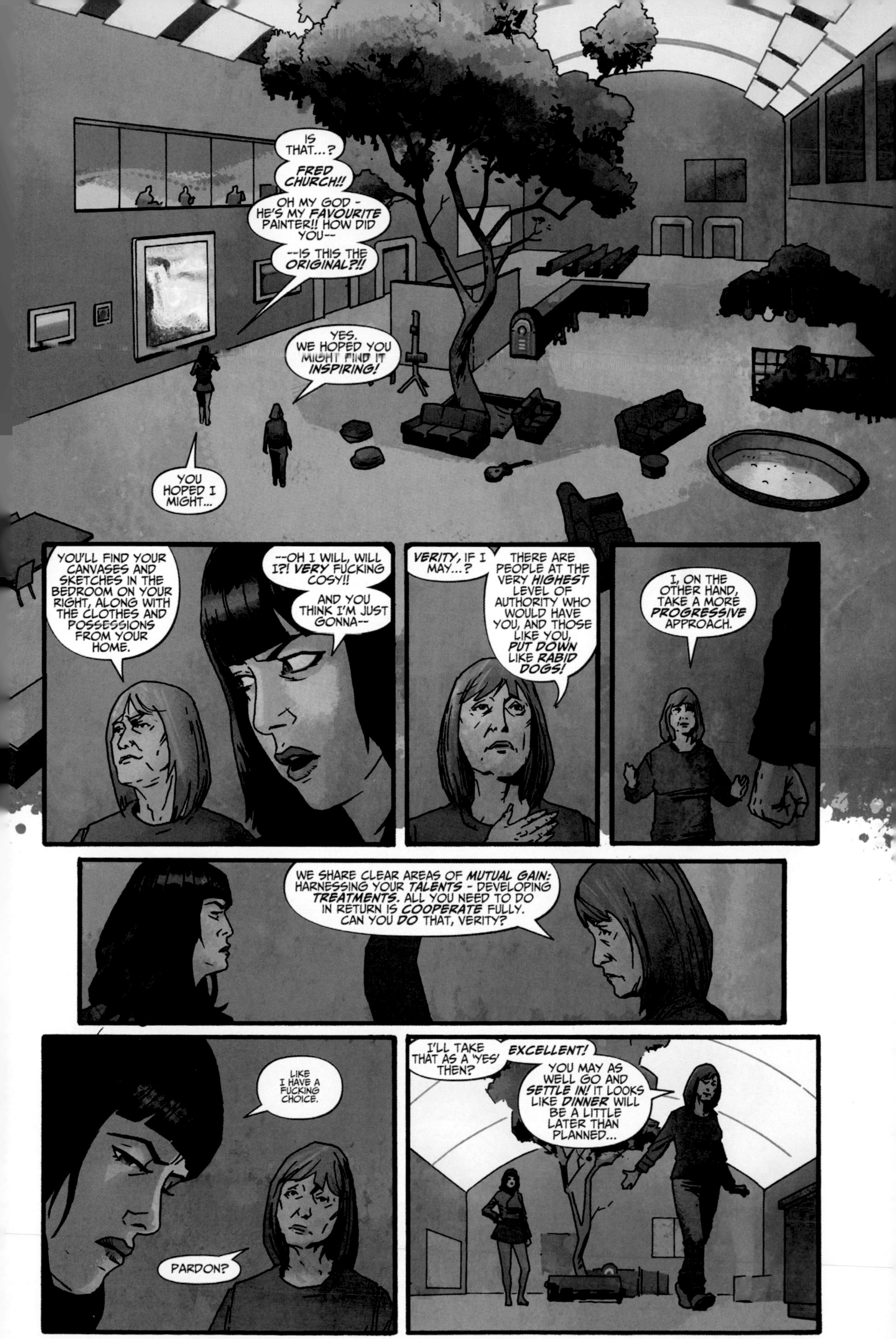
IS THAT...?
FRED CHURCH!!
OH MY GOD - HE'S MY FAVOURITE PAINTER!! HOW DID YOU--
--IS THIS THE ORIGINAL?!!
YES. WE HOPED YOU MIGHT FIND IT INSPIRING!
YOU HOPED I MIGHT...
YOU'LL FIND YOUR CANVASES AND SKETCHES IN THE BEDROOM ON YOUR RIGHT, ALONG WITH THE CLOTHES AND POSSESSIONS FROM YOUR HOME.
--OH I WILL, WILL I?! VERY FUCKING COSY!!
AND YOU THINK I'M JUST GONNA--
VERITY, IF I MAY...?
THERE ARE PEOPLE AT THE VERY HIGHEST LEVEL OF AUTHORITY WHO WOULD HAVE YOU, AND THOSE LIKE YOU, PUT DOWN LIKE RABID DOGS!
I, ON THE OTHER HAND, TAKE A MORE PROGRESSIVE APPROACH.
WE SHARE CLEAR AREAS OF MUTUAL GAIN: HARNESSING YOUR TALENTS - DEVELOPING TREATMENTS. ALL YOU NEED TO DO IN RETURN IS COOPERATE FULLY. CAN YOU DO THAT, VERITY?
LIKE I HAVE A FUCKING CHOICE.
PARDON?
I'LL TAKE THAT AS A 'YES' THEN?
EXCELLENT!
YOU MAY AS WELL GO AND SETTLE IN! IT LOOKS LIKE DINNER WILL BE A LITTLE LATER THAN PLANNED...

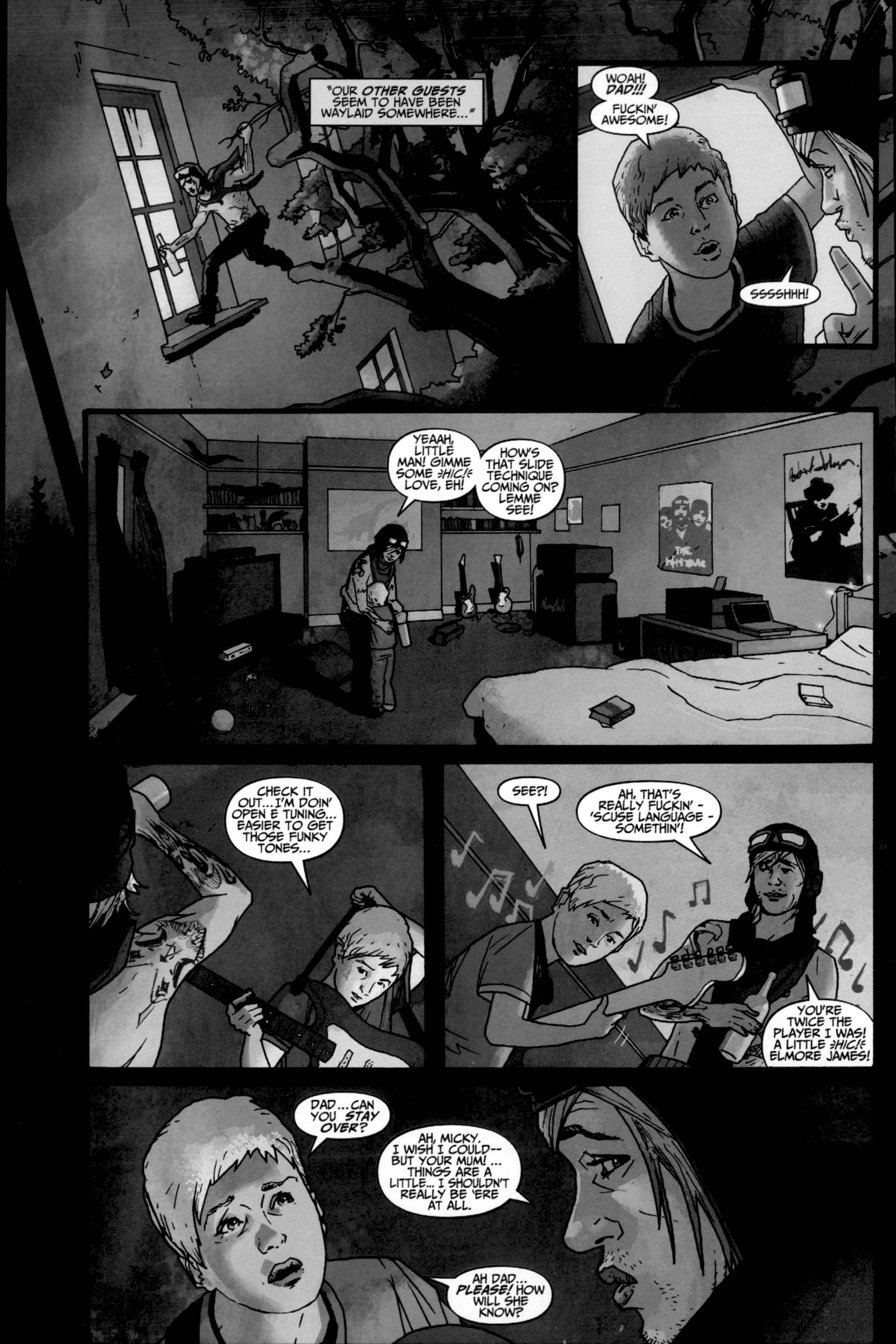
"OUR OTHER GUESTS SEEM TO HAVE BEEN WAYLAID SOMEWHERE..."
WOAH! DAD!!!
FUCKIN' AWESOME!
SSSSHHH!
YEAAH, LITTLE MAN! GIMME SOME *HIC!* LOVE, EH!
HOW'S THAT SLIDE TECHNIQUE COMING ON? LEMME SEE!
CHECK IT OUT... I'M DOIN' OPEN E TUNING... EASIER TO GET THOSE FUNKY TONES...
SEE?!
AH, THAT'S REALLY FUCKIN' - 'SCUSE LANGUAGE - SOMETHIN'!
YOU'RE TWICE THE PLAYER I WAS! A LITTLE *HIC!* ELMORE JAMES!
DAD... CAN YOU STAY OVER?
AH, MICKY. I WISH I COULD-- BUT YOUR MUM! ... THINGS ARE A LITTLE... I SHOULDN'T REALLY BE 'ERE AT ALL.
AH DAD... PLEASE! HOW WILL SHE KNOW?

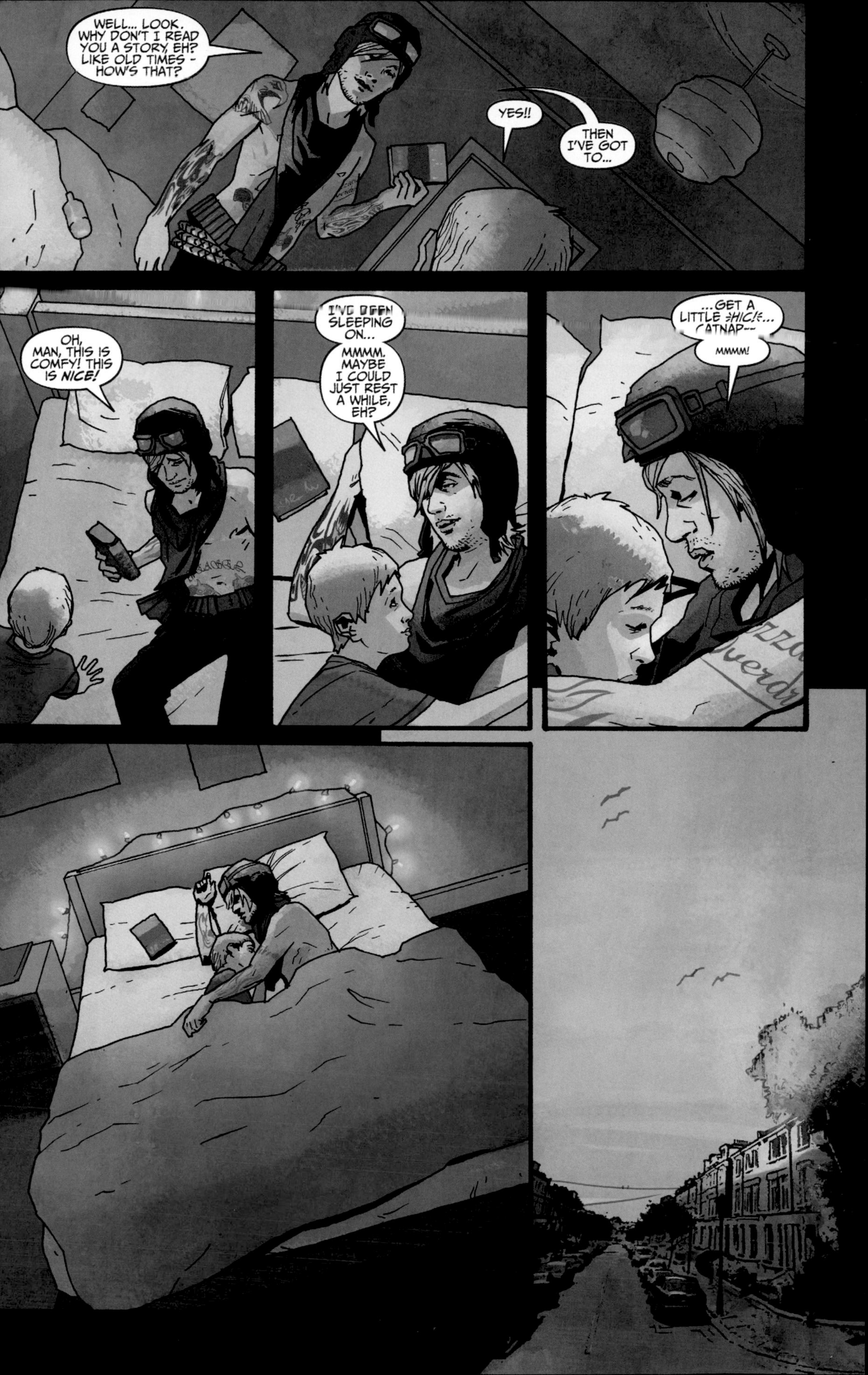
WELL... LOOK. WHY DON'T I READ YOU A STORY, EH? LIKE OLD TIMES - HOW'S THAT?
YES!!
THEN I'VE GOT TO...
OH, MAN, THIS IS COMFY! THIS IS NICE!
I'VE BEEN SLEEPING ON...
MMMM. MAYBE I COULD JUST REST A WHILE, EH?
...GET A LITTLE HIC!... CATNAP--
MMMM!

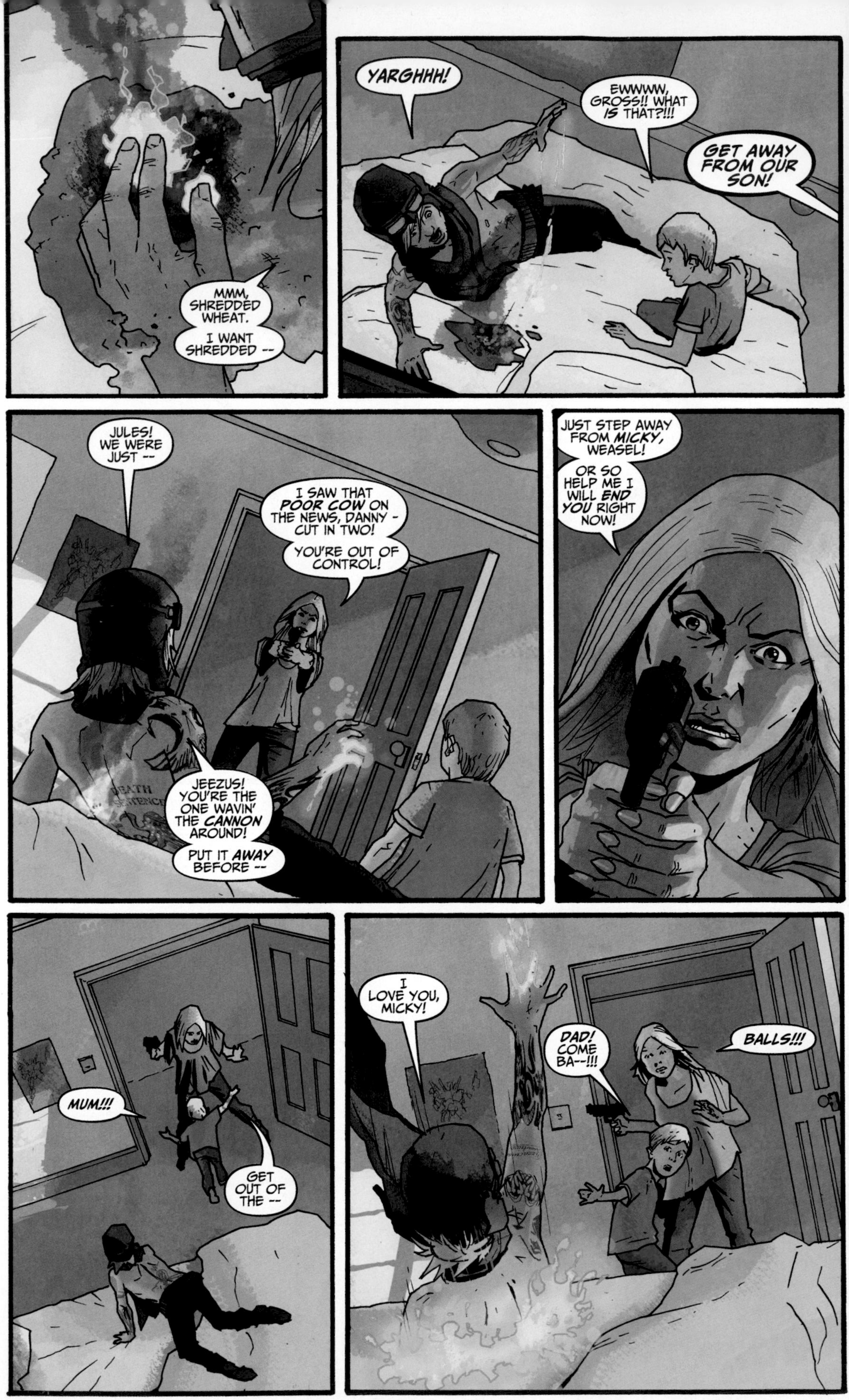
MMM, SHREDDED WHEAT.
I WANT SHREDDED --
YARGHHH!
EWWWW, GROSS!! WHAT IS THAT?!!!
GET AWAY FROM OUR SON!
JULES! WE WERE JUST --
I SAW THAT POOR COW ON THE NEWS, DANNY - CUT IN TWO!
YOU'RE OUT OF CONTROL!
JEEZUS! YOU'RE THE ONE WAVIN' THE CANNON AROUND!
PUT IT AWAY BEFORE --
JUST STEP AWAY FROM MICKY, WEASEL!
OR SO HELP ME I WILL END YOU RIGHT NOW!
MUM!!!
GET OUT OF THE --
I LOVE YOU, MICKY!
DAD! COME BA--!!!
BALLS!!!

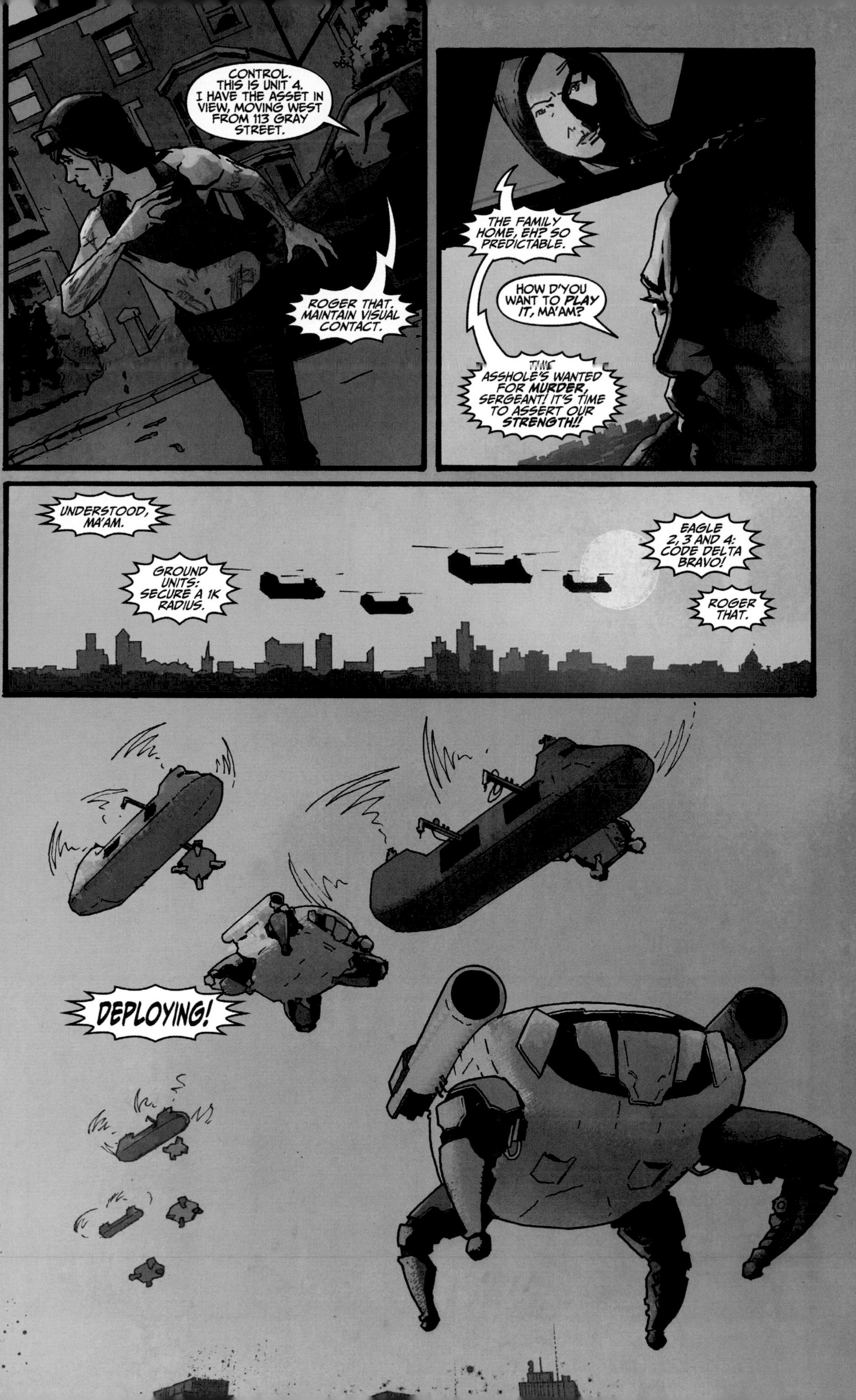
CONTROL. THIS IS UNIT 4. I HAVE THE ASSET IN VIEW, MOVING WEST FROM 113 GRAY STREET.
ROGER THAT. MAINTAIN VISUAL CONTACT.
THE FAMILY HOME, EH? SO PREDICTABLE.
HOW D'YOU WANT TO PLAY IT, MA'AM?
THIS ASSHOLE'S WANTED FOR MURDER, SERGEANT! IT'S TIME TO ASSERT OUR STRENGTH!!
UNDERSTOOD, MA'AM.
GROUND UNITS: SECURE A 1K RADIUS.
EAGLE 2, 3 AND 4: CODE DELTA BRAVO!
ROGER THAT.
DEPLOYING!

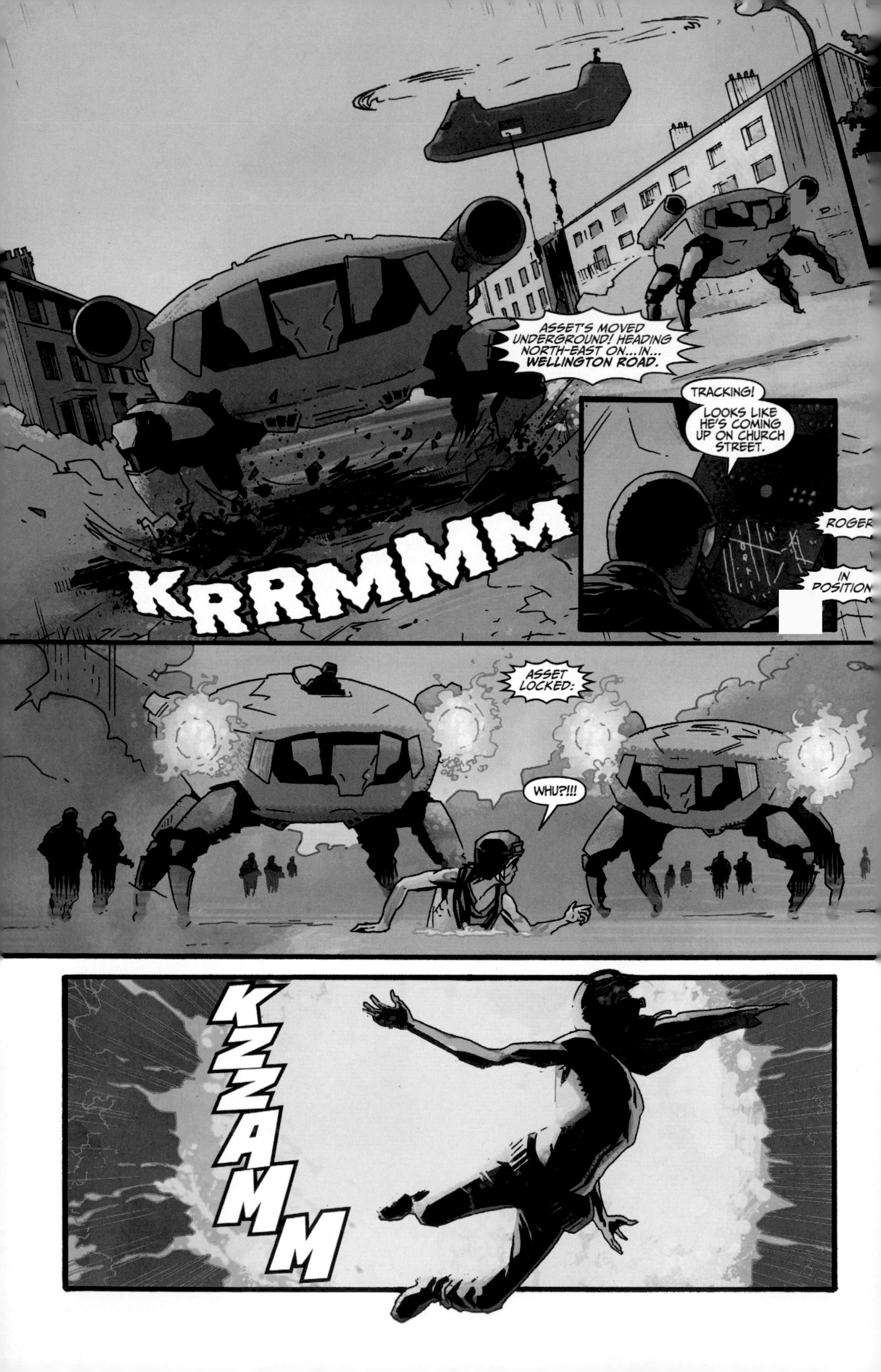

ASSET'S MOVED UNDERGROUND! HEADING NORTH-EAST ON...IN... WELLINGTON ROAD.
KRRMMMM
TRACKING!
LOOKS LIKE HE'S COMING UP ON CHURCH STREET.
ROGER
IN POSITION
ASSET LOCKED:
WHU?!!!
KZZAMMM

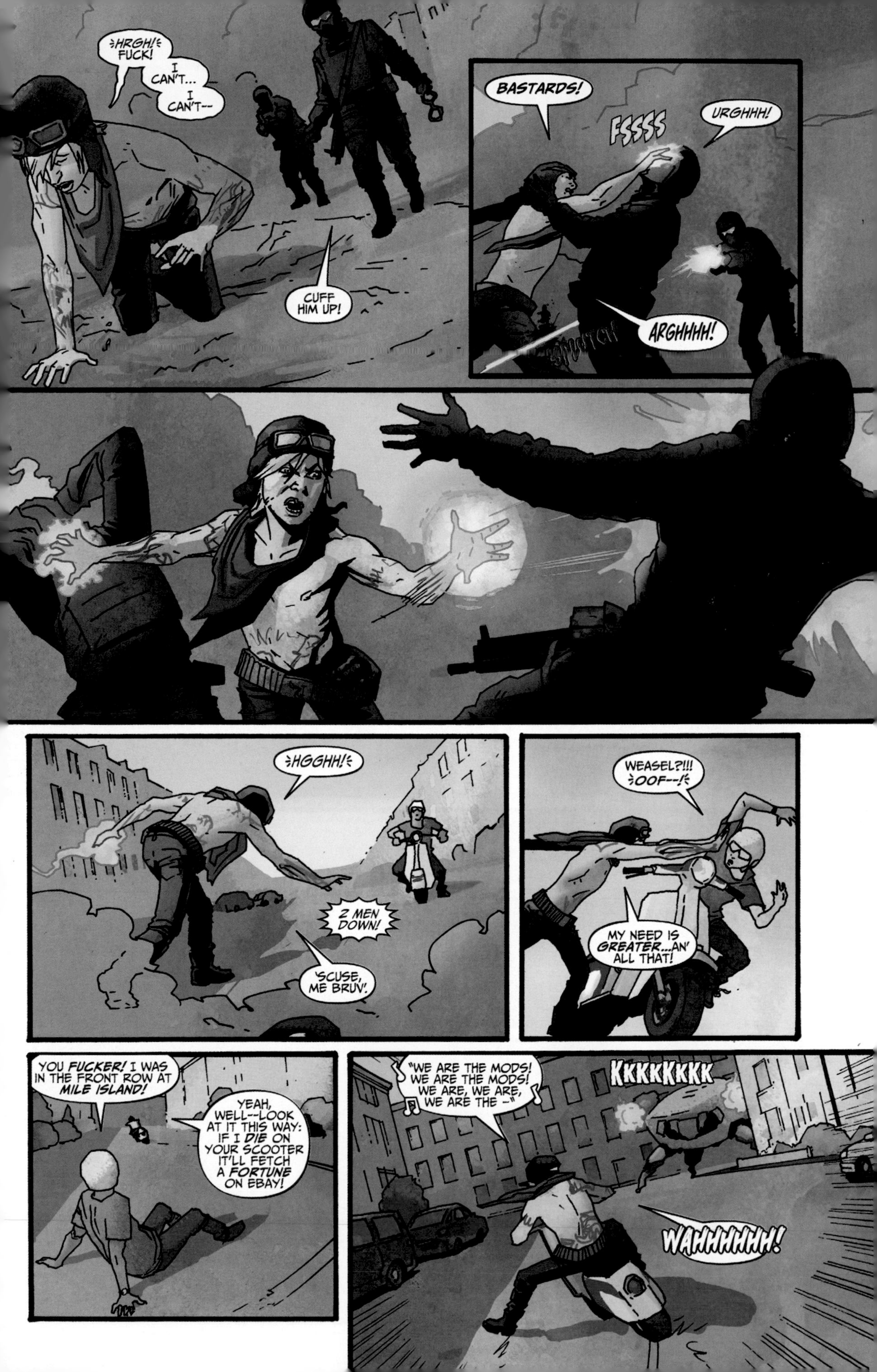
HRGH! FUCK!
I CAN'T... I CAN'T--
CUFF HIM UP!
BASTARDS!
FSSSS
URGHHH!
ARGHHHH!
HGGHH!
2 MEN DOWN!
'SCUSE, ME BRUV.
WEASEL?!!! OOF--!
MY NEED IS GREATER...AN' ALL THAT!
YOU FUCKER! I WAS IN THE FRONT ROW AT MILE ISLAND!
YEAH, WELL--LOOK AT IT THIS WAY: IF I DIE ON YOUR SCOOTER IT'LL FETCH A FORTUNE ON EBAY!
"WE ARE THE MODS! WE ARE THE MODS! WE ARE, WE ARE, WE ARE THE --"
KKKKKKKK
WAHHHHHH!

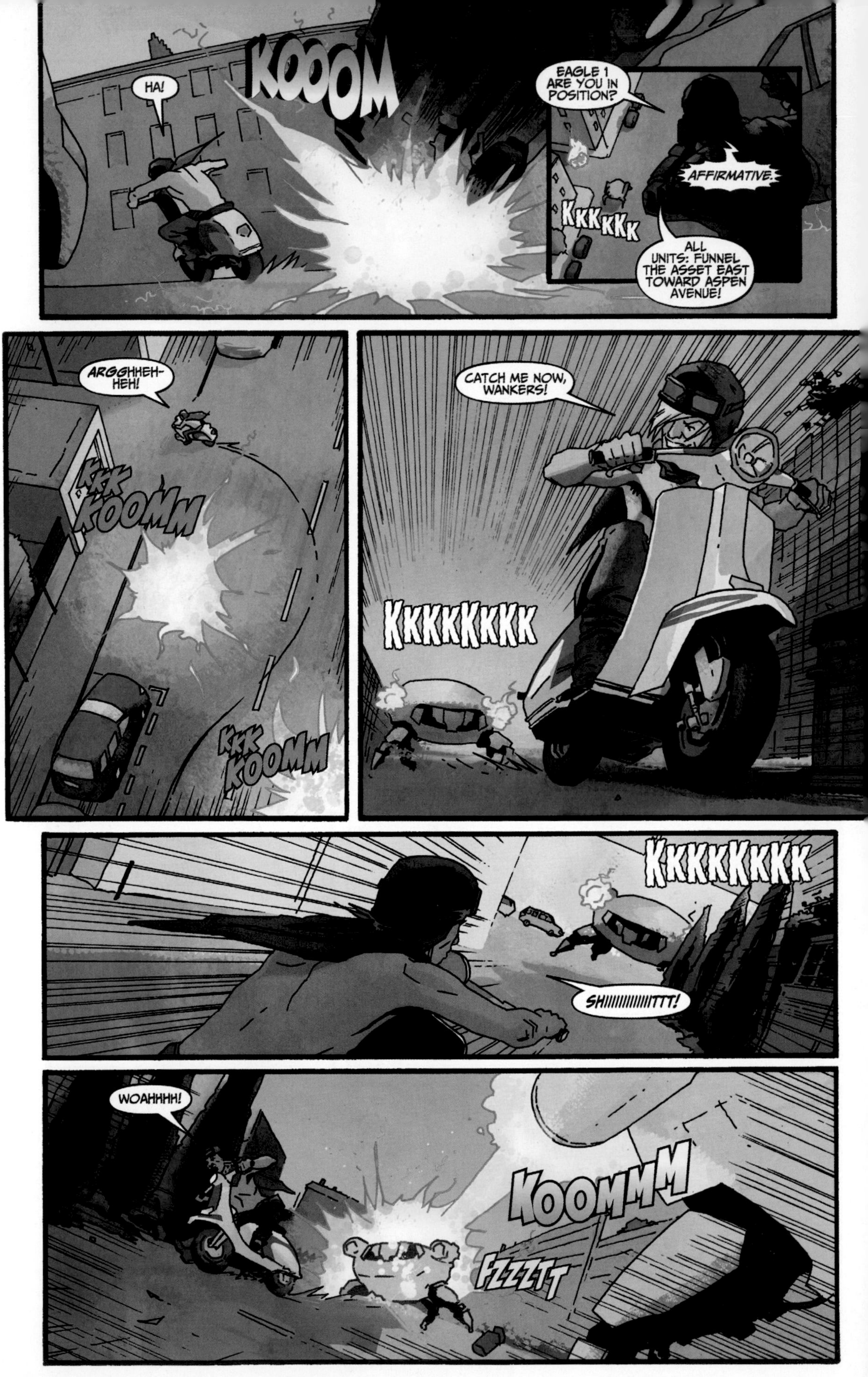
KOOOM
HA!
EAGLE 1 ARE YOU IN POSITION?
AFFIRMATIVE.
KKKKKK
ALL UNITS: FUNNEL THE ASSET EAST TOWARD ASPEN AVENUE!
ARGGHHEH-HEH!
KKK KOOMM
KKK KOOMM
CATCH ME NOW, WANKERS!
KKKKKKKK
KKKKKKKK
SHIIIIIIIIIIIIIITTT!
WOAHHHH!
KOOMMM
FZZZTT

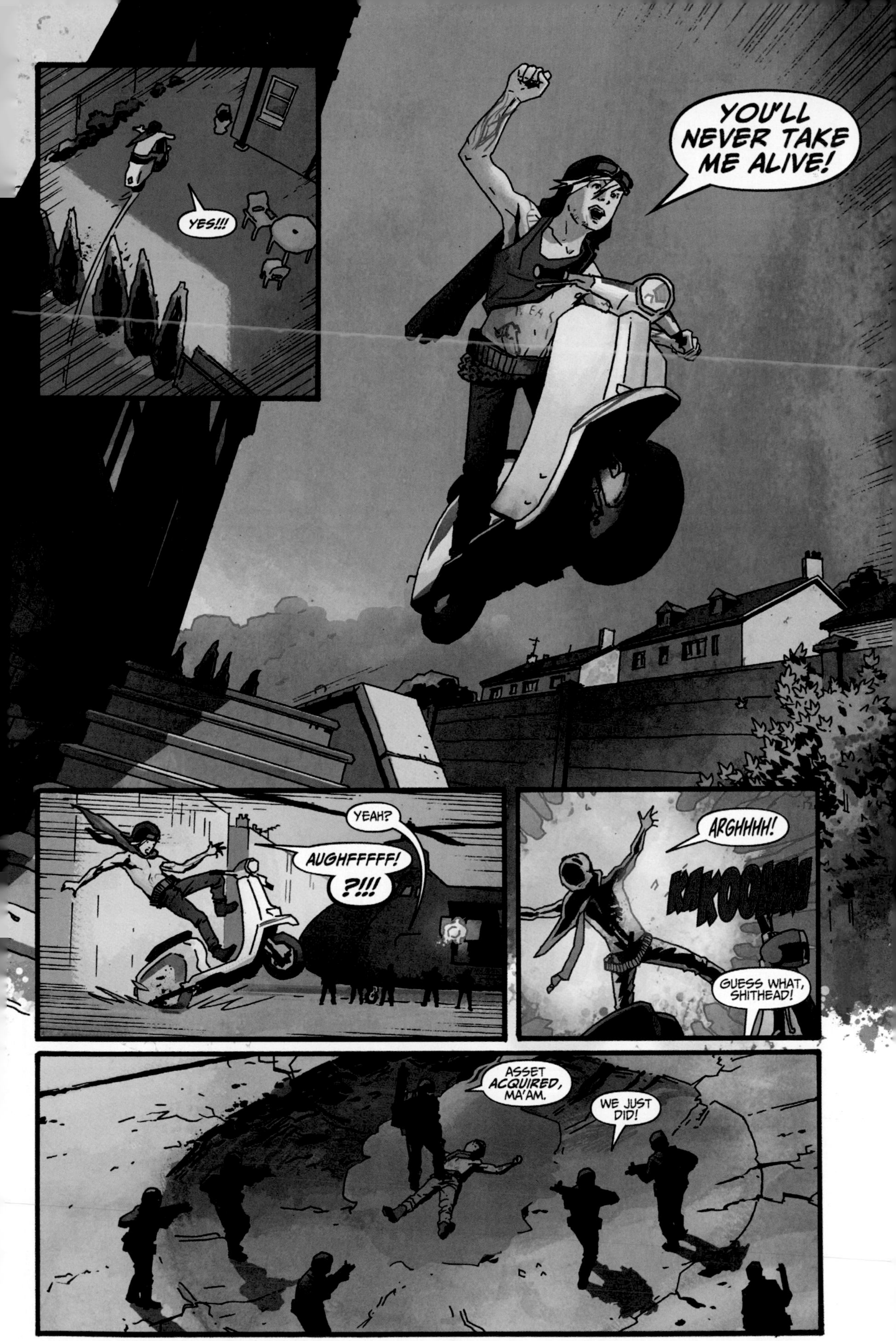
YES!!!
YOU'LL NEVER TAKE ME ALIVE!
YEAH?
AUGHFFFFF!
?!!!
ARGHHHH!
KAKOOMM
GUESS WHAT, SHITHEAD!
WE JUST DID!
ASSET ACQUIRED, MA'AM.

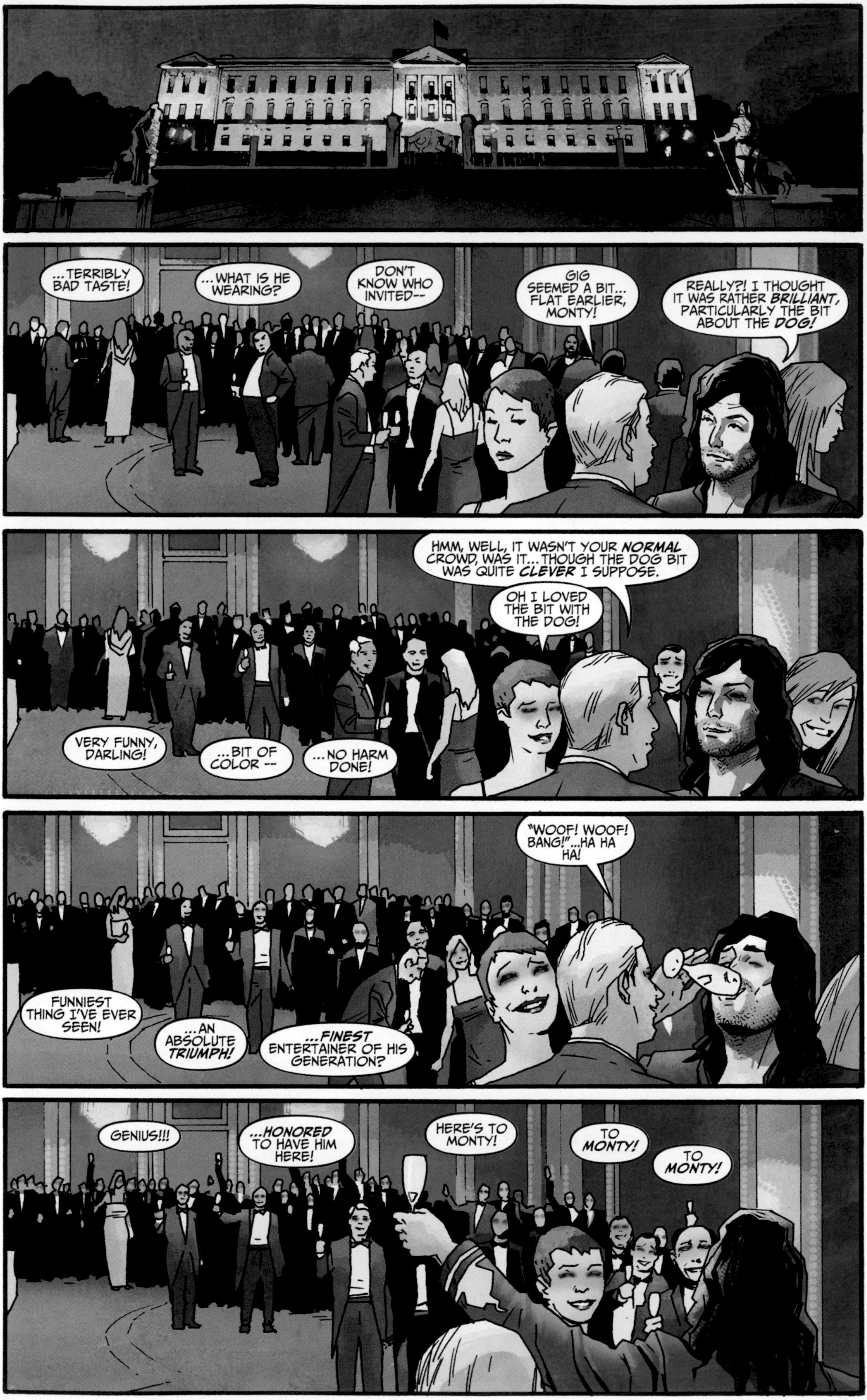
...TERRIBLY BAD TASTE!
...WHAT IS HE WEARING?
DON'T KNOW WHO INVITED--
GIG SEEMED A BIT... FLAT EARLIER, MONTY!
REALLY?! I THOUGHT IT WAS RATHER BRILLIANT, PARTICULARLY THE BIT ABOUT THE DOG!
HMM, WELL, IT WASN'T YOUR NORMAL CROWD, WAS IT... THOUGH THE DOG BIT WAS QUITE CLEVER I SUPPOSE.
OH I LOVED THE BIT WITH THE DOG!
VERY FUNNY, DARLING!
...BIT OF COLOR --
...NO HARM DONE!
"WOOF! WOOF! BANG!"...HA HA HA!
FUNNIEST THING I'VE EVER SEEN!
...AN ABSOLUTE TRIUMPH!
...FINEST ENTERTAINER OF HIS GENERATION?
GENIUS!!!
...HONORED TO HAVE HIM HERE!
HERE'S TO MONTY!
TO MONTY!
TO MONTY!

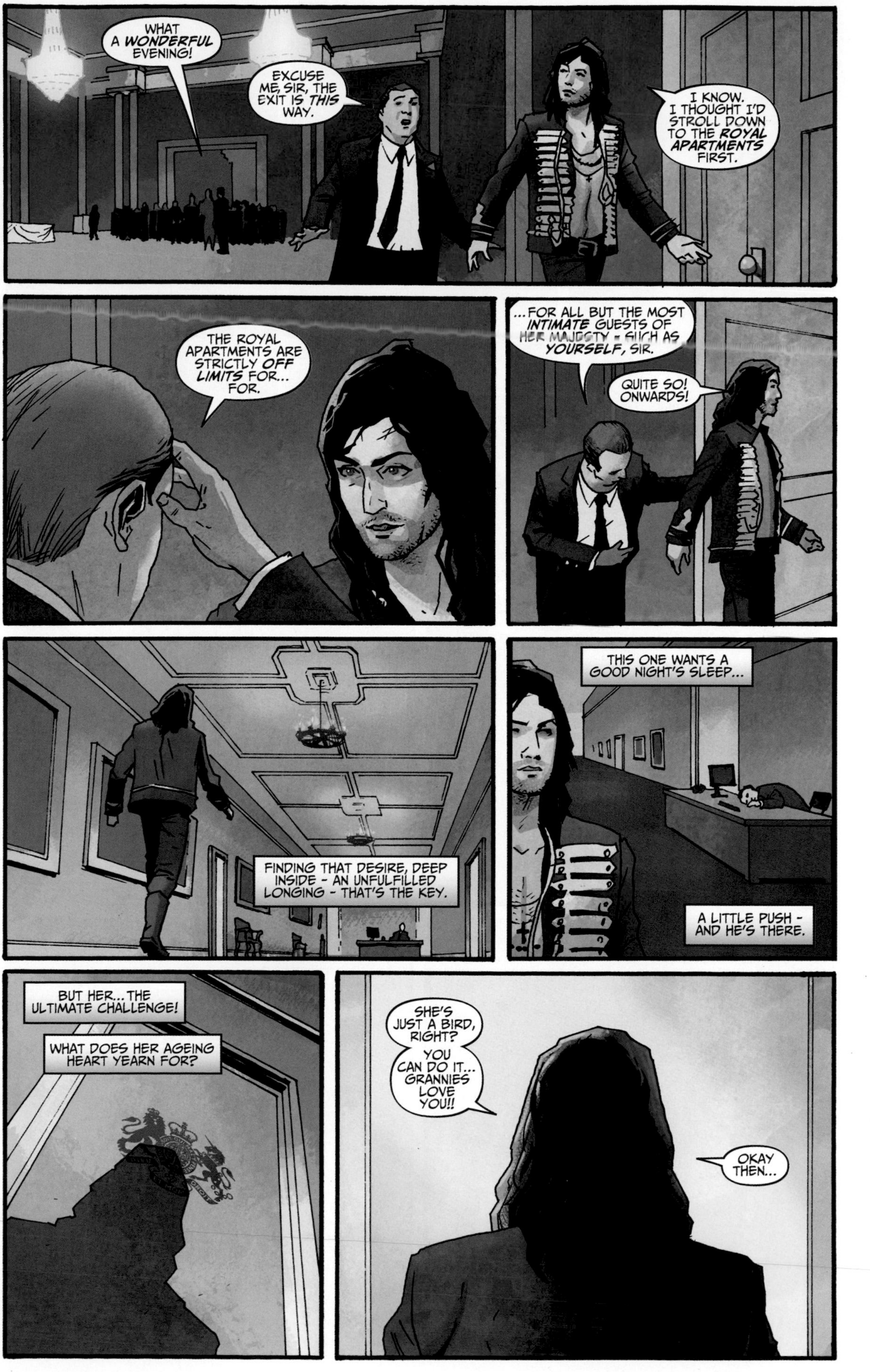
WHAT A WONDERFUL EVENING!
EXCUSE ME, SIR, THE EXIT IS THIS WAY.
I KNOW. I THOUGHT I'D STROLL DOWN TO THE ROYAL APARTMENTS FIRST.
THE ROYAL APARTMENTS ARE STRICTLY OFF LIMITS FOR... FOR.
...FOR ALL BUT THE MOST INTIMATE GUESTS OF HER MAJESTY - SUCH AS YOURSELF, SIR.
QUITE SO! ONWARDS!
FINDING THAT DESIRE, DEEP INSIDE - AN UNFULFILLED LONGING - THAT'S THE KEY.
THIS ONE WANTS A GOOD NIGHT'S SLEEP...
A LITTLE PUSH - AND HE'S THERE.
BUT HER... THE ULTIMATE CHALLENGE!
WHAT DOES HER AGEING HEART YEARN FOR?
SHE'S JUST A BIRD, RIGHT?
YOU CAN DO IT... GRANNIES LOVE YOU!!
OKAY THEN...

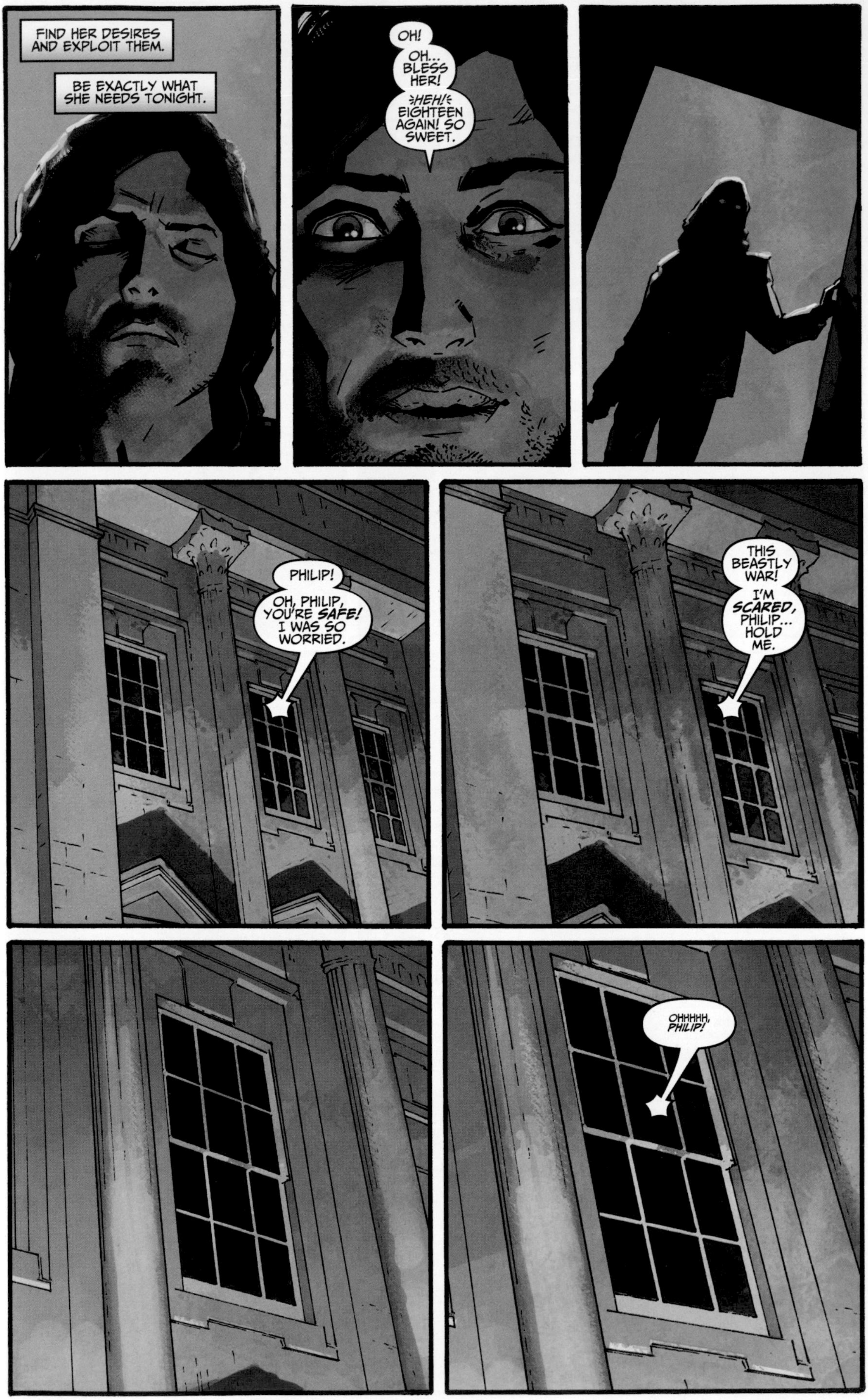
FIND HER DESIRES AND EXPLOIT THEM.
BE EXACTLY WHAT SHE NEEDS TONIGHT.
OH!
OH... BLESS HER!
HEH! EIGHTEEN AGAIN! SO SWEET.
PHILIP!
OH, PHILIP, YOU'RE SAFE! I WAS SO WORRIED.
THIS BEASTLY WAR!
I'M SCARED, PHILIP... HOLD ME.
OHHHHH, PHILIP!

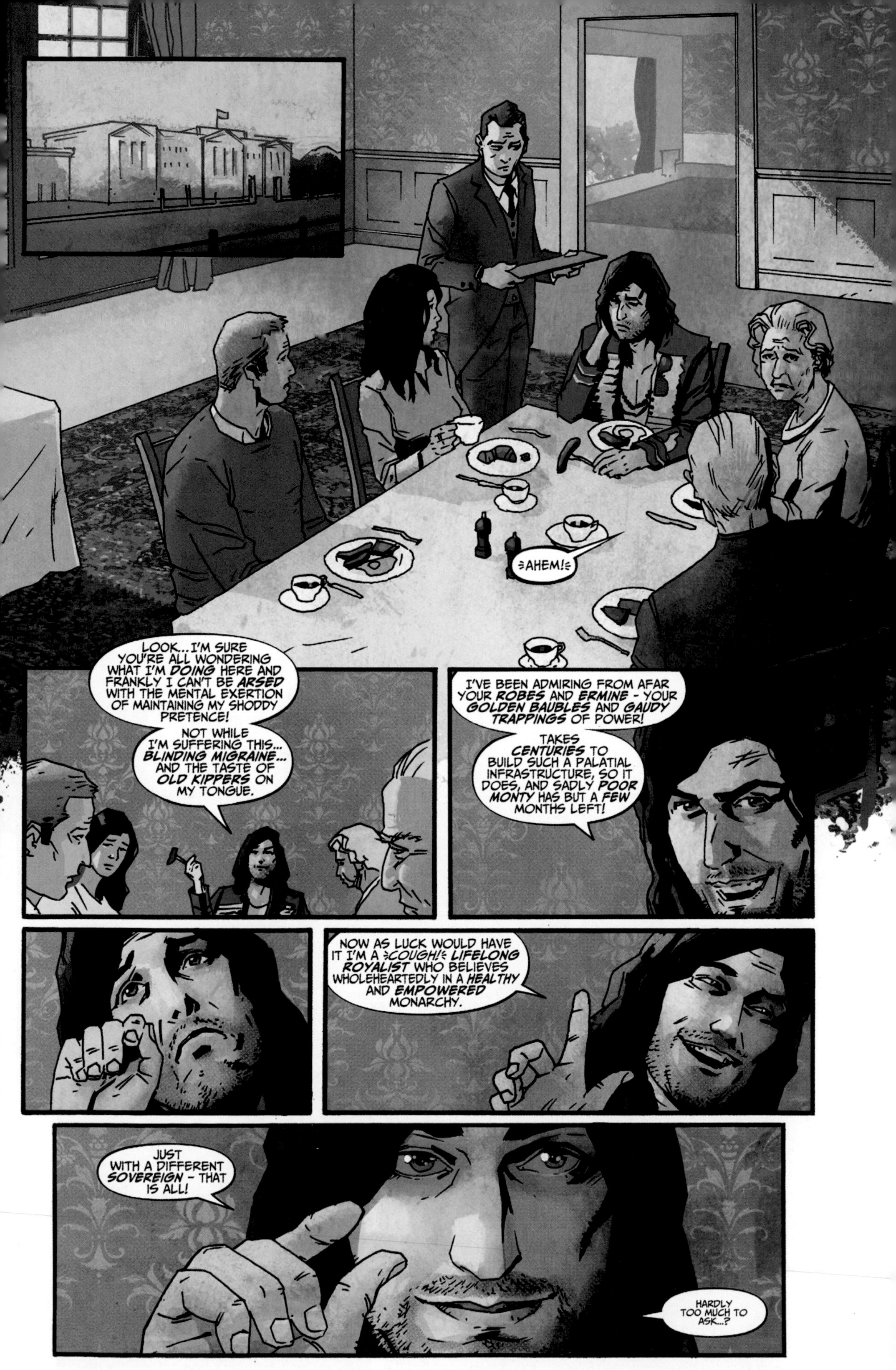

AHEM!
LOOK... I'M SURE YOU'RE ALL WONDERING WHAT I'M DOING HERE AND FRANKLY I CAN'T BE ARSED WITH THE MENTAL EXERTION OF MAINTAINING MY SHODDY PRETENCE!
NOT WHILE I'M SUFFERING THIS... BLINDING MIGRAINE... AND THE TASTE OF OLD KIPPERS ON MY TONGUE.
I'VE BEEN ADMIRING FROM AFAR YOUR ROBES AND ERMINE - YOUR GOLDEN BAUBLES AND GAUDY TRAPPINGS OF POWER!
TAKES CENTURIES TO BUILD SUCH A PALATIAL INFRASTRUCTURE, SO IT DOES, AND SADLY POOR MONTY HAS BUT A FEW MONTHS LEFT!
NOW AS LUCK WOULD HAVE IT I'M A COUGH! LIFELONG ROYALIST WHO BELIEVES WHOLEHEARTEDLY IN A HEALTHY AND EMPOWERED MONARCHY.
JUST WITH A DIFFERENT SOVEREIGN - THAT IS ALL!
HARDLY TOO MUCH TO ASK...?

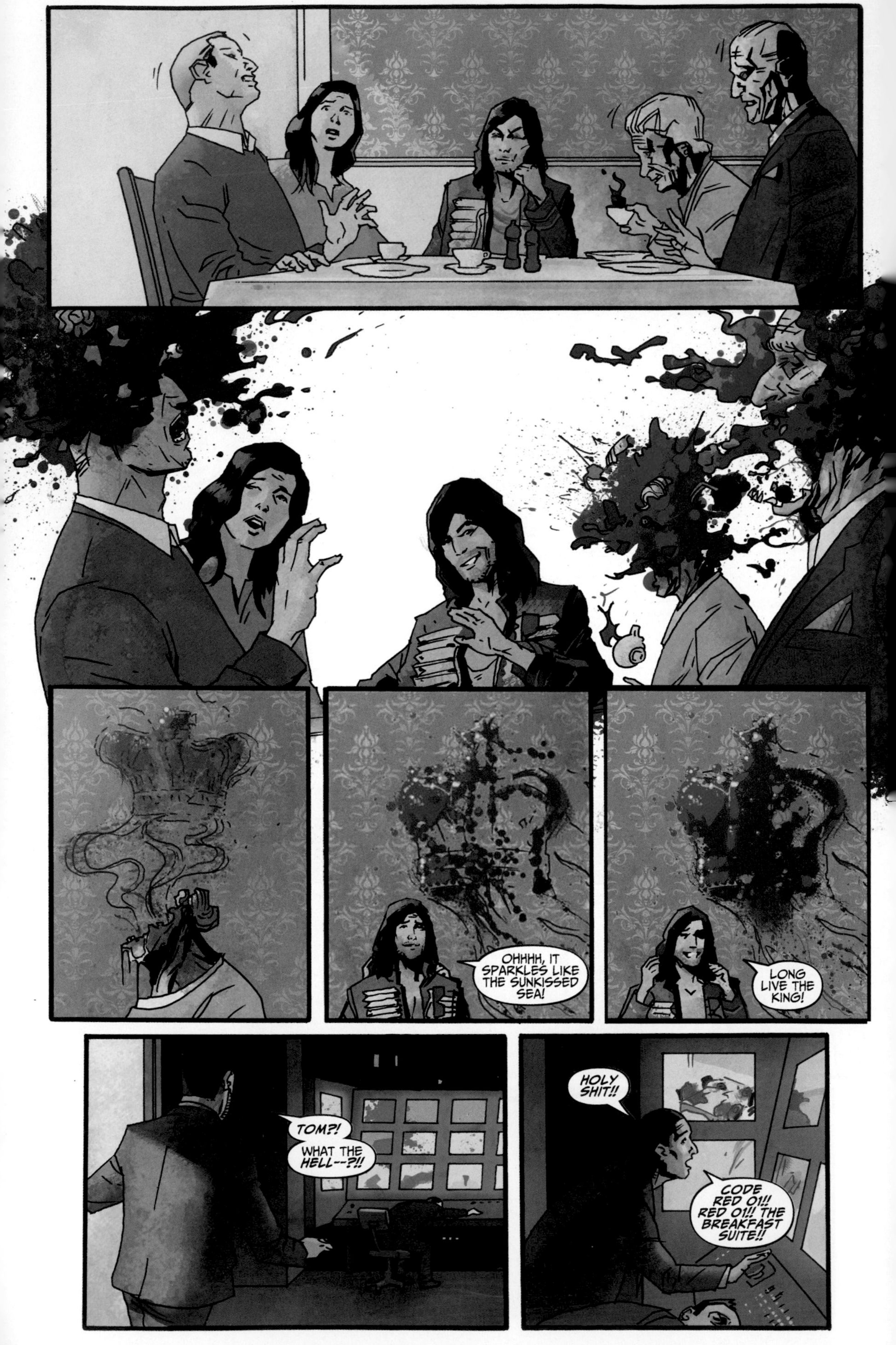
OHHHH, IT SPARKLES LIKE THE SUNKISSED SEA!
LONG LIVE THE KING!
TOM?!
WHAT THE HELL--?!!
HOLY SHIT!!
CODE RED 01!! RED 01!! THE BREAKFAST SUITE!!

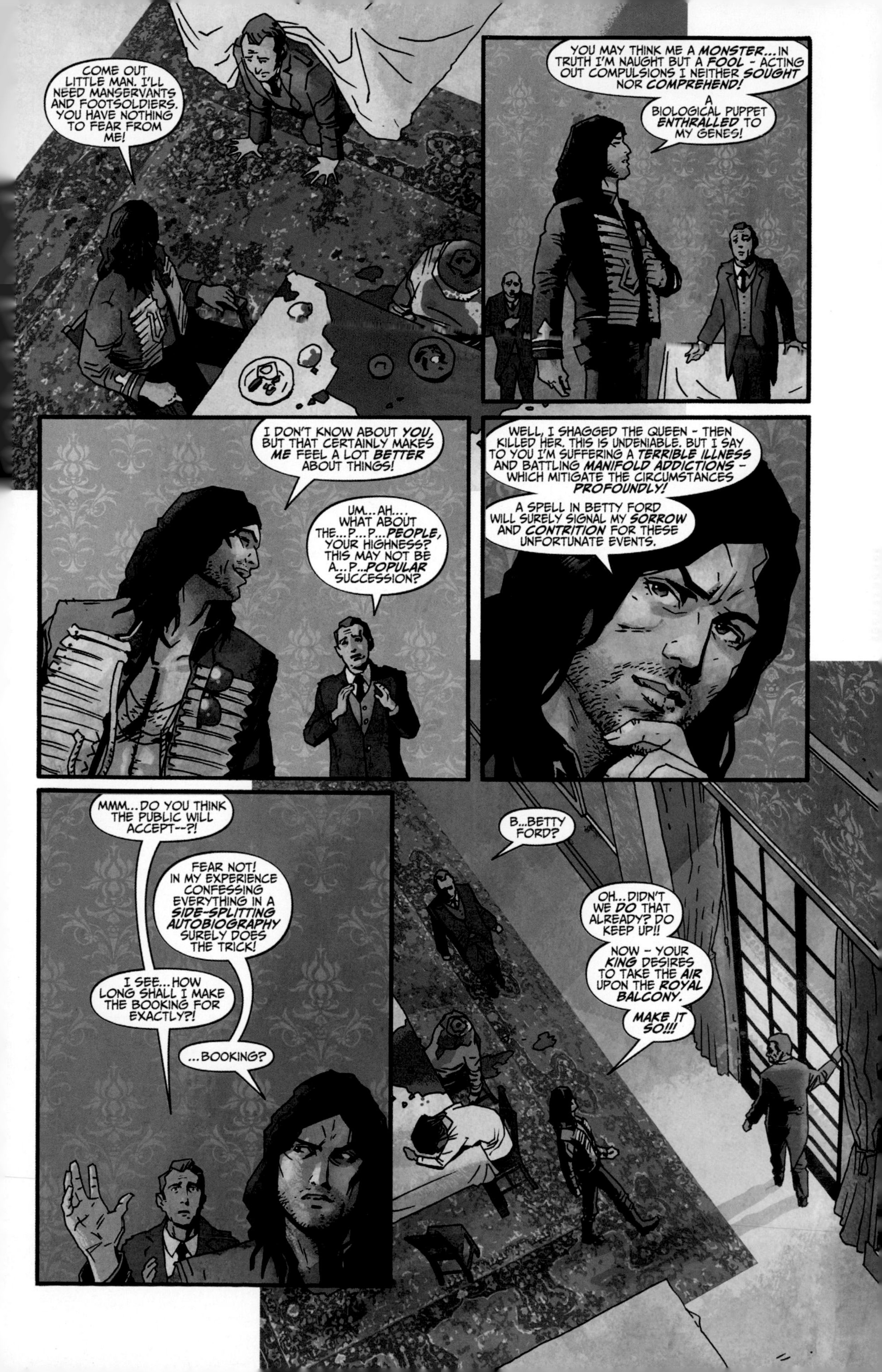
COME OUT LITTLE MAN. I'LL NEED MANSERVANTS AND FOOTSOLDIERS. YOU HAVE NOTHING TO FEAR FROM ME!
YOU MAY THINK ME A MONSTER...IN TRUTH I'M NAUGHT BUT A FOOL - ACTING OUT COMPULSIONS I NEITHER SOUGHT NOR COMPREHEND!
A BIOLOGICAL PUPPET ENTHRALLED TO MY GENES!
I DON'T KNOW ABOUT YOU, BUT THAT CERTAINLY MAKES ME FEEL A LOT BETTER ABOUT THINGS!
UM...AH.... WHAT ABOUT THE...P...P...PEOPLE, YOUR HIGHNESS? THIS MAY NOT BE A...P...POPULAR SUCCESSION?
WELL, I SHAGGED THE QUEEN - THEN KILLED HER. THIS IS UNDENIABLE. BUT I SAY TO YOU I'M SUFFERING A TERRIBLE ILLNESS AND BATTLING MANIFOLD ADDICTIONS - WHICH MITIGATE THE CIRCUMSTANCES PROFOUNDLY!
A SPELL IN BETTY FORD WILL SURELY SIGNAL MY SORROW AND CONTRITION FOR THESE UNFORTUNATE EVENTS.
MMM...DO YOU THINK THE PUBLIC WILL ACCEPT--?!
FEAR NOT! IN MY EXPERIENCE CONFESSING EVERYTHING IN A SIDE-SPLITTING AUTOBIOGRAPHY SURELY DOES THE TRICK!
I SEE...HOW LONG SHALL I MAKE THE BOOKING FOR EXACTLY?!
...BOOKING?
B...BETTY FORD?
OH...DIDN'T WE DO THAT ALREADY? DO KEEP UP!!
NOW - YOUR KING DESIRES TO TAKE THE AIR UPON THE ROYAL BALCONY.
MAKE IT SO!!!

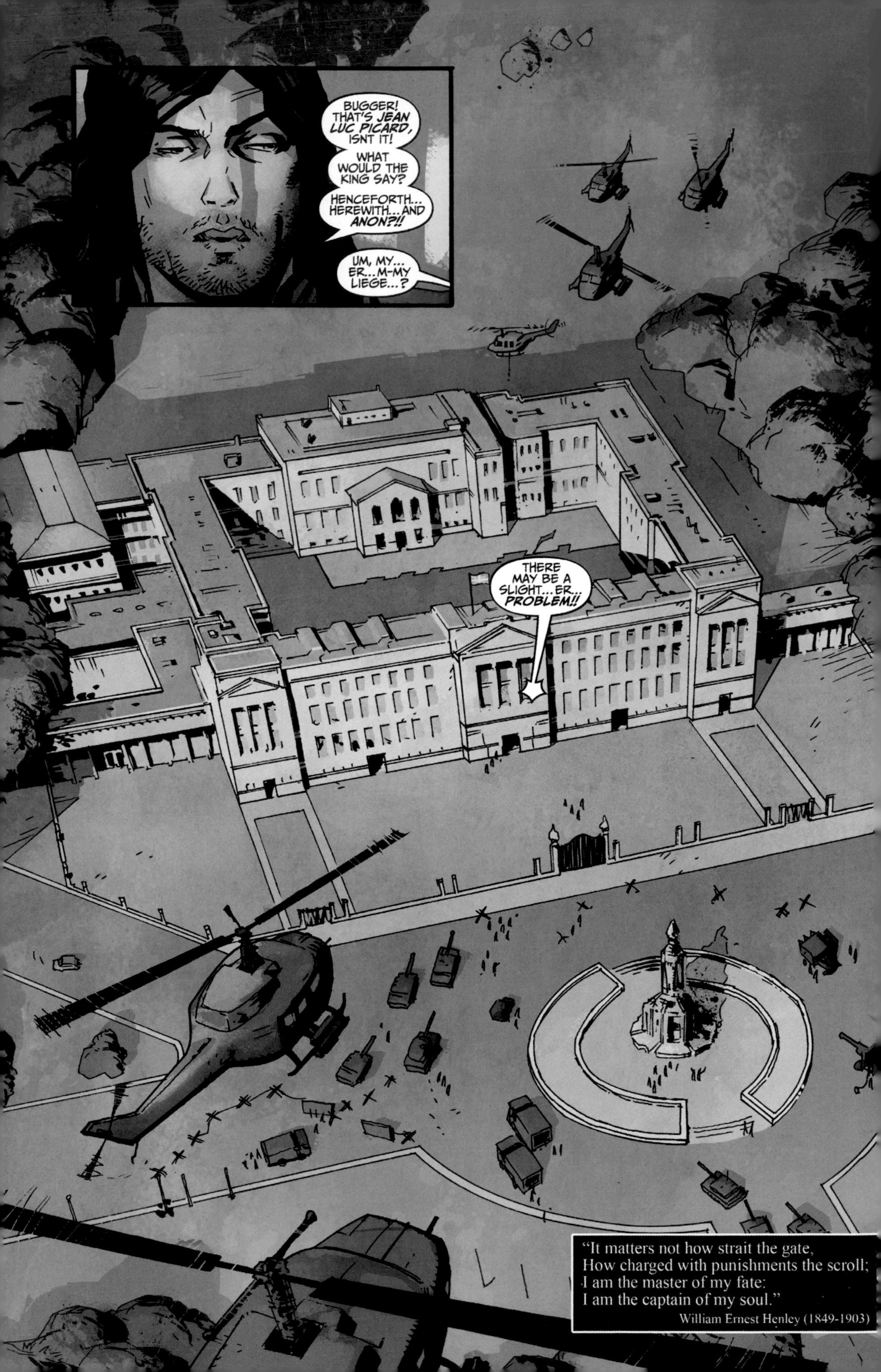
BUGGER! THAT'S JEAN LUC PICARD, ISNT IT!
WHAT WOULD THE KING SAY?
HENCEFORTH... HEREWITH... AND ANON?!!
UM, MY... ER...M-MY LIEGE...?
THERE MAY BE A SLIGHT...ER... PROBLEM!!
"It matters not how strait the gate,
How charged with punishments the scroll;
I am the master of my fate:
I am the captain of my soul."
William Ernest Henley (1849-1903)

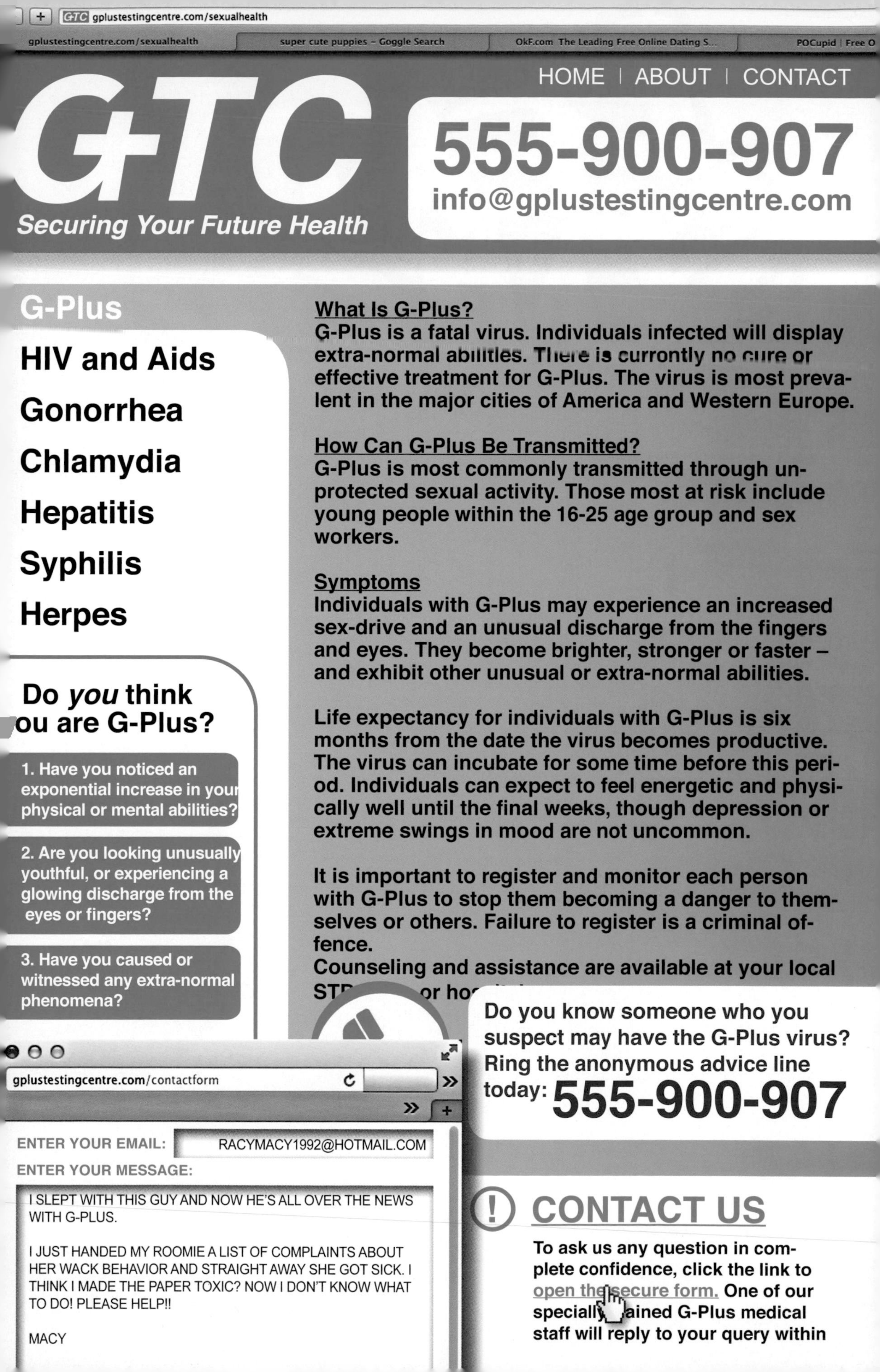

gplustestingcentre.com/sexualhealth
gplustestingcentre.com/sexualhealth
super cute puppies – Goggle Search
OkF.com The Leading Free Online Dating S...
POCupid | Free O
HOME | ABOUT | CONTACT
GTC
Securing Your Future Health
555-900-907
info@gplustestingcentre.com
G-Plus
HIV and Aids
Gonorrhea
Chlamydia
Hepatitis
Syphilis
Herpes
Do *you* think
ou are G-Plus?
1. Have you noticed an exponential increase in your physical or mental abilities?
2. Are you looking unusually youthful, or experiencing a glowing discharge from the eyes or fingers?
3. Have you caused or witnessed any extra-normal phenomena?
What Is G-Plus?
G-Plus is a fatal virus. Individuals infected will display extra-normal abilities. There is currently no cure or effective treatment for G-Plus. The virus is most prevalent in the major cities of America and Western Europe.
How Can G-Plus Be Transmitted?
G-Plus is most commonly transmitted through unprotected sexual activity. Those most at risk include young people within the 16-25 age group and sex workers.
Symptoms
Individuals with G-Plus may experience an increased sex-drive and an unusual discharge from the fingers and eyes. They become brighter, stronger or faster – and exhibit other unusual or extra-normal abilities.
Life expectancy for individuals with G-Plus is six months from the date the virus becomes productive. The virus can incubate for some time before this period. Individuals can expect to feel energetic and physically well until the final weeks, though depression or extreme swings in mood are not uncommon.
It is important to register and monitor each person with G-Plus to stop them becoming a danger to themselves or others. Failure to register is a criminal offence.
Counseling and assistance are available at your local
Do you know someone who you suspect may have the G-Plus virus? Ring the anonymous advice line today: 555-900-907
CONTACT US
To ask us any question in complete confidence, click the link to open the secure form. One of our speciall ained G-Plus medical staff will reply to your query within
gplustestingcentre.com/contactform
ENTER YOUR EMAIL: RACYMACY1992@HOTMAIL.COM
ENTER YOUR MESSAGE:
I SLEPT WITH THIS GUY AND NOW HE'S ALL OVER THE NEWS WITH G-PLUS.
I JUST HANDED MY ROOMIE A LIST OF COMPLAINTS ABOUT HER WACK BEHAVIOR AND STRAIGHT AWAY SHE GOT SICK. I THINK I MADE THE PAPER TOXIC? NOW I DON'T KNOW WHAT TO DO! PLEASE HELP!!
MACY

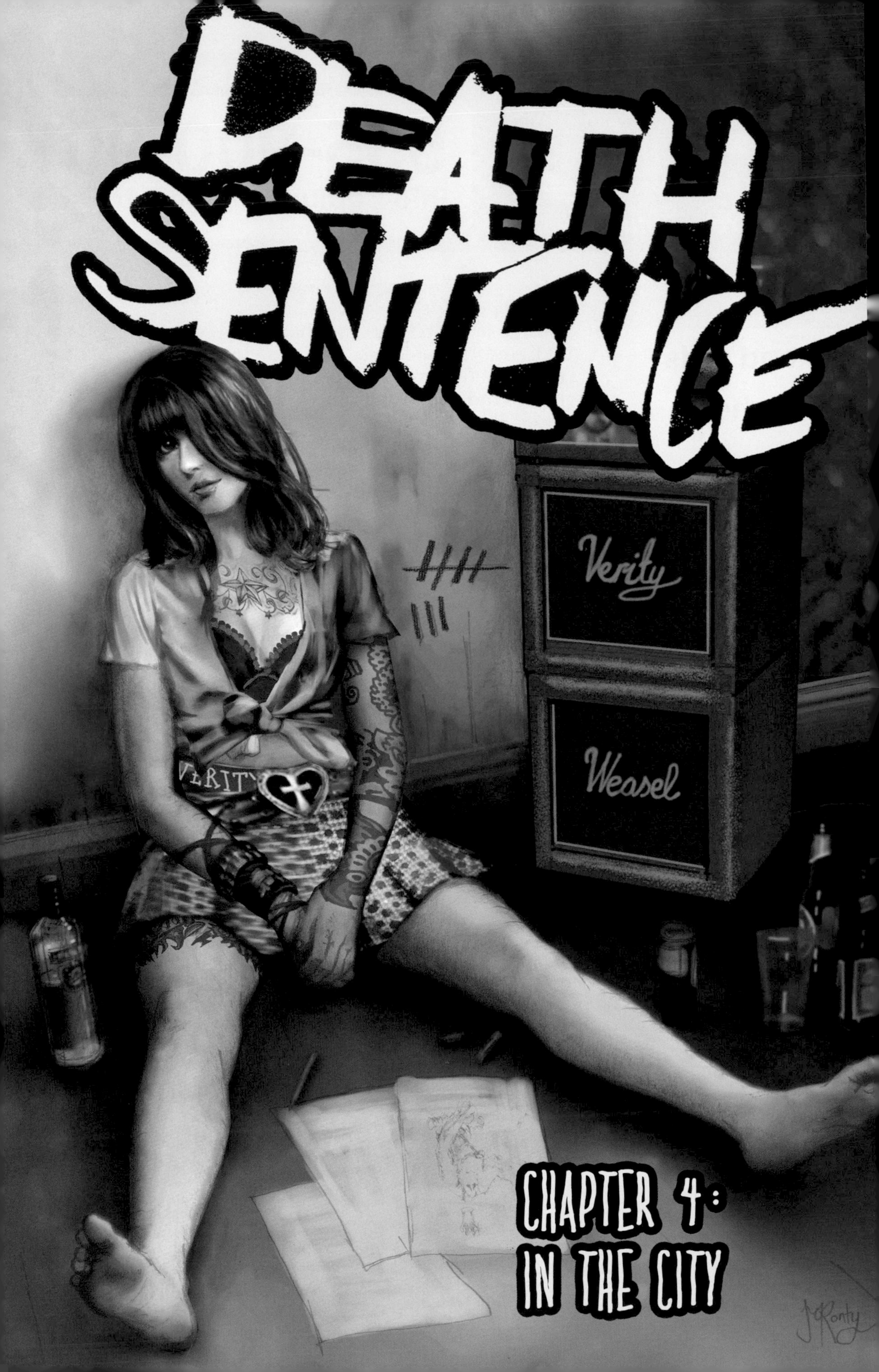
DEATH SENTENCE
Verity
Weasel
VERITY
CHAPTER 4:
IN THE CITY

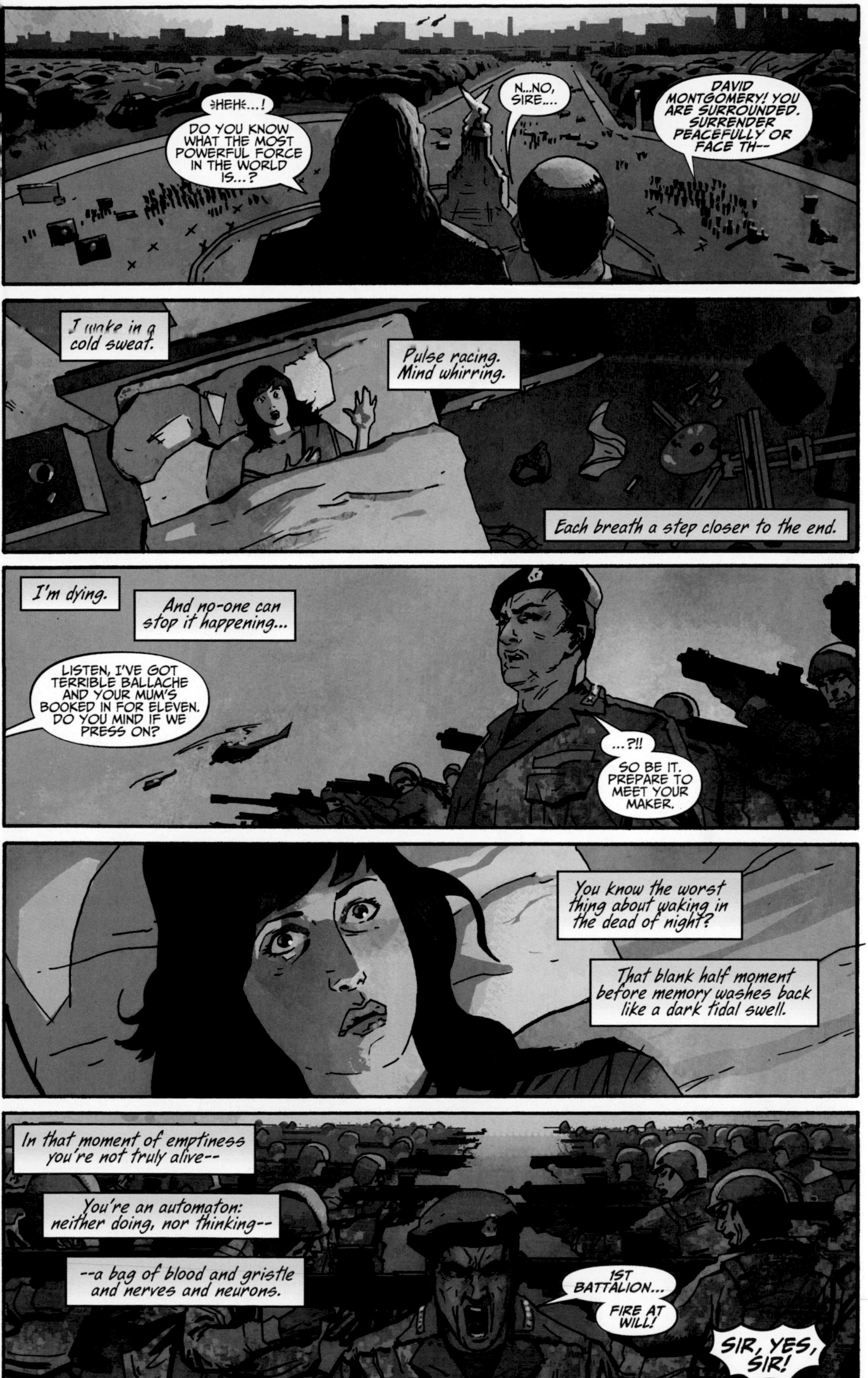
HEH...!
DO YOU KNOW WHAT THE MOST POWERFUL FORCE IN THE WORLD IS...?
N...NO, SIRE....
DAVID MONTGOMERY! YOU ARE SURROUNDED. SURRENDER PEACEFULLY OR FACE TH--
I wake in a cold sweat.
Pulse racing. Mind whirring.
Each breath a step closer to the end.
I'm dying.
And no-one can stop it happening...
LISTEN, I'VE GOT TERRIBLE BALLACHE AND YOUR MUM'S BOOKED IN FOR ELEVEN. DO YOU MIND IF WE PRESS ON?
...?!!
SO BE IT. PREPARE TO MEET YOUR MAKER.
You know the worst thing about waking in the dead of night?
That blank half moment before memory washes back like a dark tidal swell.
In that moment of emptiness you're not truly alive--
You're an automaton: neither doing, nor thinking--
--a bag of blood and gristle and nerves and neurons.
1ST BATTALION...
FIRE AT WILL!
SIR, YES, SIR!

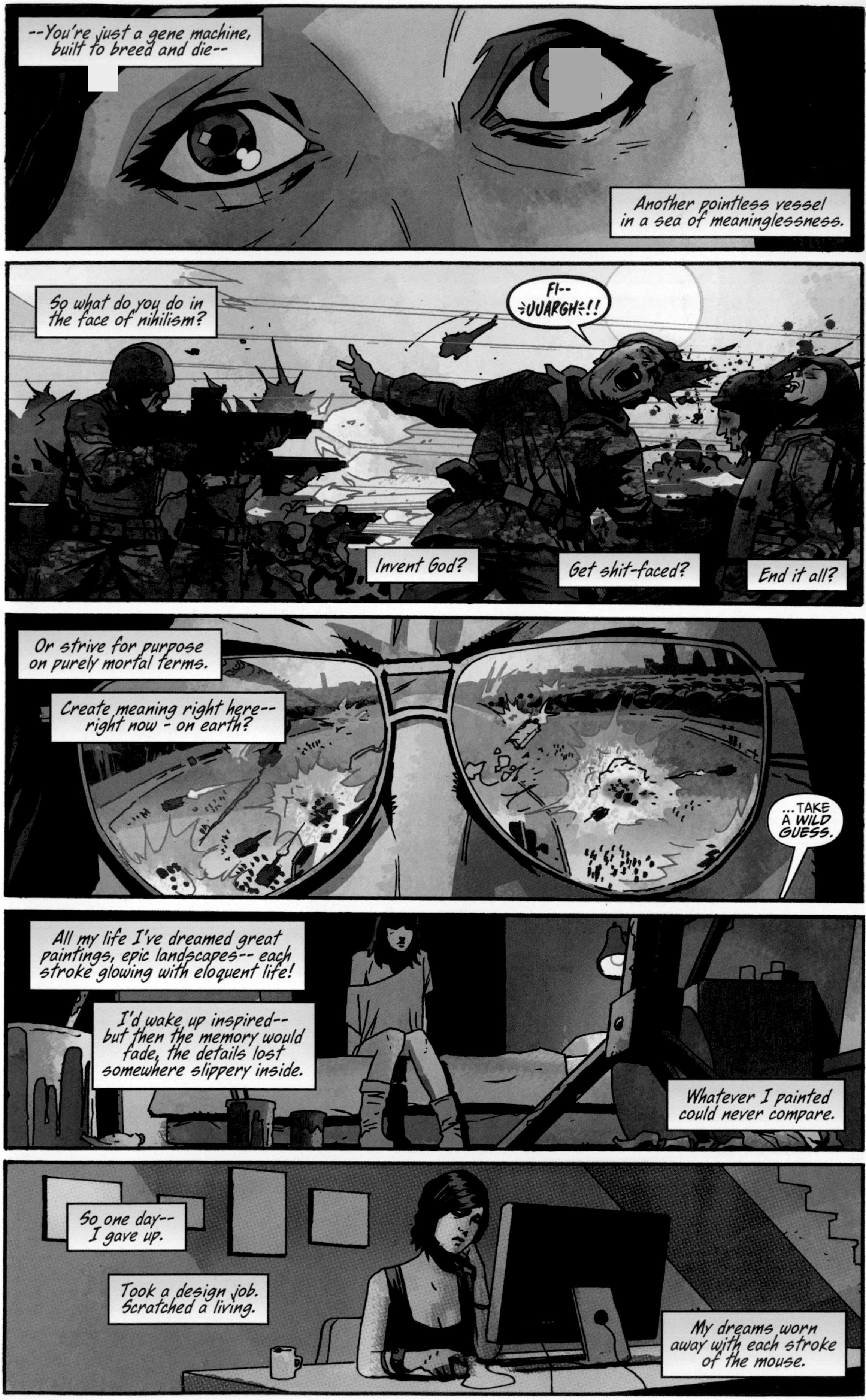
--You're just a gene machine, built to breed and die--
Another pointless vessel in a sea of meaninglessness.
So what do you do in the face of nihilism?
FI-- UUARGH!!
Invent God?
Get shit-faced?
End it all?
Or strive for purpose on purely mortal terms.
Create meaning right here-- right now - on earth?
...TAKE A WILD GUESS.
All my life I've dreamed great paintings, epic landscapes-- each stroke glowing with eloquent life!
I'd wake up inspired-- but then the memory would fade, the details lost somewhere slippery inside.
Whatever I painted could never compare.
So one day-- I gave up.
Took a design job. Scratched a living.
My dreams worn away with each stroke of the mouse.

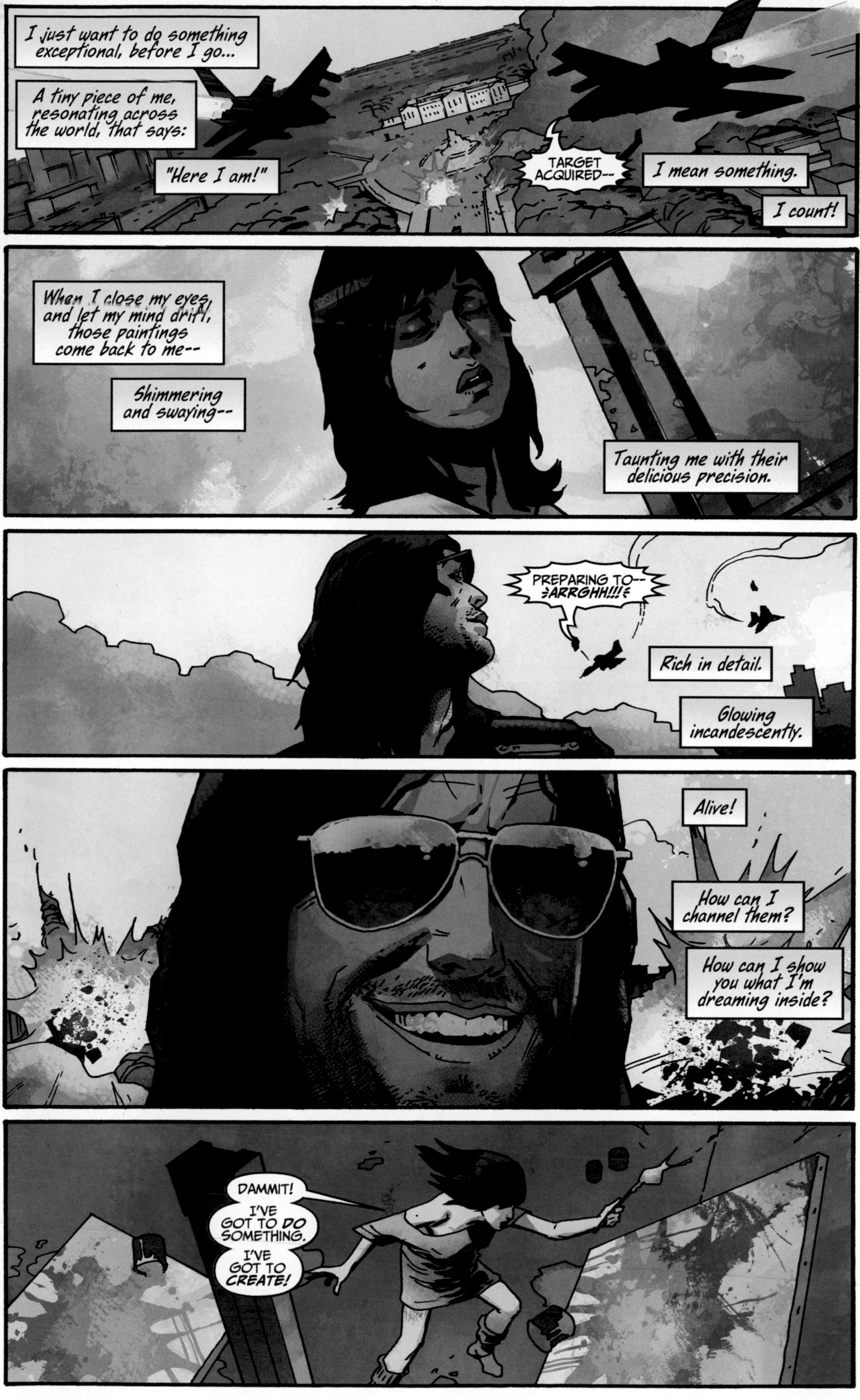

I just want to do something exceptional, before I go...
A tiny piece of me, resonating across the world, that says:
"Here I am!"
TARGET ACQUIRED--
I mean something.
I count!
When I close my eyes, and let my mind drift, those paintings come back to me--
Shimmering and swaying--
Taunting me with their delicious precision.
PREPARING TO-- ARRGHH!!!
Rich in detail.
Glowing incandescently.
Alive!
How can I channel them?
How can I show you what I'm dreaming inside?
DAMMIT!
I'VE GOT TO DO SOMETHING.
I'VE GOT TO CREATE!

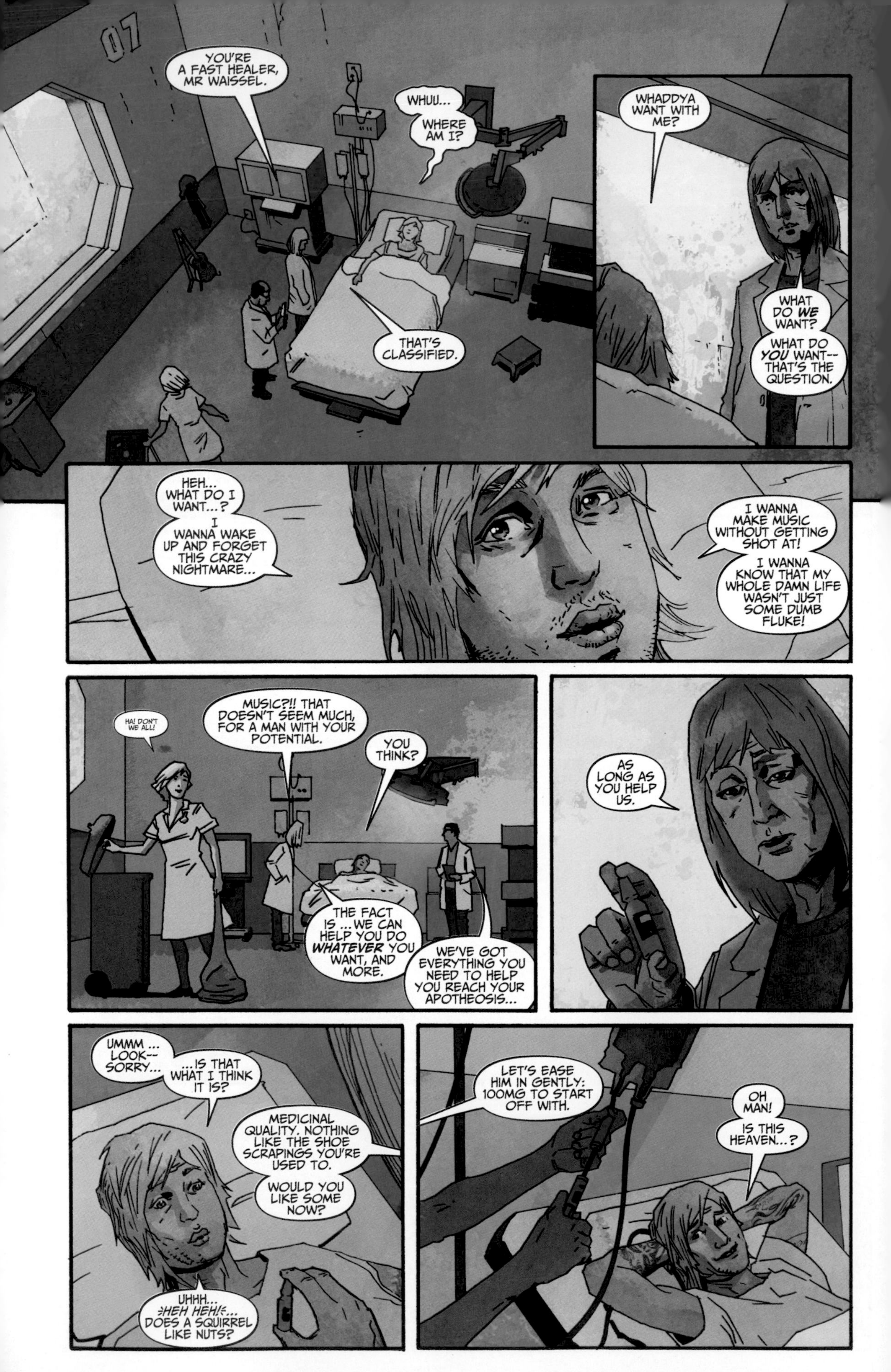

YOU'RE A FAST HEALER, MR WAISSEL.
WHUU...
WHERE AM I?
THAT'S CLASSIFIED.
WHADDYA WANT WITH ME?
WHAT DO *WE* WANT?
WHAT DO *YOU* WANT-- THAT'S THE QUESTION.
HEH... WHAT DO I WANT...?
I WANNA WAKE UP AND FORGET THIS CRAZY NIGHTMARE...
I WANNA MAKE MUSIC WITHOUT GETTING SHOT AT!
I WANNA KNOW THAT MY WHOLE DAMN LIFE WASN'T JUST SOME DUMB FLUKE!
HA! DON'T WE ALL!
MUSIC?!! THAT DOESN'T SEEM MUCH, FOR A MAN WITH YOUR POTENTIAL.
YOU THINK?
THE FACT IS ...WE CAN HELP YOU DO *WHATEVER* YOU WANT, AND MORE.
WE'VE GOT EVERYTHING YOU NEED TO HELP YOU REACH YOUR APOTHEOSIS...
AS LONG AS YOU HELP US.
UMMM ... LOOK-- SORRY...
...IS THAT WHAT I THINK IT IS?
MEDICINAL QUALITY. NOTHING LIKE THE SHOE SCRAPINGS YOU'RE USED TO.
WOULD YOU LIKE SOME NOW?
UHHH... *HEH HEH!*... DOES A SQUIRREL LIKE NUTS?
LET'S EASE HIM IN GENTLY: 100MG TO START OFF WITH.
OH MAN!
IS THIS HEAVEN...?

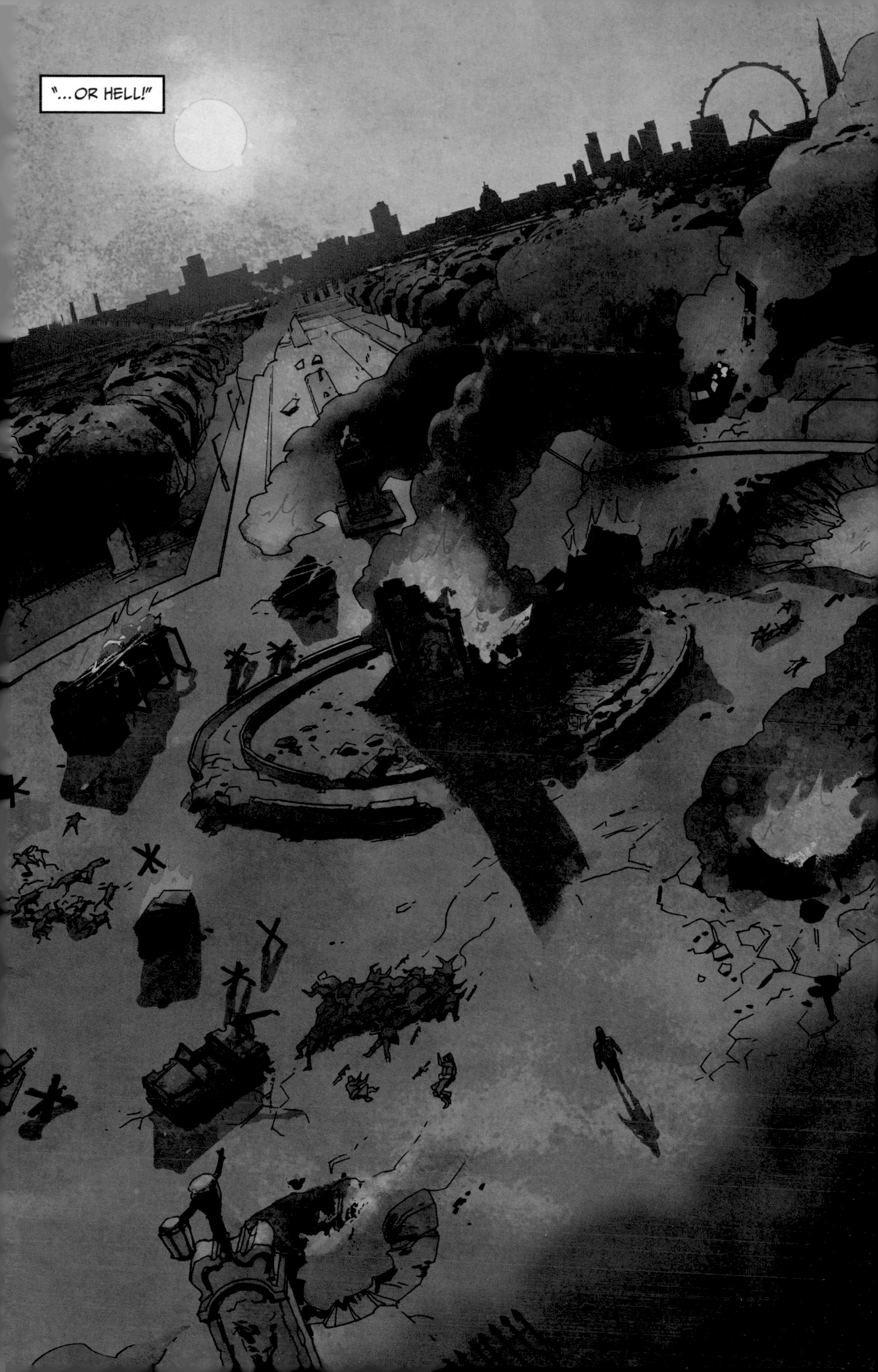
"...OR HELL!"

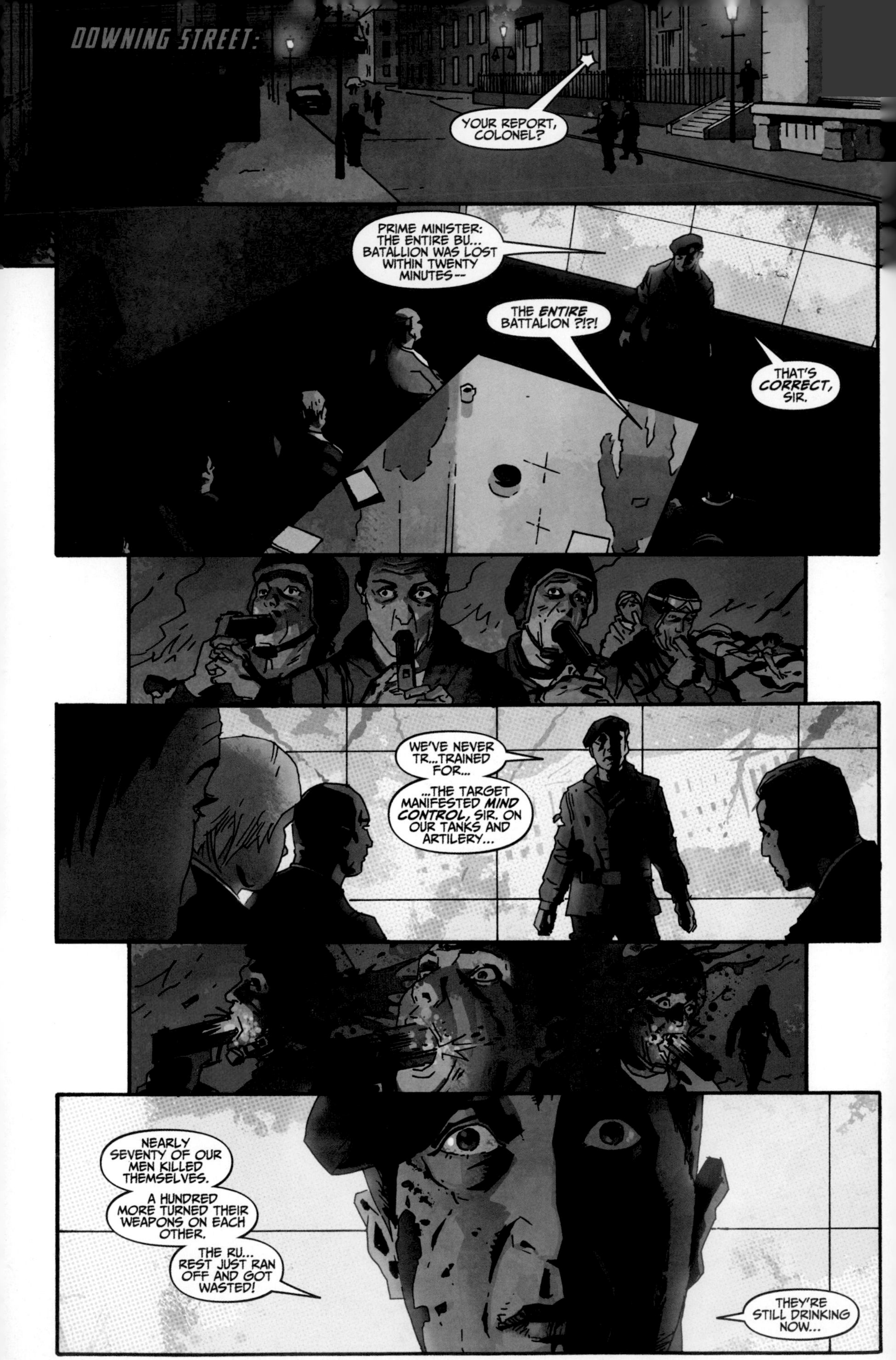
DOWNING STREET:
YOUR REPORT, COLONEL?
PRIME MINISTER: THE ENTIRE BU... BATALLION WAS LOST WITHIN TWENTY MINUTES--
THE ENTIRE BATTALION ?!?!
THAT'S CORRECT, SIR.
WE'VE NEVER TR...TRAINED FOR...
...THE TARGET MANIFESTED MIND CONTROL, SIR. ON OUR TANKS AND ARTILERY...
NEARLY SEVENTY OF OUR MEN KILLED THEMSELVES.
A HUNDRED MORE TURNED THEIR WEAPONS ON EACH OTHER.
THE RU... REST JUST RAN OFF AND GOT WASTED!
THEY'RE STILL DRINKING NOW...

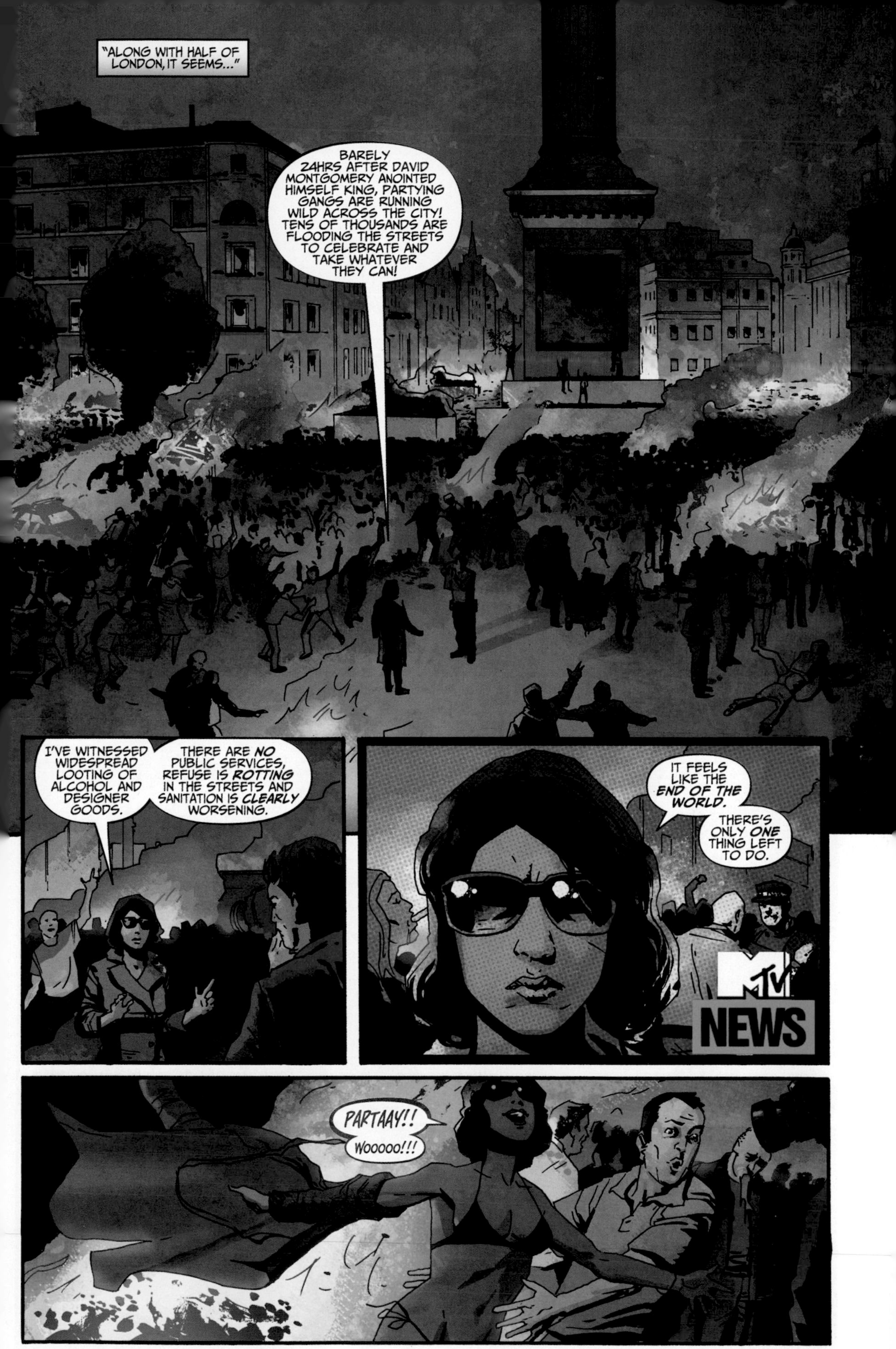
"ALONG WITH HALF OF LONDON, IT SEEMS..."
BARELY 24HRS AFTER DAVID MONTGOMERY ANOINTED HIMSELF KING, PARTYING GANGS ARE RUNNING WILD ACROSS THE CITY! TENS OF THOUSANDS ARE FLOODING THE STREETS TO CELEBRATE AND TAKE WHATEVER THEY CAN!
I'VE WITNESSED WIDESPREAD LOOTING OF ALCOHOL AND DESIGNER GOODS.
THERE ARE NO PUBLIC SERVICES, REFUSE IS ROTTING IN THE STREETS AND SANITATION IS CLEARLY WORSENING.
IT FEELS LIKE THE END OF THE WORLD.
THERE'S ONLY ONE THING LEFT TO DO.
MTV
NEWS
PARTAAY!!
WOOOOO!!!

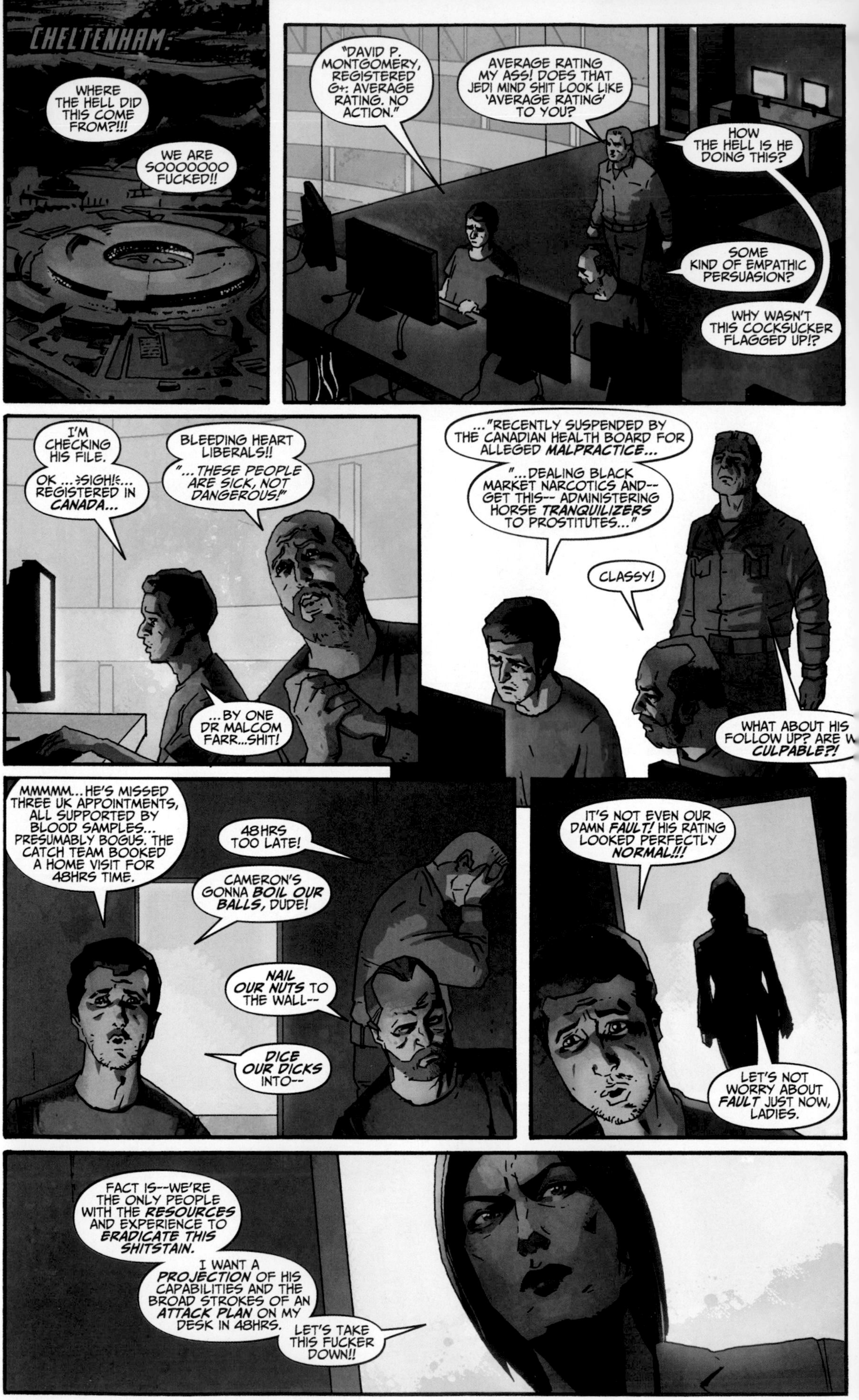
CHELTENHAM:
WHERE THE HELL DID THIS COME FROM?!!!
WE ARE SOOOOOOO FUCKED!!
"DAVID P. MONTGOMERY, REGISTERED G+: AVERAGE RATING. NO ACTION."
AVERAGE RATING MY ASS! DOES THAT JEDI MIND SHIT LOOK LIKE 'AVERAGE RATING' TO YOU?
HOW THE HELL IS HE DOING THIS?
SOME KIND OF EMPATHIC PERSUASION?
WHY WASN'T THIS COCKSUCKER FLAGGED UP!?
I'M CHECKING HIS FILE.
OK ...SIGH!... REGISTERED IN CANADA...
BLEEDING HEART LIBERALS!! "...THESE PEOPLE ARE SICK, NOT DANGEROUS!"
...BY ONE DR MALCOM FARR...SHIT!
..."RECENTLY SUSPENDED BY THE CANADIAN HEALTH BOARD FOR ALLEGED MALPRACTICE...
"...DEALING BLACK MARKET NARCOTICS AND--GET THIS-- ADMINISTERING HORSE TRANQUILIZERS TO PROSTITUTES..."
CLASSY!
WHAT ABOUT HIS FOLLOW UP? ARE W CULPABLE?!
MMMMM...HE'S MISSED THREE UK APPOINTMENTS, ALL SUPPORTED BY BLOOD SAMPLES... PRESUMABLY BOGUS. THE CATCH TEAM BOOKED A HOME VISIT FOR 48HRS TIME.
48HRS TOO LATE!
CAMERON'S GONNA BOIL OUR BALLS, DUDE!
NAIL OUR NUTS TO THE WALL--
DICE OUR DICKS INTO--
IT'S NOT EVEN OUR DAMN FAULT! HIS RATING LOOKED PERFECTLY NORMAL!!!
LET'S NOT WORRY ABOUT FAULT JUST NOW, LADIES.
FACT IS--WE'RE THE ONLY PEOPLE WITH THE RESOURCES AND EXPERIENCE TO ERADICATE THIS SHITSTAIN.
I WANT A PROJECTION OF HIS CAPABILITIES AND THE BROAD STROKES OF AN ATTACK PLAN ON MY DESK IN 48HRS.
LET'S TAKE THIS FUCKER DOWN!!

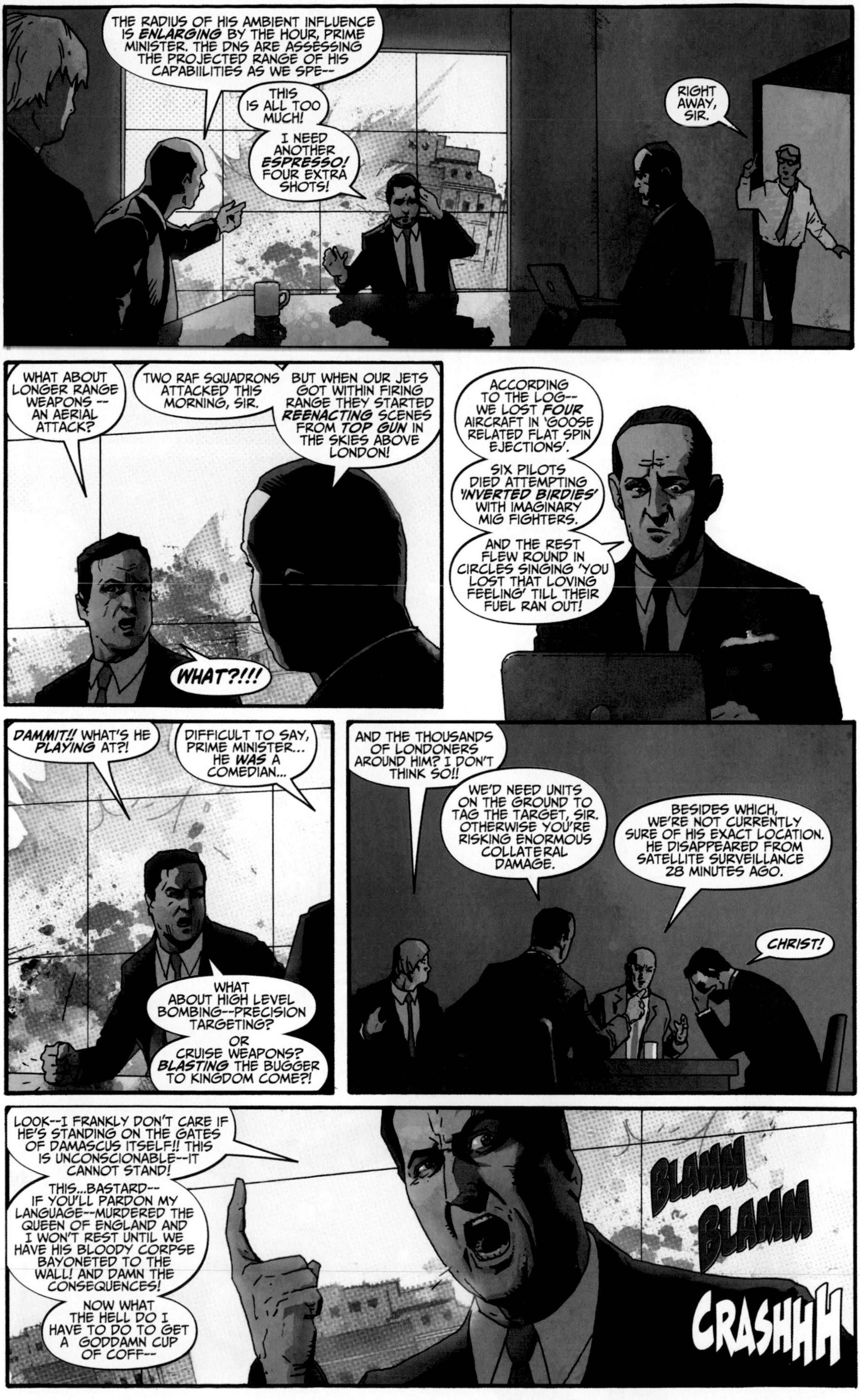
THE RADIUS OF HIS AMBIENT INFLUENCE IS ENLARGING BY THE HOUR, PRIME MINISTER. THE DNS ARE ASSESSING THE PROJECTED RANGE OF HIS CAPABIILITIES AS WE SPE--
THIS IS ALL TOO MUCH!
I NEED ANOTHER ESPRESSO! FOUR EXTRA SHOTS!
RIGHT AWAY, SIR.
WHAT ABOUT LONGER RANGE WEAPONS -- AN AERIAL ATTACK?
TWO RAF SQUADRONS ATTACKED THIS MORNING, SIR.
BUT WHEN OUR JETS GOT WITHIN FIRING RANGE THEY STARTED REENACTING SCENES FROM TOP GUN IN THE SKIES ABOVE LONDON!
WHAT?!!!
ACCORDING TO THE LOG-- WE LOST FOUR AIRCRAFT IN 'GOOSE RELATED FLAT SPIN EJECTIONS'.
SIX PILOTS DIED ATTEMPTING 'INVERTED BIRDIES' WITH IMAGINARY MIG FIGHTERS.
AND THE REST FLEW ROUND IN CIRCLES SINGING 'YOU LOST THAT LOVING FEELING' TILL THEIR FUEL RAN OUT!
DAMMIT!! WHAT'S HE PLAYING AT?!
DIFFICULT TO SAY, PRIME MINISTER... HE WAS A COMEDIAN...
WHAT ABOUT HIGH LEVEL BOMBING--PRECISION TARGETING?
OR CRUISE WEAPONS? BLASTING THE BUGGER TO KINGDOM COME?!
AND THE THOUSANDS OF LONDONERS AROUND HIM? I DON'T THINK SO!!
WE'D NEED UNITS ON THE GROUND TO TAG THE TARGET, SIR. OTHERWISE YOU'RE RISKING ENORMOUS COLLATERAL DAMAGE.
BESIDES WHICH, WE'RE NOT CURRENTLY SURE OF HIS EXACT LOCATION. HE DISAPPEARED FROM SATELLITE SURVEILLANCE 28 MINUTES AGO.
CHRIST!
LOOK--I FRANKLY DON'T CARE IF HE'S STANDING ON THE GATES OF DAMASCUS ITSELF!! THIS IS UNCONSCIONABLE--IT CANNOT STAND!
THIS...BASTARD-- IF YOU'LL PARDON MY LANGUAGE--MURDERED THE QUEEN OF ENGLAND AND I WON'T REST UNTIL WE HAVE HIS BLOODY CORPSE BAYONETED TO THE WALL! AND DAMN THE CONSEQUENCES!
NOW WHAT THE HELL DO I HAVE TO DO TO GET A GODDAMN CUP OF COFF--
BLAMM
BLAMM
CRASHHH

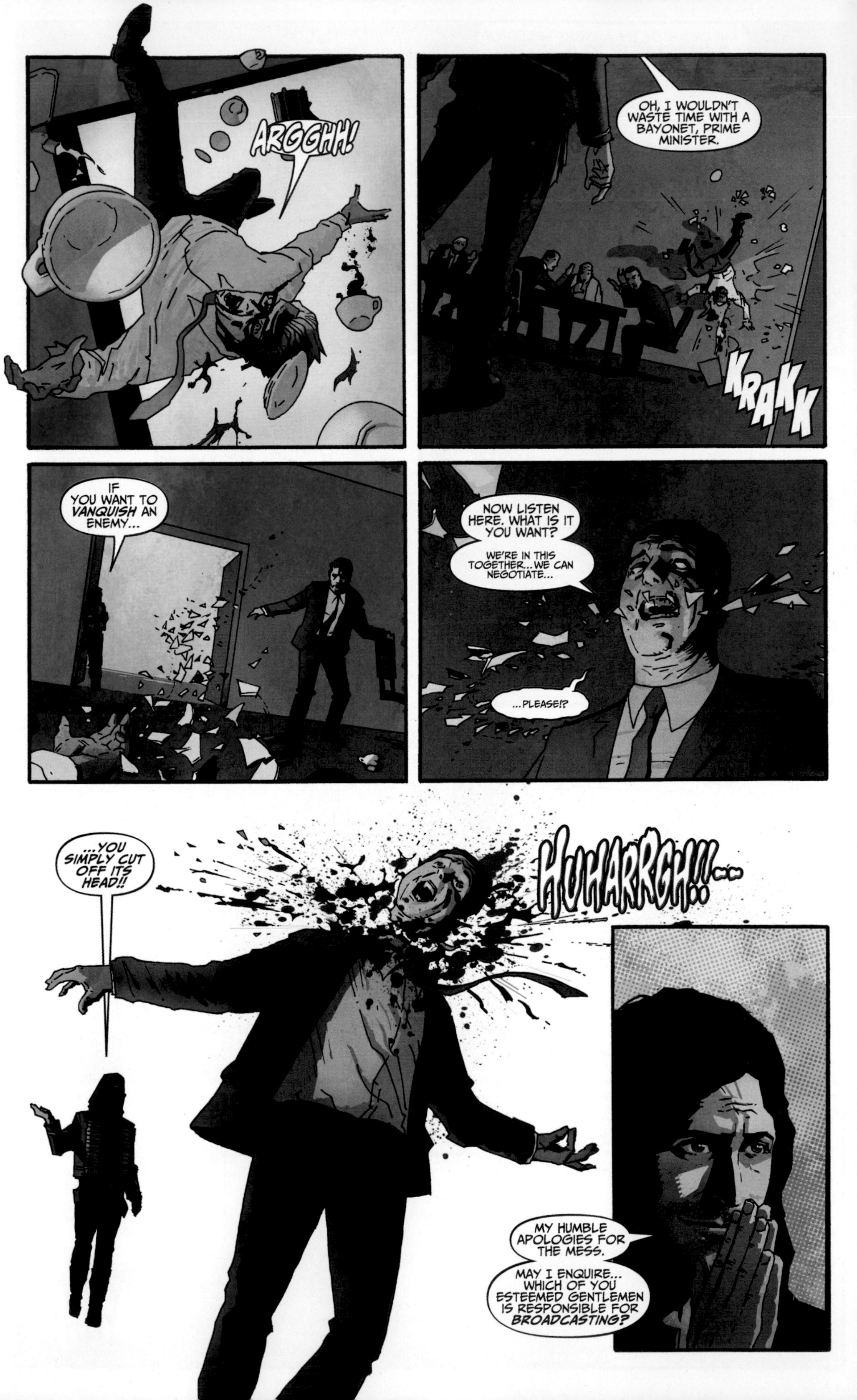
ARGGHH!
OH, I WOULDN'T WASTE TIME WITH A BAYONET, PRIME MINISTER.
KRAKK
IF YOU WANT TO VANQUISH AN ENEMY...
NOW LISTEN HERE. WHAT IS IT YOU WANT?
WE'RE IN THIS TOGETHER...WE CAN NEGOTIATE...
...PLEASE!?
...YOU SIMPLY CUT OFF ITS HEAD!!
HUHARRGH!!..
MY HUMBLE APOLOGIES FOR THE MESS.
MAY I ENQUIRE... WHICH OF YOU ESTEEMED GENTLEMEN IS RESPONSIBLE FOR BROADCASTING?

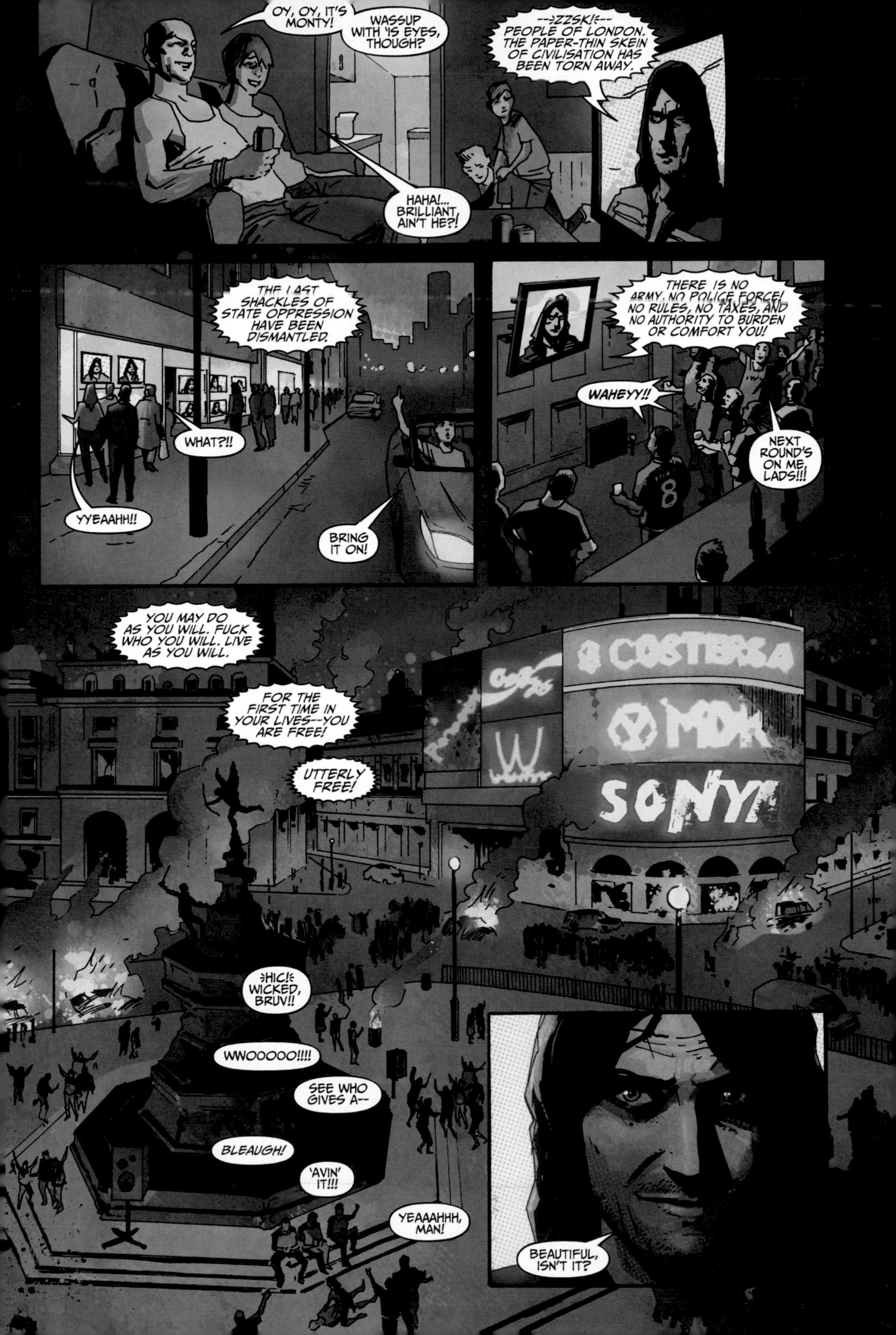
OY, OY, IT'S MONTY!
WASSUP WITH 'IS EYES, THOUGH?
HAHA!... BRILLIANT, AIN'T HE?!
--ZZSK!--
PEOPLE OF LONDON. THE PAPER-THIN SKEIN OF CIVILISATION HAS BEEN TORN AWAY.
THE LAST SHACKLES OF STATE OPPRESSION HAVE BEEN DISMANTLED.
WHAT?!!
YYEAAHH!!
BRING IT ON!
THERE IS NO ARMY, NO POLICE FORCE! NO RULES, NO TAXES, AND NO AUTHORITY TO BURDEN OR COMFORT YOU!
WAHEYY!!
NEXT ROUND'S ON ME, LADS!!!
YOU MAY DO AS YOU WILL. FUCK WHO YOU WILL. LIVE AS YOU WILL.
FOR THE FIRST TIME IN YOUR LIVES--YOU ARE FREE!
UTTERLY FREE!
COSTERSA
MDR
SONY
HIC! WICKED, BRUV!!
WWOOOOO!!!!
SEE WHO GIVES A--
BLEAUGH!
'AVIN' IT!!!
YEAAAHHH, MAN!
BEAUTIFUL, ISN'T IT?

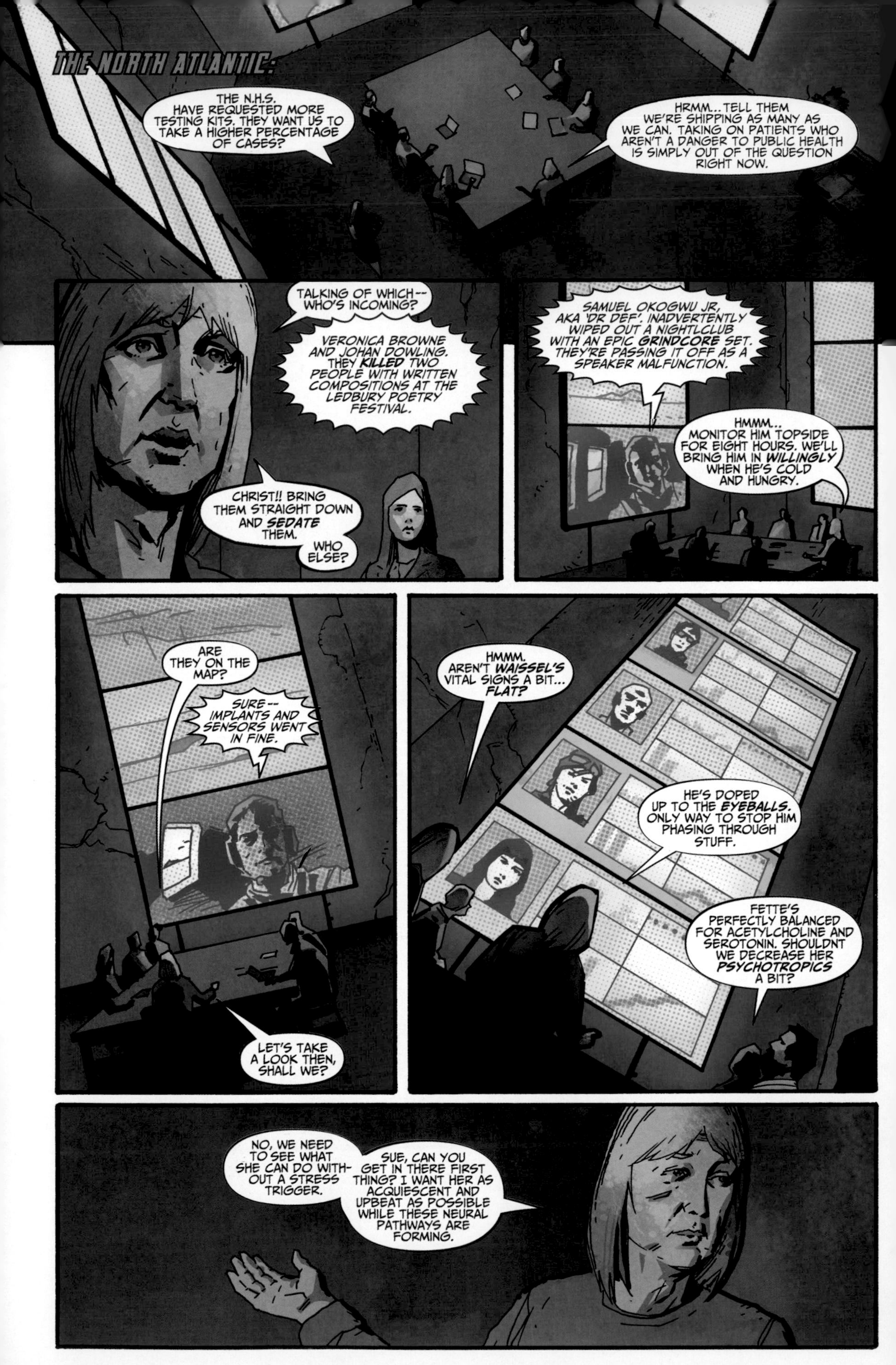
THE NORTH ATLANTIC:
THE N.H.S. HAVE REQUESTED MORE TESTING KITS. THEY WANT US TO TAKE A HIGHER PERCENTAGE OF CASES?
HRMM... TELL THEM WE'RE SHIPPING AS MANY AS WE CAN. TAKING ON PATIENTS WHO AREN'T A DANGER TO PUBLIC HEALTH IS SIMPLY OUT OF THE QUESTION RIGHT NOW.
TALKING OF WHICH-- WHO'S INCOMING?
VERONICA BROWNE AND JOHAN DOWLING. THEY KILLED TWO PEOPLE WITH WRITTEN COMPOSITIONS AT THE LEDBURY POETRY FESTIVAL.
CHRIST!! BRING THEM STRAIGHT DOWN AND SEDATE THEM.
WHO ELSE?
SAMUEL OKOGWU JR, AKA 'DR DEF'. INADVERTENTLY WIPED OUT A NIGHTLCLUB WITH AN EPIC GRINDCORE SET. THEY'RE PASSING IT OFF AS A SPEAKER MALFUNCTION.
HMMM.. MONITOR HIM TOPSIDE FOR EIGHT HOURS. WE'LL BRING HIM IN WILLINGLY WHEN HE'S COLD AND HUNGRY.
ARE THEY ON THE MAP?
SURE-- IMPLANTS AND SENSORS WENT IN FINE.
LET'S TAKE A LOOK THEN, SHALL WE?
HMMM. AREN'T WAISSEL'S VITAL SIGNS A BIT... FLAT?
HE'S DOPED UP TO THE EYEBALLS. ONLY WAY TO STOP HIM PHASING THROUGH STUFF.
FETTE'S PERFECTLY BALANCED FOR ACETYLCHOLINE AND SEROTONIN. SHOULDNT WE DECREASE HER PSYCHOTROPICS A BIT?
NO, WE NEED TO SEE WHAT SHE CAN DO WITH-OUT A STRESS TRIGGER.
SUE, CAN YOU GET IN THERE FIRST THING? I WANT HER AS ACQUIESCENT AND UPBEAT AS POSSIBLE WHILE THESE NEURAL PATHWAYS ARE FORMING.

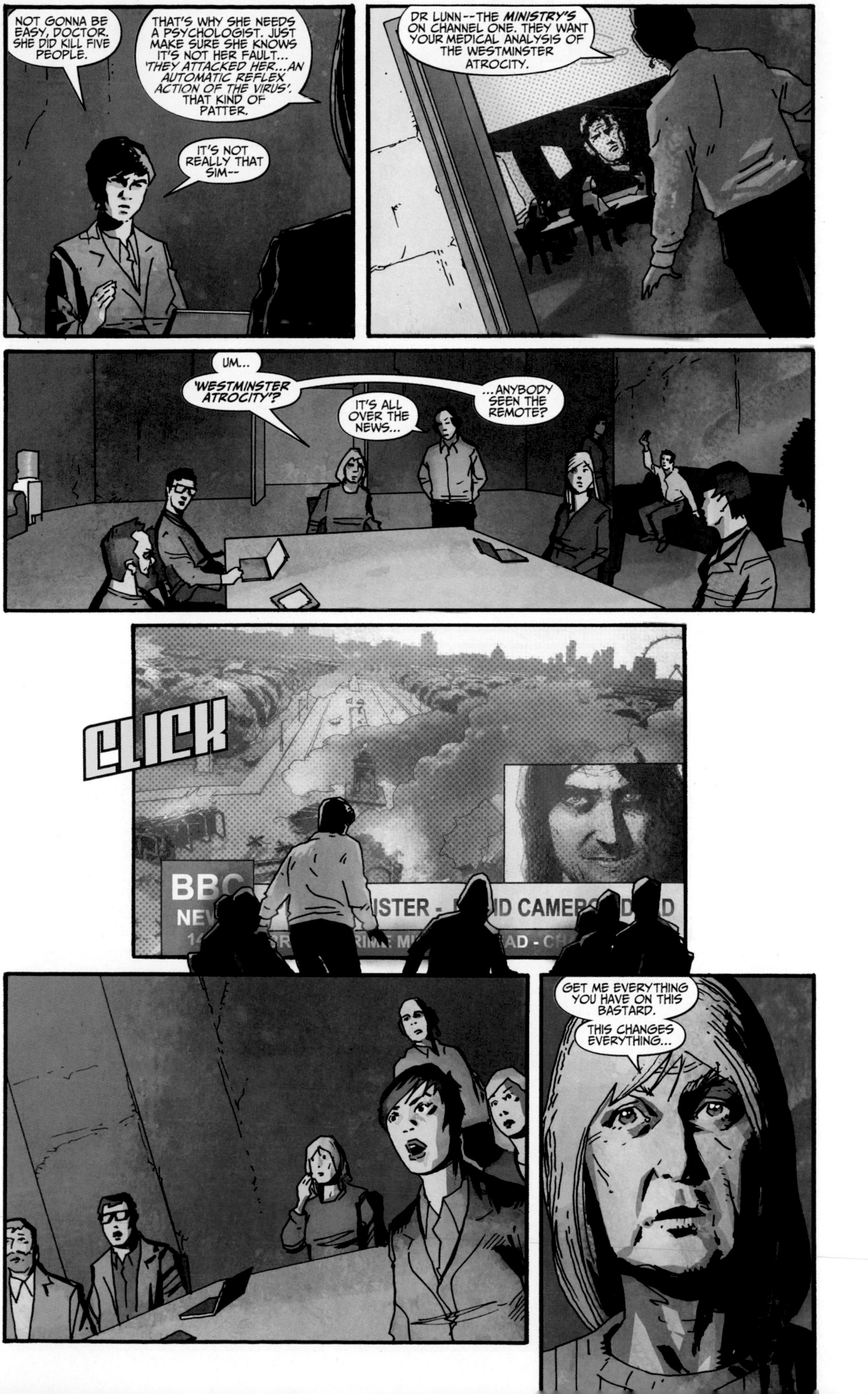
NOT GONNA BE EASY, DOCTOR. SHE DID KILL FIVE PEOPLE.
THAT'S WHY SHE NEEDS A PSYCHOLOGIST. JUST MAKE SURE SHE KNOWS IT'S NOT HER FAULT... *'THEY ATTACKED HER...AN AUTOMATIC REFLEX ACTION OF THE VIRUS'.* THAT KIND OF PATTER.
IT'S NOT REALLY THAT SIM--
DR LUNN--THE *MINISTRY'S* ON CHANNEL ONE. THEY WANT YOUR MEDICAL ANALYSIS OF THE WESTMINSTER ATROCITY.
UM...
'WESTMINSTER ATROCITY'?
...ANYBODY SEEN THE REMOTE?
IT'S ALL OVER THE NEWS...
CLICK
BBC
GET ME EVERYTHING YOU HAVE ON THIS BASTARD.
THIS CHANGES EVERYTHING...

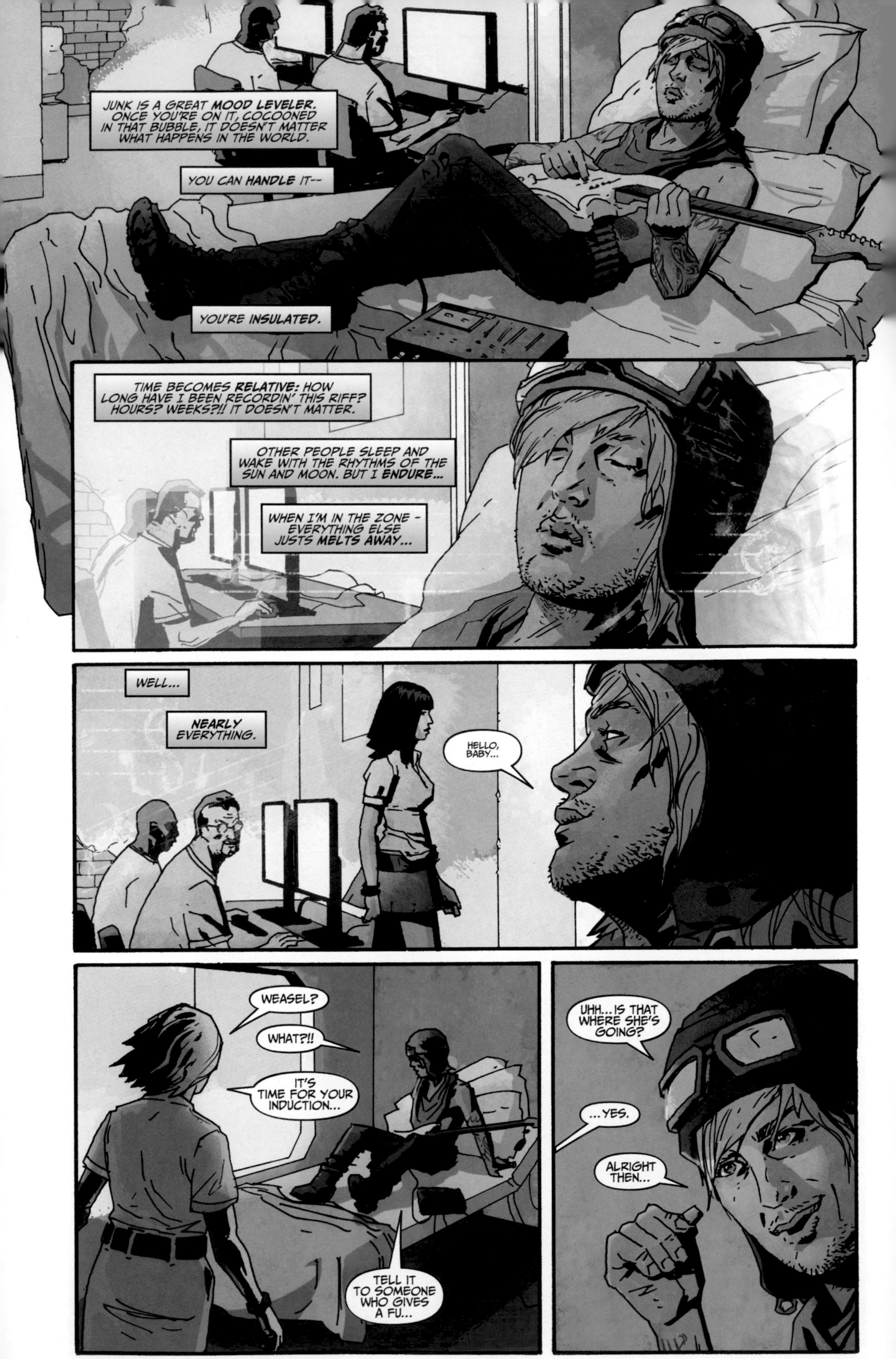
JUNK IS A GREAT MOOD LEVELER. ONCE YOU'RE ON IT, COCOONED IN THAT BUBBLE, IT DOESN'T MATTER WHAT HAPPENS IN THE WORLD.
YOU CAN HANDLE IT--
YOU'RE INSULATED.
TIME BECOMES RELATIVE: HOW LONG HAVE I BEEN RECORDIN' THIS RIFF? HOURS? WEEKS?!! IT DOESN'T MATTER.
OTHER PEOPLE SLEEP AND WAKE WITH THE RHYTHMS OF THE SUN AND MOON. BUT I ENDURE...
WHEN I'M IN THE ZONE - EVERYTHING ELSE JUSTS MELTS AWAY...
WELL...
NEARLY EVERYTHING.
HELLO, BABY...
WEASEL?
WHAT?!!
IT'S TIME FOR YOUR INDUCTION...
TELL IT TO SOMEONE WHO GIVES A FU...
UHH... IS THAT WHERE SHE'S GOING?
...YES.
ALRIGHT THEN...

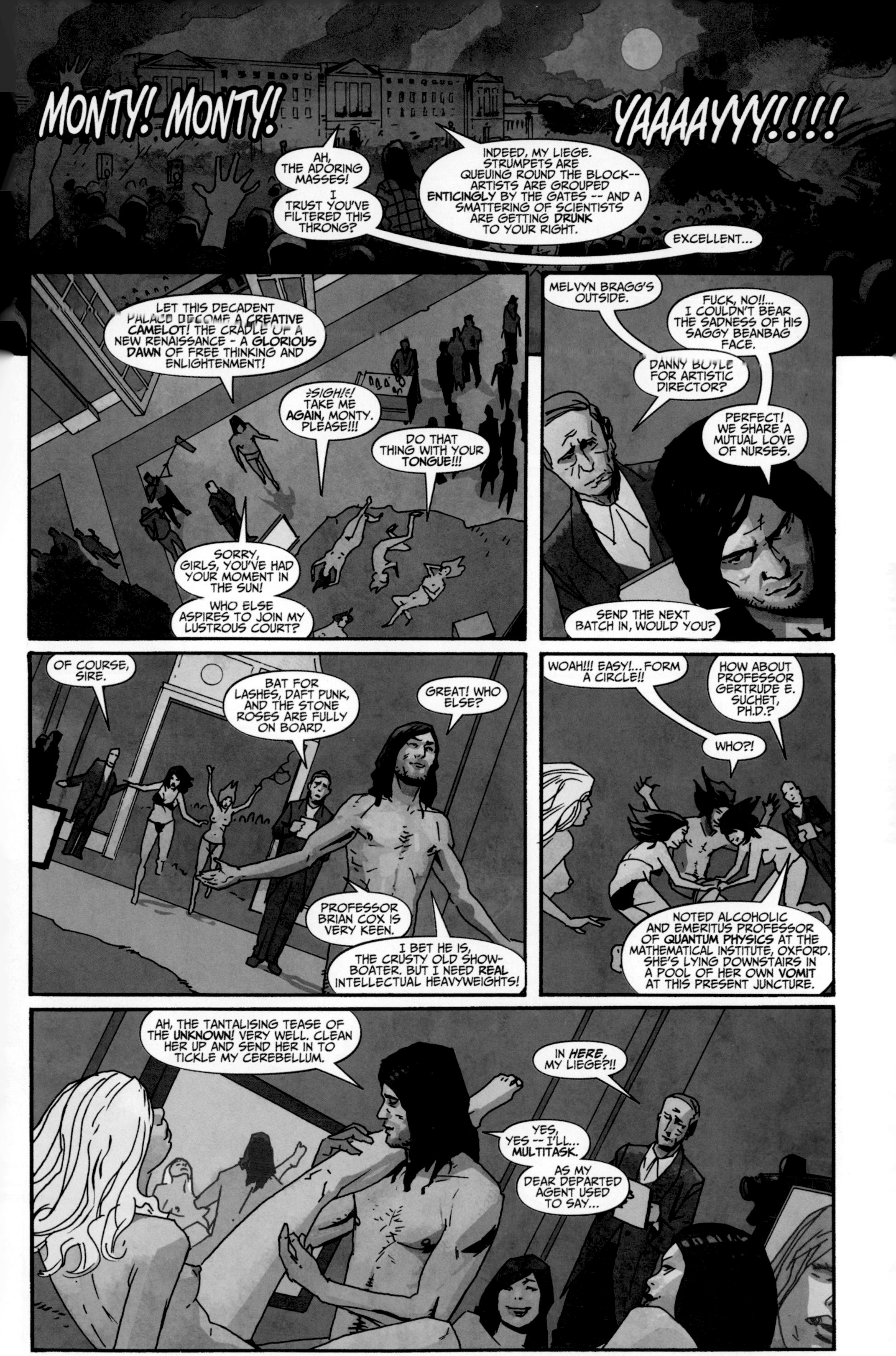
MONTY! MONTY!
YAAAAYYY!!!!
AH, THE ADORING MASSES!
I TRUST YOU'VE FILTERED THIS THRONG?
INDEED, MY LIEGE. STRUMPETS ARE QUEUING ROUND THE BLOCK-- ARTISTS ARE GROUPED **ENTICINGLY** BY THE GATES -- AND A SMATTERING OF SCIENTISTS ARE GETTING **DRUNK** TO YOUR RIGHT.
EXCELLENT...
LET THIS DECADENT PALACE BECOME A **CREATIVE CAMELOT**! THE CRADLE OF A NEW RENAISSANCE - A **GLORIOUS DAWN** OF FREE THINKING AND ENLIGHTENMENT!
SIGH! TAKE ME **AGAIN**, MONTY. PLEASE!!!
DO THAT THING WITH YOUR **TONGUE**!!!
SORRY, GIRLS, YOU'VE HAD YOUR MOMENT IN THE SUN!
WHO ELSE ASPIRES TO JOIN MY LUSTROUS COURT?
MELVYN BRAGG'S OUTSIDE.
FUCK, NO!!... I COULDN'T BEAR THE SADNESS OF HIS SAGGY BEANBAG FACE.
DANNY BOYLE FOR ARTISTIC DIRECTOR?
PERFECT! WE SHARE A MUTUAL LOVE OF NURSES.
SEND THE NEXT BATCH IN, WOULD YOU?
OF COURSE, SIRE.
BAT FOR LASHES, DAFT PUNK, AND THE STONE ROSES ARE FULLY ON BOARD.
GREAT! WHO ELSE?
PROFESSOR BRIAN COX IS VERY KEEN.
I BET HE IS, THE CRUSTY OLD SHOW-BOATER. BUT I NEED **REAL** INTELLECTUAL HEAVYWEIGHTS!
WOAH!!! EASY!...FORM A CIRCLE!!
HOW ABOUT PROFESSOR GERTRUDE E. SUCHET, PH.D.?
WHO?!
NOTED ALCOHOLIC AND EMERITUS PROFESSOR OF **QUANTUM PHYSICS** AT THE MATHEMATICAL INSTITUTE, OXFORD. SHE'S LYING DOWNSTAIRS IN A POOL OF HER OWN **VOMIT** AT THIS PRESENT JUNCTURE.
AH, THE TANTALISING TEASE OF THE **UNKNOWN**! VERY WELL. CLEAN HER UP AND SEND HER IN TO TICKLE MY CEREBELLUM.
IN ***HERE***, MY LIEGE?!!
YES, YES -- I'LL... **MULTITASK**.
AS MY DEAR DEPARTED AGENT USED TO SAY...

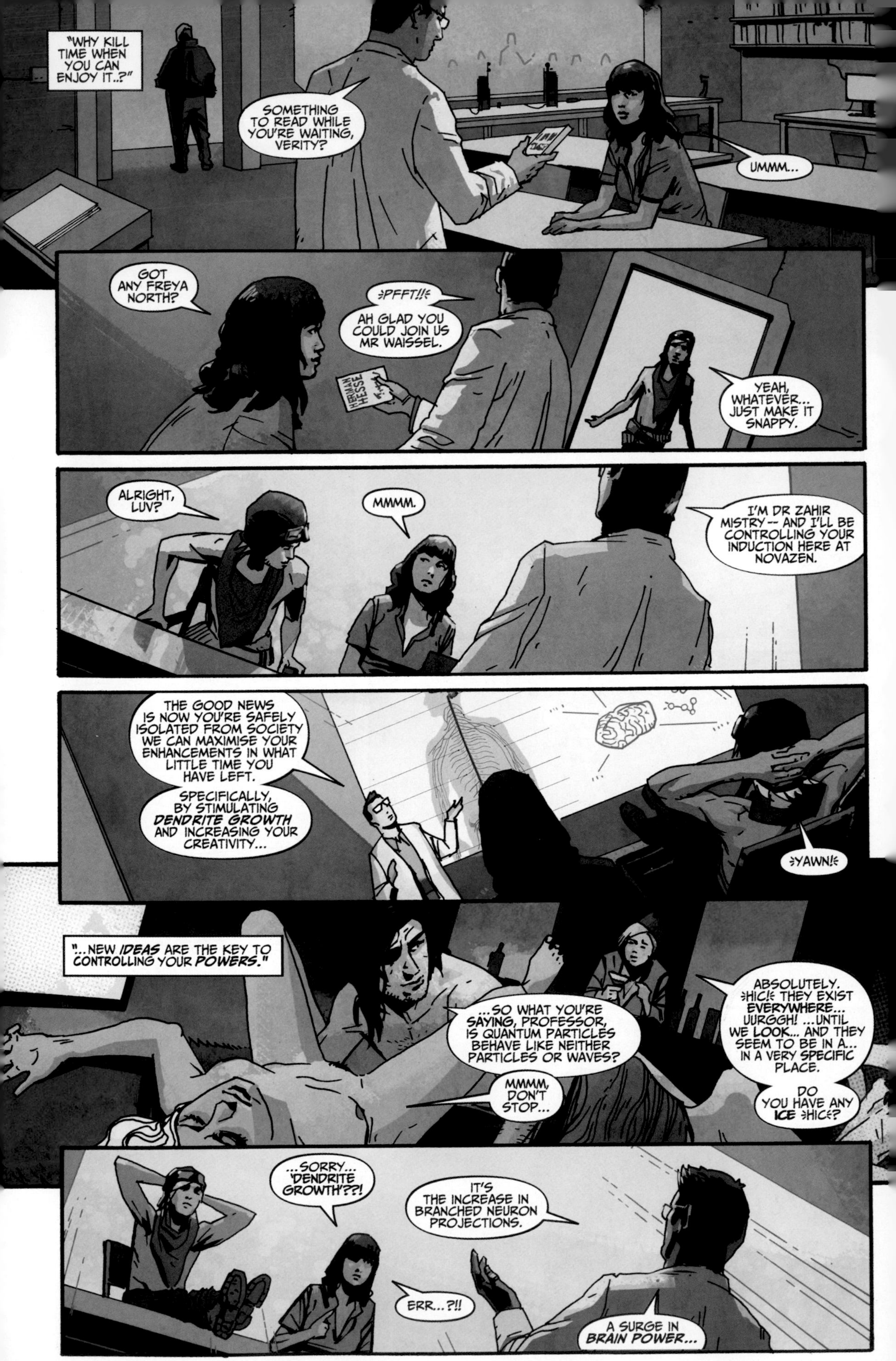
"WHY KILL TIME WHEN YOU CAN ENJOY IT..?"
SOMETHING TO READ WHILE YOU'RE WAITING, VERITY?
UMMM...
GOT ANY FREYA NORTH?
PFFT!!
AH GLAD YOU COULD JOIN US MR WAISSEL.
HERMAN HESSE
YEAH, WHATEVER... JUST MAKE IT SNAPPY.
ALRIGHT, LUV?
MMMM.
I'M DR ZAHIR MISTRY -- AND I'LL BE CONTROLLING YOUR INDUCTION HERE AT NOVAZEN.
THE GOOD NEWS IS NOW YOU'RE SAFELY ISOLATED FROM SOCIETY WE CAN MAXIMISE YOUR ENHANCEMENTS IN WHAT LITTLE TIME YOU HAVE LEFT.
SPECIFICALLY, BY STIMULATING DENDRITE GROWTH AND INCREASING YOUR CREATIVITY...
YAWN!
"...NEW IDEAS ARE THE KEY TO CONTROLLING YOUR POWERS."
...SO WHAT YOU'RE SAYING, PROFESSOR, IS QUANTUM PARTICLES BEHAVE LIKE NEITHER PARTICLES OR WAVES?
MMMM, DON'T STOP...
ABSOLUTELY. HIC! THEY EXIST EVERYWHERE... UURGGH! ...UNTIL WE LOOK... AND THEY SEEM TO BE IN A... IN A VERY SPECIFIC PLACE.
DO YOU HAVE ANY ICE HIC?
...SORRY... 'DENDRITE GROWTH'??!
IT'S THE INCREASE IN BRANCHED NEURON PROJECTIONS.
ERR...?!!
A SURGE IN BRAIN POWER...

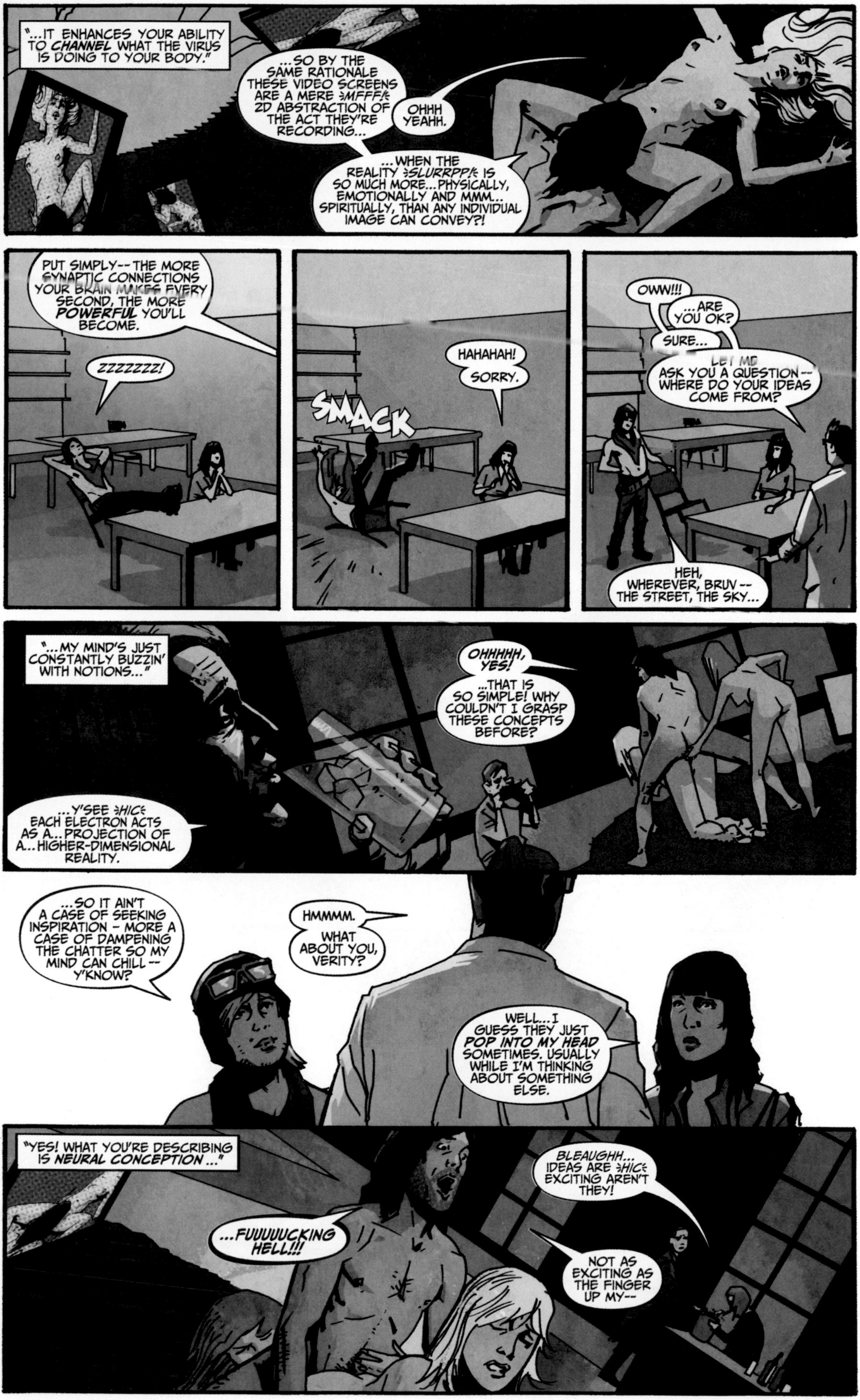
"...IT ENHANCES YOUR ABILITY TO CHANNEL WHAT THE VIRUS IS DOING TO YOUR BODY."
...SO BY THE SAME RATIONALE THESE VIDEO SCREENS ARE A MERE *MFFF* 2D ABSTRACTION OF THE ACT THEY'RE RECORDING...
OHHH YEAHH.
...WHEN THE REALITY *SLURRPP* IS SO MUCH MORE...PHYSICALLY, EMOTIONALLY AND MMM.. SPIRITUALLY, THAN ANY INDIVIDUAL IMAGE CAN CONVEY?!
PUT SIMPLY-- THE MORE SYNAPTIC CONNECTIONS YOUR BRAIN MAKES EVERY SECOND, THE MORE POWERFUL YOU'LL BECOME.
ZZZZZZZ!
SMACK
HAHAHAH!
SORRY.
OWW!!!
...ARE YOU OK?
SURE...
LET ME ASK YOU A QUESTION-- WHERE DO YOUR IDEAS COME FROM?
HEH, WHEREVER, BRUV-- THE STREET, THE SKY...
"...MY MIND'S JUST CONSTANTLY BUZZIN' WITH NOTIONS..."
OHHHHH, YES!
...THAT IS SO SIMPLE! WHY COULDN'T I GRASP THESE CONCEPTS BEFORE?
...Y'SEE *HIC* EACH ELECTRON ACTS AS A...PROJECTION OF A...HIGHER-DIMENSIONAL REALITY.
...SO IT AIN'T A CASE OF SEEKING INSPIRATION - MORE A CASE OF DAMPENING THE CHATTER SO MY MIND CAN CHILL-- Y'KNOW?
HMMMM.
WHAT ABOUT YOU, VERITY?
WELL...I GUESS THEY JUST POP INTO MY HEAD SOMETIMES. USUALLY WHILE I'M THINKING ABOUT SOMETHING ELSE.
"YES! WHAT YOU'RE DESCRIBING IS NEURAL CONCEPTION..."
...FUUUUUCKING HELL!!!
BLEAUGHH... IDEAS ARE *HIC* EXCITING AREN'T THEY!
NOT AS EXCITING AS THE FINGER UP MY--

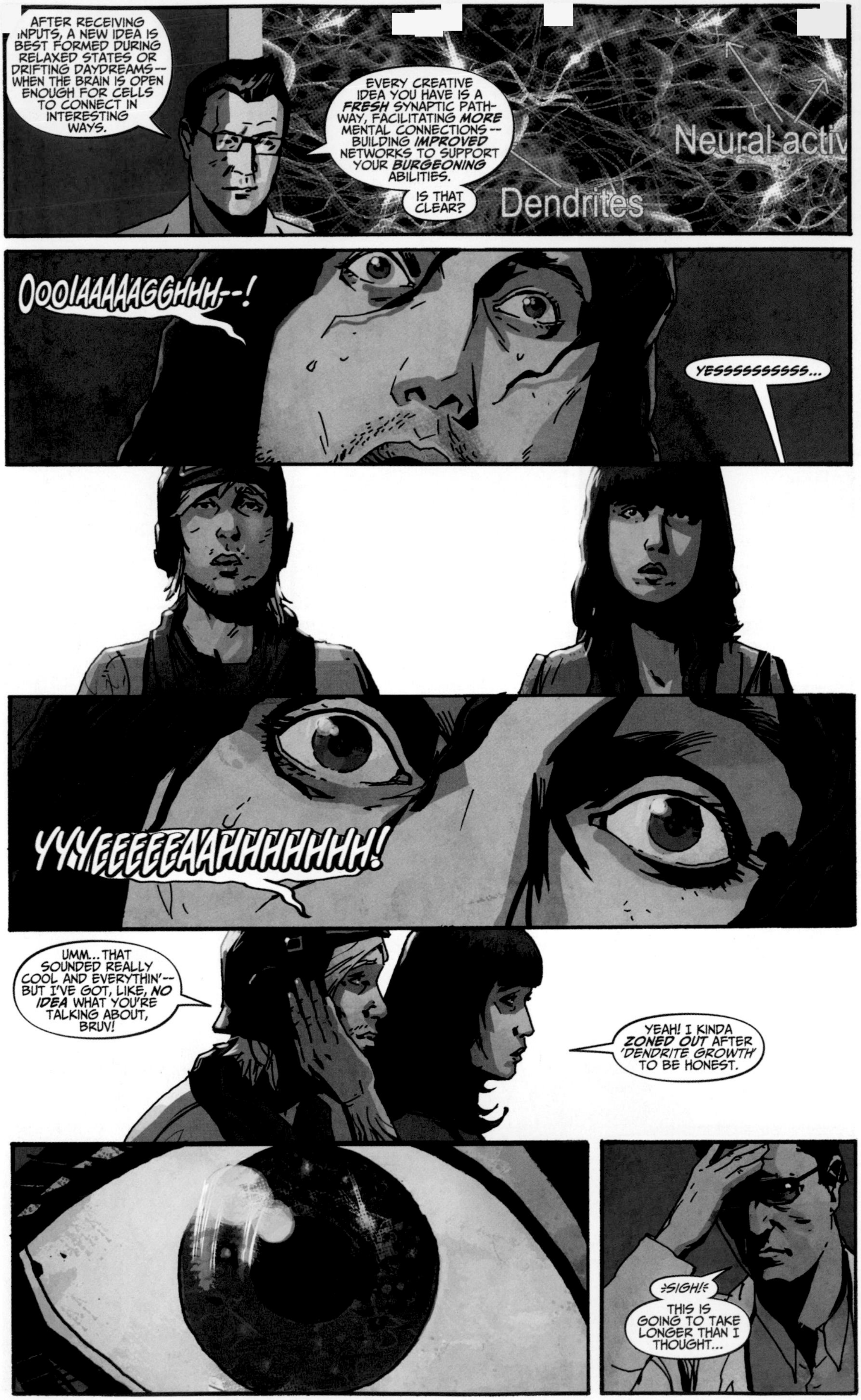
AFTER RECEIVING INPUTS, A NEW IDEA IS BEST FORMED DURING RELAXED STATES OR DRIFTING DAYDREAMS-- WHEN THE BRAIN IS OPEN ENOUGH FOR CELLS TO CONNECT IN INTERESTING WAYS.
EVERY CREATIVE IDEA YOU HAVE IS A FRESH SYNAPTIC PATHWAY, FACILITATING MORE MENTAL CONNECTIONS-- BUILDING IMPROVED NETWORKS TO SUPPORT YOUR BURGEONING ABILITIES.
IS THAT CLEAR?
Neural activ
Dendrites
OOOIAAAAAGGHHH--!
YESSSSSSSSSS...
YYYEEEEEAAHHHHHHH!
UMM...THAT SOUNDED REALLY COOL AND EVERYTHIN'-- BUT I'VE GOT, LIKE, NO IDEA WHAT YOU'RE TALKING ABOUT, BRUV!
YEAH! I KINDA ZONED OUT AFTER 'DENDRITE GROWTH' TO BE HONEST.
SIGH!
THIS IS GOING TO TAKE LONGER THAN I THOUGHT...

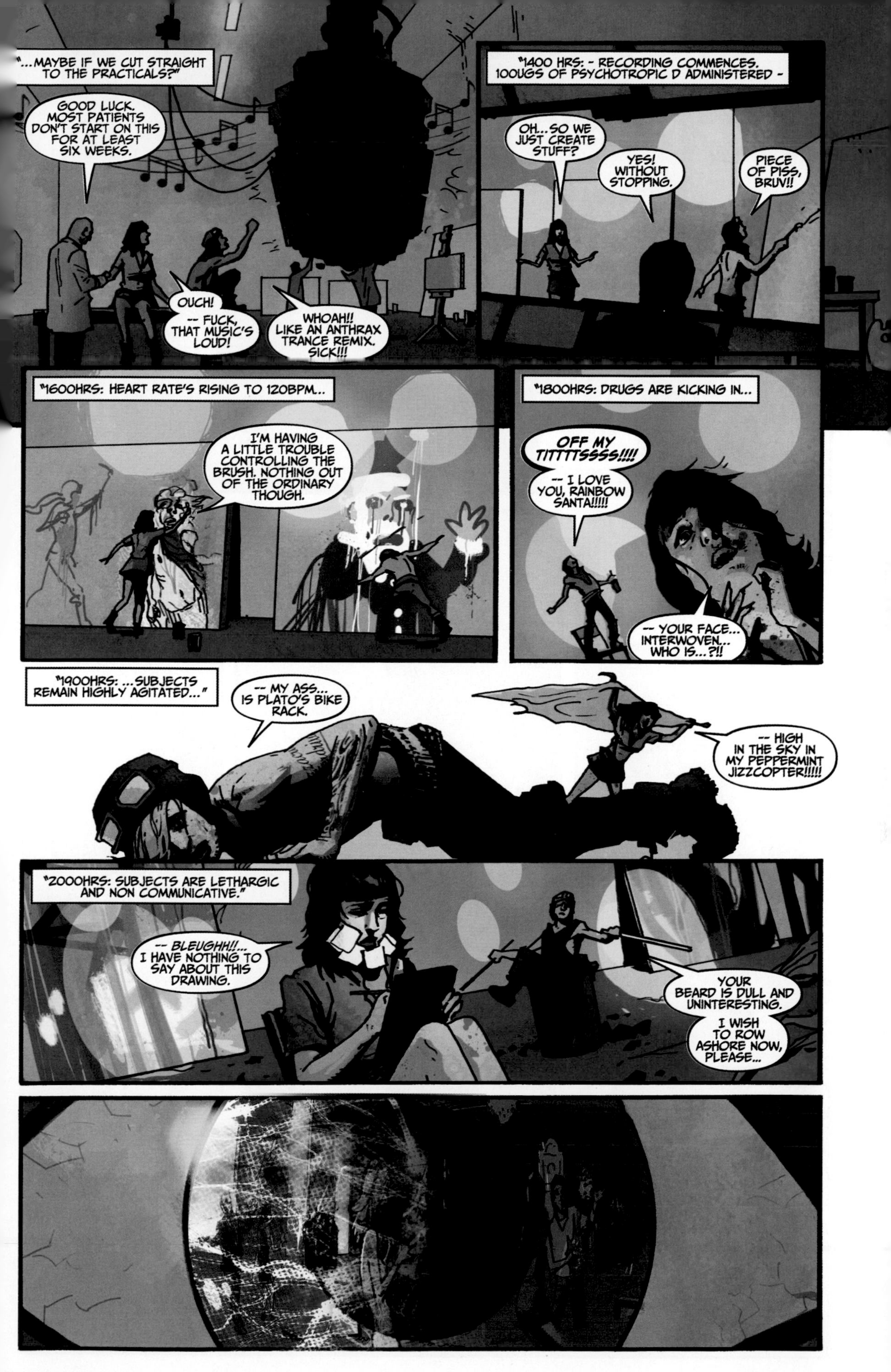
"...MAYBE IF WE CUT STRAIGHT TO THE PRACTICALS?"
GOOD LUCK. MOST PATIENTS DON'T START ON THIS FOR AT LEAST SIX WEEKS.
OUCH! -- FUCK, THAT MUSIC'S LOUD!
WHOAH!! LIKE AN ANTHRAX TRANCE REMIX. SICK!!!
"1400 HRS: - RECORDING COMMENCES. 100UGS OF PSYCHOTROPIC D ADMINISTERED -
OH... SO WE JUST CREATE STUFF?
YES! WITHOUT STOPPING.
PIECE OF PISS, BRUV!!
"1600HRS: HEART RATE'S RISING TO 120BPM...
I'M HAVING A LITTLE TROUBLE CONTROLLING THE BRUSH. NOTHING OUT OF THE ORDINARY THOUGH.
"1800HRS: DRUGS ARE KICKING IN...
OFF MY TITTTTSSSS!!!!
-- I LOVE YOU, RAINBOW SANTA!!!!!
-- YOUR FACE... INTERWOVEN... WHO IS...?!!
"1900HRS: ...SUBJECTS REMAIN HIGHLY AGITATED..."
-- MY ASS... IS PLATO'S BIKE RACK.
-- HIGH IN THE SKY IN MY PEPPERMINT JIZZCOPTER!!!!!
"2000HRS: SUBJECTS ARE LETHARGIC AND NON COMMUNICATIVE."
-- BLEUGHH!!... I HAVE NOTHING TO SAY ABOUT THIS DRAWING.
YOUR BEARD IS DULL AND UNINTERESTING.
I WISH TO ROW ASHORE NOW, PLEASE...

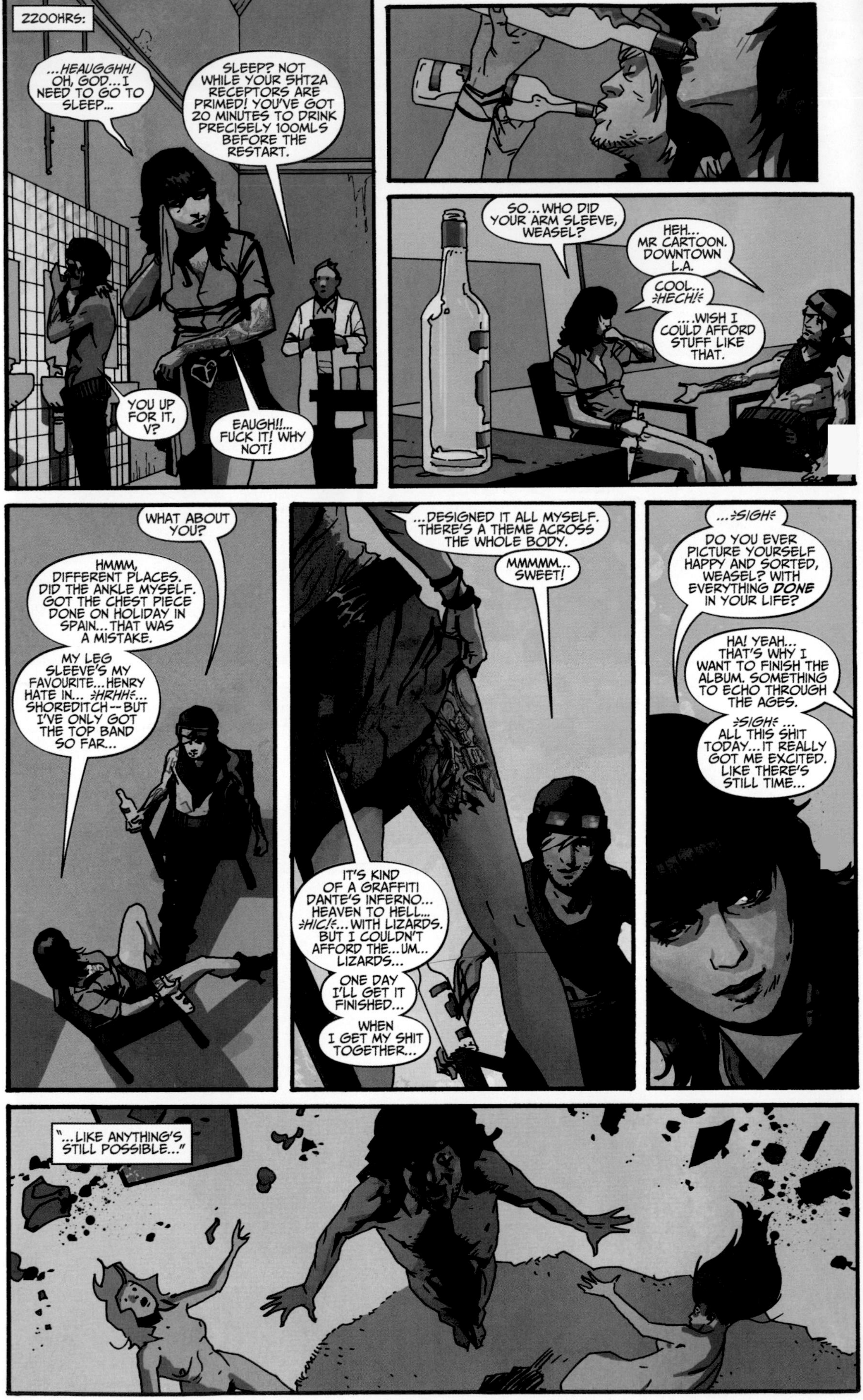

2200HRS:
...HEAUGGHH! OH, GOD...I NEED TO GO TO SLEEP...
SLEEP? NOT WHILE YOUR SHTZA RECEPTORS ARE PRIMED! YOU'VE GOT 20 MINUTES TO DRINK PRECISELY 100MLS BEFORE THE RESTART.
YOU UP FOR IT, V?
EAUGH!!... FUCK IT! WHY NOT!
SO...WHO DID YOUR ARM SLEEVE, WEASEL?
HEH... MR CARTOON. DOWNTOWN L.A.
COOL... ≋HECH!≋
...WISH I COULD AFFORD STUFF LIKE THAT.
WHAT ABOUT YOU?
HMMM, DIFFERENT PLACES. DID THE ANKLE MYSELF. GOT THE CHEST PIECE DONE ON HOLIDAY IN SPAIN...THAT WAS A MISTAKE.
MY LEG SLEEVE'S MY FAVOURITE...HENRY HATE IN... ≋HRHH≋... SHOREDITCH--BUT I'VE ONLY GOT THE TOP BAND SO FAR...
...DESIGNED IT ALL MYSELF. THERE'S A THEME ACROSS THE WHOLE BODY.
MMMMM... SWEET!
IT'S KIND OF A GRAFFITI DANTE'S INFERNO... HEAVEN TO HELL... ≋HIC!≋...WITH LIZARDS. BUT I COULDN'T AFFORD THE...UM... LIZARDS...
ONE DAY I'LL GET IT FINISHED...
WHEN I GET MY SHIT TOGETHER...
...≋SIGH≋
DO YOU EVER PICTURE YOURSELF HAPPY AND SORTED, WEASEL? WITH EVERYTHING DONE IN YOUR LIFE?
HA! YEAH... THAT'S WHY I WANT TO FINISH THE ALBUM. SOMETHING TO ECHO THROUGH THE AGES.
≋SIGH≋ ... ALL THIS SHIT TODAY...IT REALLY GOT ME EXCITED. LIKE THERE'S STILL TIME...
"...LIKE ANYTHING'S STILL POSSIBLE..."

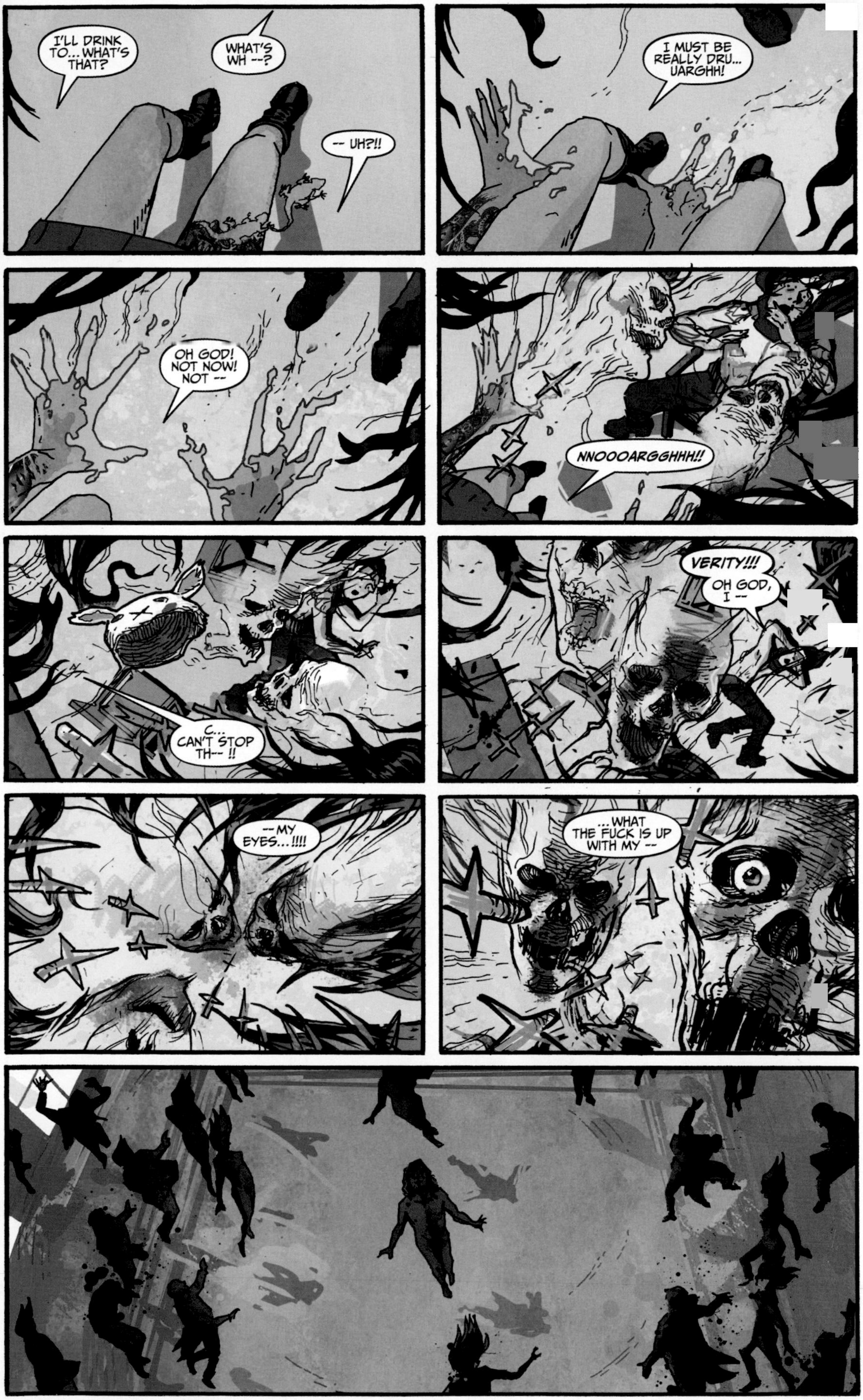
I'LL DRINK TO... WHAT'S THAT?
WHAT'S WH --?
-- UH?!!
I MUST BE REALLY DRU... UARGHH!
OH GOD! NOT NOW! NOT --
NNOOOARGGHHH!!
C... CAN'T STOP TH-- !!
VERITY!!! OH GOD, I --
--MY EYES...!!!!
...WHAT THE FUCK IS UP WITH MY --

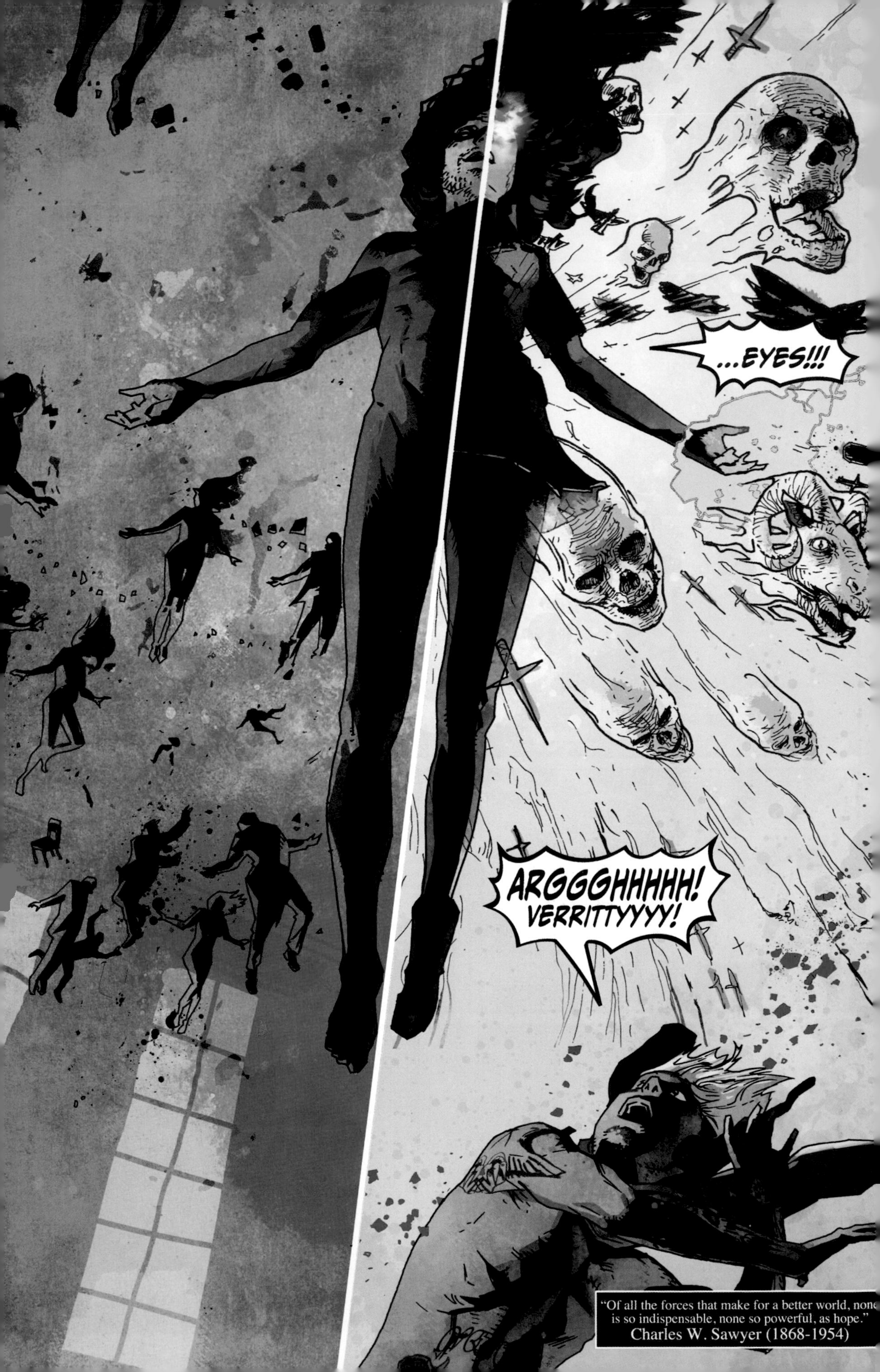
...EYES!!!
ARGGGHHHHH! VERRITTYYYY!
"Of all the forces that make for a better world, none is so indispensable, none so powerful, as hope."
Charles W. Sawyer (1868-1954)

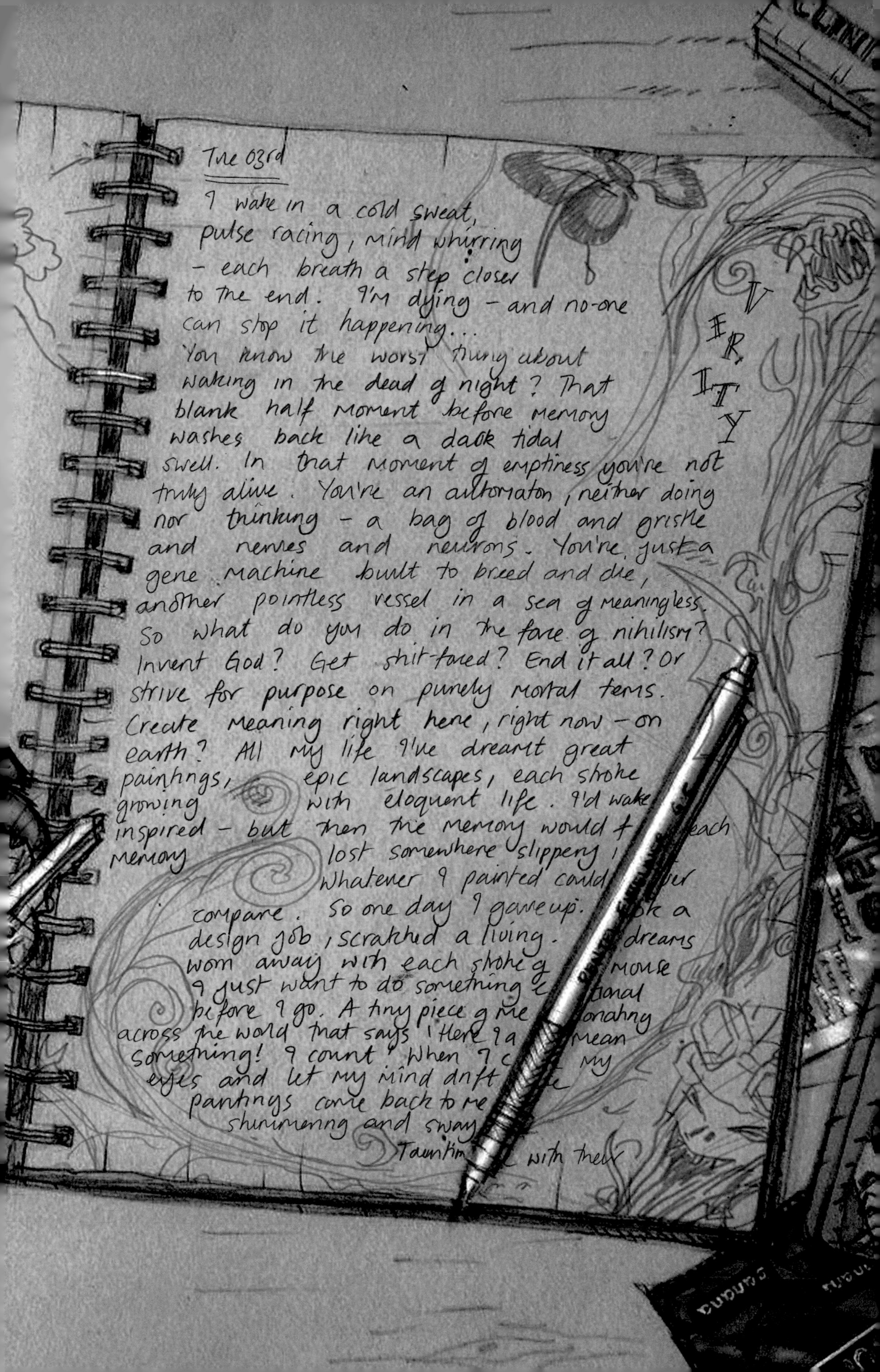
Tue 03rd
I wake in a cold sweat,
pulse racing, mind whirring
– each breath a step closer
to the end. I'm dying – and no-one
can stop it happening...
You know the worst thing about
waking in the dead of night? That
blank half moment before memory
washes back like a dark tidal
swell. In that moment of emptiness you're not
truly alive. You're an automaton, neither doing
nor thinking – a bag of blood and gristle
and nerves and neurons. You're just a
gene machine built to breed and die,
another pointless vessel in a sea of meaningless.
So what do you do in the face of nihilism?
Invent God? Get shit-faced? End it all? Or
strive for purpose on purely mortal terms.
Create meaning right here, right now – on
earth? All my life I've dreamt great
paintings, epic landscapes, each stroke
growing with eloquent life. I'd wake
inspired – but then the memory would f each
memory lost somewhere slippery
Whatever I painted could er
compare. So one day I gave up. k a
design job, scratched a living. dreams
worn away with each stroke of mouse
I just want to do something tional
before I go. A tiny piece of me onating
across the world that says 'Here I a mean
something! I count' When I c my
eyes and let my mind drift e
paintings come back to me
shimmering and sway
Taunting with their
VERITY

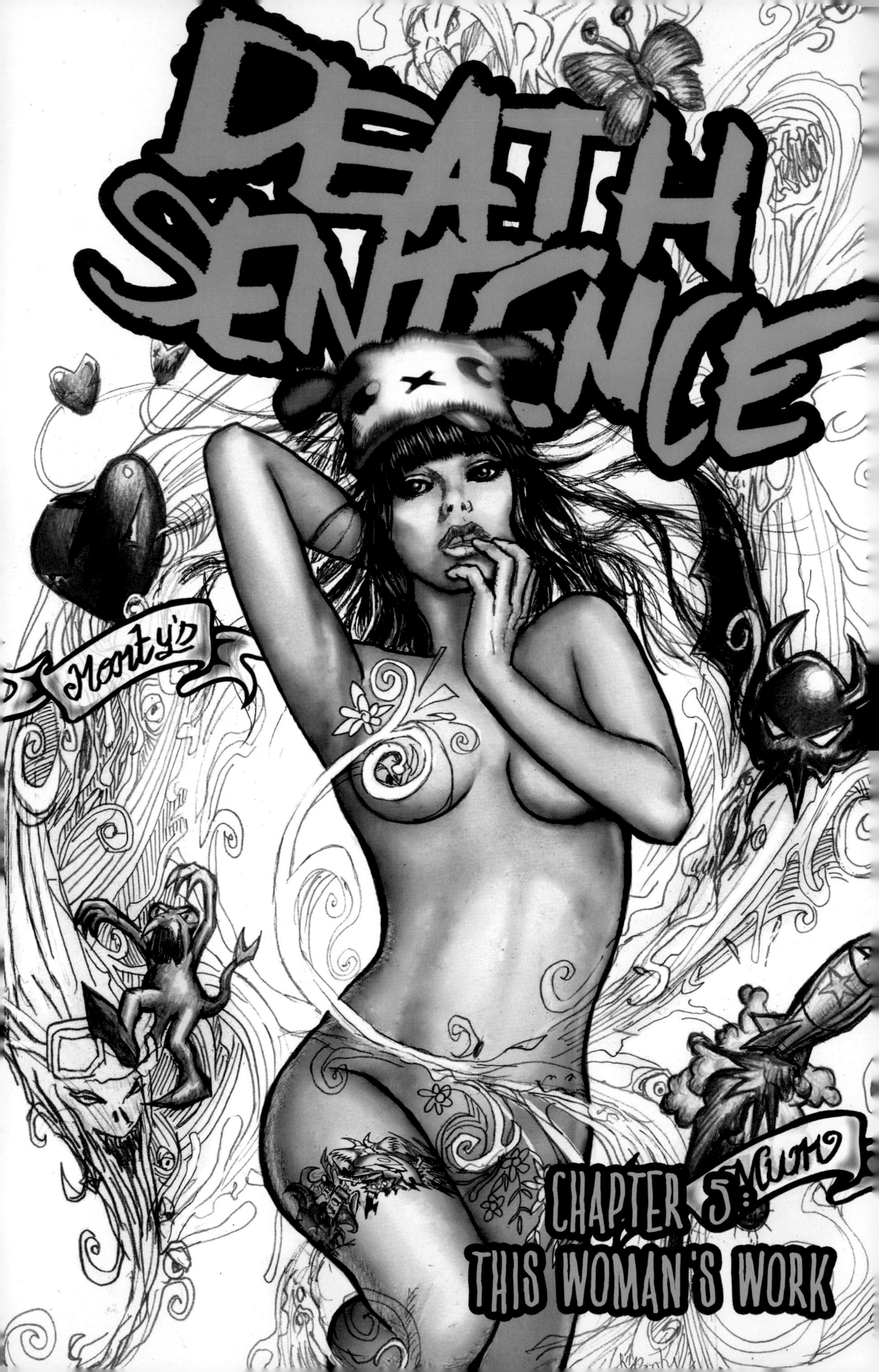
DEATH SENTENCE
Monty's
CHAPTER 5
THIS WOMAN'S WORK

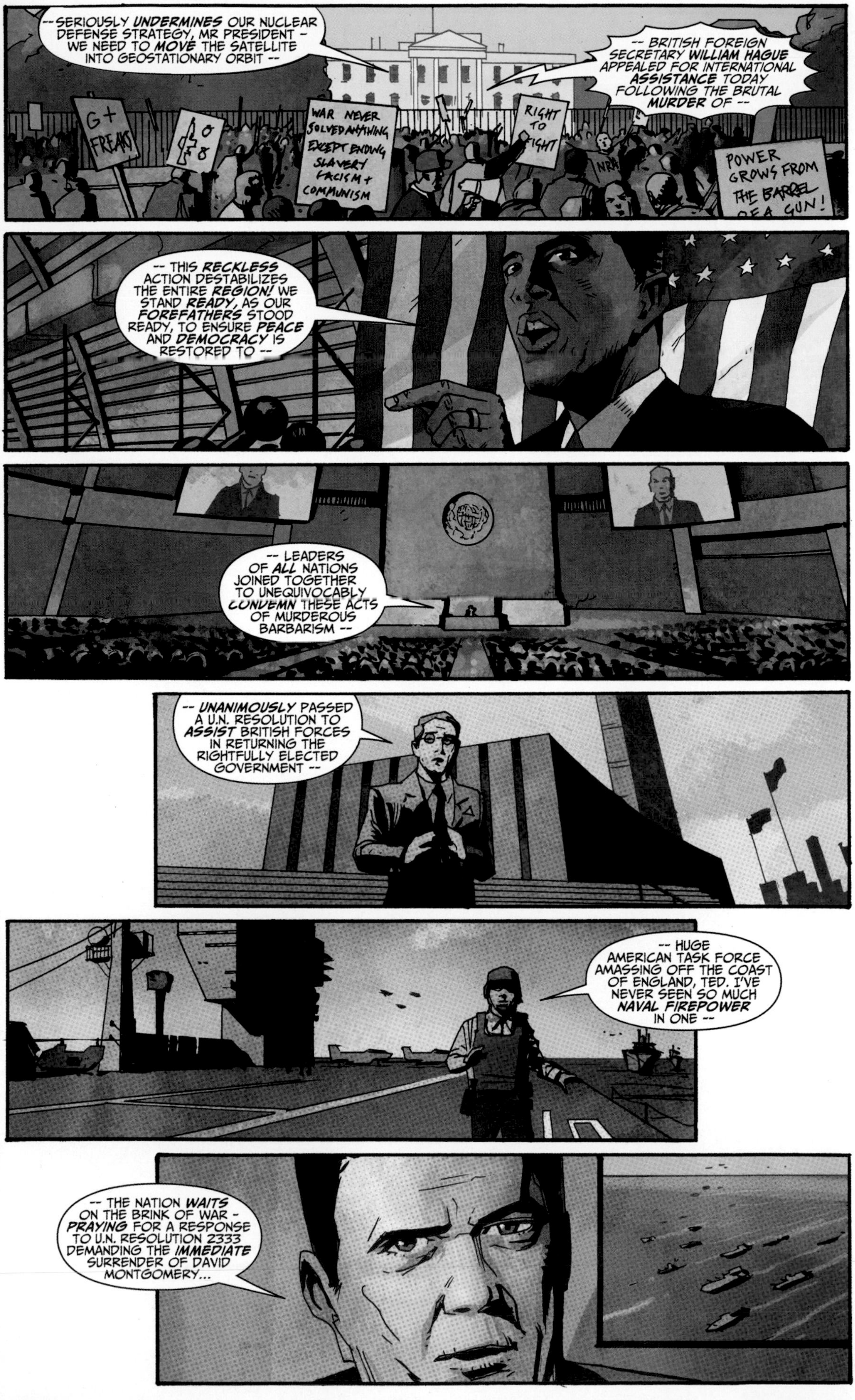
--SERIOUSLY UNDERMINES OUR NUCLEAR DEFENSE STRATEGY, MR PRESIDENT - WE NEED TO MOVE THE SATELLITE INTO GEOSTATIONARY ORBIT --
-- BRITISH FOREIGN SECRETARY WILLIAM HAGUE APPEALED FOR INTERNATIONAL ASSISTANCE TODAY FOLLOWING THE BRUTAL MURDER OF --
G+ FREAKS
WAR NEVER SOLVED ANYTHING EXCEPT ENDING SLAVERY RACISM + COMMUNISM
RIGHT TO FIGHT
NRA
POWER GROWS FROM THE BARREL OF A GUN!
-- THIS RECKLESS ACTION DESTABILIZES THE ENTIRE REGION! WE STAND READY, AS OUR FOREFATHERS STOOD READY, TO ENSURE PEACE AND DEMOCRACY IS RESTORED TO --
-- LEADERS OF ALL NATIONS JOINED TOGETHER TO UNEQUIVOCABLY CONDEMN THESE ACTS OF MURDEROUS BARBARISM --
-- UNANIMOUSLY PASSED A U.N. RESOLUTION TO ASSIST BRITISH FORCES IN RETURNING THE RIGHTFULLY ELECTED GOVERNMENT --
-- HUGE AMERICAN TASK FORCE AMASSING OFF THE COAST OF ENGLAND, TED. I'VE NEVER SEEN SO MUCH NAVAL FIREPOWER IN ONE --
-- THE NATION WAITS ON THE BRINK OF WAR - PRAYING FOR A RESPONSE TO U.N. RESOLUTION 2333 DEMANDING THE IMMEDIATE SURRENDER OF DAVID MONTGOMERY...

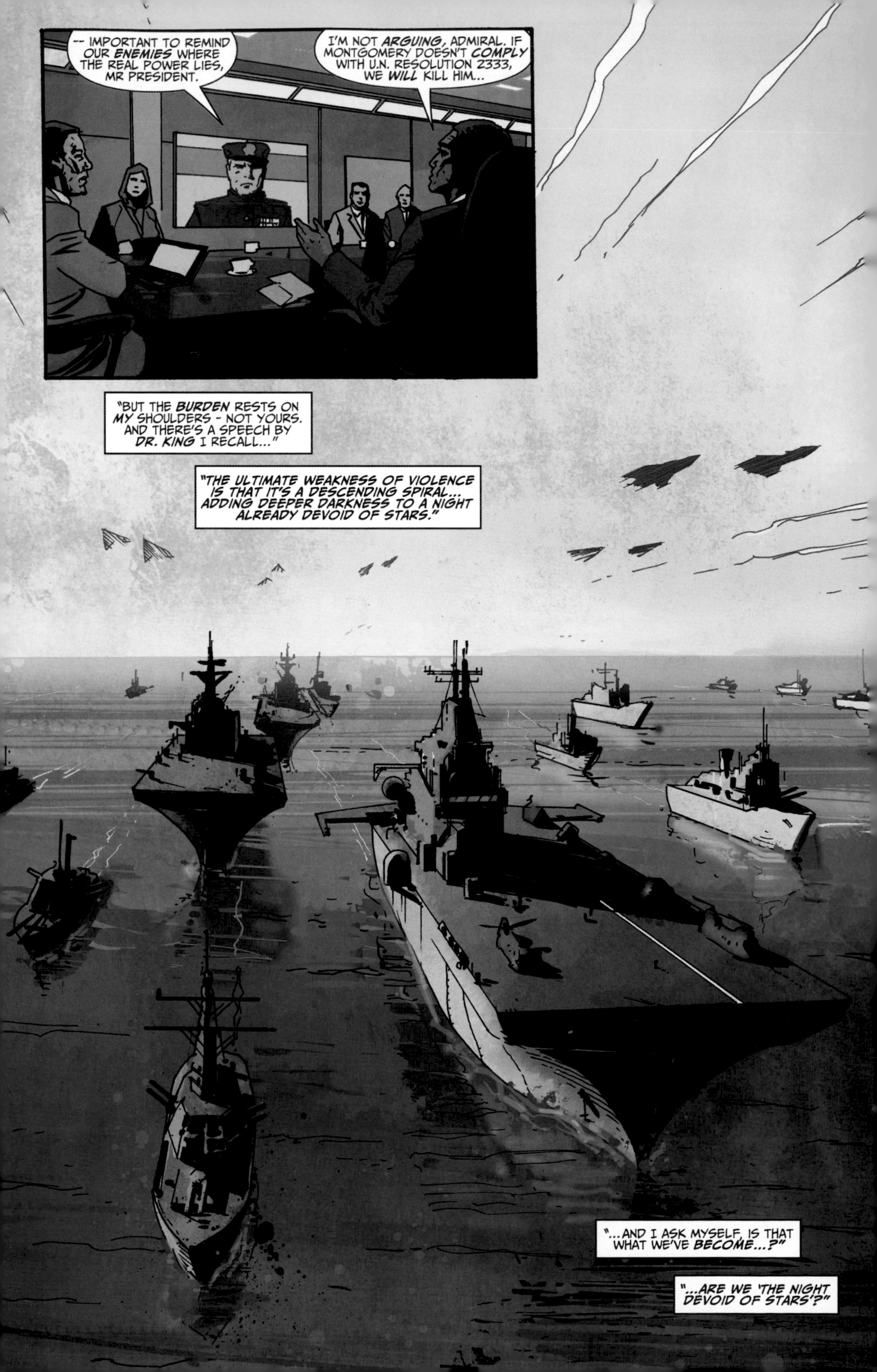
-- IMPORTANT TO REMIND OUR ENEMIES WHERE THE REAL POWER LIES, MR PRESIDENT.
I'M NOT ARGUING, ADMIRAL. IF MONTGOMERY DOESN'T COMPLY WITH U.N. RESOLUTION 2333, WE WILL KILL HIM...
"BUT THE BURDEN RESTS ON MY SHOULDERS - NOT YOURS. AND THERE'S A SPEECH BY DR. KING I RECALL..."
"THE ULTIMATE WEAKNESS OF VIOLENCE IS THAT IT'S A DESCENDING SPIRAL... ADDING DEEPER DARKNESS TO A NIGHT ALREADY DEVOID OF STARS."
"...AND I ASK MYSELF, IS THAT WHAT WE'VE BECOME...?"
"...ARE WE 'THE NIGHT DEVOID OF STARS'?"

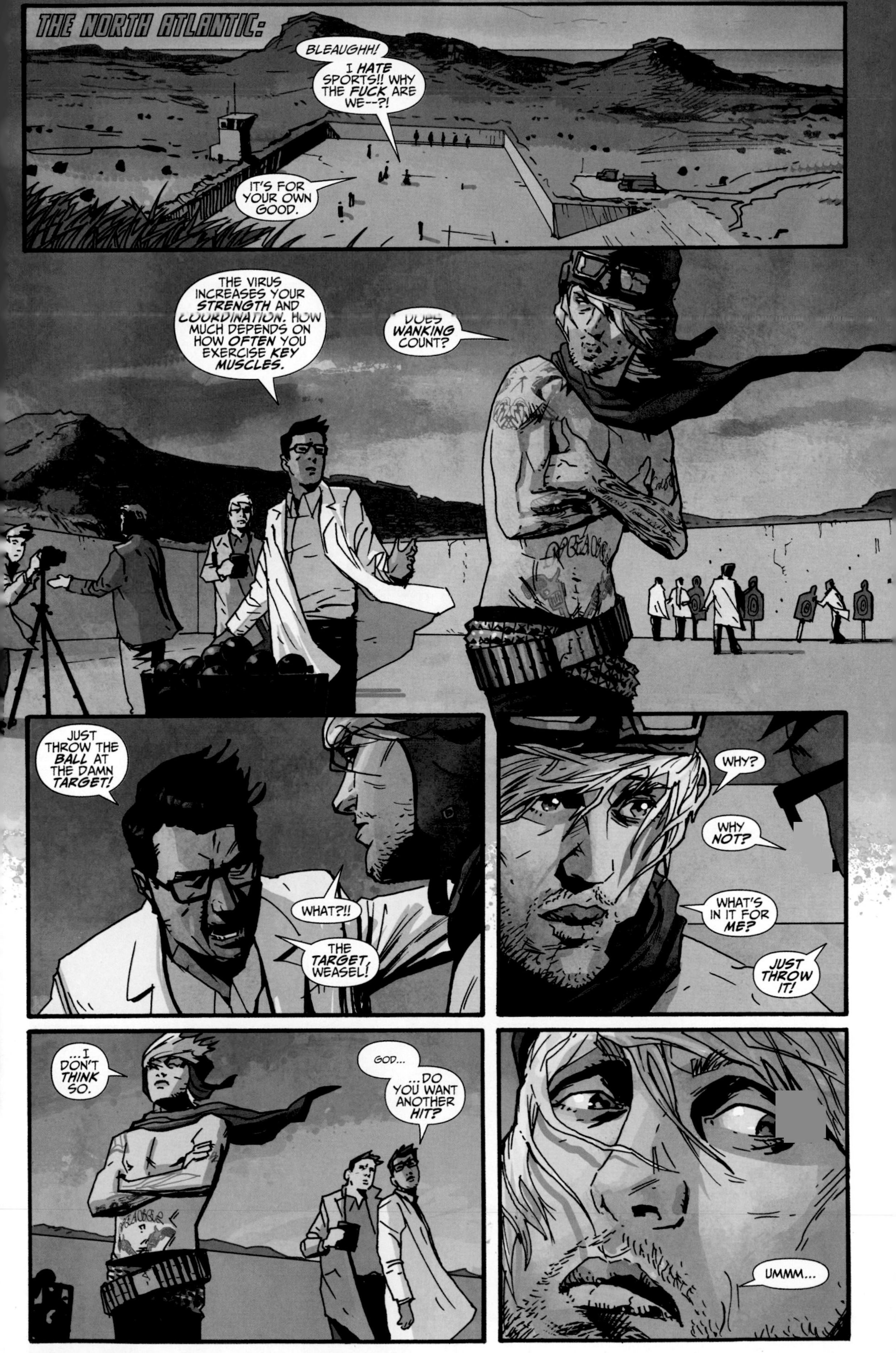
THE NORTH ATLANTIC:
BLEAUGHH!
I HATE SPORTS!! WHY THE FUCK ARE WE--?!
IT'S FOR YOUR OWN GOOD.
THE VIRUS INCREASES YOUR STRENGTH AND COORDINATION. HOW MUCH DEPENDS ON HOW OFTEN YOU EXERCISE KEY MUSCLES.
DOES WANKING COUNT?
JUST THROW THE BALL AT THE DAMN TARGET!
WHAT?!!
THE TARGET, WEASEL!
WHY?
WHY NOT?
WHAT'S IN IT FOR ME?
JUST THROW IT!
...I DON'T THINK SO.
GOD...
...DO YOU WANT ANOTHER HIT?
UMMM...

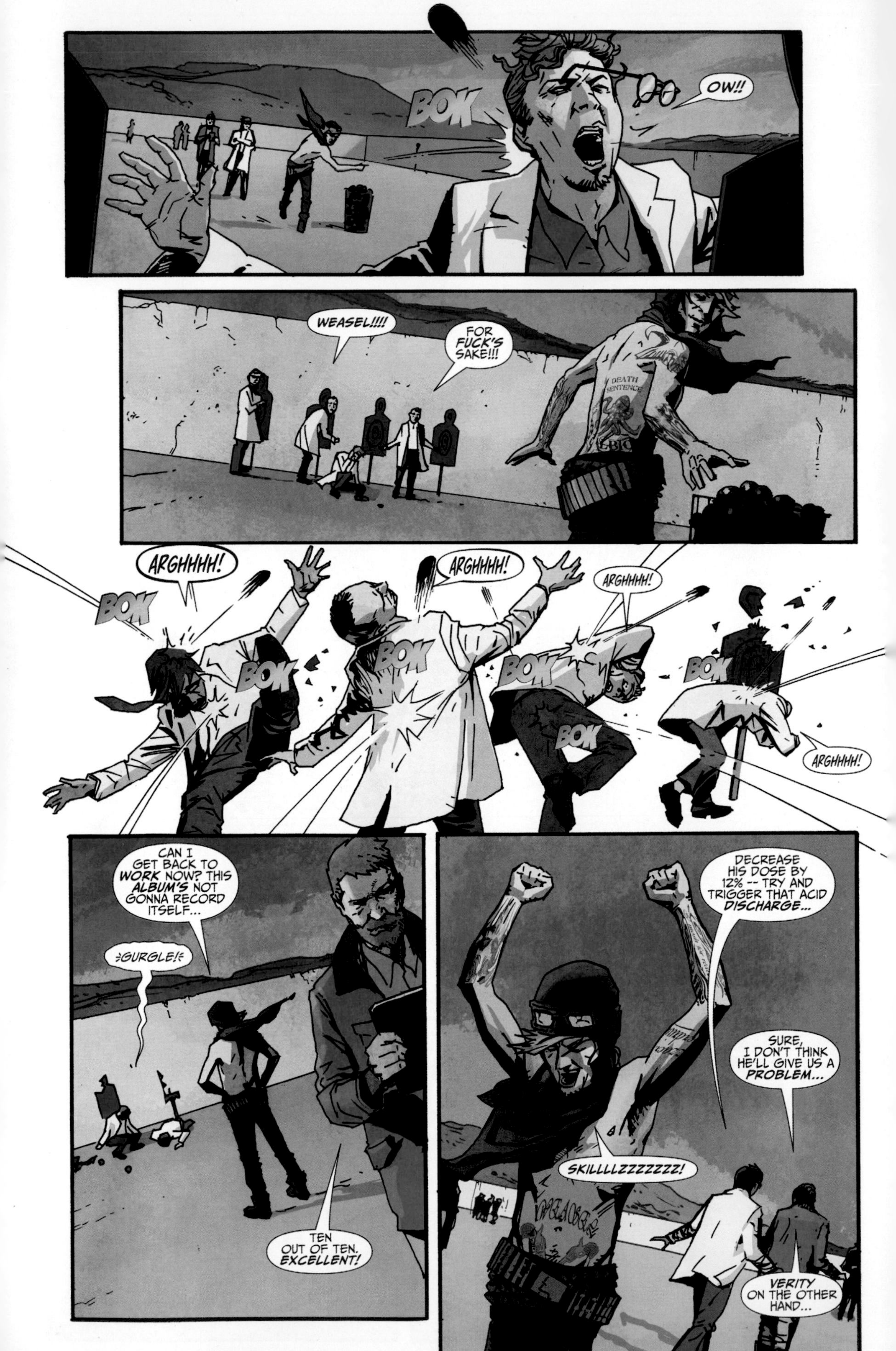
BOK
OW!!
WEASEL!!!!
FOR FUCK'S SAKE!!!
DEATH SENTENCE
ARGHHHH!
BOK
ARGHHHH!
BOK
BOK
ARGHHHH!
BOK
BOK
BOK
ARGHHHH!
CAN I GET BACK TO WORK NOW? THIS ALBUM'S NOT GONNA RECORD ITSELF...
GURGLE!
TEN OUT OF TEN. EXCELLENT!
DECREASE HIS DOSE BY 12% -- TRY AND TRIGGER THAT ACID DISCHARGE...
SURE, I DON'T THINK HE'LL GIVE US A PROBLEM...
SKILLLLZZZZZZZ!
VERITY ON THE OTHER HAND...

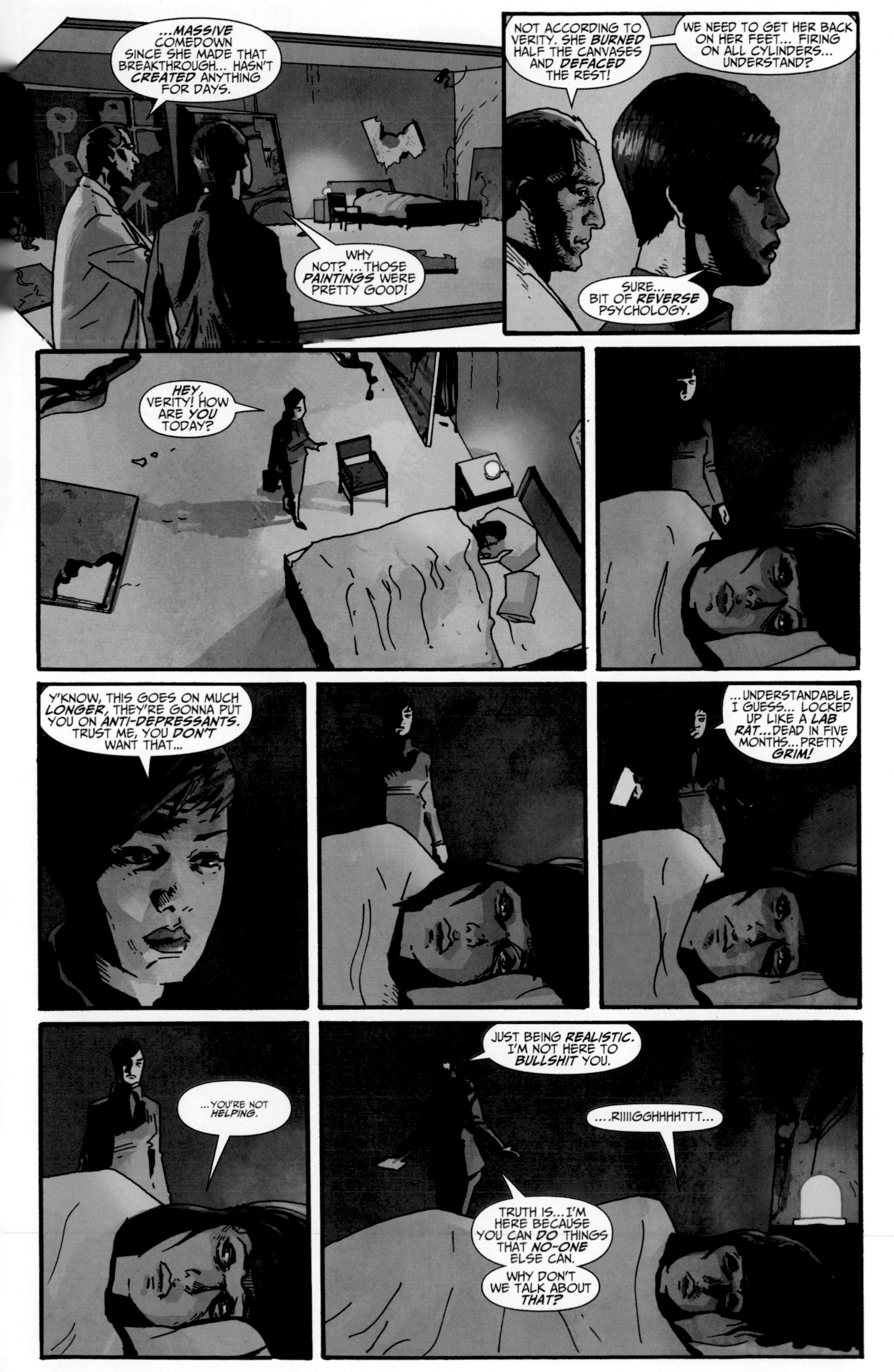
...MASSIVE COMEDOWN SINCE SHE MADE THAT BREAKTHROUGH... HASN'T CREATED ANYTHING FOR DAYS.
WHY NOT? ...THOSE PAINTINGS WERE PRETTY GOOD!
NOT ACCORDING TO VERITY. SHE BURNED HALF THE CANVASES AND DEFACED THE REST!
WE NEED TO GET HER BACK ON HER FEET... FIRING ON ALL CYLINDERS... UNDERSTAND?
SURE... BIT OF REVERSE PSYCHOLOGY.
HEY, VERITY! HOW ARE YOU TODAY?
Y'KNOW, THIS GOES ON MUCH LONGER, THEY'RE GONNA PUT YOU ON ANTI-DEPRESSANTS. TRUST ME, YOU DON'T WANT THAT...
...UNDERSTANDABLE, I GUESS... LOCKED UP LIKE A LAB RAT...DEAD IN FIVE MONTHS...PRETTY GRIM!
...YOU'RE NOT HELPING.
JUST BEING REALISTIC. I'M NOT HERE TO BULLSHIT YOU.
....RIIIIGGHHHHTTT...
TRUTH IS...I'M HERE BECAUSE YOU CAN DO THINGS THAT NO-ONE ELSE CAN.
WHY DON'T WE TALK ABOUT THAT?

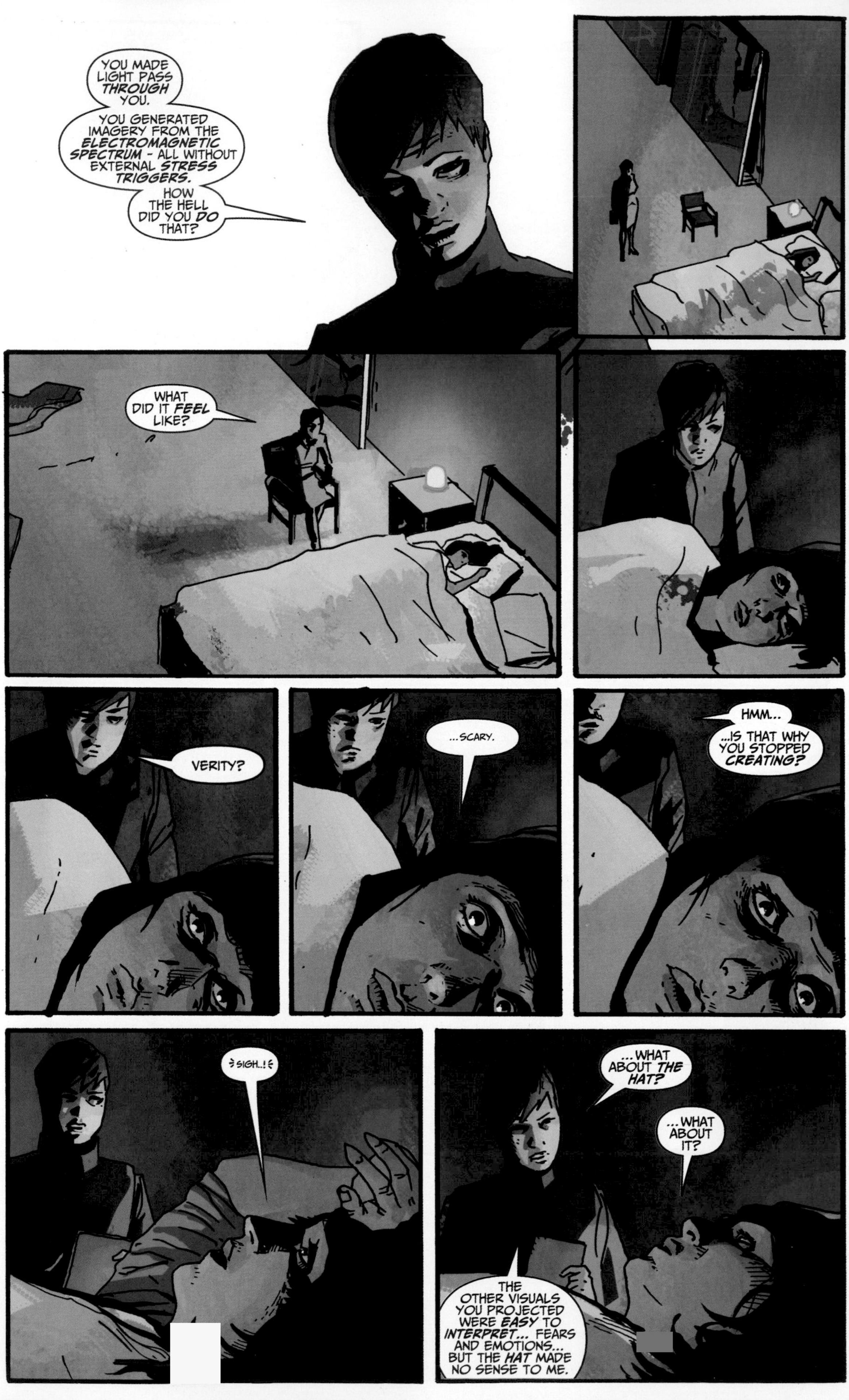

YOU MADE LIGHT PASS THROUGH YOU.
YOU GENERATED IMAGERY FROM THE ELECTROMAGNETIC SPECTRUM - ALL WITHOUT EXTERNAL STRESS TRIGGERS.
HOW THE HELL DID YOU DO THAT?
WHAT DID IT FEEL LIKE?
VERITY?
...SCARY.
HMM...
...IS THAT WHY YOU STOPPED CREATING?
SIGH..!
...WHAT ABOUT THE HAT?
...WHAT ABOUT IT?
THE OTHER VISUALS YOU PROJECTED WERE EASY TO INTERPRET... FEARS AND EMOTIONS... BUT THE HAT MADE NO SENSE TO ME.

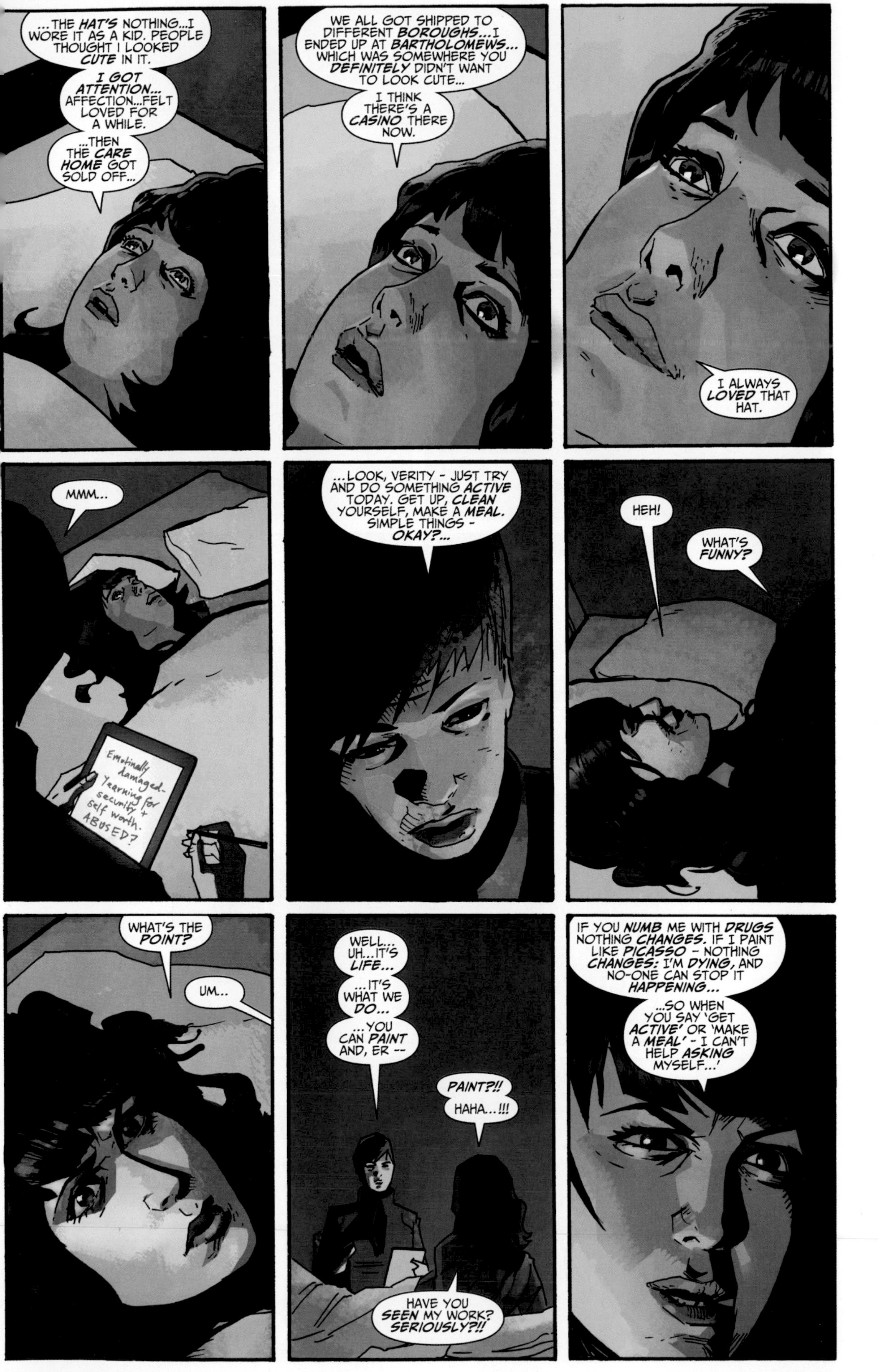
...THE HAT'S NOTHING...I WORE IT AS A KID. PEOPLE THOUGHT I LOOKED CUTE IN IT.
I GOT ATTENTION... AFFECTION...FELT LOVED FOR A WHILE.
...THEN THE CARE HOME GOT SOLD OFF...
WE ALL GOT SHIPPED TO DIFFERENT BOROUGHS...I ENDED UP AT BARTHOLOMEWS... WHICH WAS SOMEWHERE YOU DEFINITELY DIDN'T WANT TO LOOK CUTE...
I THINK THERE'S A CASINO THERE NOW.
I ALWAYS LOVED THAT HAT.
MMM...
Emotionally damaged- Yearning for security + self worth. ABUSED?
...LOOK, VERITY - JUST TRY AND DO SOMETHING ACTIVE TODAY. GET UP, CLEAN YOURSELF, MAKE A MEAL. SIMPLE THINGS - OKAY?...
HEH!
WHAT'S FUNNY?
WHAT'S THE POINT?
UM...
WELL... UH...IT'S LIFE...
...IT'S WHAT WE DO...
...YOU CAN PAINT AND, ER --
PAINT?!!
HAHA...!!!
HAVE YOU SEEN MY WORK? SERIOUSLY?!!
IF YOU NUMB ME WITH DRUGS NOTHING CHANGES. IF I PAINT LIKE PICASSO - NOTHING CHANGES: I'M DYING, AND NO-ONE CAN STOP IT HAPPENING...
...SO WHEN YOU SAY 'GET ACTIVE' OR 'MAKE A MEAL' - I CAN'T HELP ASKING MYSELF...'

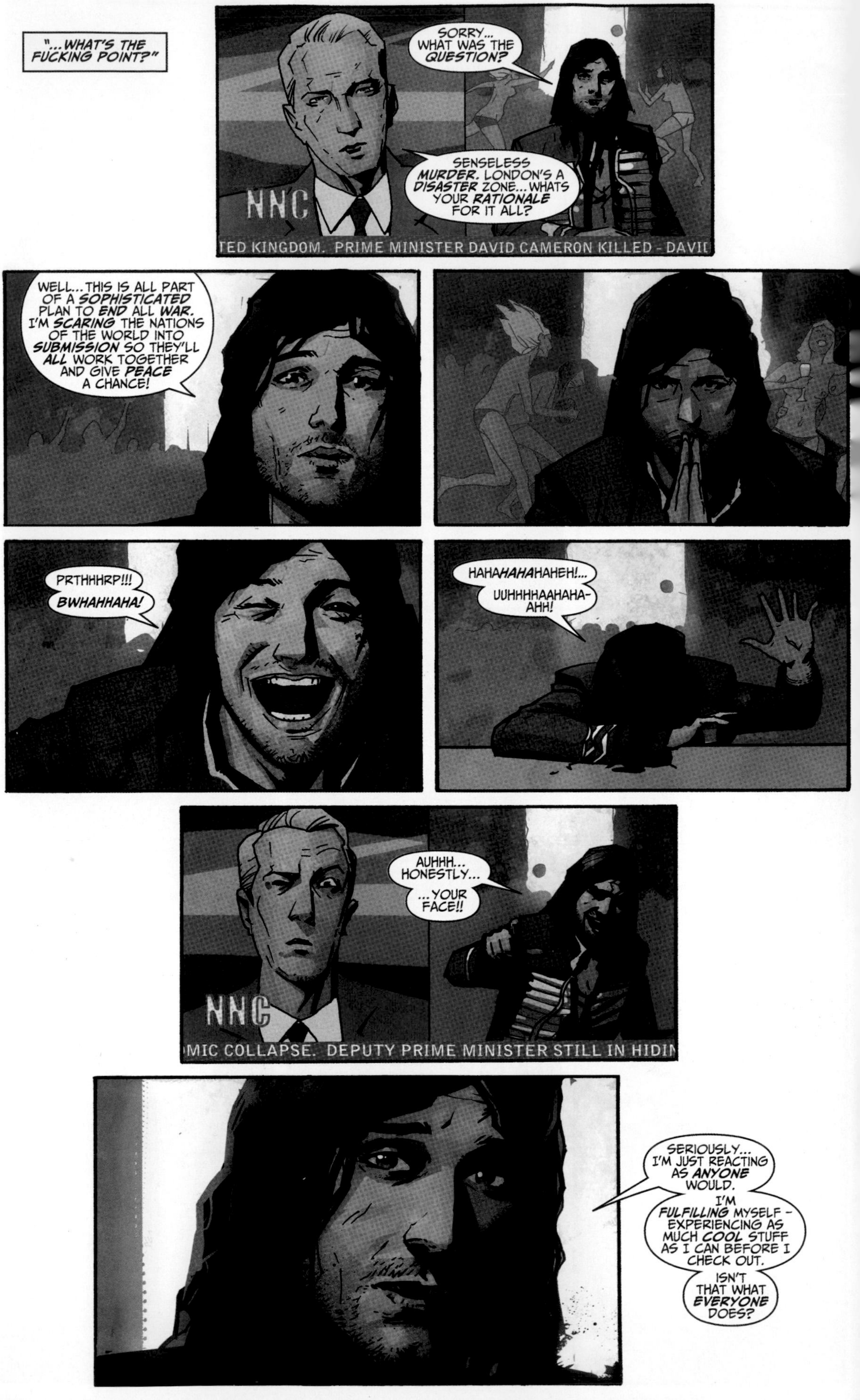
"...WHAT'S THE FUCKING POINT?"
SORRY... WHAT WAS THE QUESTION?
SENSELESS MURDER. LONDON'S A DISASTER ZONE... WHATS YOUR RATIONALE FOR IT ALL?
NNC
TED KINGDOM. PRIME MINISTER DAVID CAMERON KILLED - DAVI
WELL... THIS IS ALL PART OF A SOPHISTICATED PLAN TO END ALL WAR. I'M SCARING THE NATIONS OF THE WORLD INTO SUBMISSION SO THEY'LL ALL WORK TOGETHER AND GIVE PEACE A CHANCE!
PRTHHHRP!!! BWHAHHAHA!
HAHAHAHAHAHEH!... UUHHHHAAHAHA-AHH!
AUHHH... HONESTLY...
...YOUR FACE!!
NNC
MIC COLLAPSE. DEPUTY PRIME MINISTER STILL IN HIDIN
SERIOUSLY... I'M JUST REACTING AS ANYONE WOULD.
I'M FULFILLING MYSELF - EXPERIENCING AS MUCH COOL STUFF AS I CAN BEFORE I CHECK OUT.
ISN'T THAT WHAT EVERYONE DOES?

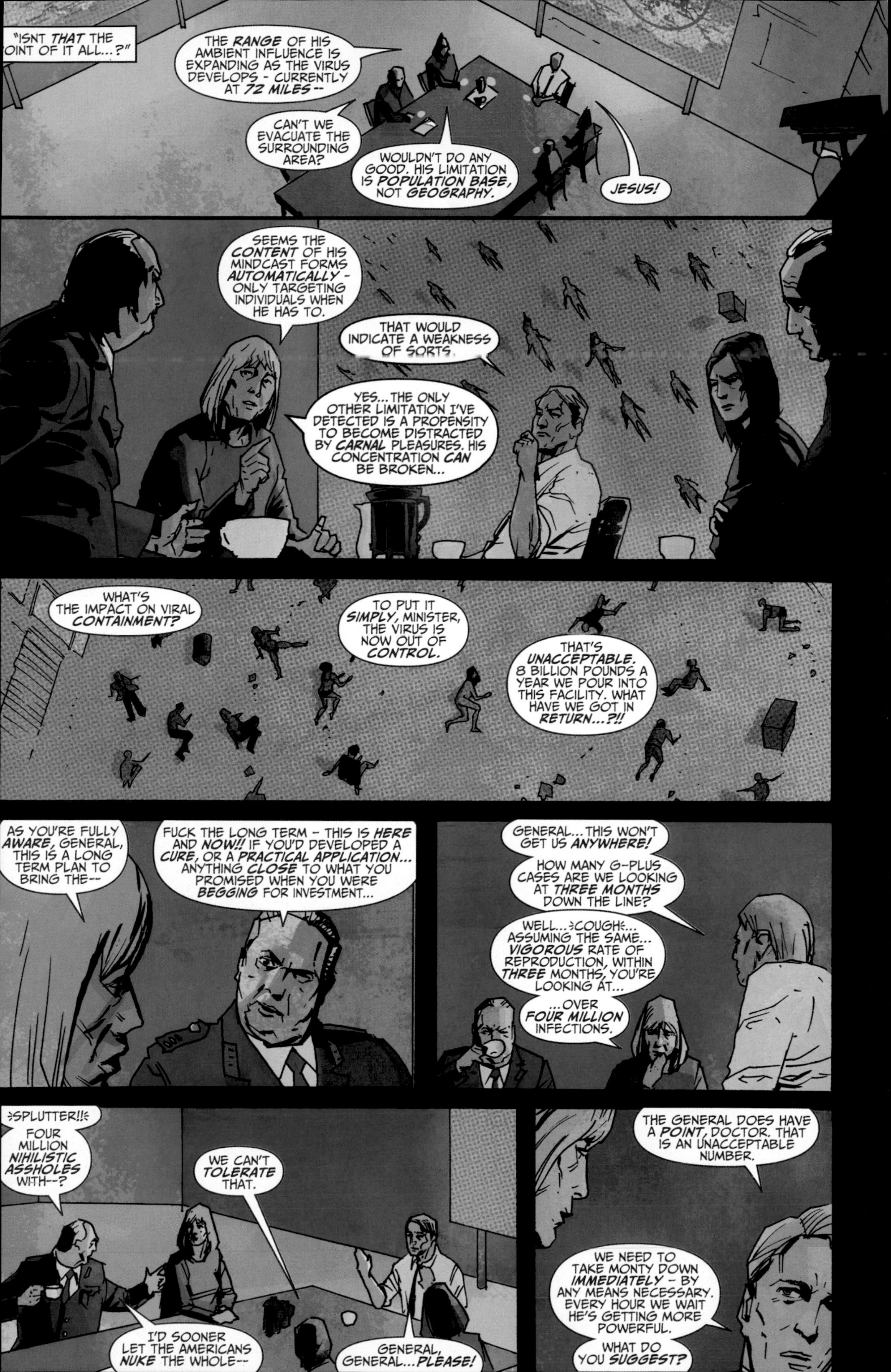
"ISNT THAT THE
OINT OF IT ALL...?"
THE RANGE OF HIS AMBIENT INFLUENCE IS EXPANDING AS THE VIRUS DEVELOPS - CURRENTLY AT 72 MILES --
CAN'T WE EVACUATE THE SURROUNDING AREA?
WOULDN'T DO ANY GOOD. HIS LIMITATION IS POPULATION BASE, NOT GEOGRAPHY.
JESUS!
SEEMS THE CONTENT OF HIS MINDCAST FORMS AUTOMATICALLY - ONLY TARGETING INDIVIDUALS WHEN HE HAS TO.
THAT WOULD INDICATE A WEAKNESS OF SORTS.
YES... THE ONLY OTHER LIMITATION I'VE DETECTED IS A PROPENSITY TO BECOME DISTRACTED BY CARNAL PLEASURES. HIS CONCENTRATION CAN BE BROKEN...
WHAT'S THE IMPACT ON VIRAL CONTAINMENT?
TO PUT IT SIMPLY, MINISTER, THE VIRUS IS NOW OUT OF CONTROL.
THAT'S UNACCEPTABLE. 8 BILLION POUNDS A YEAR WE POUR INTO THIS FACILITY. WHAT HAVE WE GOT IN RETURN...?!!
AS YOU'RE FULLY AWARE, GENERAL, THIS IS A LONG TERM PLAN TO BRING THE--
FUCK THE LONG TERM - THIS IS HERE AND NOW!! IF YOU'D DEVELOPED A CURE, OR A PRACTICAL APPLICATION... ANYTHING CLOSE TO WHAT YOU PROMISED WHEN YOU WERE BEGGING FOR INVESTMENT...
GENERAL... THIS WON'T GET US ANYWHERE!
HOW MANY G-PLUS CASES ARE WE LOOKING AT THREE MONTHS DOWN THE LINE?
WELL... ›COUGH‹... ASSUMING THE SAME... VIGOROUS RATE OF REPRODUCTION, WITHIN THREE MONTHS, YOU'RE LOOKING AT...
...OVER FOUR MILLION INFECTIONS.
›SPLUTTER!!‹
FOUR MILLION NIHILISTIC ASSHOLES WITH--?
WE CAN'T TOLERATE THAT.
I'D SOONER LET THE AMERICANS NUKE THE WHOLE--
GENERAL, GENERAL... PLEASE!
THE GENERAL DOES HAVE A POINT, DOCTOR. THAT IS AN UNACCEPTABLE NUMBER.
WE NEED TO TAKE MONTY DOWN IMMEDIATELY - BY ANY MEANS NECESSARY. EVERY HOUR WE WAIT HE'S GETTING MORE POWERFUL.
WHAT DO YOU SUGGEST?

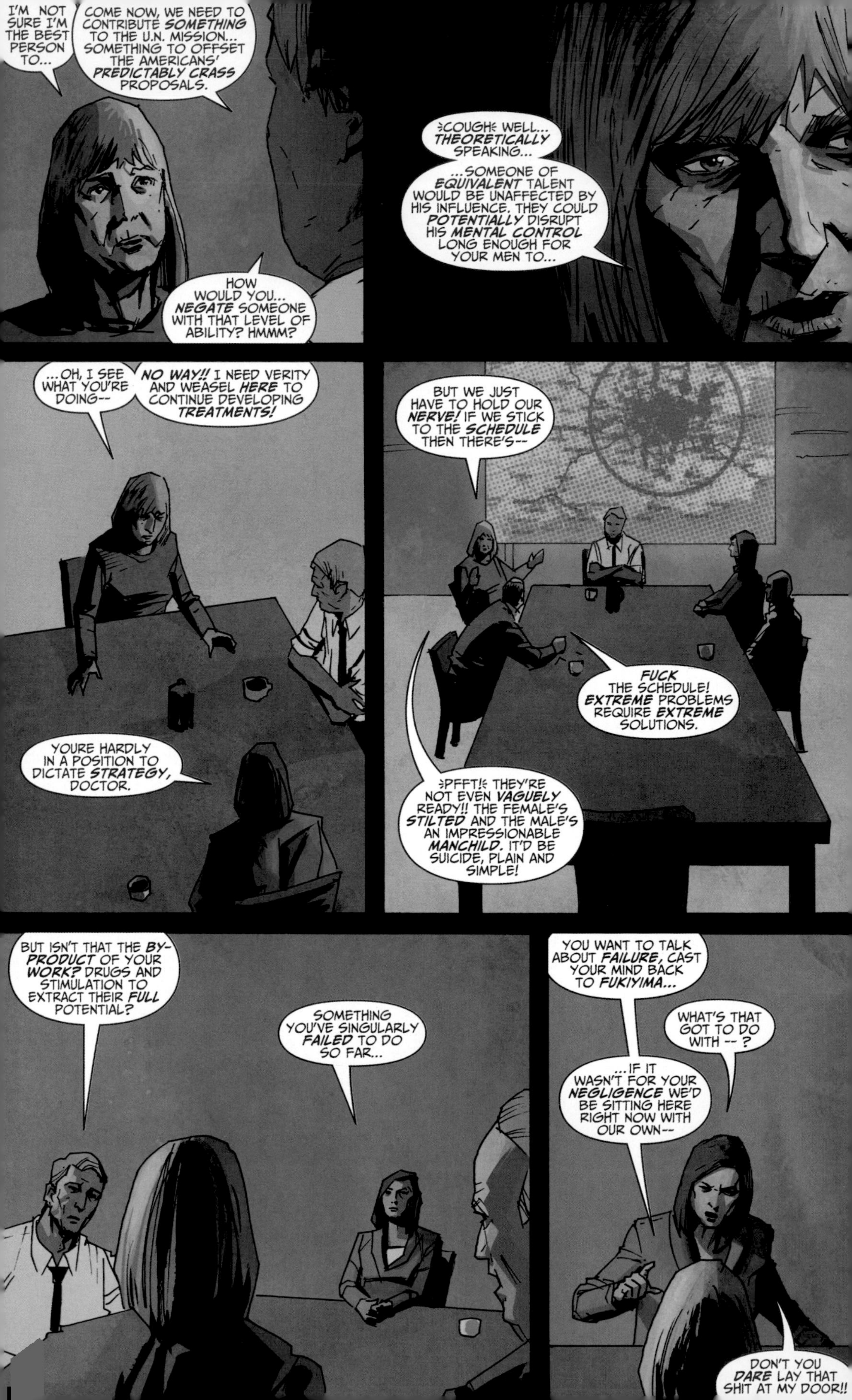
I'M NOT SURE I'M THE BEST PERSON TO...
COME NOW, WE NEED TO CONTRIBUTE SOMETHING TO THE U.N. MISSION... SOMETHING TO OFFSET THE AMERICANS' PREDICTABLY CRASS PROPOSALS.
HOW WOULD YOU... NEGATE SOMEONE WITH THAT LEVEL OF ABILITY? HMMM?
COUGH WELL... THEORETICALLY SPEAKING...
...SOMEONE OF EQUIVALENT TALENT WOULD BE UNAFFECTED BY HIS INFLUENCE. THEY COULD POTENTIALLY DISRUPT HIS MENTAL CONTROL LONG ENOUGH FOR YOUR MEN TO...
...OH, I SEE WHAT YOU'RE DOING--
NO WAY!! I NEED VERITY AND WEASEL HERE TO CONTINUE DEVELOPING TREATMENTS!
YOURE HARDLY IN A POSITION TO DICTATE STRATEGY, DOCTOR.
BUT WE JUST HAVE TO HOLD OUR NERVE! IF WE STICK TO THE SCHEDULE THEN THERE'S--
FUCK THE SCHEDULE! EXTREME PROBLEMS REQUIRE EXTREME SOLUTIONS.
PFFT! THEY'RE NOT EVEN VAGUELY READY!! THE FEMALE'S STILTED AND THE MALE'S AN IMPRESSIONABLE MANCHILD. IT'D BE SUICIDE, PLAIN AND SIMPLE!
BUT ISN'T THAT THE BY-PRODUCT OF YOUR WORK? DRUGS AND STIMULATION TO EXTRACT THEIR FULL POTENTIAL?
SOMETHING YOU'VE SINGULARLY FAILED TO DO SO FAR...
YOU WANT TO TALK ABOUT FAILURE, CAST YOUR MIND BACK TO FUKIYIMA...
WHAT'S THAT GOT TO DO WITH --?
...IF IT WASN'T FOR YOUR NEGLIGENCE WE'D BE SITTING HERE RIGHT NOW WITH OUR OWN--
DON'T YOU DARE LAY THAT SHIT AT MY DOOR!!

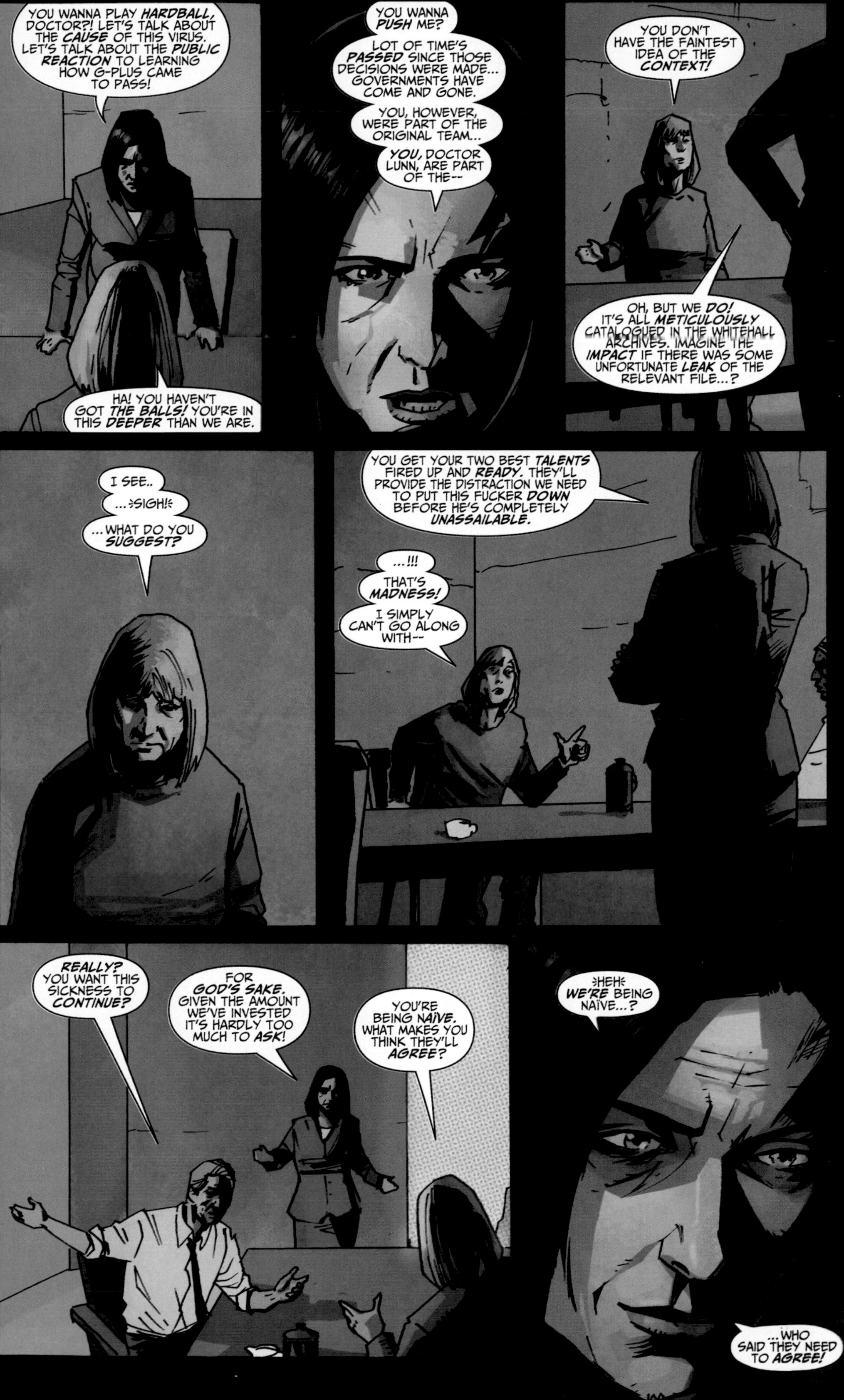

YOU WANNA PLAY HARDBALL, DOCTOR?! LET'S TALK ABOUT THE CAUSE OF THIS VIRUS. LET'S TALK ABOUT THE PUBLIC REACTION TO LEARNING HOW G-PLUS CAME TO PASS!
HA! YOU HAVEN'T GOT THE BALLS! YOU'RE IN THIS DEEPER THAN WE ARE.
YOU WANNA PUSH ME?
LOT OF TIME'S PASSED SINCE THOSE DECISIONS WERE MADE... GOVERNMENTS HAVE COME AND GONE.
YOU, HOWEVER, WERE PART OF THE ORIGINAL TEAM...
YOU, DOCTOR LUNN, ARE PART OF THE--
YOU DON'T HAVE THE FAINTEST IDEA OF THE CONTEXT!
OH, BUT WE DO! IT'S ALL METICULOUSLY CATALOGUED IN THE WHITEHALL ARCHIVES. IMAGINE THE IMPACT IF THERE WAS SOME UNFORTUNATE LEAK OF THE RELEVANT FILE...?
I SEE..
...SIGH!
...WHAT DO YOU SUGGEST?
YOU GET YOUR TWO BEST TALENTS FIRED UP AND READY. THEY'LL PROVIDE THE DISTRACTION WE NEED TO PUT THIS FUCKER DOWN BEFORE HE'S COMPLETELY UNASSAILABLE.
...!!!
THAT'S MADNESS!
I SIMPLY CAN'T GO ALONG WITH--
REALLY? YOU WANT THIS SICKNESS TO CONTINUE?
FOR GOD'S SAKE. GIVEN THE AMOUNT WE'VE INVESTED IT'S HARDLY TOO MUCH TO ASK!
YOU'RE BEING NAÏVE. WHAT MAKES YOU THINK THEY'LL AGREE?
HEH
WE'RE BEING NAÏVE...?
...WHO SAID THEY NEED TO AGREE!

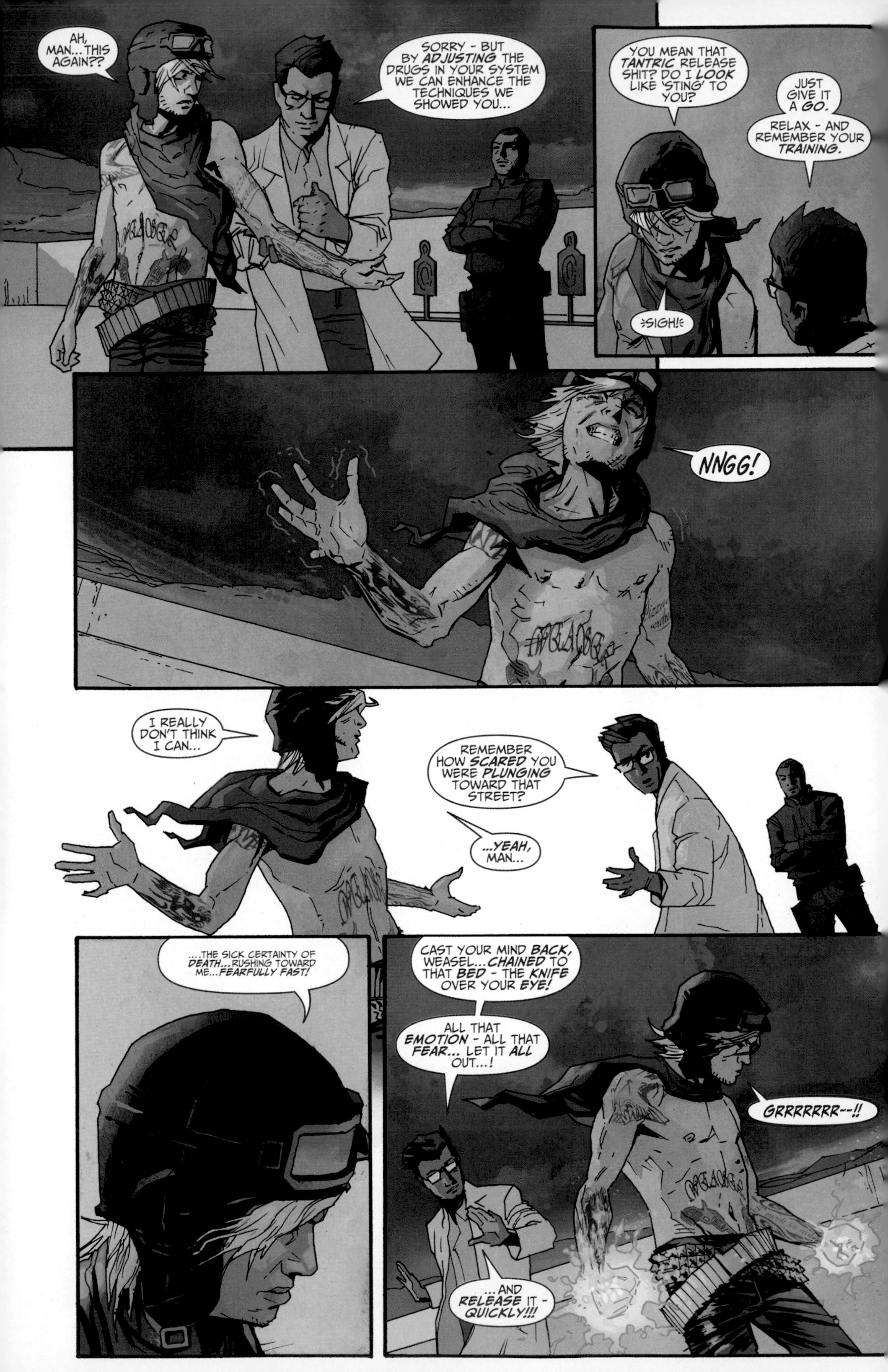
AH, MAN... THIS AGAIN??
SORRY - BUT BY ADJUSTING THE DRUGS IN YOUR SYSTEM WE CAN ENHANCE THE TECHNIQUES WE SHOWED YOU...
YOU MEAN THAT TANTRIC RELEASE SHIT? DO I LOOK LIKE 'STING' TO YOU?
JUST GIVE IT A GO.
RELAX - AND REMEMBER YOUR TRAINING.
SIGH!
NNGG!
I REALLY DON'T THINK I CAN...
REMEMBER HOW SCARED YOU WERE PLUNGING TOWARD THAT STREET?
...YEAH, MAN...
...THE SICK CERTAINTY OF DEATH...RUSHING TOWARD ME...FEARFULLY FAST!
CAST YOUR MIND BACK, WEASEL...CHAINED TO THAT BED - THE KNIFE OVER YOUR EYE!
ALL THAT EMOTION - ALL THAT FEAR... LET IT ALL OUT...!
GRRRRRRR--!!
...AND RELEASE IT - QUICKLY!!!

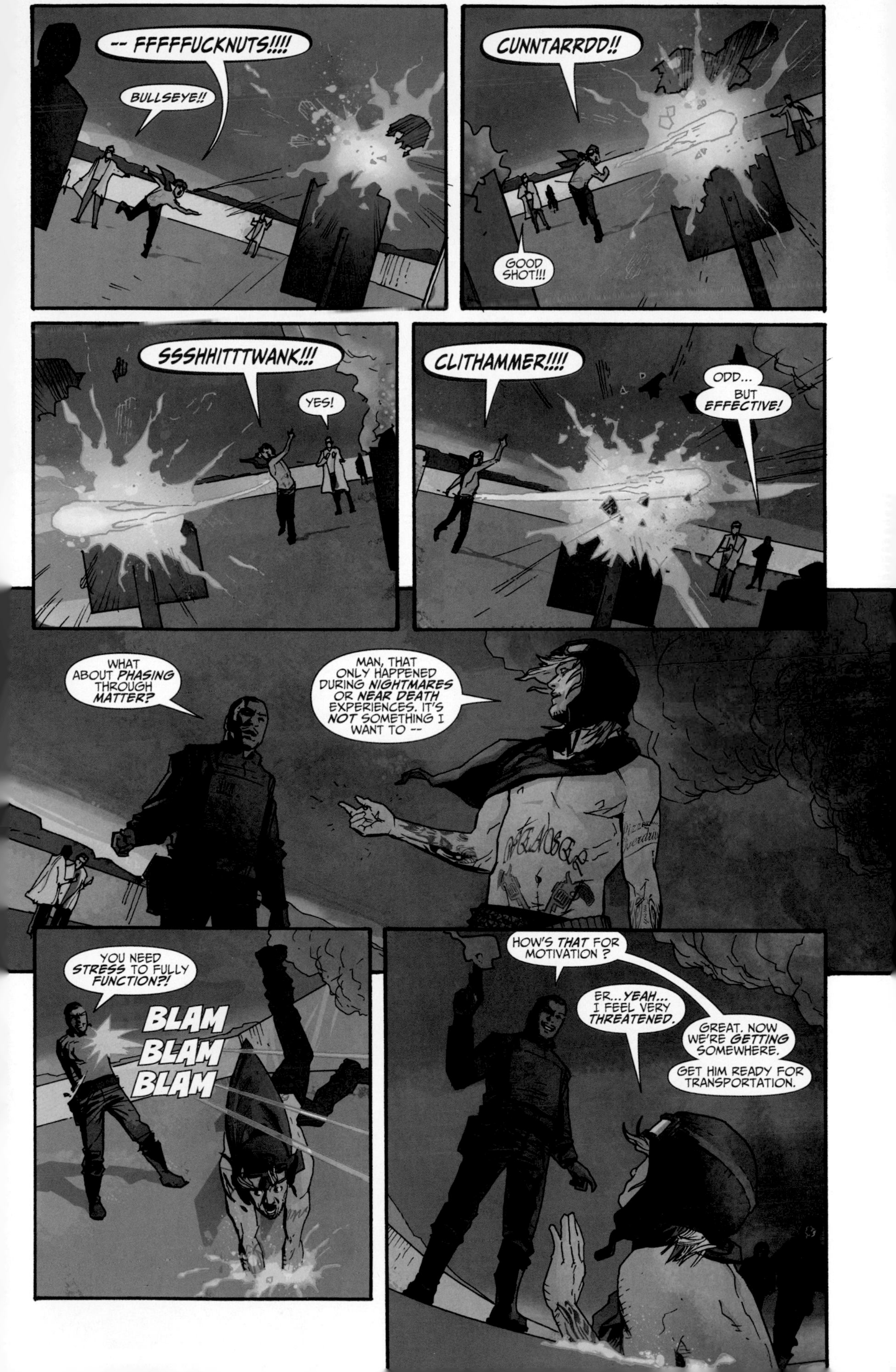
-- FFFFFUCKNUTS!!!!
BULLSEYE!!
CUNNTARRDD!!
GOOD SHOT!!!
SSSHHITTTWANK!!!
YES!
CLITHAMMER!!!!
ODD... BUT EFFECTIVE!
WHAT ABOUT PHASING THROUGH MATTER?
MAN, THAT ONLY HAPPENED DURING NIGHTMARES OR NEAR DEATH EXPERIENCES. IT'S NOT SOMETHING I WANT TO --
YOU NEED STRESS TO FULLY FUNCTION?!
BLAM
BLAM
BLAM
HOW'S THAT FOR MOTIVATION ?
ER...YEAH... I FEEL VERY THREATENED.
GREAT. NOW WE'RE GETTING SOMEWHERE.
GET HIM READY FOR TRANSPORTATION.

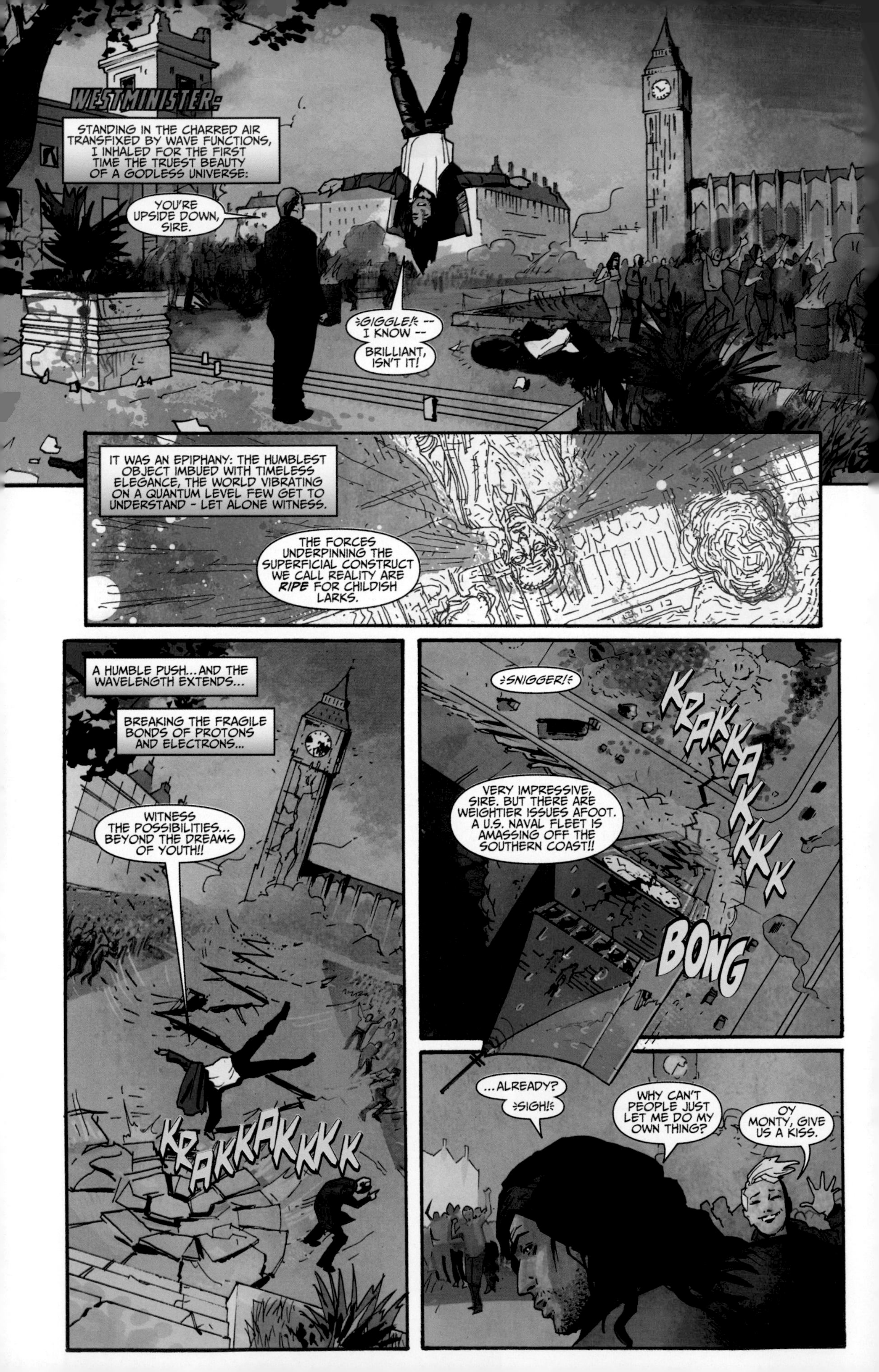
WESTMINISTER:
STANDING IN THE CHARRED AIR TRANSFIXED BY WAVE FUNCTIONS, I INHALED FOR THE FIRST TIME THE TRUEST BEAUTY OF A GODLESS UNIVERSE:
YOU'RE UPSIDE DOWN, SIRE.
GIGGLE! -- I KNOW --
BRILLIANT, ISN'T IT!
IT WAS AN EPIPHANY: THE HUMBLEST OBJECT IMBUED WITH TIMELESS ELEGANCE, THE WORLD VIBRATING ON A QUANTUM LEVEL FEW GET TO UNDERSTAND - LET ALONE WITNESS.
THE FORCES UNDERPINNING THE SUPERFICIAL CONSTRUCT WE CALL REALITY ARE RIPE FOR CHILDISH LARKS.
A HUMBLE PUSH... AND THE WAVELENGTH EXTENDS...
BREAKING THE FRAGILE BONDS OF PROTONS AND ELECTRONS...
WITNESS THE POSSIBILITIES... BEYOND THE DREAMS OF YOUTH!!
KRAKKAKKKK
SNIGGER!
KRAKKAKKKK
VERY IMPRESSIVE, SIRE. BUT THERE ARE WEIGHTIER ISSUES AFOOT. A U.S. NAVAL FLEET IS AMASSING OFF THE SOUTHERN COAST!!
BONG
...ALREADY?
SIGH!
WHY CAN'T PEOPLE JUST LET ME DO MY OWN THING?
OY MONTY, GIVE US A KISS.

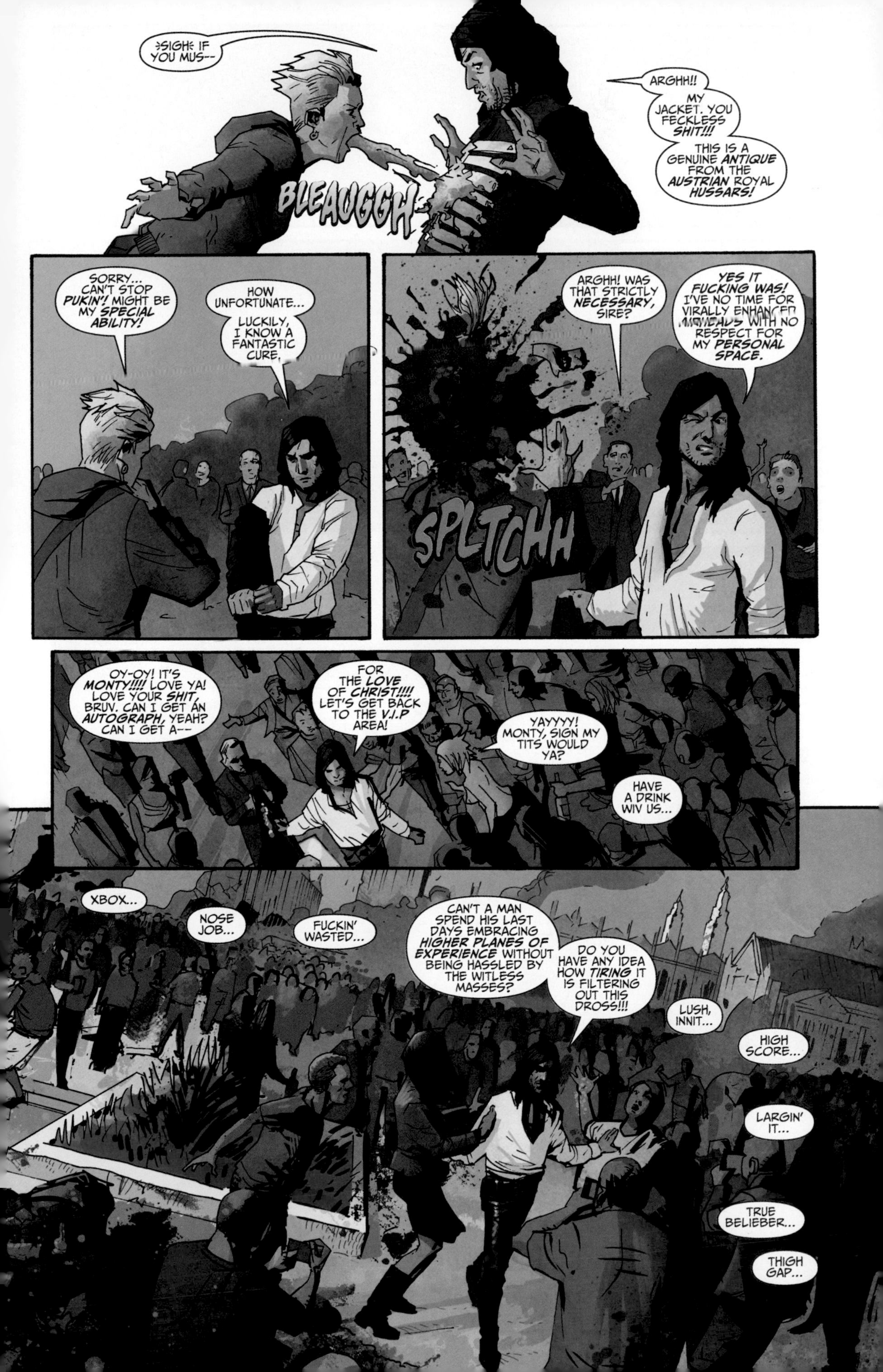

SIGH IF YOU MUS--
BLEAUGGH
ARGHH!! MY JACKET. YOU FECKLESS SHIT!!!
THIS IS A GENUINE ANTIQUE FROM THE AUSTRIAN ROYAL HUSSARS!
SORRY... CAN'T STOP PUKIN'! MIGHT BE MY SPECIAL ABILITY!
HOW UNFORTUNATE...
LUCKILY, I KNOW A FANTASTIC CURE.
ARGHH! WAS THAT STRICTLY NECESSARY, SIRE?
YES IT FUCKING WAS! I'VE NO TIME FOR VIRALLY ENHANCED MONGS WITH NO RESPECT FOR MY PERSONAL SPACE.
SPLTCHH
OY-OY! IT'S MONTY!!!! LOVE YA! LOVE YOUR SHIT, BRUV. CAN I GET AN AUTOGRAPH, YEAH? CAN I GET A--
FOR THE LOVE OF CHRIST!!!! LET'S GET BACK TO THE V.I.P AREA!
YAYYYY! MONTY, SIGN MY TITS WOULD YA?
HAVE A DRINK WIV US...
XBOX...
NOSE JOB...
FUCKIN' WASTED...
CAN'T A MAN SPEND HIS LAST DAYS EMBRACING HIGHER PLANES OF EXPERIENCE WITHOUT BEING HASSLED BY THE WITLESS MASSES?
DO YOU HAVE ANY IDEA HOW TIRING IT IS FILTERING OUT THIS DROSS!!!
LUSH, INNIT...
HIGH SCORE...
LARGIN' IT...
TRUE BELIEBER...
THIGH GAP...

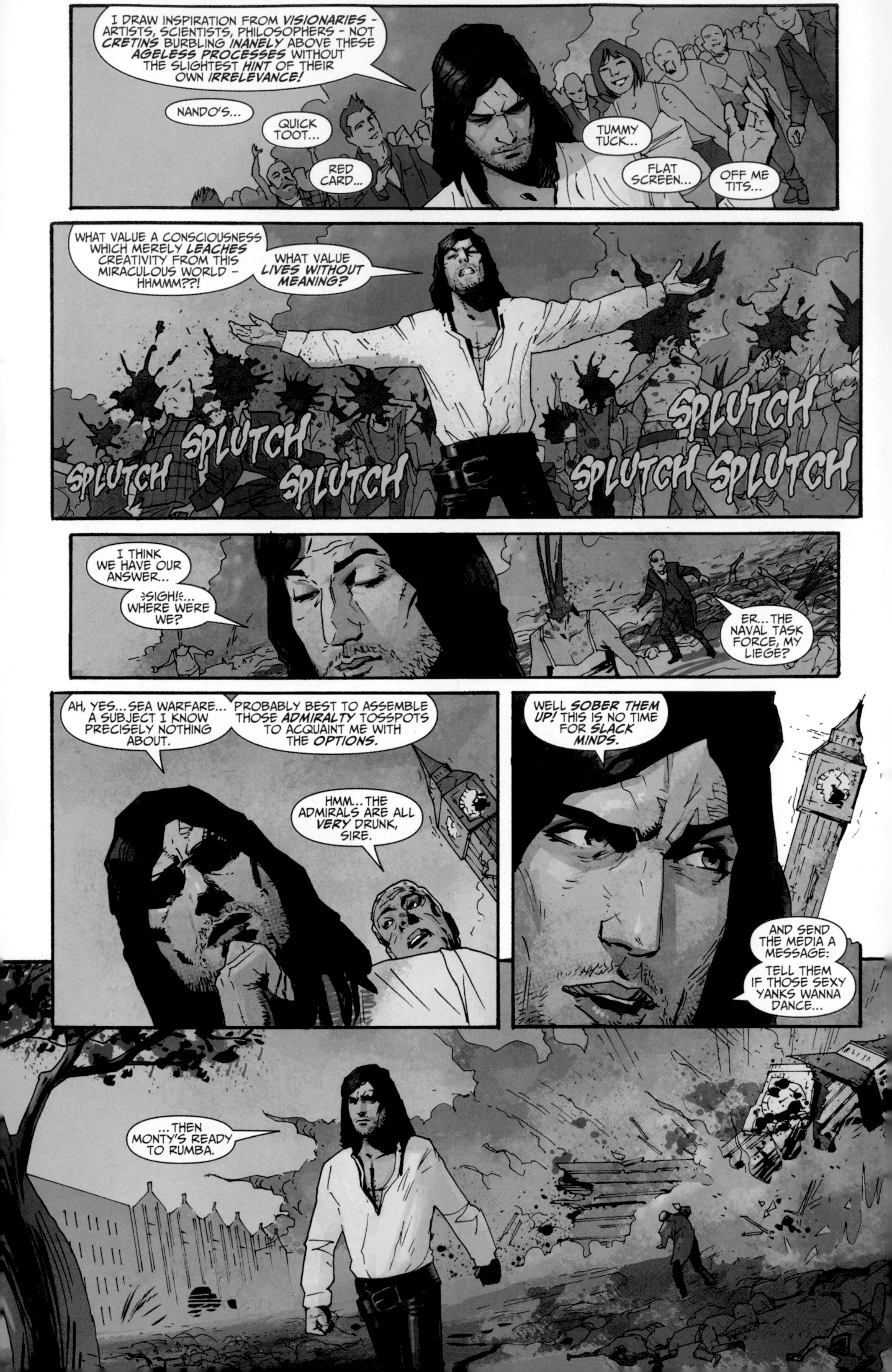

I DRAW INSPIRATION FROM VISIONARIES - ARTISTS, SCIENTISTS, PHILOSOPHERS - NOT CRETINS BURBLING INANELY ABOVE THESE AGELESS PROCESSES WITHOUT THE SLIGHTEST HINT OF THEIR OWN IRRELEVANCE!
NANDO'S...
QUICK TOOT...
RED CARD...
TUMMY TUCK...
FLAT SCREEN...
OFF ME TITS...
WHAT VALUE A CONSCIOUSNESS WHICH MERELY LEACHES CREATIVITY FROM THIS MIRACULOUS WORLD - HHMMM??!
WHAT VALUE LIVES WITHOUT MEANING?
SPLUTCH
SPLUTCH
SPLUTCH
SPLUTCH
SPLUTCH
SPLUTCH
I THINK WE HAVE OUR ANSWER...
SIGH!... WHERE WERE WE?
ER... THE NAVAL TASK FORCE, MY LIEGE?
AH, YES... SEA WARFARE... A SUBJECT I KNOW PRECISELY NOTHING ABOUT.
PROBABLY BEST TO ASSEMBLE THOSE ADMIRALTY TOSSPOTS TO ACQUAINT ME WITH THE OPTIONS.
HMM... THE ADMIRALS ARE ALL VERY DRUNK, SIRE.
WELL SOBER THEM UP! THIS IS NO TIME FOR SLACK MINDS.
AND SEND THE MEDIA A MESSAGE: TELL THEM IF THOSE SEXY YANKS WANNA DANCE...
...THEN MONTY'S READY TO RUMBA.

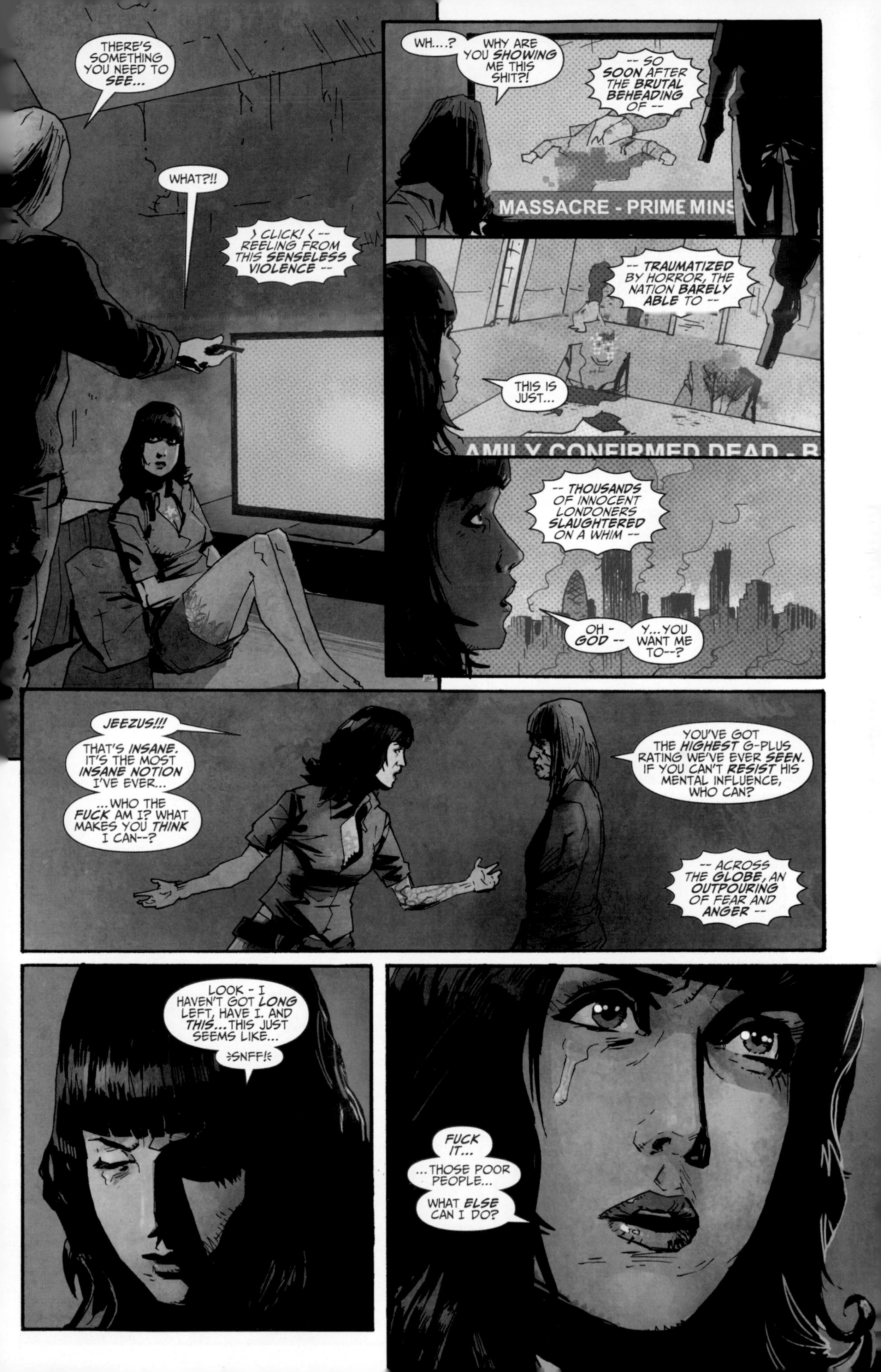

THERE'S SOMETHING YOU NEED TO SEE...
WHAT?!!
›CLICK!‹ -- REELING FROM THIS SENSELESS VIOLENCE --
WH....?
WHY ARE YOU SHOWING ME THIS SHIT?!
-- SO SOON AFTER THE BRUTAL BEHEADING OF --
MASSACRE - PRIME MINS
-- TRAUMATIZED BY HORROR, THE NATION BARELY ABLE TO --
THIS IS JUST...
AMILY CONFIRMED DEAD - B
-- THOUSANDS OF INNOCENT LONDONERS SLAUGHTERED ON A WHIM --
OH - GOD --
Y...YOU WANT ME TO--?
JEEZUS!!!
THAT'S INSANE. IT'S THE MOST INSANE NOTION I'VE EVER...
...WHO THE FUCK AM I? WHAT MAKES YOU THINK I CAN--?
YOU'VE GOT THE HIGHEST G-PLUS RATING WE'VE EVER SEEN. IF YOU CAN'T RESIST HIS MENTAL INFLUENCE, WHO CAN?
-- ACROSS THE GLOBE, AN OUTPOURING OF FEAR AND ANGER --
LOOK - I HAVEN'T GOT LONG LEFT, HAVE I. AND THIS...THIS JUST SEEMS LIKE...
›SNFF!‹
FUCK IT...
...THOSE POOR PEOPLE...
WHAT ELSE CAN I DO?

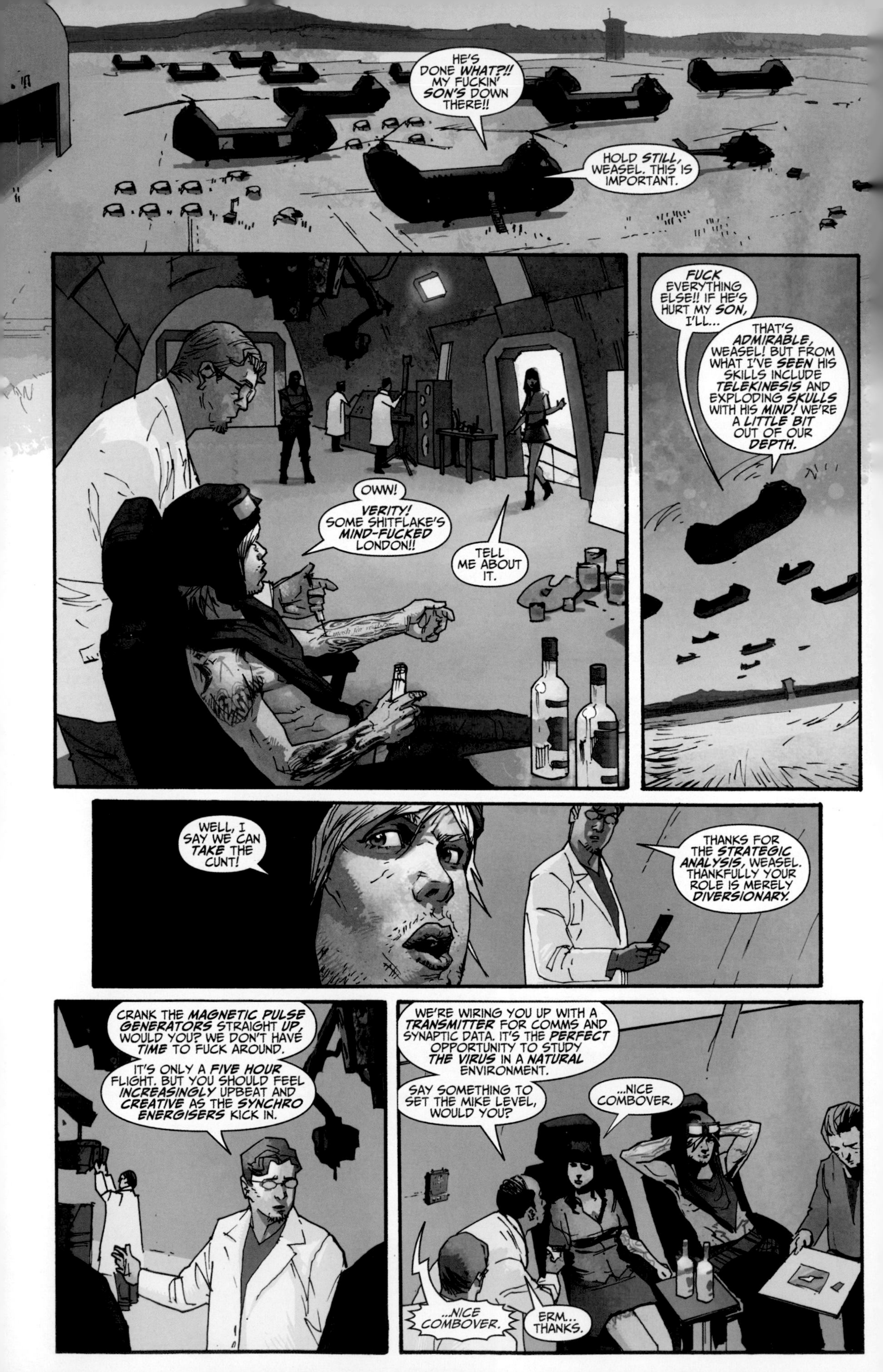
HE'S DONE WHAT?!! MY FUCKIN' SON'S DOWN THERE!!
HOLD STILL, WEASEL. THIS IS IMPORTANT.
OWW! VERITY! SOME SHITFLAKE'S MIND-FUCKED LONDON!!
TELL ME ABOUT IT.
FUCK EVERYTHING ELSE!! IF HE'S HURT MY SON, I'LL...
THAT'S ADMIRABLE, WEASEL! BUT FROM WHAT I'VE SEEN HIS SKILLS INCLUDE TELEKINESIS AND EXPLODING SKULLS WITH HIS MIND! WE'RE A LITTLE BIT OUT OF OUR DEPTH.
WELL, I SAY WE CAN TAKE THE CUNT!
THANKS FOR THE STRATEGIC ANALYSIS, WEASEL. THANKFULLY YOUR ROLE IS MERELY DIVERSIONARY.
CRANK THE MAGNETIC PULSE GENERATORS STRAIGHT UP, WOULD YOU? WE DON'T HAVE TIME TO FUCK AROUND.
IT'S ONLY A FIVE HOUR FLIGHT. BUT YOU SHOULD FEEL INCREASINGLY UPBEAT AND CREATIVE AS THE SYNCHRO ENERGISERS KICK IN.
WE'RE WIRING YOU UP WITH A TRANSMITTER FOR COMMS AND SYNAPTIC DATA. IT'S THE PERFECT OPPORTUNITY TO STUDY THE VIRUS IN A NATURAL ENVIRONMENT.
SAY SOMETHING TO SET THE MIKE LEVEL, WOULD YOU?
...NICE COMBOVER.
...NICE COMBOVER.
ERM... THANKS.

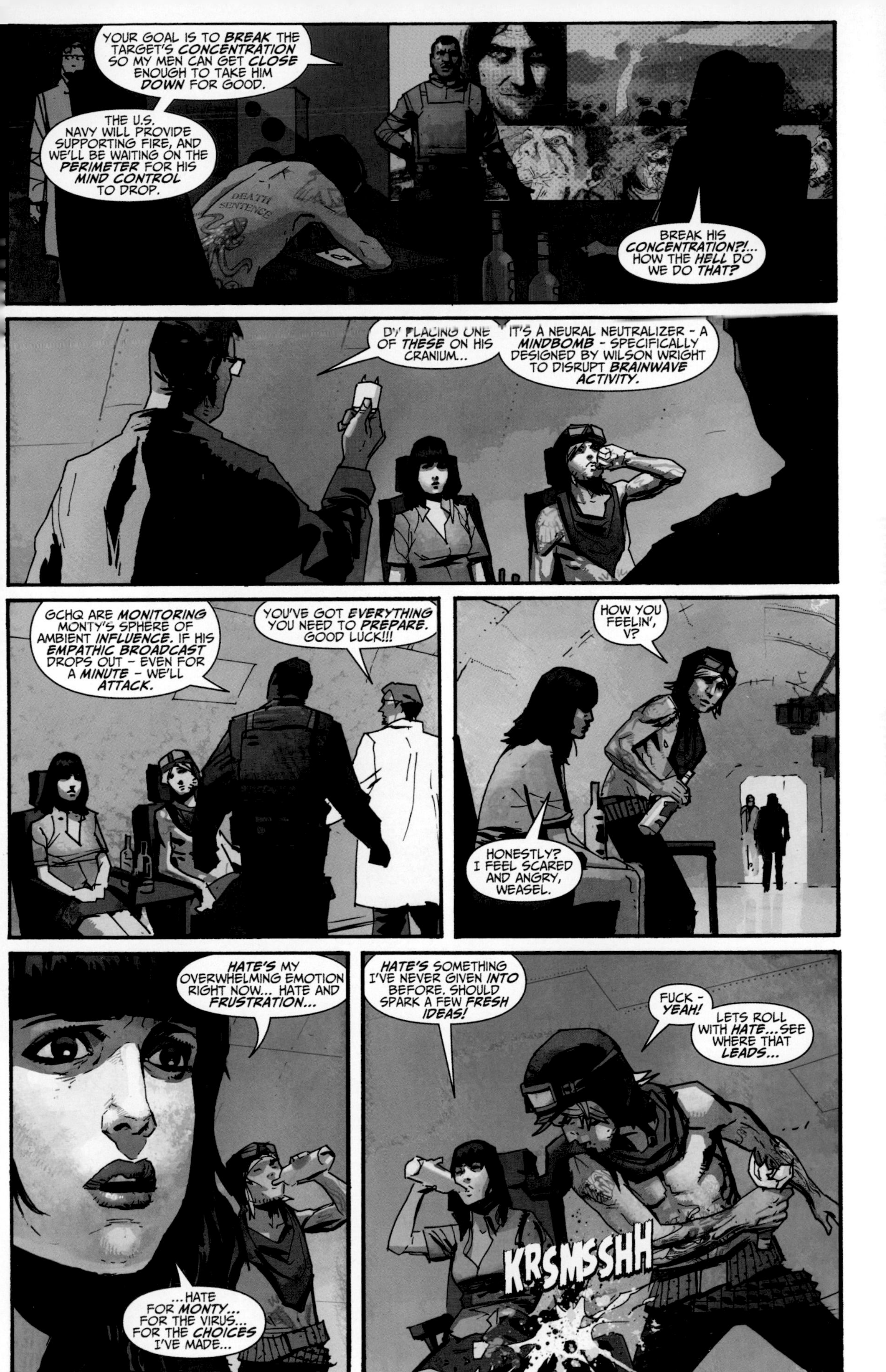
YOUR GOAL IS TO BREAK THE TARGET'S CONCENTRATION SO MY MEN CAN GET CLOSE ENOUGH TO TAKE HIM DOWN FOR GOOD.
THE U.S. NAVY WILL PROVIDE SUPPORTING FIRE, AND WE'LL BE WAITING ON THE PERIMETER FOR HIS MIND CONTROL TO DROP.
DEATH SENTENCE
BREAK HIS CONCENTRATION?!... HOW THE HELL DO WE DO THAT?
BY PLACING ONE OF THESE ON HIS CRANIUM...
IT'S A NEURAL NEUTRALIZER - A MINDBOMB - SPECIFICALLY DESIGNED BY WILSON WRIGHT TO DISRUPT BRAINWAVE ACTIVITY.
GCHQ ARE MONITORING MONTY'S SPHERE OF AMBIENT INFLUENCE. IF HIS EMPATHIC BROADCAST DROPS OUT - EVEN FOR A MINUTE - WE'LL ATTACK.
YOU'VE GOT EVERYTHING YOU NEED TO PREPARE. GOOD LUCK!!!
HOW YOU FEELIN', V?
HONESTLY? I FEEL SCARED AND ANGRY, WEASEL.
HATE'S MY OVERWHELMING EMOTION RIGHT NOW... HATE AND FRUSTRATION...
...HATE FOR MONTY... FOR THE VIRUS... FOR THE CHOICES I'VE MADE...
HATE'S SOMETHING I'VE NEVER GIVEN INTO BEFORE. SHOULD SPARK A FEW FRESH IDEAS!
FUCK - YEAH!
LETS ROLL WITH HATE... SEE WHERE THAT LEADS...
KRSMSSHH

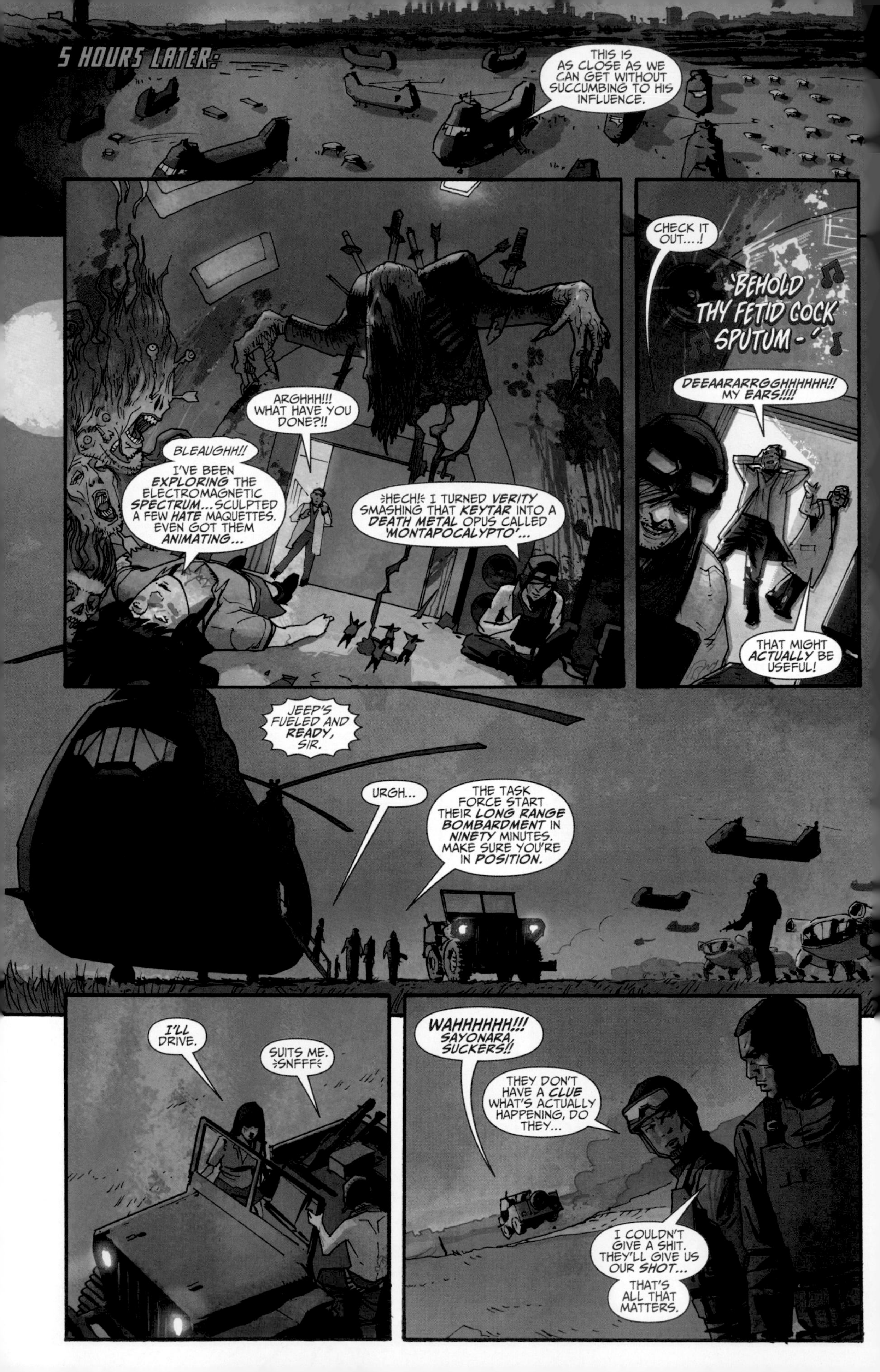
5 HOURS LATER:
THIS IS AS CLOSE AS WE CAN GET WITHOUT SUCCUMBING TO HIS INFLUENCE.
ARGHHH!!! WHAT HAVE YOU DONE?!!
BLEAUGHH!!
I'VE BEEN EXPLORING THE ELECTROMAGNETIC SPECTRUM... SCULPTED A FEW HATE MAQUETTES. EVEN GOT THEM ANIMATING...
HECH! I TURNED VERITY SMASHING THAT KEYTAR INTO A DEATH METAL OPUS CALLED 'MONTAPOCALYPTO'...
CHECK IT OUT...!
'BEHOLD THY FETID COCK SPUTUM -'
DEEAARARRGGHHHHHH!! MY EARS!!!!
THAT MIGHT ACTUALLY BE USEFUL!
JEEP'S FUELED AND READY, SIR.
URGH...
THE TASK FORCE START THEIR LONG RANGE BOMBARDMENT IN NINETY MINUTES. MAKE SURE YOU'RE IN POSITION.
I'LL DRIVE.
SUITS ME. SNFFF
WAHHHHHH!!! SAYONARA, SUCKERS!!
THEY DON'T HAVE A CLUE WHAT'S ACTUALLY HAPPENING, DO THEY...
I COULDN'T GIVE A SHIT. THEY'LL GIVE US OUR SHOT...
THAT'S ALL THAT MATTERS.

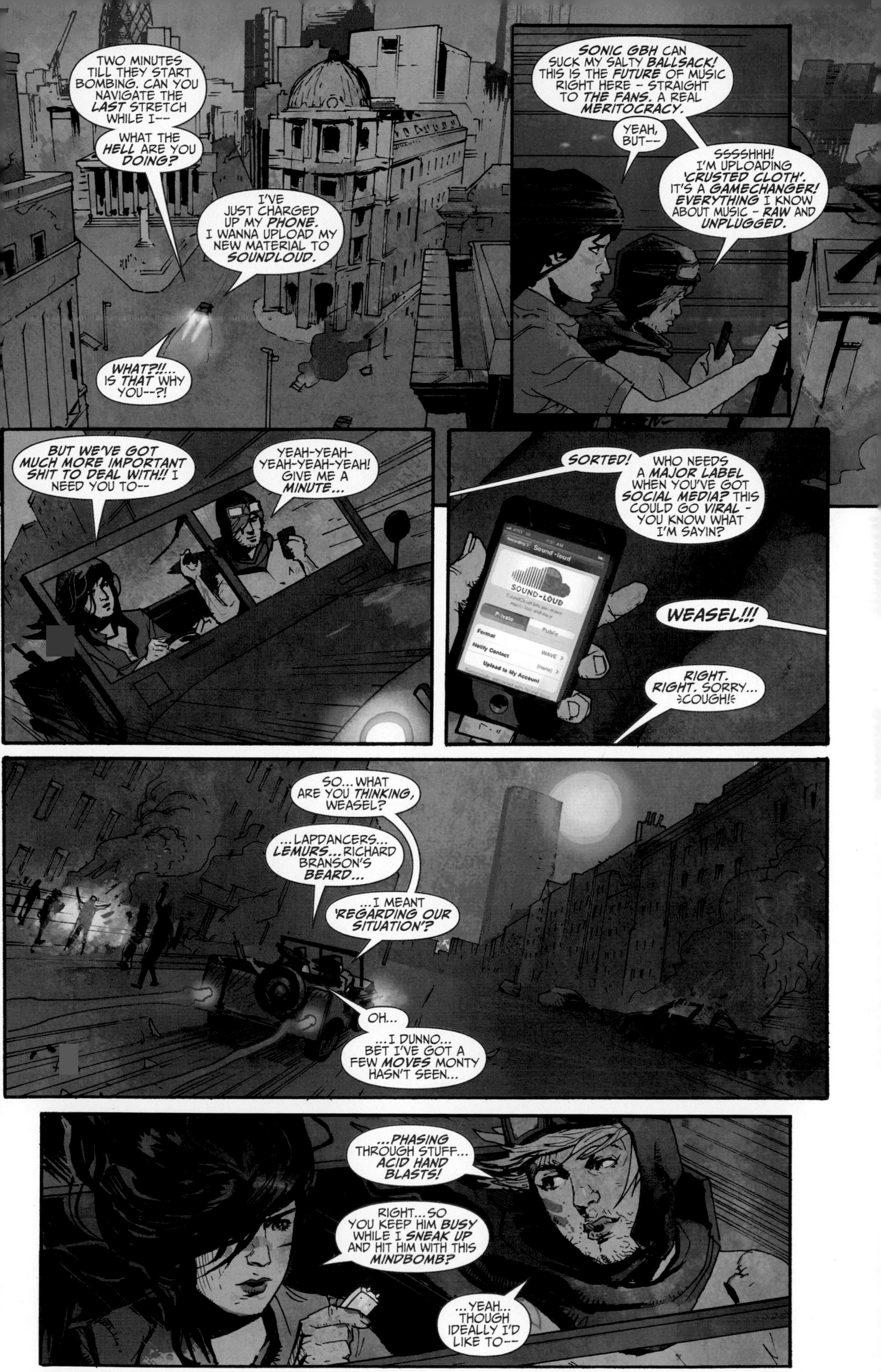
TWO MINUTES TILL THEY START BOMBING. CAN YOU NAVIGATE THE LAST STRETCH WHILE I--
WHAT THE HELL ARE YOU DOING?
I'VE JUST CHARGED UP MY PHONE. I WANNA UPLOAD MY NEW MATERIAL TO SOUNDLOUD.
WHAT?!!... IS THAT WHY YOU--?!
SONIC GBH CAN SUCK MY SALTY BALLSACK! THIS IS THE FUTURE OF MUSIC RIGHT HERE - STRAIGHT TO THE FANS. A REAL MERITOCRACY.
YEAH, BUT--
SSSSHHH! I'M UPLOADING 'CRUSTED CLOTH'. IT'S A GAMECHANGER! EVERYTHING I KNOW ABOUT MUSIC - RAW AND UNPLUGGED.
BUT WE'VE GOT MUCH MORE IMPORTANT SHIT TO DEAL WITH!! I NEED YOU TO--
YEAH-YEAH-YEAH-YEAH-YEAH! GIVE ME A MINUTE...
SORTED!
WHO NEEDS A MAJOR LABEL WHEN YOU'VE GOT SOCIAL MEDIA? THIS COULD GO VIRAL - YOU KNOW WHAT I'M SAYIN?
SOUND-LOUD
WEASEL!!!
RIGHT. RIGHT. SORRY... *COUGH!*
SO... WHAT ARE YOU THINKING, WEASEL?
...LAPDANCERS... LEMURS... RICHARD BRANSON'S BEARD...
...I MEANT 'REGARDING OUR SITUATION'?
OH...
...I DUNNO... BET I'VE GOT A FEW MOVES MONTY HASN'T SEEN...
...PHASING THROUGH STUFF... ACID HAND BLASTS!
RIGHT... SO YOU KEEP HIM BUSY WHILE I SNEAK UP AND HIT HIM WITH THIS MINDBOMB?
...YEAH... THOUGH IDEALLY I'D LIKE TO--

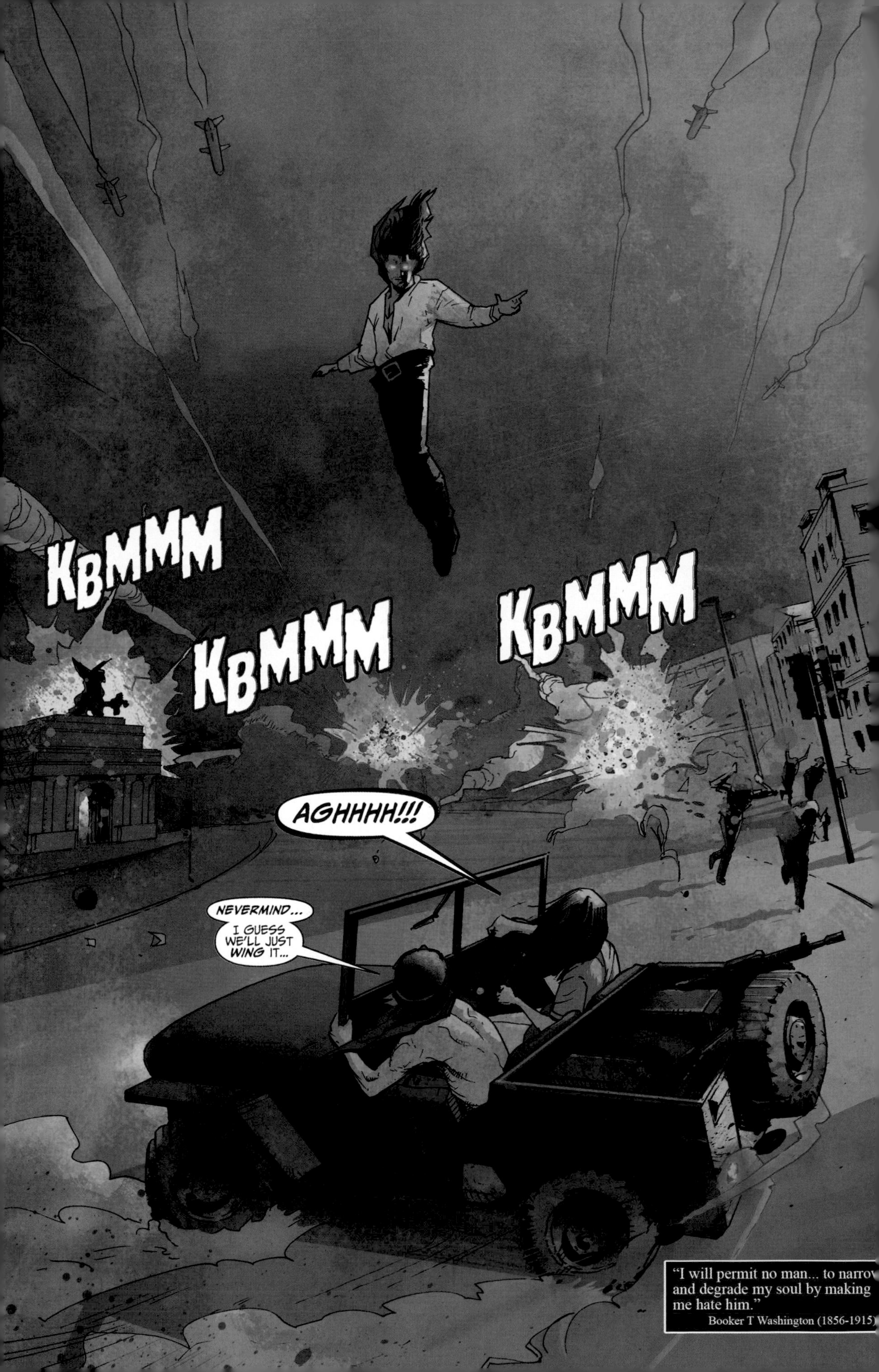
KBMMM
KBMMM
KBMMM
AGHHHH!!!
NEVERMIND... I GUESS WE'LL JUST WING IT...

"I will permit no man... to narrow and degrade my soul by making me hate him."
Booker T Washington (1856-1915)

Defense Intelligence Agency
Office of the Inspector General
Office for Investigations

CLASSIFIED

Date: [redacted] [redacted] **Time: 1020**

Name of Contact: [redacted] **Office/Division:** [redacted] **Phone** [redacted]

Address of Organization: [redacted]

Employee Name: [redacted] **Office/Division: IG** **Phone #:** [redacted]

...le One
...E/I **CALLED/VISITED** DR. WILSON WRIGHT

Subject: INTERCEPT OF TRANSCRIPT

What was said:

FROM A [redacted] THE FIELD OF [redacted] AND [redacted] IS FRAUGHT WITH DIFFICULTY. THE PROBLEMS ARE WELL ESTABLISHED. FIRSTLY, A 'NEW' VIRUS IS SIMPLY THE SUBTLE MUTATION OF AN EXISTING VIRUS, AND ONE THAT WILL SURELY MUTATE AGAIN IN TIME. SECONDLY, A VIRUS AND ITS HOST ARE INTERDEPENDENT. AS EACH VIRUS EVOLVES SO THE HUMAN BODY REFINES ITS DEFENCES, AN ENDLESS CYCLE OF ATTACK AND COUNTER THAT HAS PLAYED OUT FOR GENERATIONS.

VIRUSES MUTATE BY VIRTUE OF [redacted] RARE BUT INEVITABLE ERRORS IN REPRODUCTION, ERRORS THAT OCCASIONALLY PROVE [redacted] SURVIVAL [redacted]
THE HOST ORGANISM REMAINS A [redacted]. IF THE VIRUS IS TOO POTENT, THE HOST ORGANISM IS WIPED [redacted] VIRUS CAN SPREAD. IF THE [redacted] IS TOO POWERFUL, THE VIRUS IS WIPED OUT BEFORE TAKING HOLD. AN EFFECTIVE VIRUS THEREFORE NEEDS TO EVOLVE IN BALANCE WITH THE DEFENCES OF HOST ORGANISMS, AN EVOLUTION THAT CANNOT BE [redacted]

VIRUSES EVOLVE FASTER THAN HUMANS, PRODUCING THOUSANDS OF OFFSPRING DAILY. THE AVERAGE WESTERN MAN HAS 2.4 DESCENDANTS EVERY 20 OR MORE YEARS. IN NORMAL CIRCUMSTANCES IT WOULD

CNTD.

Reviewed by: [handwritten initials and date]

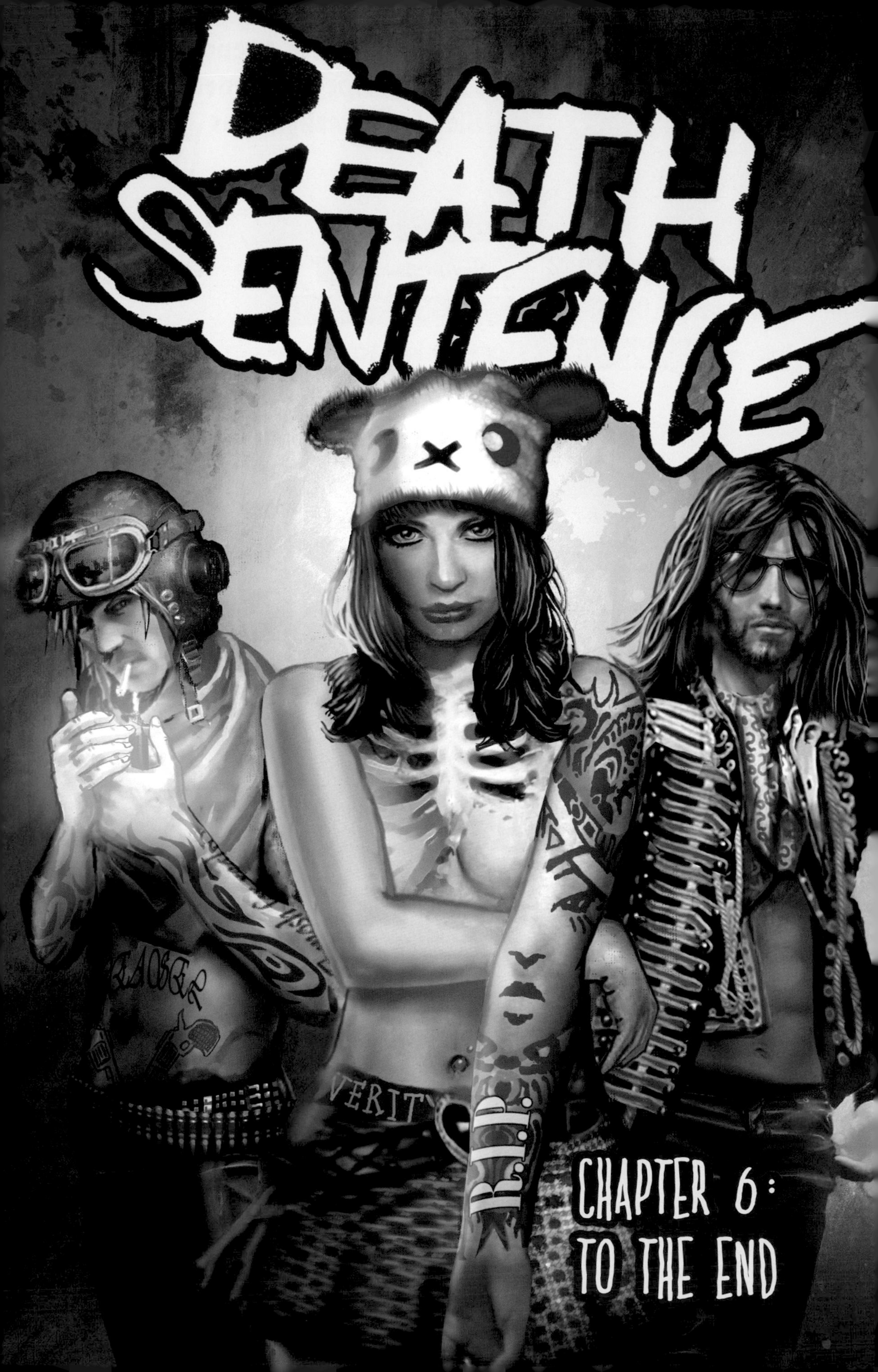
DEATH SENTENCE
CHAPTER 6:
TO THE END

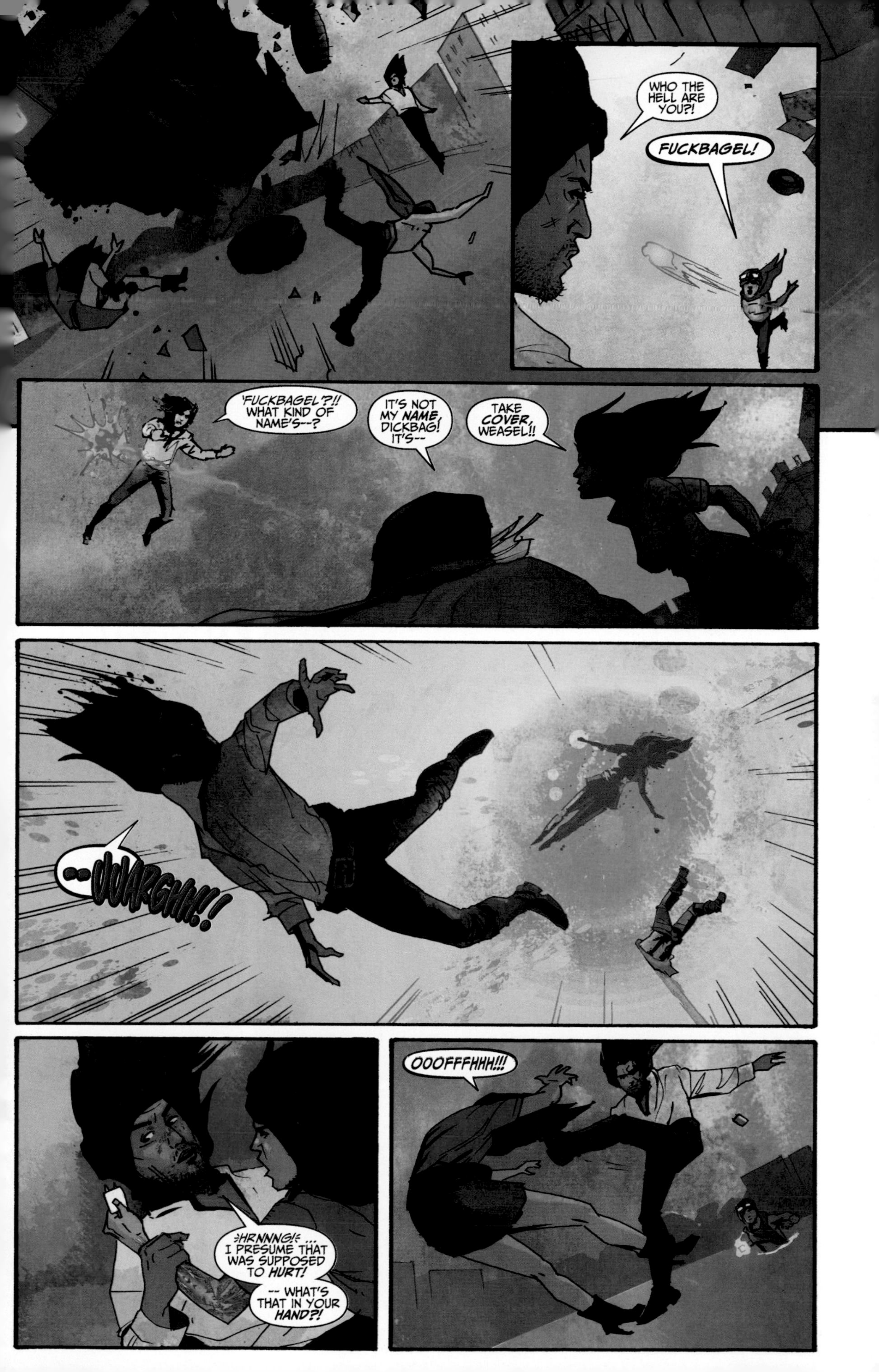
WHO THE HELL ARE YOU?!
FUCKBAGEL!
'FUCKBAGEL'?!! WHAT KIND OF NAME'S--?
IT'S NOT MY NAME, DICKBAG! IT'S--
TAKE COVER, WEASEL!!
--UUARGHH!!
HRNNNG! ... I PRESUME THAT WAS SUPPOSED TO HURT!
-- WHAT'S THAT IN YOUR HAND?!
OOOFFFHHH!!!

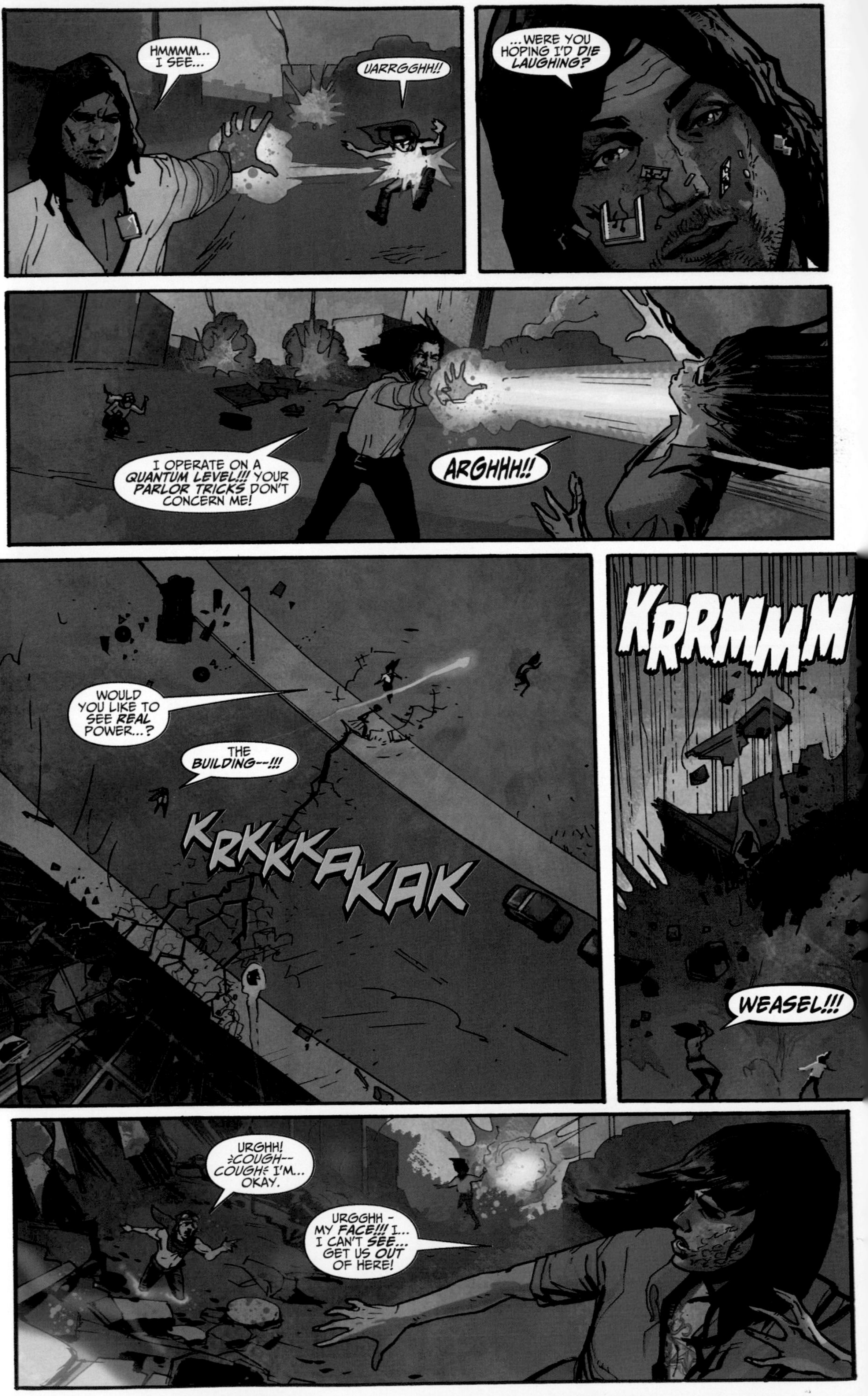
HMMMM... I SEE...
UARRGGHH!!
...WERE YOU HOPING I'D DIE LAUGHING?
I OPERATE ON A QUANTUM LEVEL!!! YOUR PARLOR TRICKS DON'T CONCERN ME!
ARGHHH!!
WOULD YOU LIKE TO SEE REAL POWER...?
THE BUILDING--!!!
KRKKKAKAK
KRRMMM
WEASEL!!!
URGHH! COUGH--COUGH I'M... OKAY.
URGGHH - MY FACE!!! I... I CAN'T SEE... GET US OUT OF HERE!

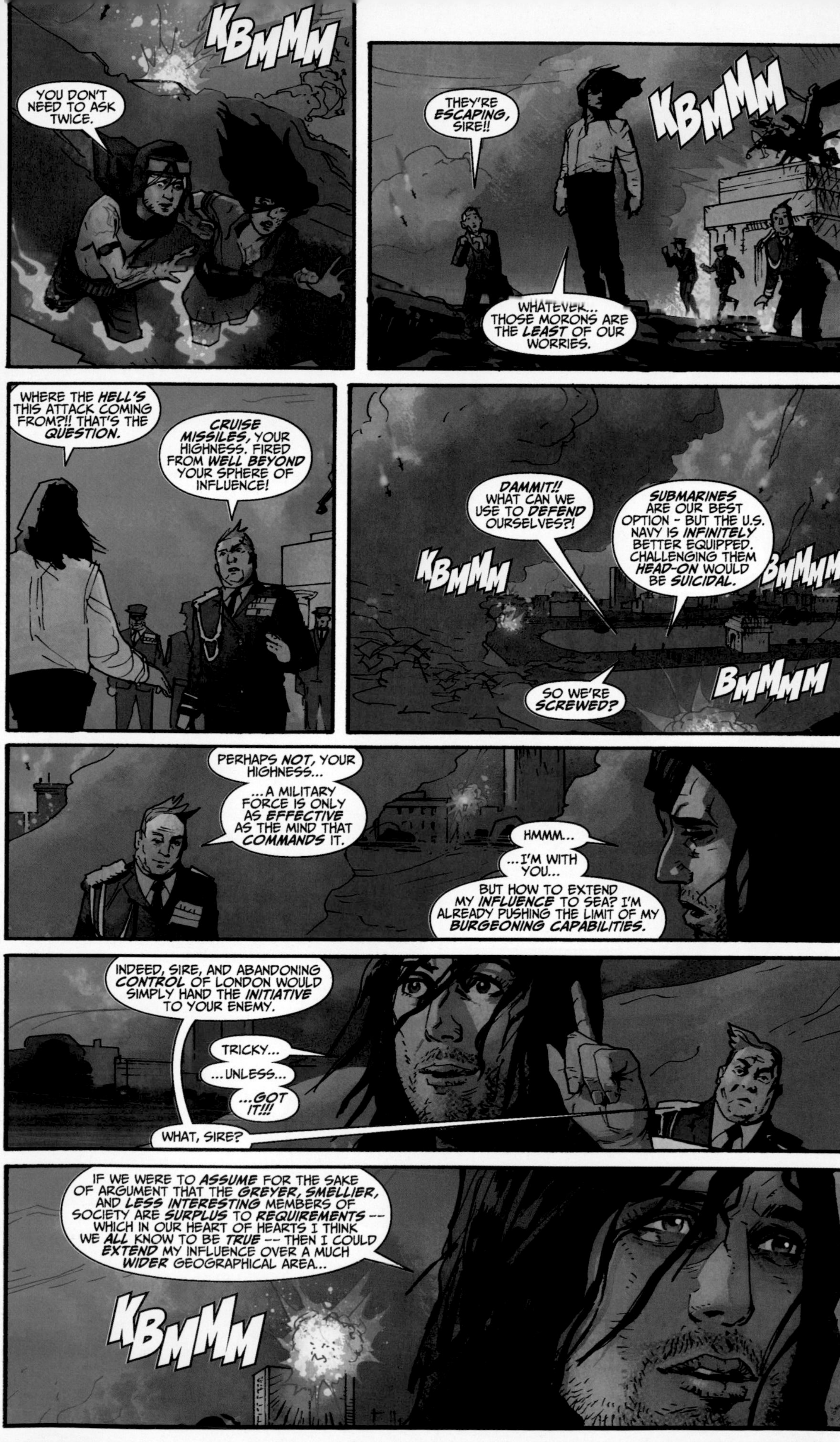
KBMMM
YOU DON'T NEED TO ASK TWICE.
THEY'RE ESCAPING, SIRE!!
KBMMM
WHATEVER... THOSE MORONS ARE THE LEAST OF OUR WORRIES.
WHERE THE HELL'S THIS ATTACK COMING FROM?!! THAT'S THE QUESTION.
CRUISE MISSILES, YOUR HIGHNESS. FIRED FROM WELL BEYOND YOUR SPHERE OF INFLUENCE!
DAMMIT!! WHAT CAN WE USE TO DEFEND OURSELVES?!
SUBMARINES ARE OUR BEST OPTION - BUT THE U.S. NAVY IS INFINITELY BETTER EQUIPPED. CHALLENGING THEM HEAD-ON WOULD BE SUICIDAL.
KBMMM
BMMMM
SO WE'RE SCREWED?
BMMMM
PERHAPS NOT, YOUR HIGHNESS...
...A MILITARY FORCE IS ONLY AS EFFECTIVE AS THE MIND THAT COMMANDS IT.
HMMM...
...I'M WITH YOU...
BUT HOW TO EXTEND MY INFLUENCE TO SEA? I'M ALREADY PUSHING THE LIMIT OF MY BURGEONING CAPABILITIES.
INDEED, SIRE, AND ABANDONING CONTROL OF LONDON WOULD SIMPLY HAND THE INITIATIVE TO YOUR ENEMY.
TRICKY...
...UNLESS...
...GOT IT!!!
WHAT, SIRE?
IF WE WERE TO ASSUME FOR THE SAKE OF ARGUMENT THAT THE GREYER, SMELLIER, AND LESS INTERESTING MEMBERS OF SOCIETY ARE SURPLUS TO REQUIREMENTS -- WHICH IN OUR HEART OF HEARTS I THINK WE ALL KNOW TO BE TRUE -- THEN I COULD EXTEND MY INFLUENCE OVER A MUCH WIDER GEOGRAPHICAL AREA...
KBMMM

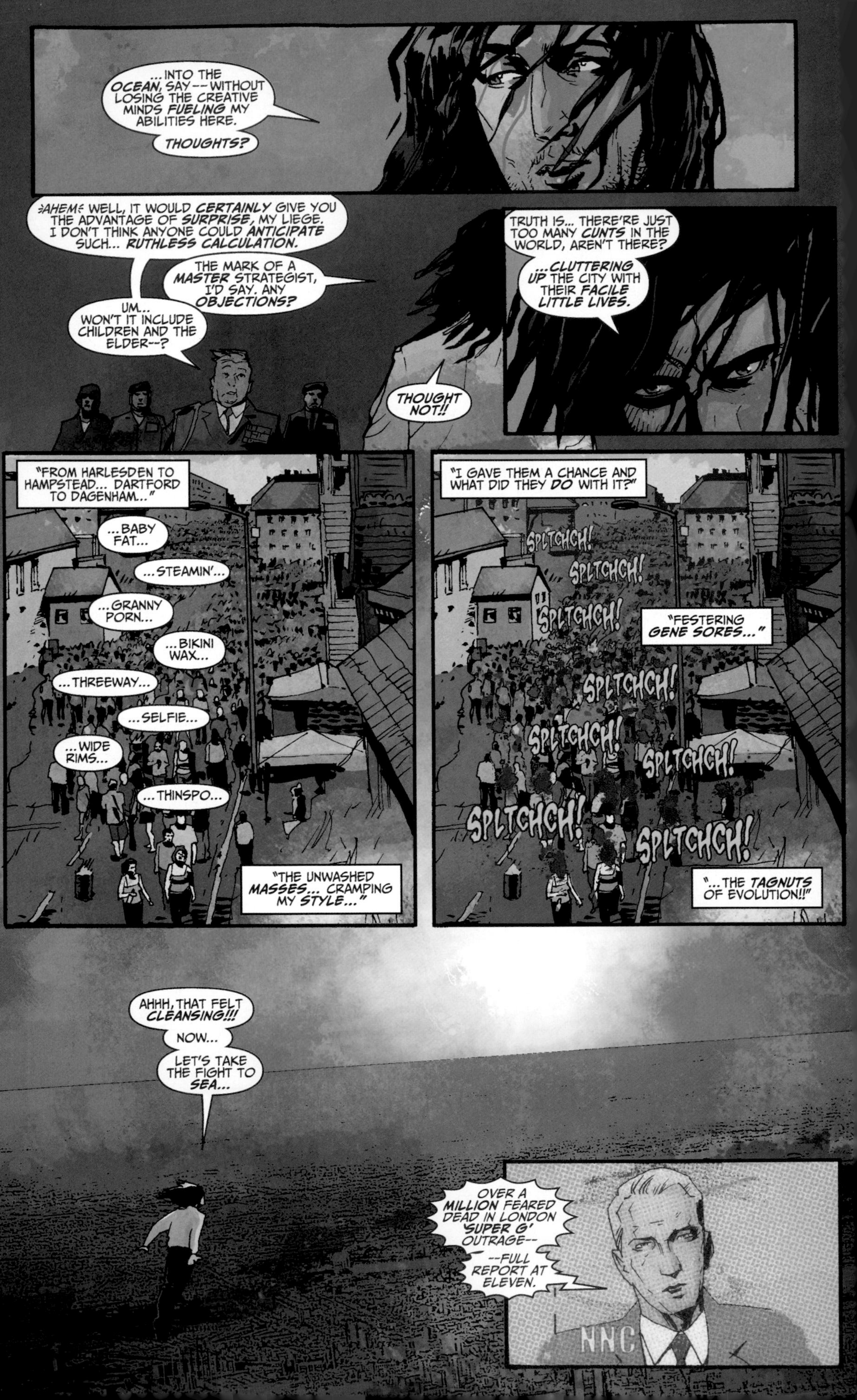
...INTO THE OCEAN, SAY--WITHOUT LOSING THE CREATIVE MINDS FUELING MY ABILITIES HERE.
THOUGHTS?
AHEM WELL, IT WOULD CERTAINLY GIVE YOU THE ADVANTAGE OF SURPRISE, MY LIEGE. I DON'T THINK ANYONE COULD ANTICIPATE SUCH... RUTHLESS CALCULATION.
THE MARK OF A MASTER STRATEGIST, I'D SAY. ANY OBJECTIONS?
UM... WON'T IT INCLUDE CHILDREN AND THE ELDER--?
TRUTH IS... THERE'RE JUST TOO MANY CUNTS IN THE WORLD, AREN'T THERE?
...CLUTTERING UP THE CITY WITH THEIR FACILE LITTLE LIVES.
THOUGHT NOT!!
"FROM HARLESDEN TO HAMPSTEAD... DARTFORD TO DAGENHAM..."
...BABY FAT...
...STEAMIN'...
...GRANNY PORN...
...BIKINI WAX...
...THREEWAY...
...SELFIE...
...WIDE RIMS...
...THINSPO...
"THE UNWASHED MASSES... CRAMPING MY STYLE..."
"I GAVE THEM A CHANCE AND WHAT DID THEY DO WITH IT?"
SPLTCHCH!
SPLTCHCH!
SPLTCHCH!
"FESTERING GENE SORES..."
SPLTCHCH!
SPLTCHCH!
SPLTCHCH!
SPLTCHCH!
SPLTCHCH!
"...THE TAGNUTS OF EVOLUTION!!"
AHHH, THAT FELT CLEANSING!!!
NOW...
LET'S TAKE THE FIGHT TO SEA...
OVER A MILLION FEARED DEAD IN LONDON 'SUPER G' OUTRAGE--
--FULL REPORT AT ELEVEN.
NNC

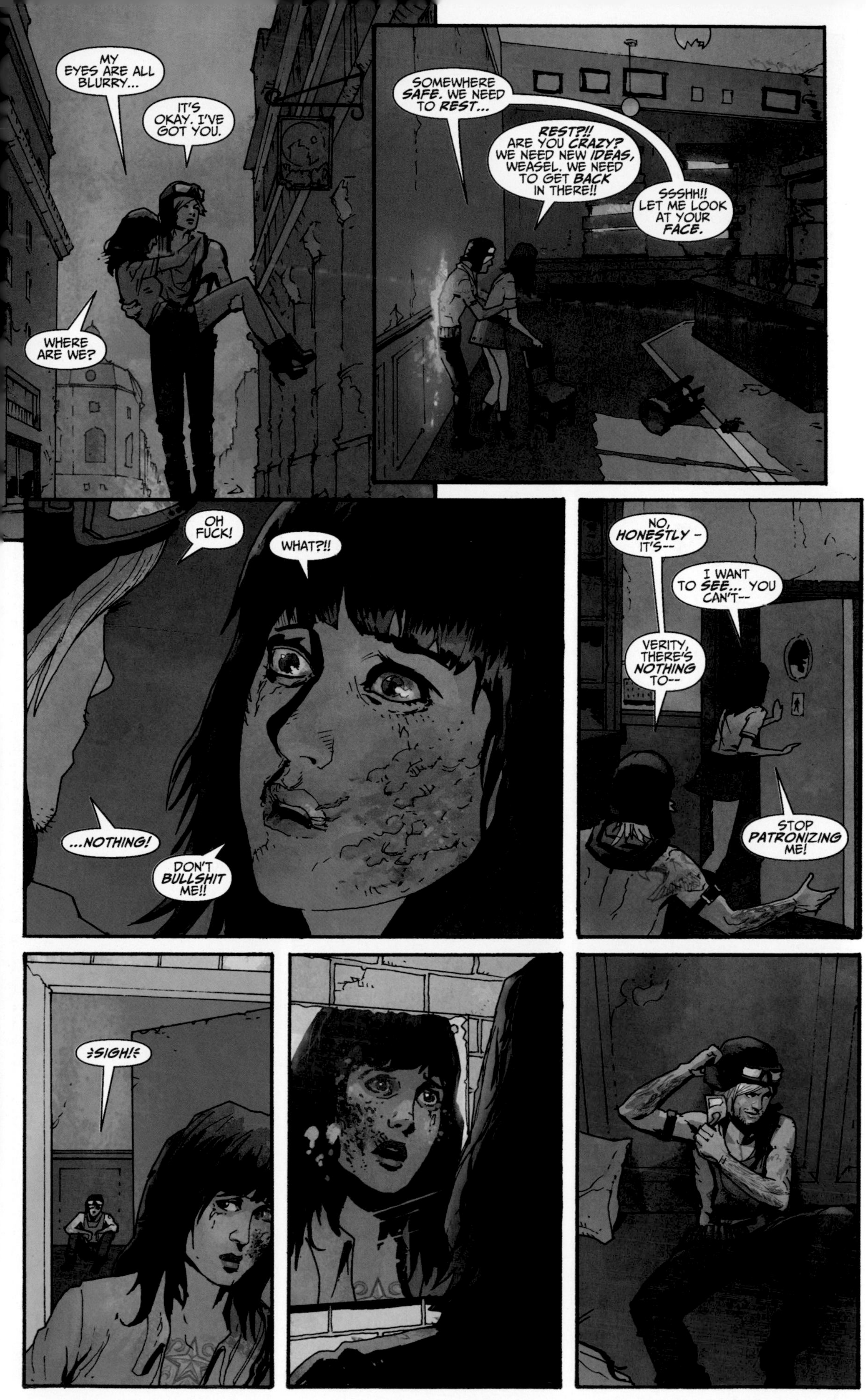

MY EYES ARE ALL BLURRY...
IT'S OKAY. I'VE GOT YOU.
WHERE ARE WE?
SOMEWHERE SAFE. WE NEED TO REST...
REST?!! ARE YOU CRAZY? WE NEED NEW IDEAS, WEASEL. WE NEED TO GET BACK IN THERE!!
SSSHH!! LET ME LOOK AT YOUR FACE.
OH FUCK!
WHAT?!!
...NOTHING!
DON'T BULLSHIT ME!!
NO, HONESTLY - IT'S--
I WANT TO SEE... YOU CAN'T--
VERITY, THERE'S NOTHING TO--
STOP PATRONIZING ME!
SIGH!

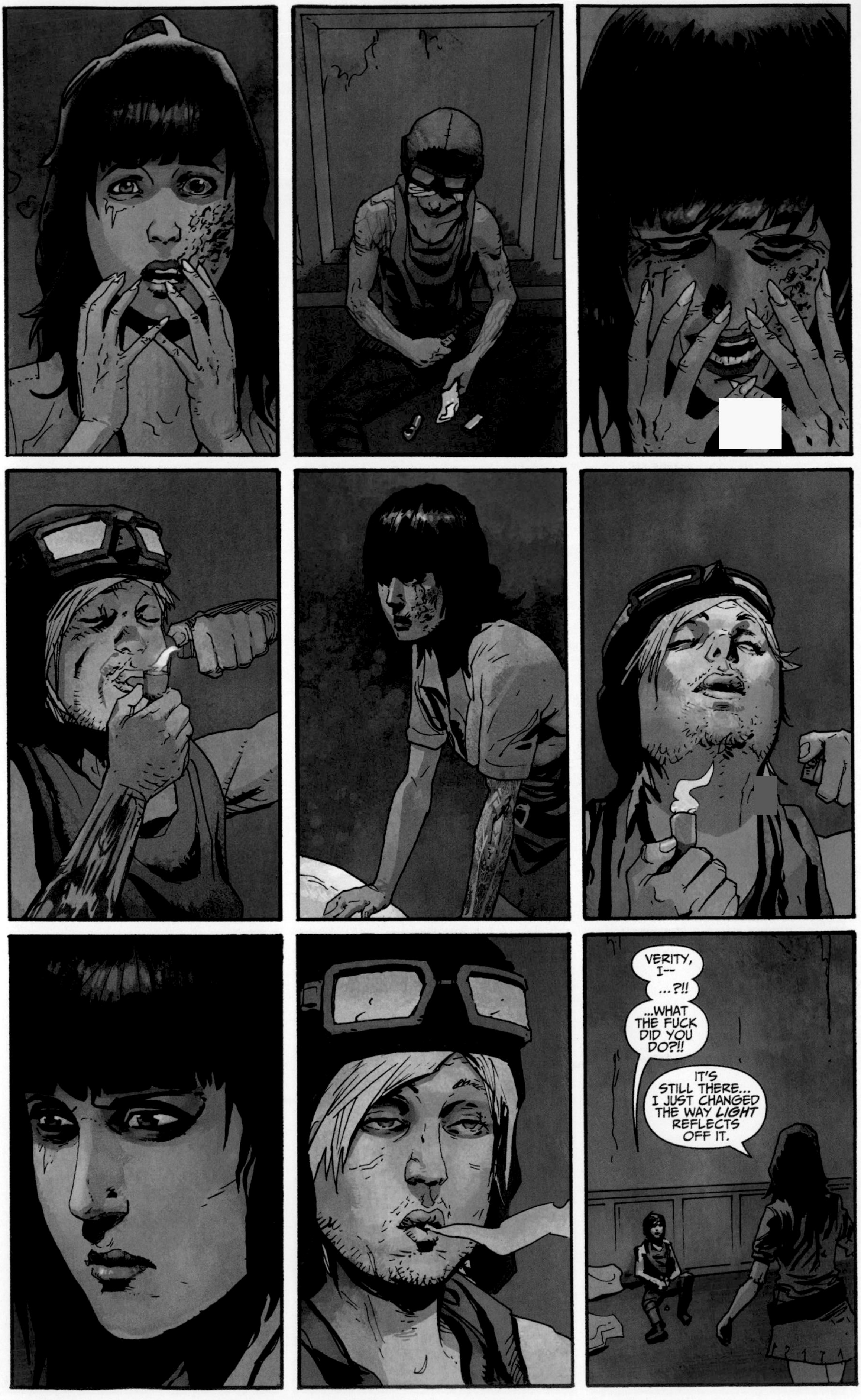
VERITY, I--
...?!!
...WHAT THE FUCK DID YOU DO?!!
IT'S STILL THERE... I JUST CHANGED THE WAY LIGHT REFLECTS OFF IT.

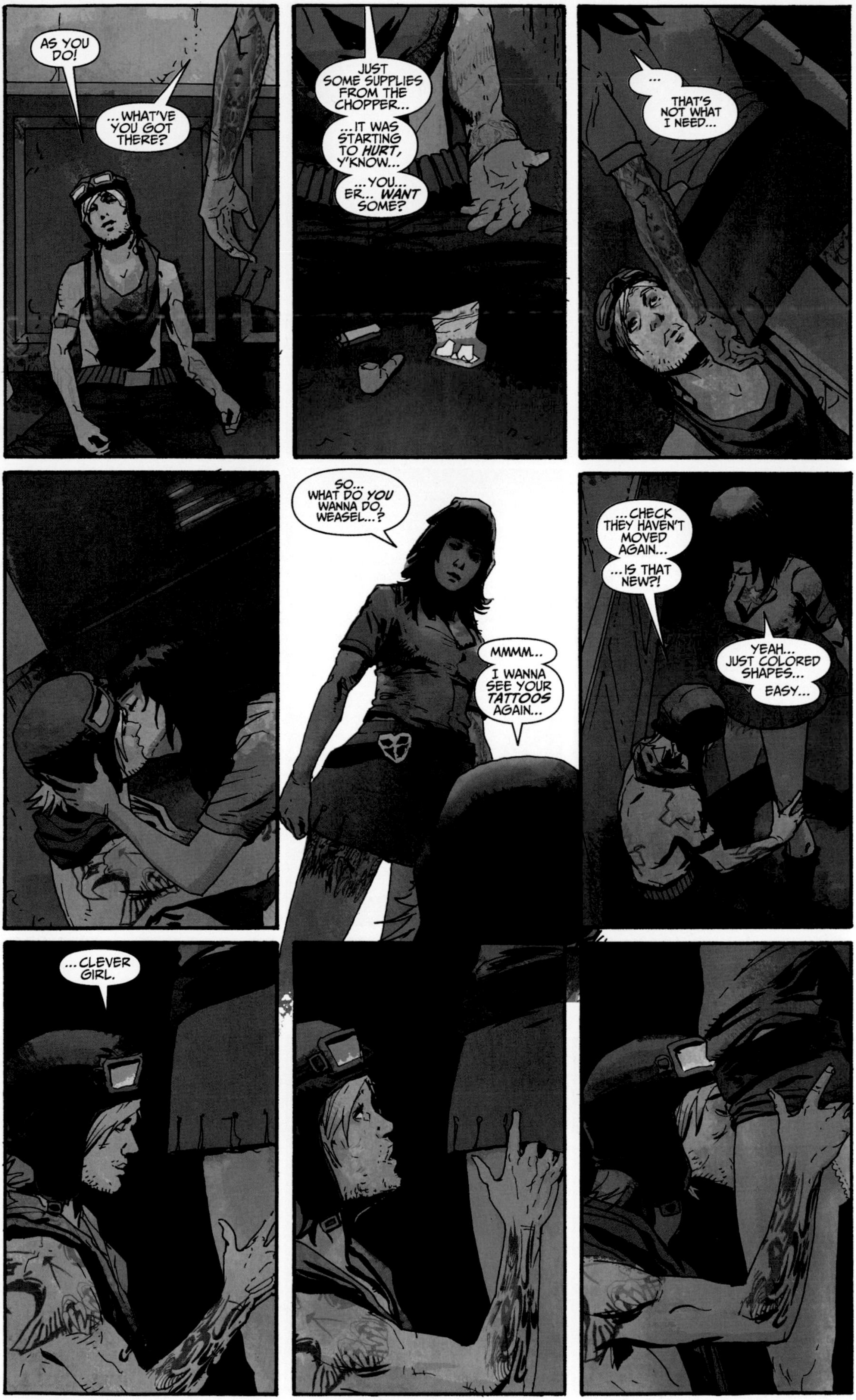
AS YOU DO!
...WHAT'VE YOU GOT THERE?
JUST SOME SUPPLIES FROM THE CHOPPER...
...IT WAS STARTING TO HURT, Y'KNOW...
...YOU... ER... WANT SOME?
...
THAT'S NOT WHAT I NEED...
SO... WHAT DO YOU WANNA DO, WEASEL...?
MMMM...
I WANNA SEE YOUR TATTOOS AGAIN...
...CHECK THEY HAVEN'T MOVED AGAIN...
...IS THAT NEW?!
YEAH... JUST COLORED SHAPES...
EASY...
...CLEVER GIRL.

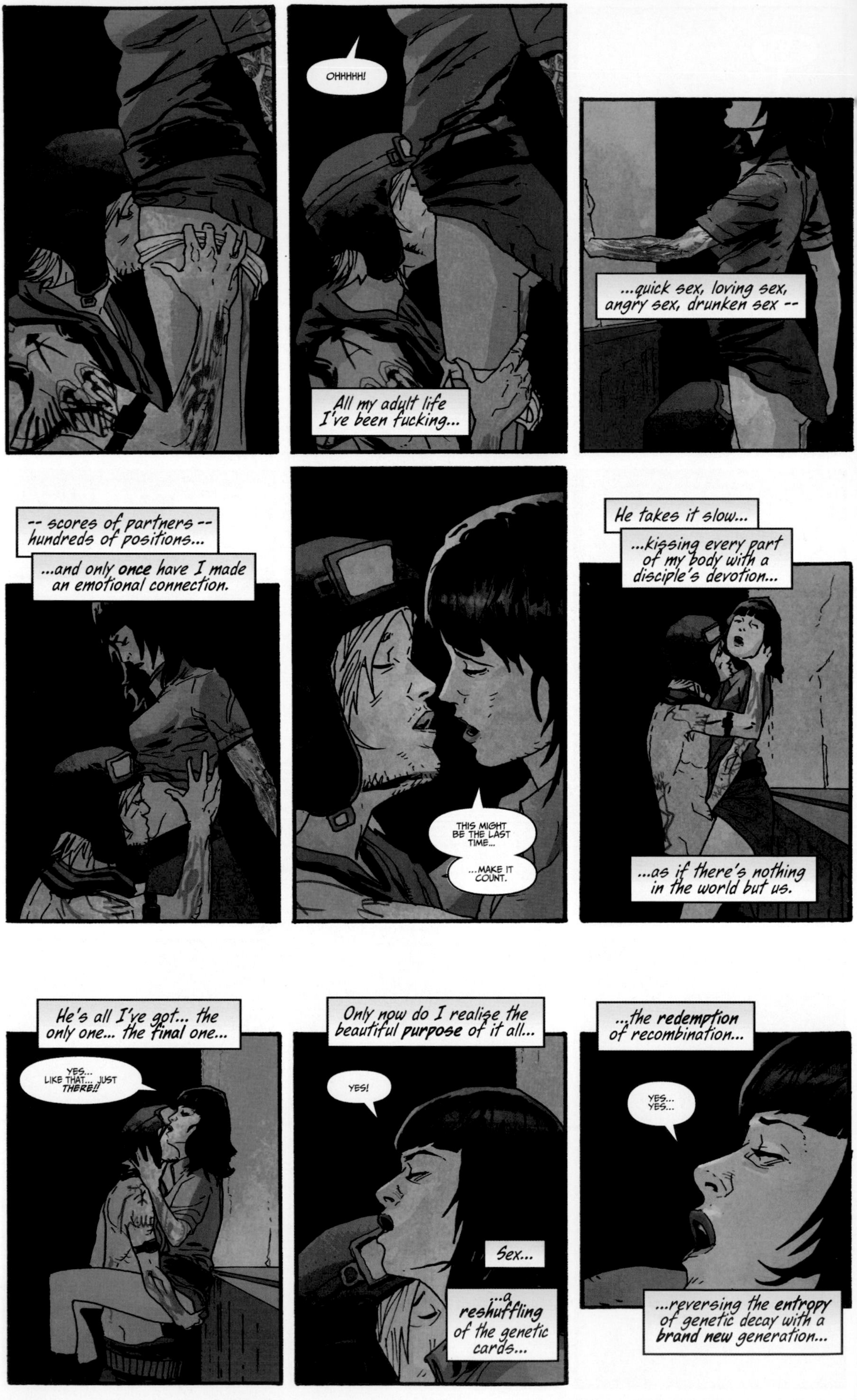
OHHHHH!
All my adult life I've been fucking...
...quick sex, loving sex, angry sex, drunken sex --
-- scores of partners -- hundreds of positions...
...and only **once** have I made an emotional connection.
THIS MIGHT BE THE LAST TIME...
...MAKE IT COUNT.
He takes it slow...
...kissing every part of my body with a disciple's devotion...
...as if there's nothing in the world but us.
He's all I've got... the only one... the final one...
YES... LIKE THAT... JUST *THERE!!*
Only now do I realise the beautiful **purpose** of it all...
YES!
Sex...
...a **reshuffling** of the genetic cards...
...the **redemption** of recombination...
YES... YES...
...reversing the **entropy** of genetic decay with a **brand new** generation...

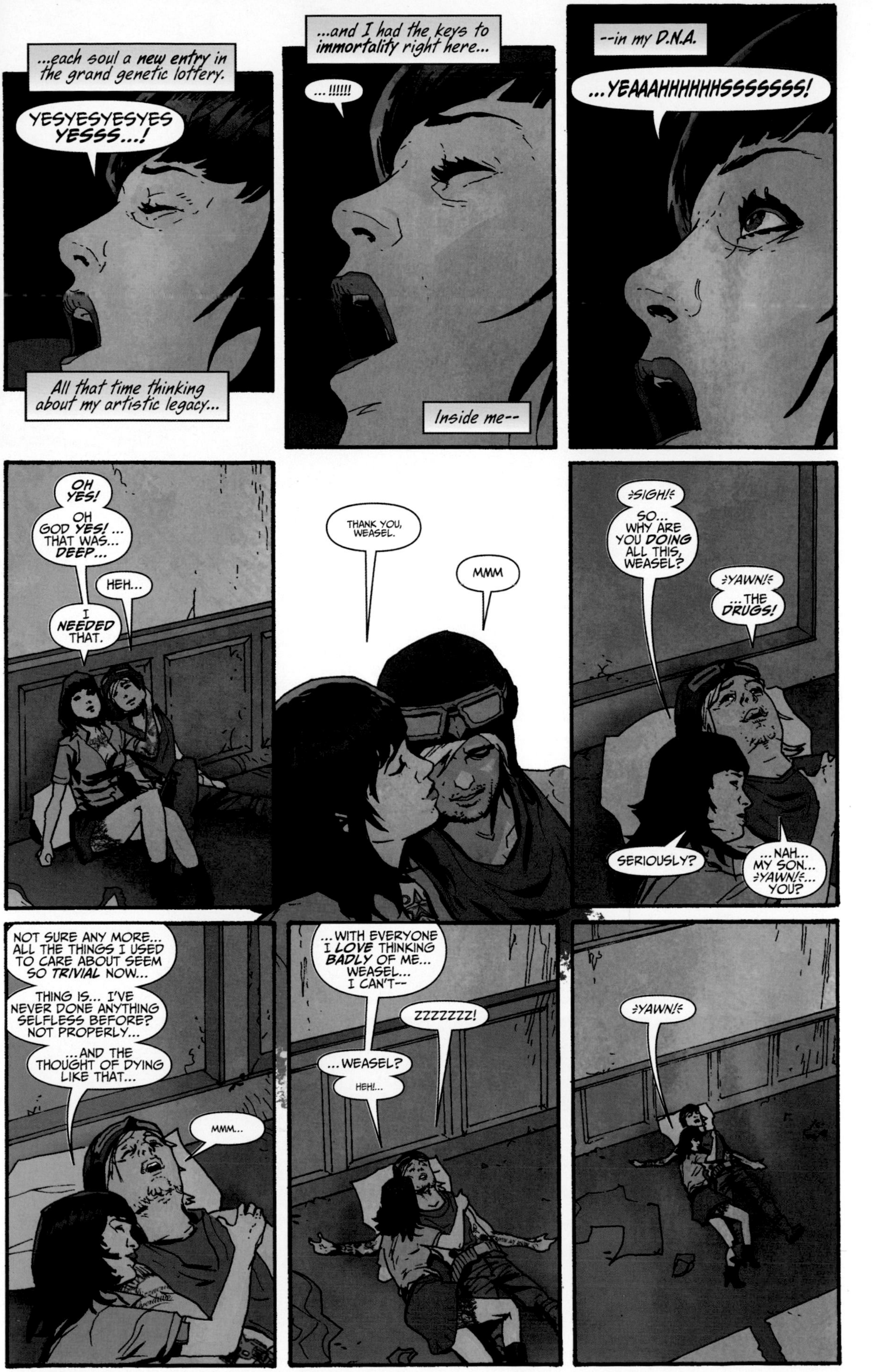
...each soul a new entry in the grand genetic lottery.
YESYESYESYES YESSS...!
All that time thinking about my artistic legacy...
...and I had the keys to immortality right here...
...!!!!!!
Inside me--
--in my D.N.A.
...YEAAAHHHHHHSSSSSSS!
OH YES!
OH GOD YES! ... THAT WAS... DEEP...
HEH...
I NEEDED THAT.
THANK YOU, WEASEL.
MMM
SIGH!
SO... WHY ARE YOU DOING ALL THIS, WEASEL?
YAWN! ...THE DRUGS!
SERIOUSLY?
...NAH... MY SON... *YAWN!*... YOU?
NOT SURE ANY MORE... ALL THE THINGS I USED TO CARE ABOUT SEEM SO TRIVIAL NOW...
THING IS... I'VE NEVER DONE ANYTHING SELFLESS BEFORE? NOT PROPERLY...
...AND THE THOUGHT OF DYING LIKE THAT...
MMM...
...WITH EVERYONE I LOVE THINKING BADLY OF ME... WEASEL... I CAN'T--
ZZZZZZZ!
...WEASEL?
HEH!...
YAWN!

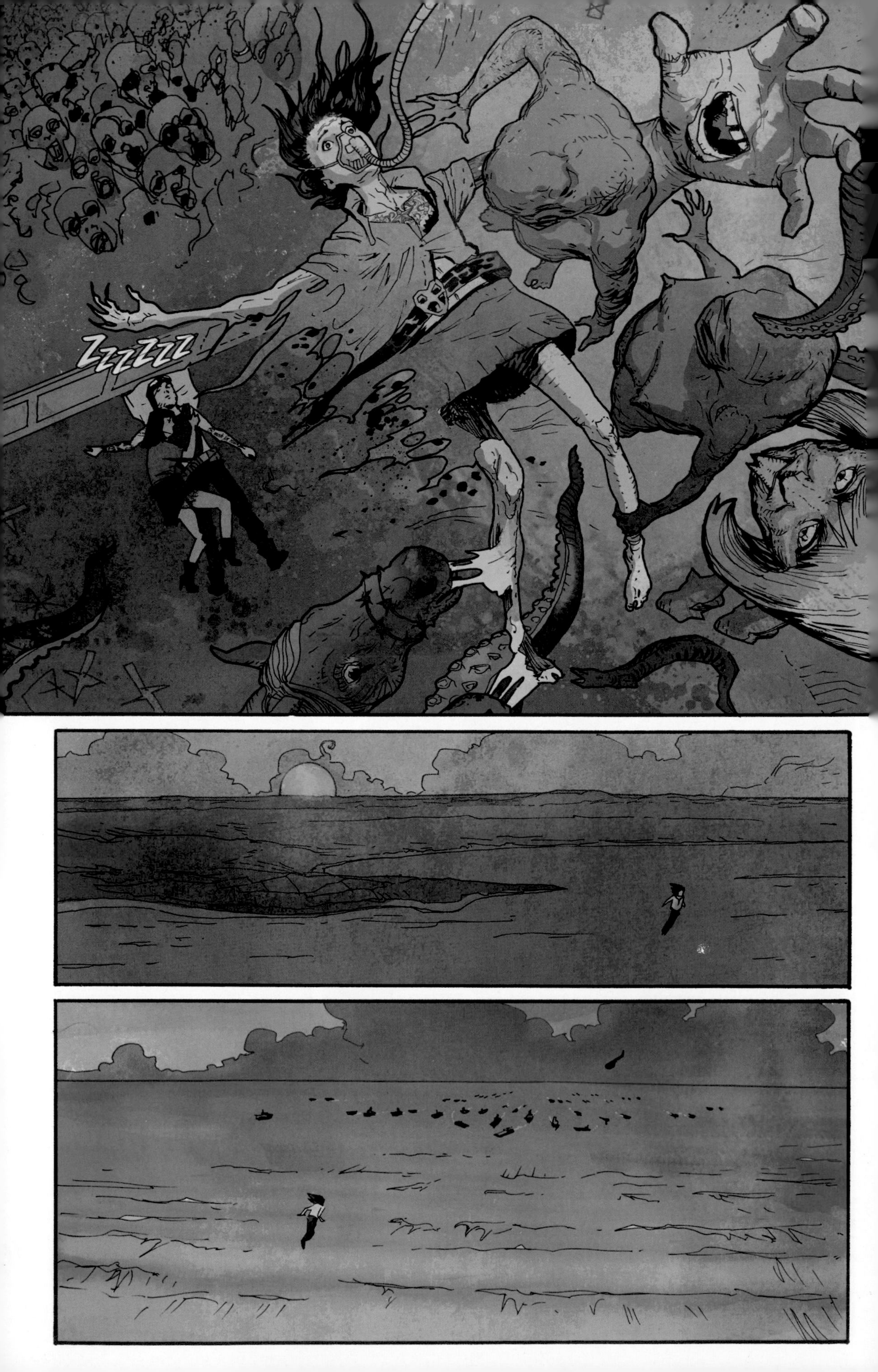
ZzzZzzz

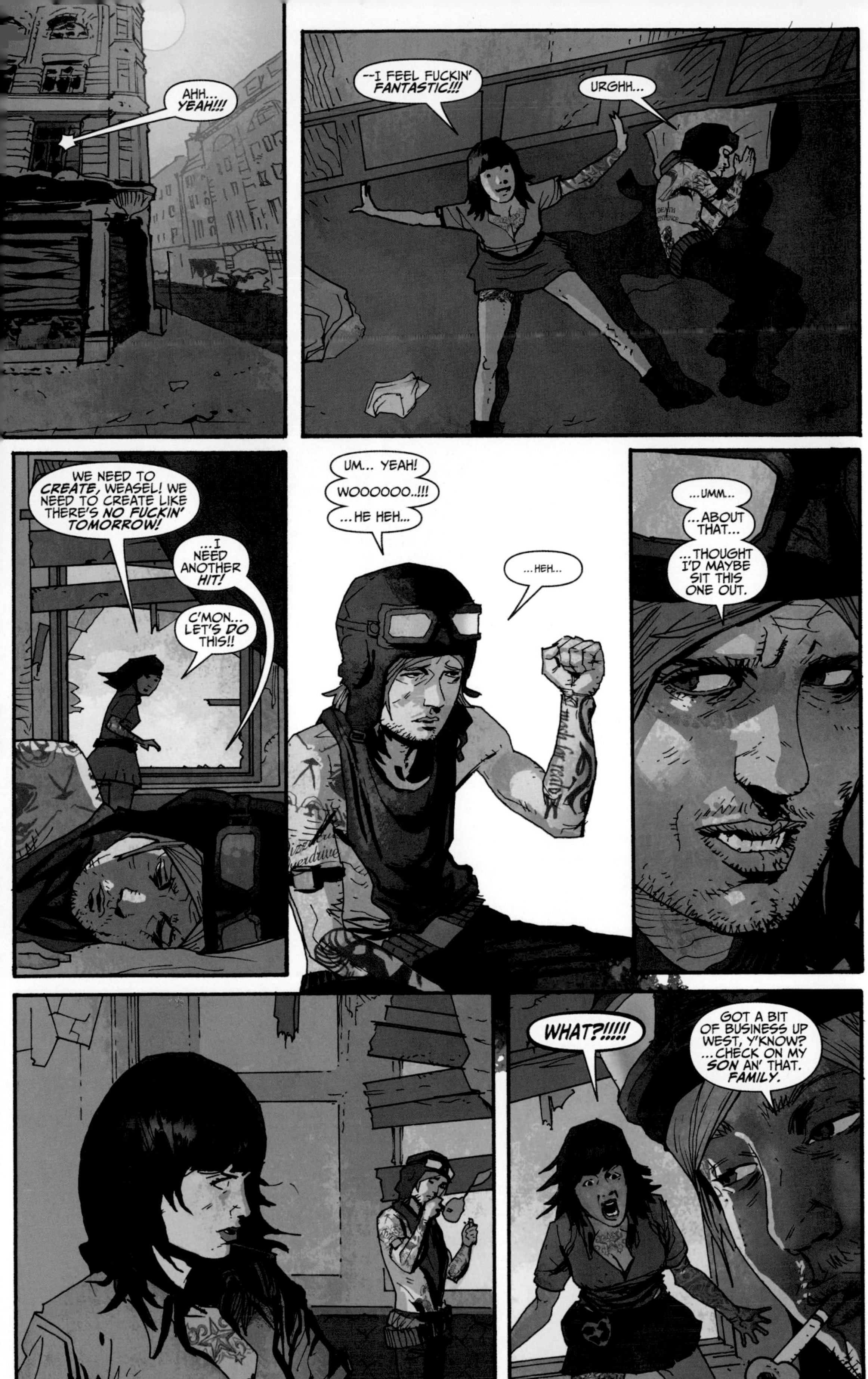

AHH... YEAH!!!
--I FEEL FUCKIN' FANTASTIC!!!
URGHH...
WE NEED TO CREATE, WEASEL! WE NEED TO CREATE LIKE THERE'S NO FUCKIN' TOMORROW!
...I NEED ANOTHER HIT!
C'MON... LET'S DO THIS!!
UM... YEAH!
WOOOOOO..!!!
...HE HEH...
...HEH...
...UMM...
...ABOUT THAT...
...THOUGHT I'D MAYBE SIT THIS ONE OUT.
WHAT?!!!!!
GOT A BIT OF BUSINESS UP WEST, Y'KNOW? ...CHECK ON MY SON AN' THAT. FAMILY.

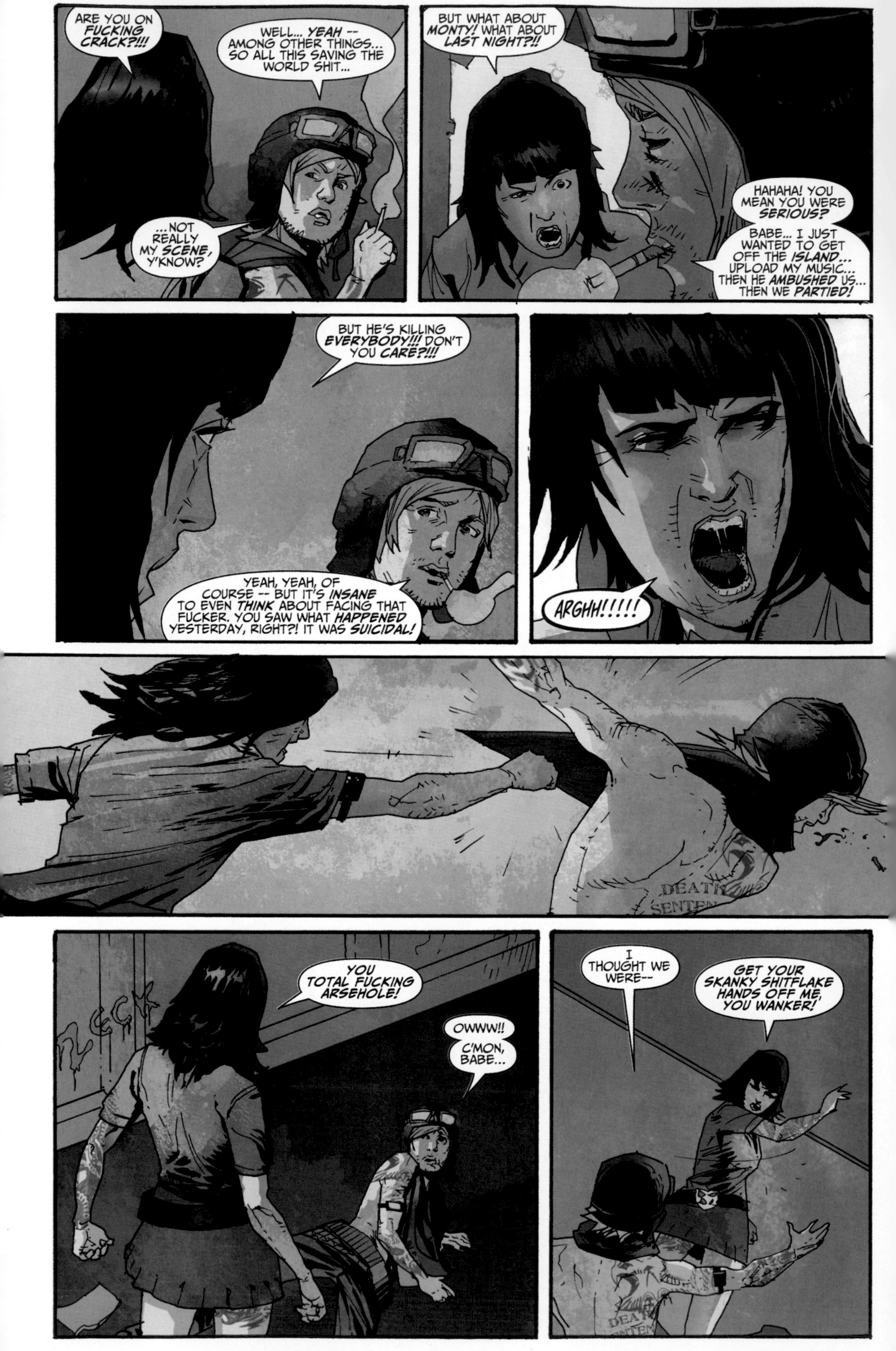
ARE YOU ON FUCKING CRACK?!!!
WELL... YEAH -- AMONG OTHER THINGS... SO ALL THIS SAVING THE WORLD SHIT...
...NOT REALLY MY SCENE, Y'KNOW?
BUT WHAT ABOUT MONTY! WHAT ABOUT LAST NIGHT?!!
HAHAHA! YOU MEAN YOU WERE SERIOUS?
BABE... I JUST WANTED TO GET OFF THE ISLAND... UPLOAD MY MUSIC... THEN HE AMBUSHED US... THEN WE PARTIED!
BUT HE'S KILLING EVERYBODY!!! DON'T YOU CARE?!!!
YEAH, YEAH, OF COURSE -- BUT IT'S INSANE TO EVEN THINK ABOUT FACING THAT FUCKER. YOU SAW WHAT HAPPENED YESTERDAY, RIGHT?! IT WAS SUICIDAL!
ARGHH!!!!!
DEATH SENTEN
YOU TOTAL FUCKING ARSEHOLE!
OWWW!! C'MON, BABE...
I THOUGHT WE WERE--
GET YOUR SKANKY SHITFLAKE HANDS OFF ME, YOU WANKER!

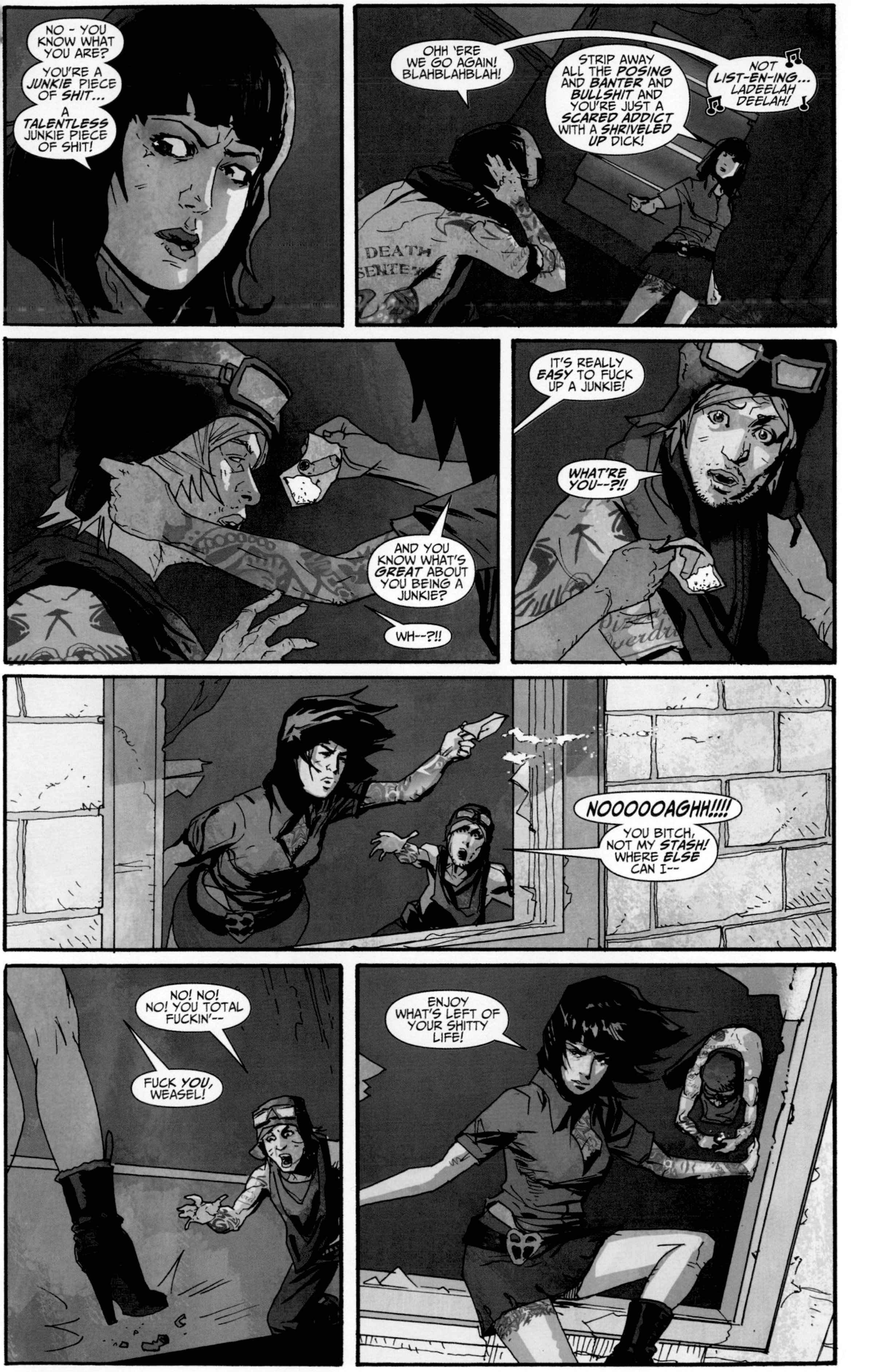
NO - YOU KNOW WHAT YOU ARE?
YOU'RE A JUNKIE PIECE OF SHIT...
A TALENTLESS JUNKIE PIECE OF SHIT!
OHH 'ERE WE GO AGAIN! BLAHBLAHBLAH!
STRIP AWAY ALL THE POSING AND BANTER AND BULLSHIT AND YOU'RE JUST A SCARED ADDICT WITH A SHRIVELED UP DICK!
NOT LIST-EN-ING... LADEELAH DEELAH!
DEATH SENTE
AND YOU KNOW WHAT'S GREAT ABOUT YOU BEING A JUNKIE?
WH--?!!
IT'S REALLY EASY TO FUCK UP A JUNKIE!
WHAT'RE YOU--?!!
NOOOOOAGHH!!!!
YOU BITCH, NOT MY STASH! WHERE ELSE CAN I--
NO! NO! NO! YOU TOTAL FUCKIN'--
FUCK YOU, WEASEL!
ENJOY WHAT'S LEFT OF YOUR SHITTY LIFE!

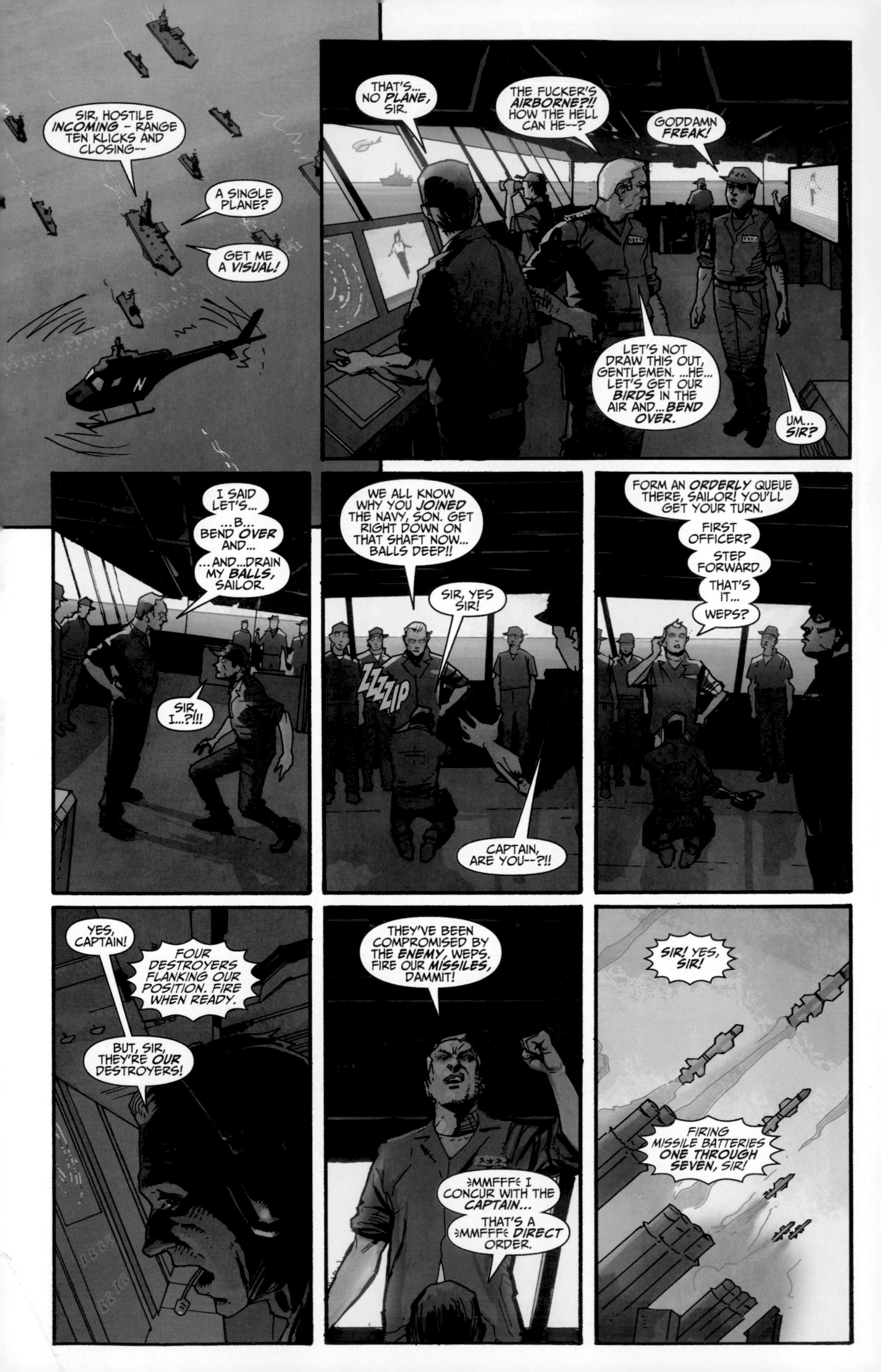
SIR, HOSTILE INCOMING – RANGE TEN KLICKS AND CLOSING--
A SINGLE PLANE?
GET ME A VISUAL!
THAT'S... NO PLANE, SIR.
THE FUCKER'S AIRBORNE?!! HOW THE HELL CAN HE--?
GODDAMN FREAK!
LET'S NOT DRAW THIS OUT, GENTLEMEN. ...HE... LET'S GET OUR BIRDS IN THE AIR AND...BEND OVER.
UM... SIR?
I SAID LET'S...
...B... BEND OVER AND...
...AND...DRAIN MY BALLS, SAILOR.
SIR, I...?!!!
WE ALL KNOW WHY YOU JOINED THE NAVY, SON. GET RIGHT DOWN ON THAT SHAFT NOW... BALLS DEEP!!
SIR, YES SIR!
ZZZZIP
CAPTAIN, ARE YOU--?!!
FORM AN ORDERLY QUEUE THERE, SAILOR! YOU'LL GET YOUR TURN.
FIRST OFFICER?
STEP FORWARD.
THAT'S IT...
WEPS?
YES, CAPTAIN!
FOUR DESTROYERS FLANKING OUR POSITION. FIRE WHEN READY.
BUT, SIR, THEY'RE OUR DESTROYERS!
THEY'VE BEEN COMPROMISED BY THE ENEMY, WEPS. FIRE OUR MISSILES, DAMMIT!
MMFFF I CONCUR WITH THE CAPTAIN...
THAT'S A MMFFF DIRECT ORDER.
SIR! YES, SIR!
FIRING MISSILE BATTERIES ONE THROUGH SEVEN, SIR!

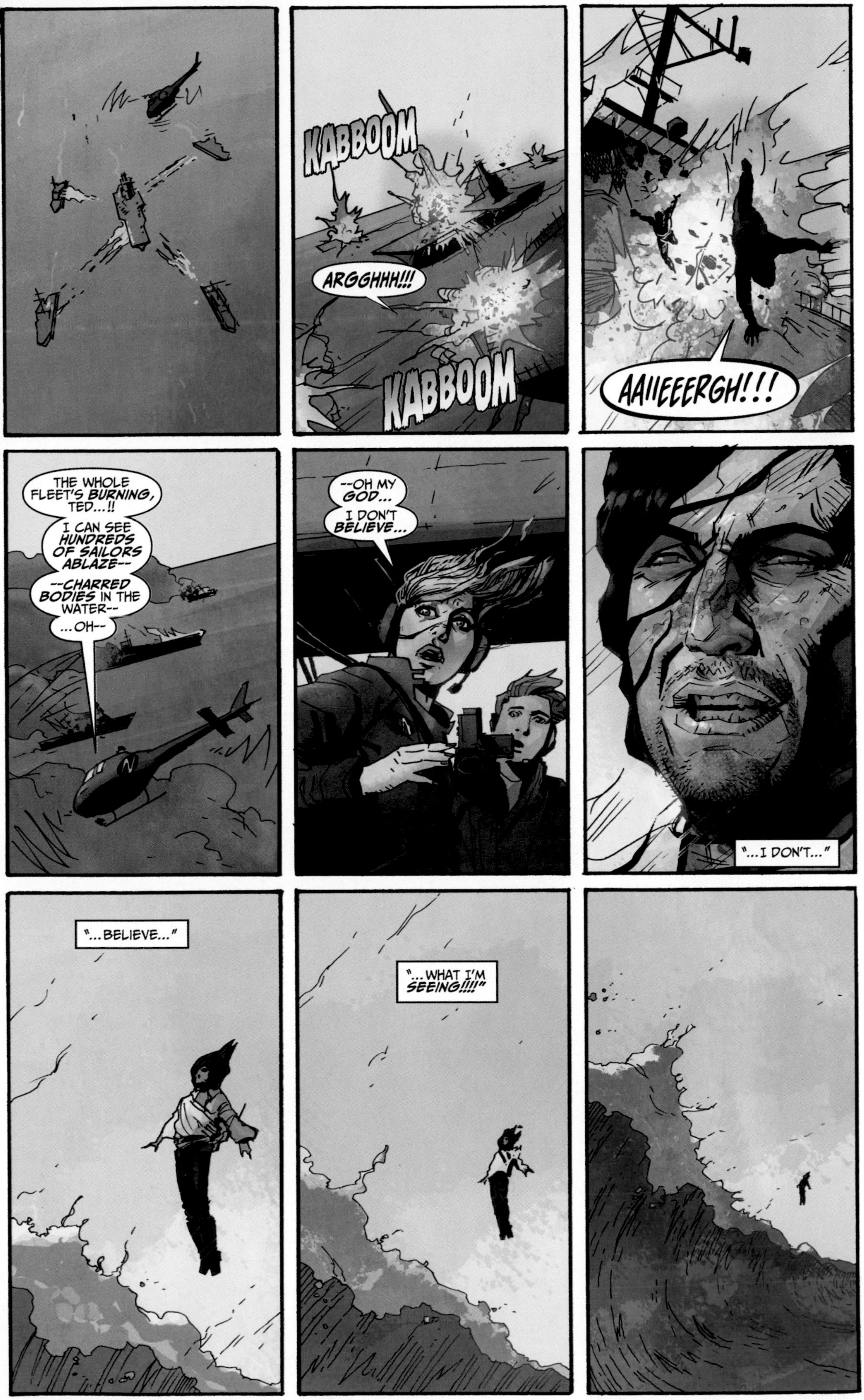
KABBOOM
ARGGHHH!!!
KABBOOM
AAIIEEERGH!!!
THE WHOLE FLEET'S BURNING, TED...!!
I CAN SEE HUNDREDS OF SAILORS ABLAZE--
--CHARRED BODIES IN THE WATER--
...OH--
--OH MY GOD... I DON'T BELIEVE...
"...I DON'T..."
"...BELIEVE..."
"...WHAT I'M SEEING!!!!"

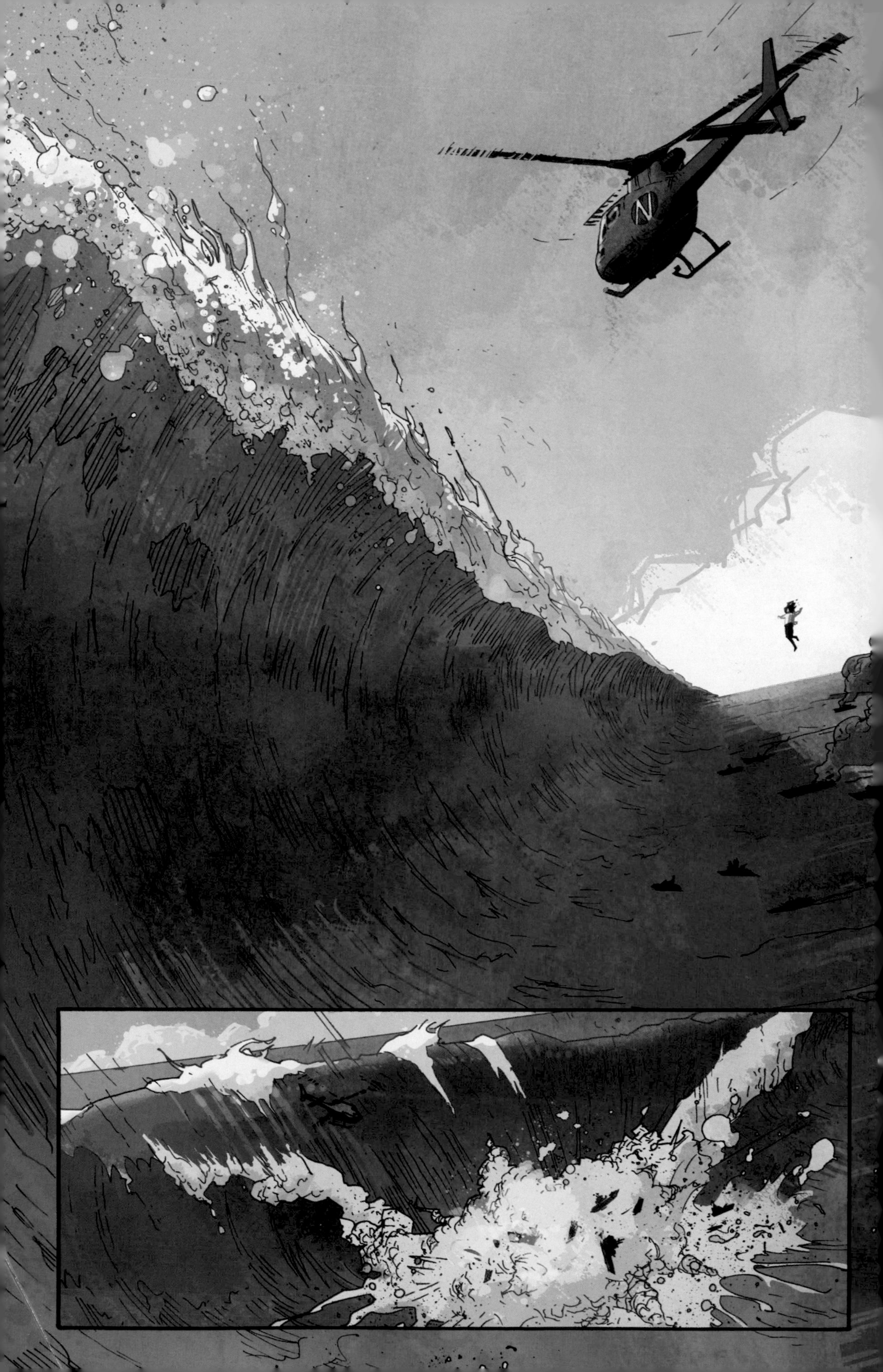

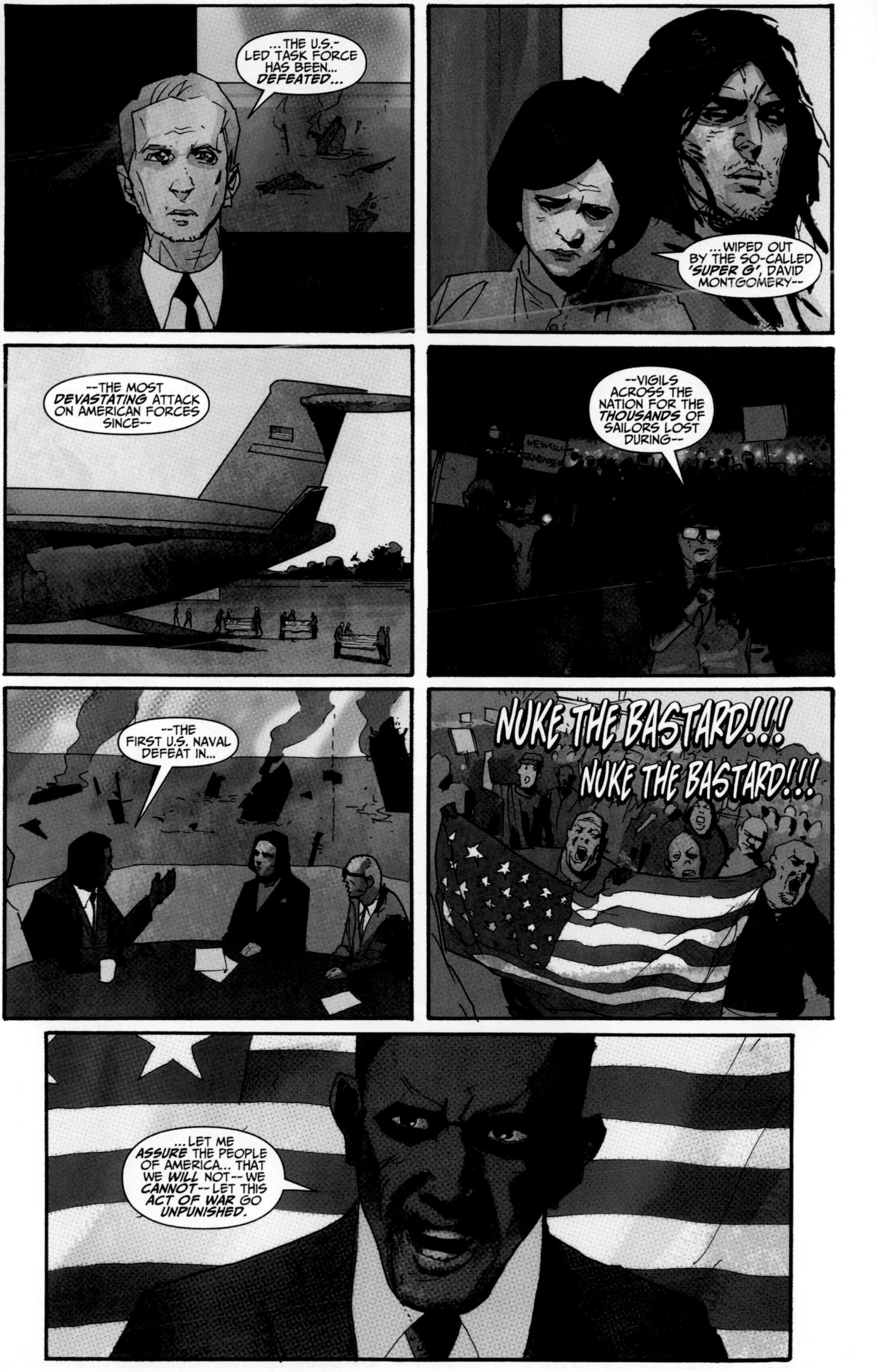
...THE U.S.-LED TASK FORCE HAS BEEN... DEFEATED...
...WIPED OUT BY THE SO-CALLED 'SUPER G', DAVID MONTGOMERY--
--THE MOST DEVASTATING ATTACK ON AMERICAN FORCES SINCE--
--VIGILS ACROSS THE NATION FOR THE THOUSANDS OF SAILORS LOST DURING--
--THE FIRST U.S. NAVAL DEFEAT IN...
NUKE THE BASTARD!!!
NUKE THE BASTARD!!!
...LET ME ASSURE THE PEOPLE OF AMERICA... THAT WE WILL NOT--WE CANNOT--LET THIS ACT OF WAR GO UNPUNISHED.

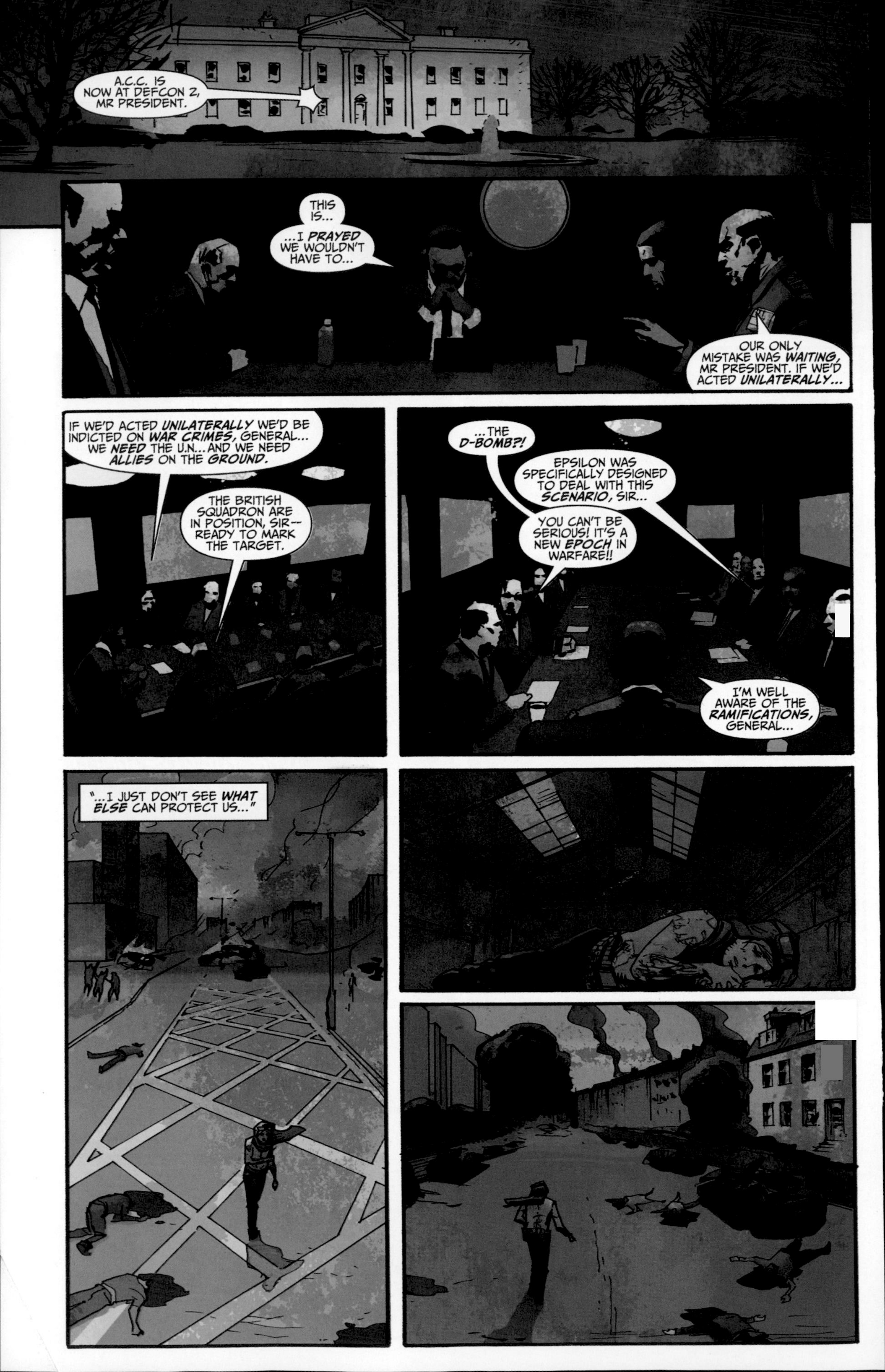
A.C.C. IS NOW AT DEFCON 2, MR PRESIDENT.
THIS IS...
...I PRAYED WE WOULDN'T HAVE TO...
OUR ONLY MISTAKE WAS WAITING, MR PRESIDENT. IF WE'D ACTED UNILATERALLY...
IF WE'D ACTED UNILATERALLY WE'D BE INDICTED ON WAR CRIMES, GENERAL... WE NEED THE U.N... AND WE NEED ALLIES ON THE GROUND.
THE BRITISH SQUADRON ARE IN POSITION, SIR-- READY TO MARK THE TARGET.
...THE D-BOMB?!
EPSILON WAS SPECIFICALLY DESIGNED TO DEAL WITH THIS SCENARIO, SIR...
YOU CAN'T BE SERIOUS! IT'S A NEW EPOCH IN WARFARE!!
I'M WELL AWARE OF THE RAMIFICATIONS, GENERAL...
"...I JUST DON'T SEE WHAT ELSE CAN PROTECT US..."

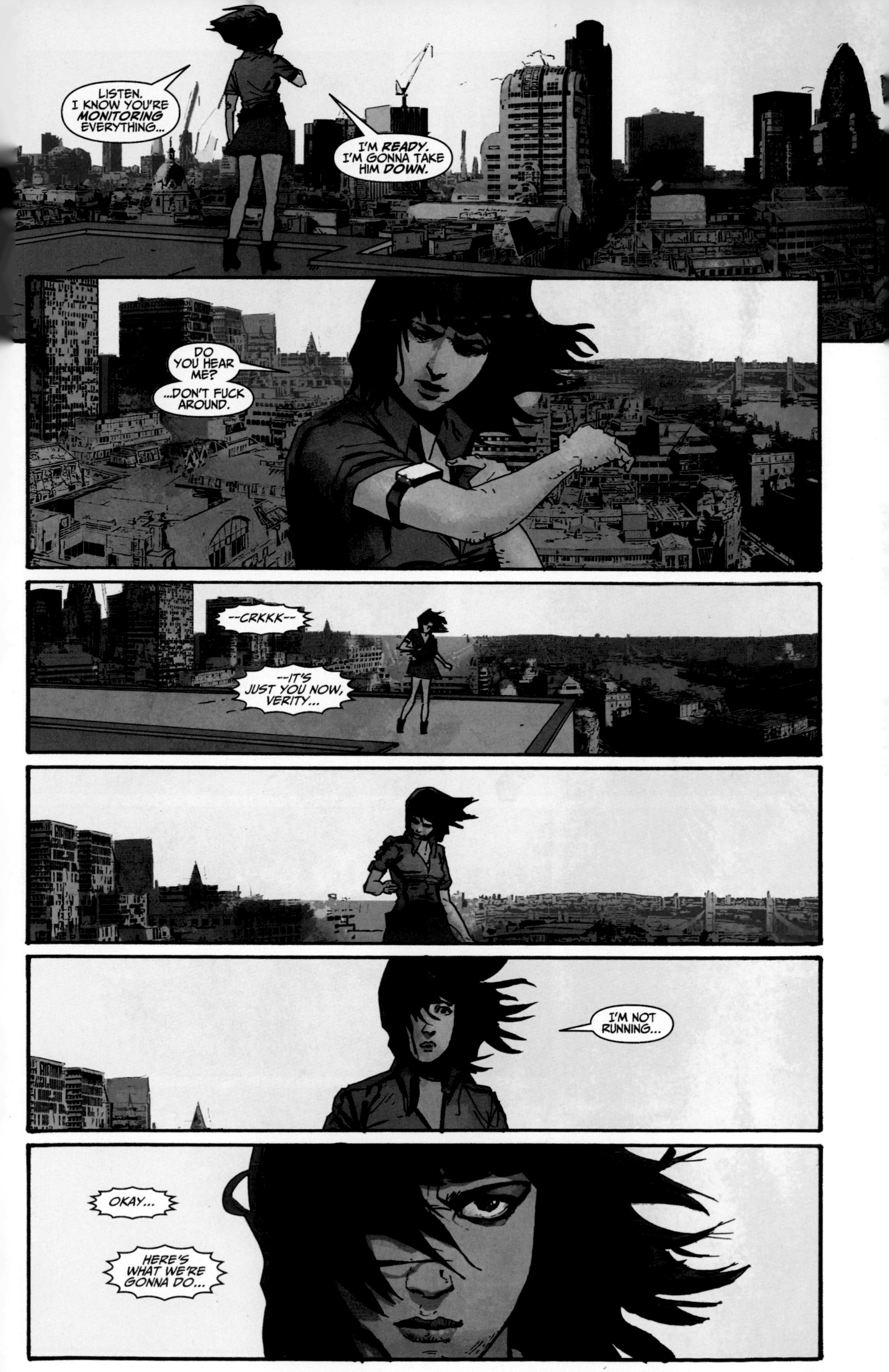
LISTEN. I KNOW YOU'RE MONITORING EVERYTHING...
I'M READY. I'M GONNA TAKE HIM DOWN.
DO YOU HEAR ME? ...DON'T FUCK AROUND.
--CRKKK--
--IT'S JUST YOU NOW, VERITY...
I'M NOT RUNNING...
OKAY...
HERE'S WHAT WE'RE GONNA DO...

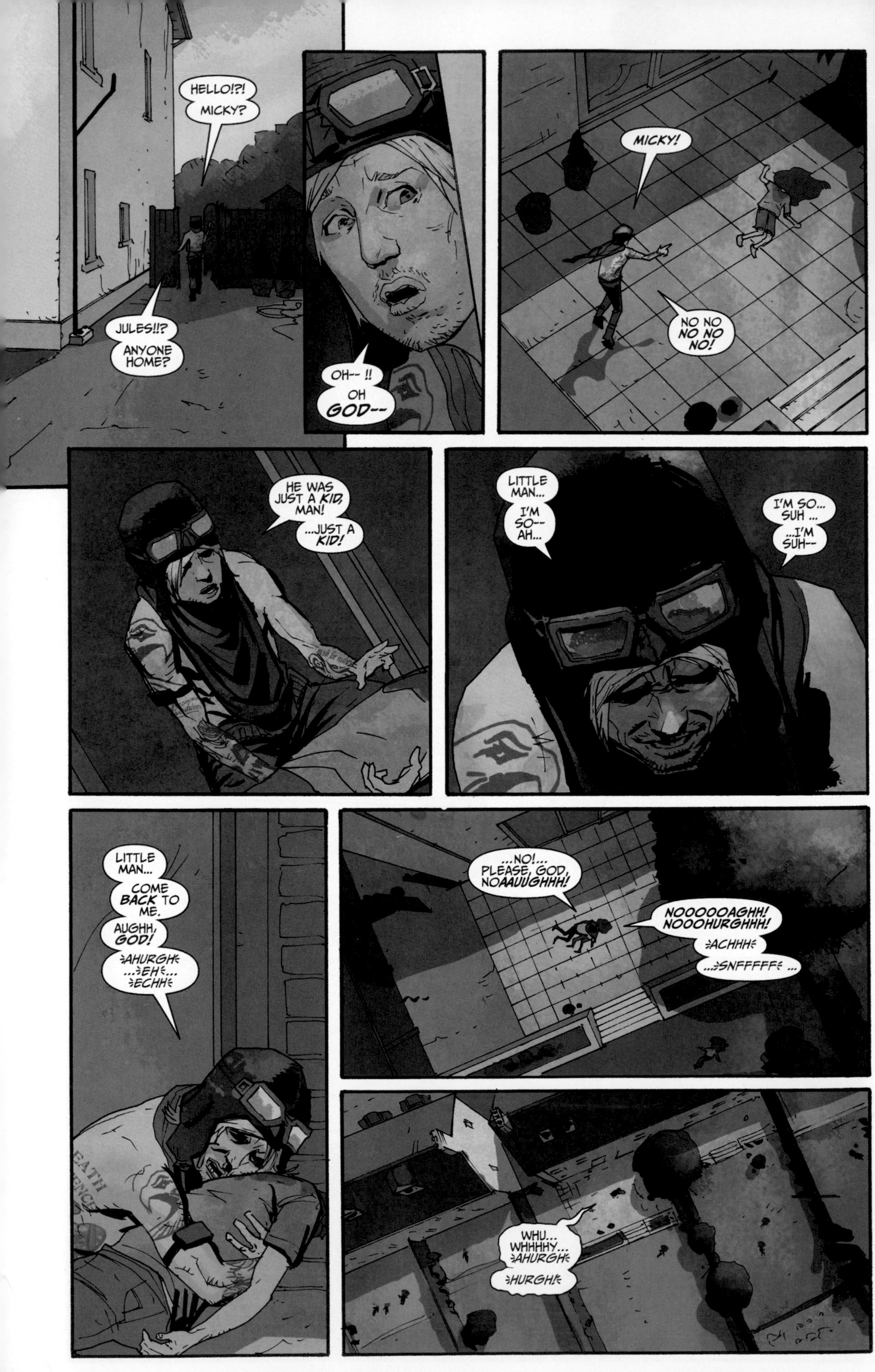
HELLO!?! MICKY?
JULES!!? ANYONE HOME?
OH-- !! OH GOD--
MICKY!
NO NO NO NO NO!
HE WAS JUST A KID, MAN!
...JUST A KID!
LITTLE MAN... I'M SO-- AH...
I'M SO... SUH ...
...I'M SUH--
LITTLE MAN... COME BACK TO ME.
AUGHH, GOD!
AHURGH ...EH... ECHH
...NO!... PLEASE, GOD, NOAAUUGHHH!
NOOOOOAGHH! NOOOHURGHHH!
ACHHH
...SNFFFFF ...
WHU... WHHHHY... AHURGH
HURGH!

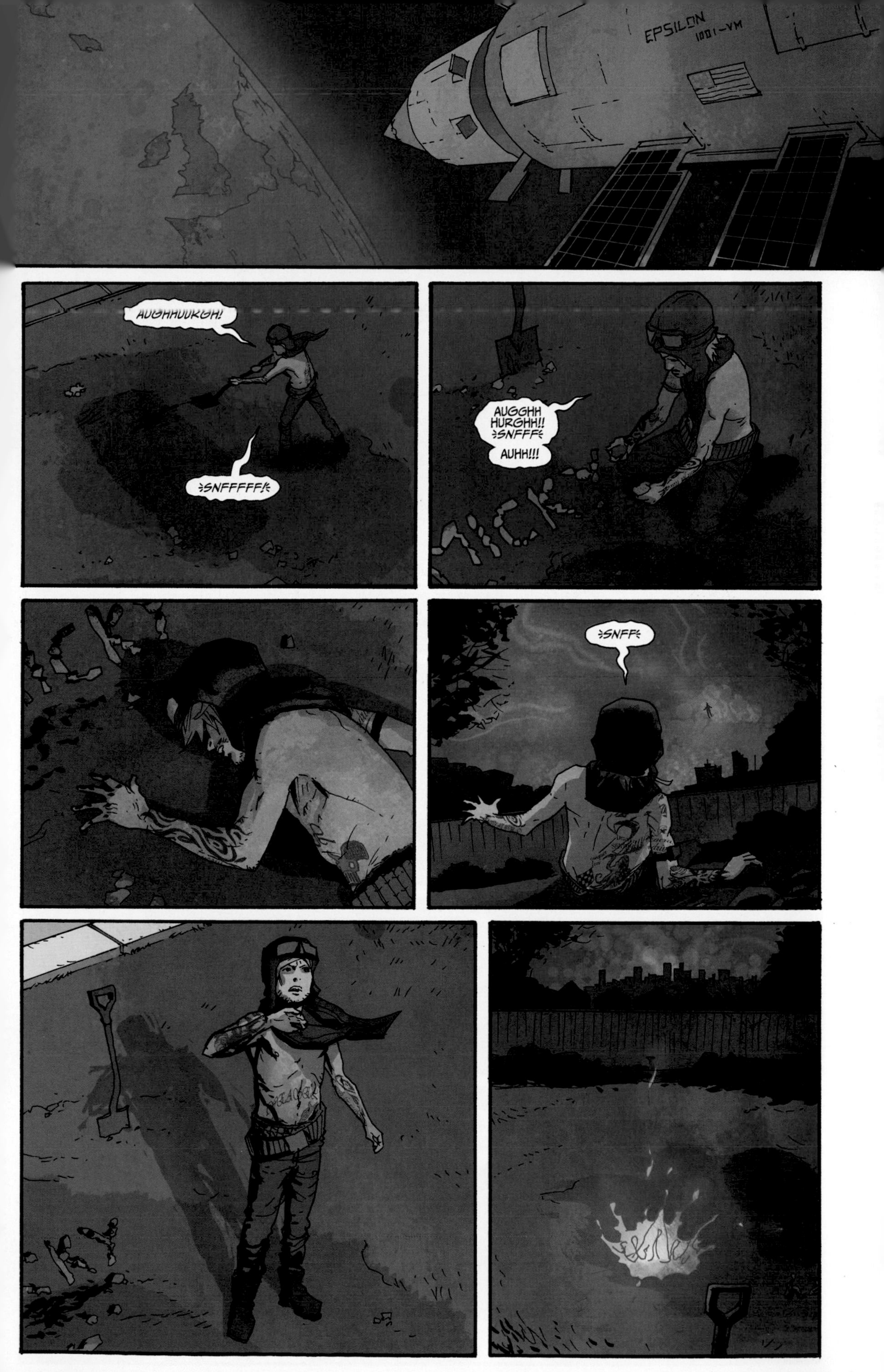
EPSILON
1001-VM
AUGHHUURGH!
SNFFFFF!
AUGGHH
HURGHH!!
SNFFF
AUHH!!!
SNFF

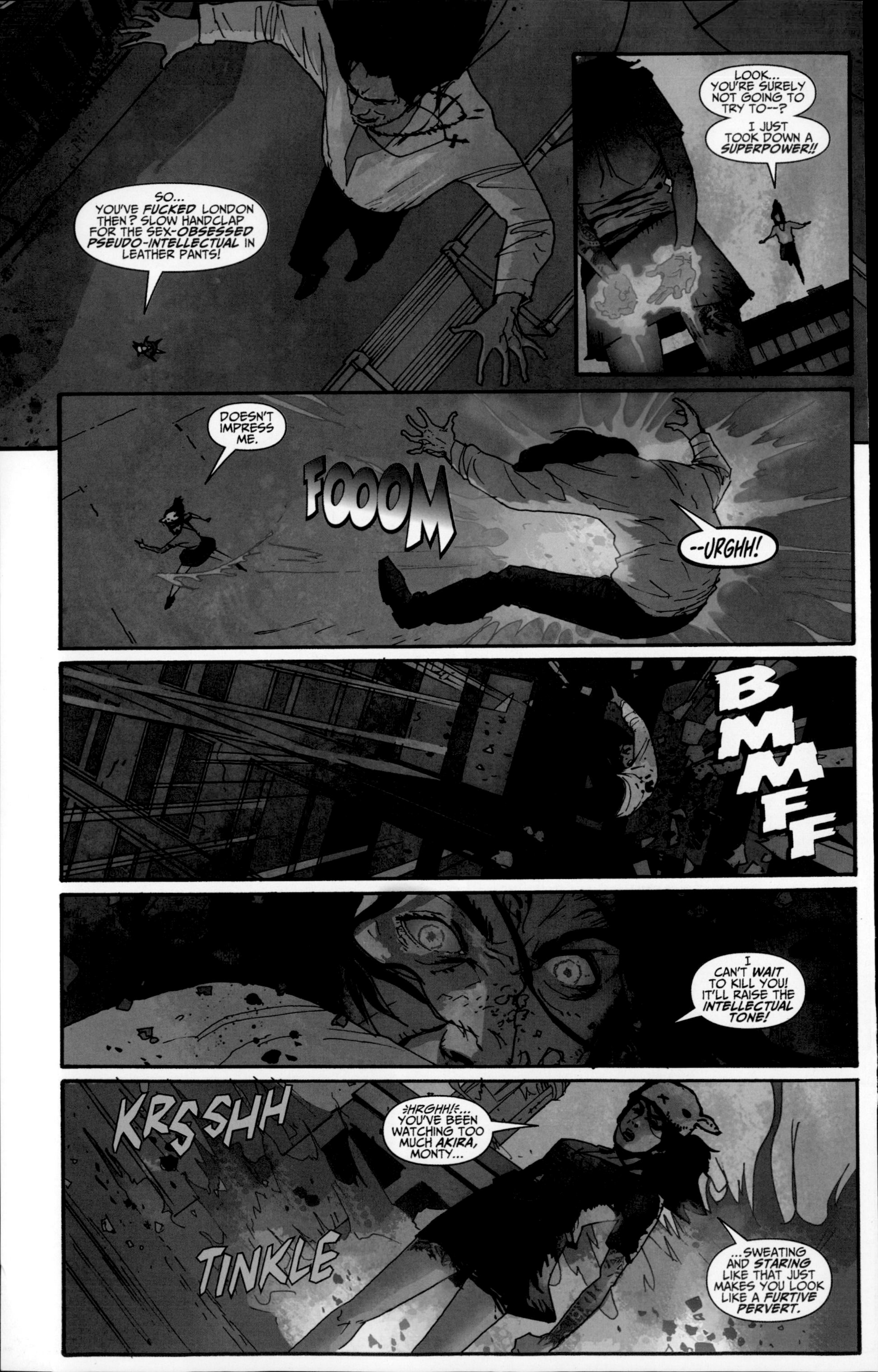
SO... YOU'VE FUCKED LONDON THEN? SLOW HANDCLAP FOR THE SEX-OBSESSED PSEUDO-INTELLECTUAL IN LEATHER PANTS!
LOOK... YOU'RE SURELY NOT GOING TO TRY TO--?
I JUST TOOK DOWN A SUPERPOWER!!
DOESN'T IMPRESS ME.
FOOOM
--URGHH!
BMMFF
I CAN'T WAIT TO KILL YOU! IT'LL RAISE THE INTELLECTUAL TONE!
KRSSHH
HRGHH!... YOU'VE BEEN WATCHING TOO MUCH AKIRA, MONTY...
...SWEATING AND STARING LIKE THAT JUST MAKES YOU LOOK LIKE A FURTIVE PERVERT.
TINKLE

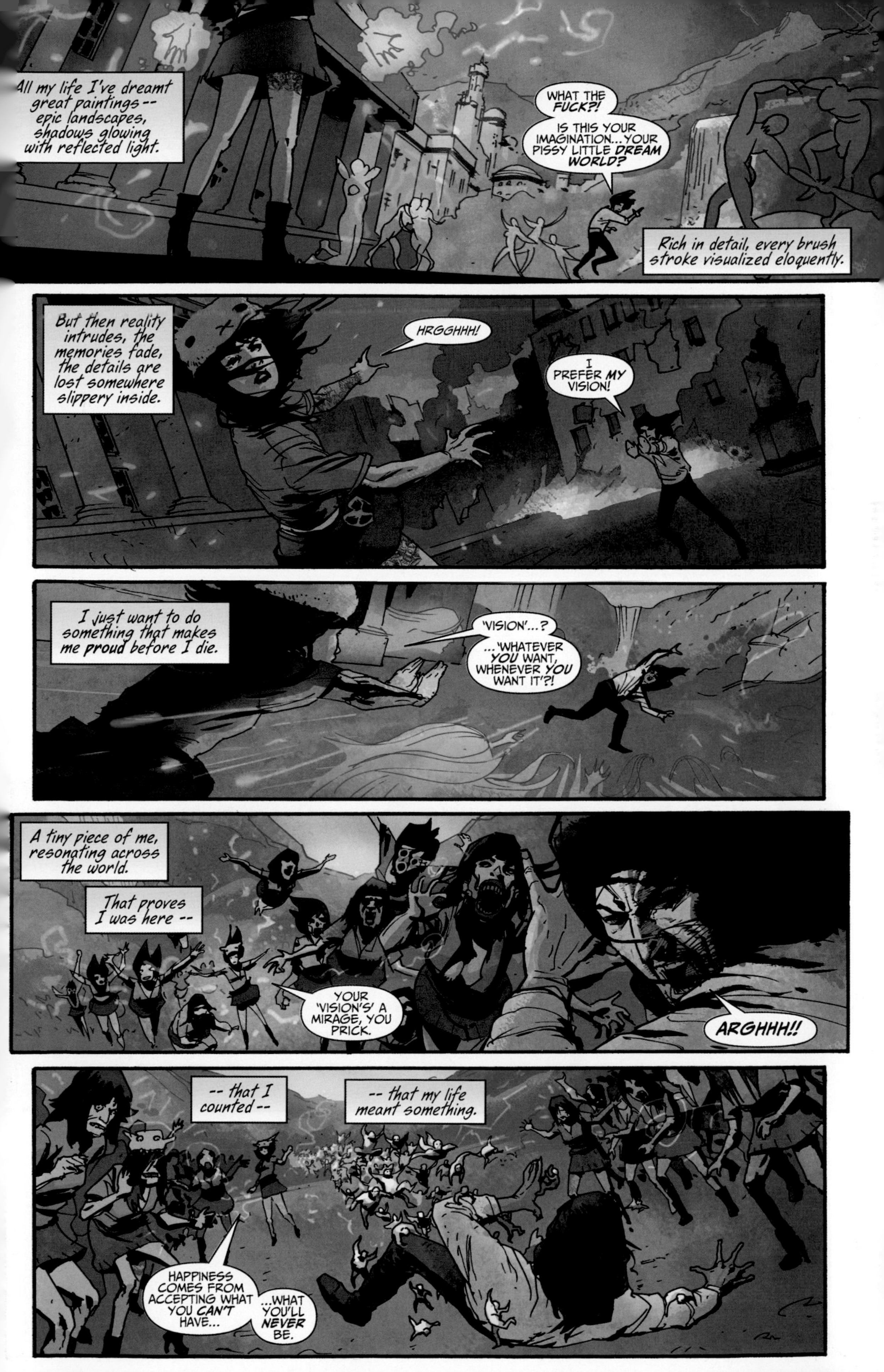
All my life I've dreamt great paintings -- epic landscapes, shadows glowing with reflected light.
WHAT THE FUCK?!
IS THIS YOUR IMAGINATION... YOUR PISSY LITTLE DREAM WORLD?
Rich in detail, every brush stroke visualized eloquently.
But then reality intrudes, the memories fade, the details are lost somewhere slippery inside.
HRGGHHH!
I PREFER MY VISION!
I just want to do something that makes me proud before I die.
'VISION'...?
...'WHATEVER YOU WANT, WHENEVER YOU WANT IT'?!
A tiny piece of me, resonating across the world.
That proves I was here --
YOUR 'VISION'S' A MIRAGE, YOU PRICK.
ARGHHH!!
-- that I counted --
-- that my life meant something.
HAPPINESS COMES FROM ACCEPTING WHAT YOU CAN'T HAVE...
...WHAT YOU'LL NEVER BE.

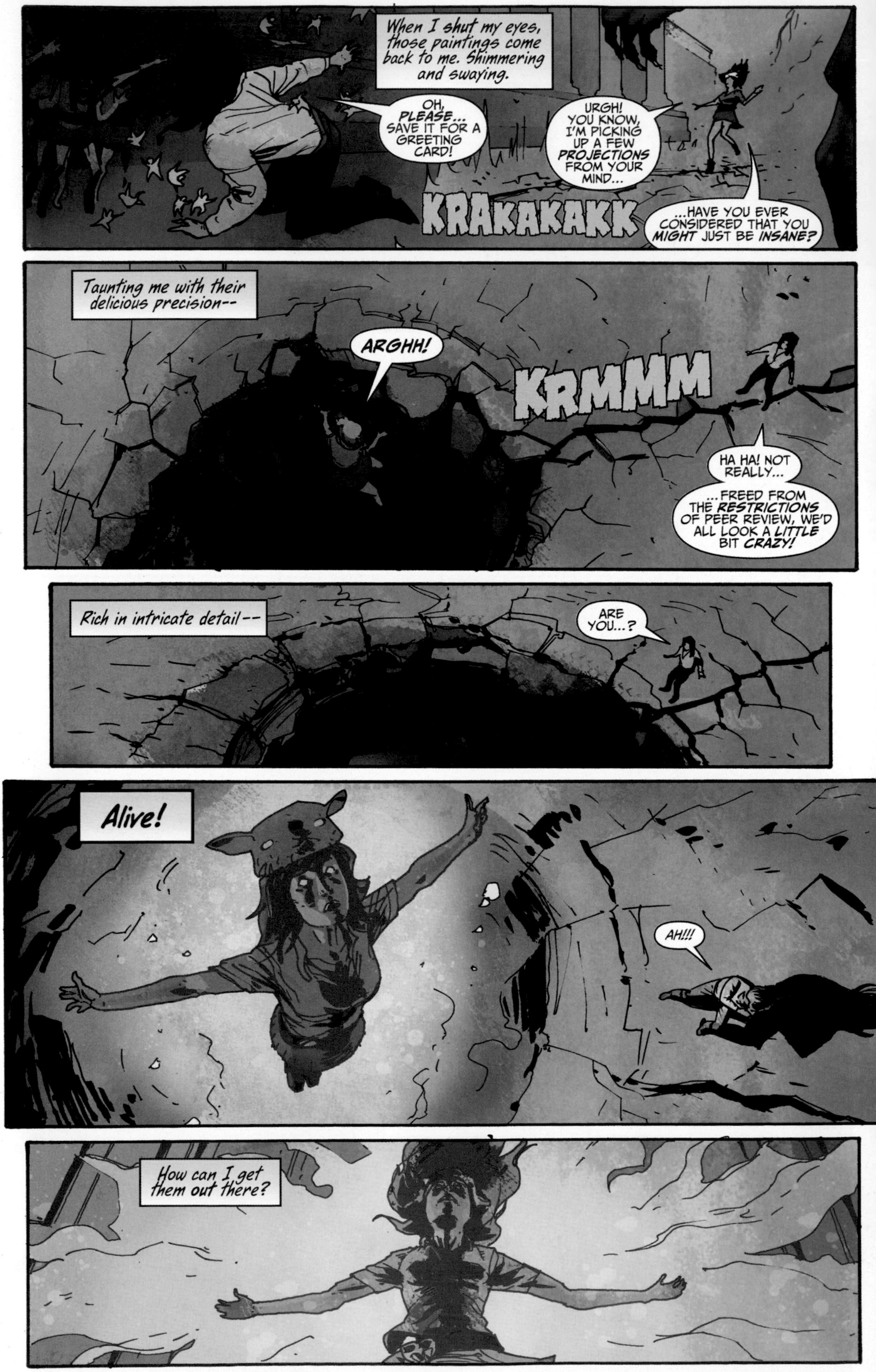
When I shut my eyes, those paintings come back to me. Shimmering and swaying.
OH, PLEASE... SAVE IT FOR A GREETING CARD!
URGH! YOU KNOW, I'M PICKING UP A FEW PROJECTIONS FROM YOUR MIND...
KRAKAKAKK
...HAVE YOU EVER CONSIDERED THAT YOU MIGHT JUST BE INSANE?
Taunting me with their delicious precision--
ARGHH!
KRMMM
HA HA! NOT REALLY...
...FREED FROM THE RESTRICTIONS OF PEER REVIEW, WE'D ALL LOOK A LITTLE BIT CRAZY!
Rich in intricate detail--
ARE YOU...?
Alive!
AH!!!
How can I get them out there?

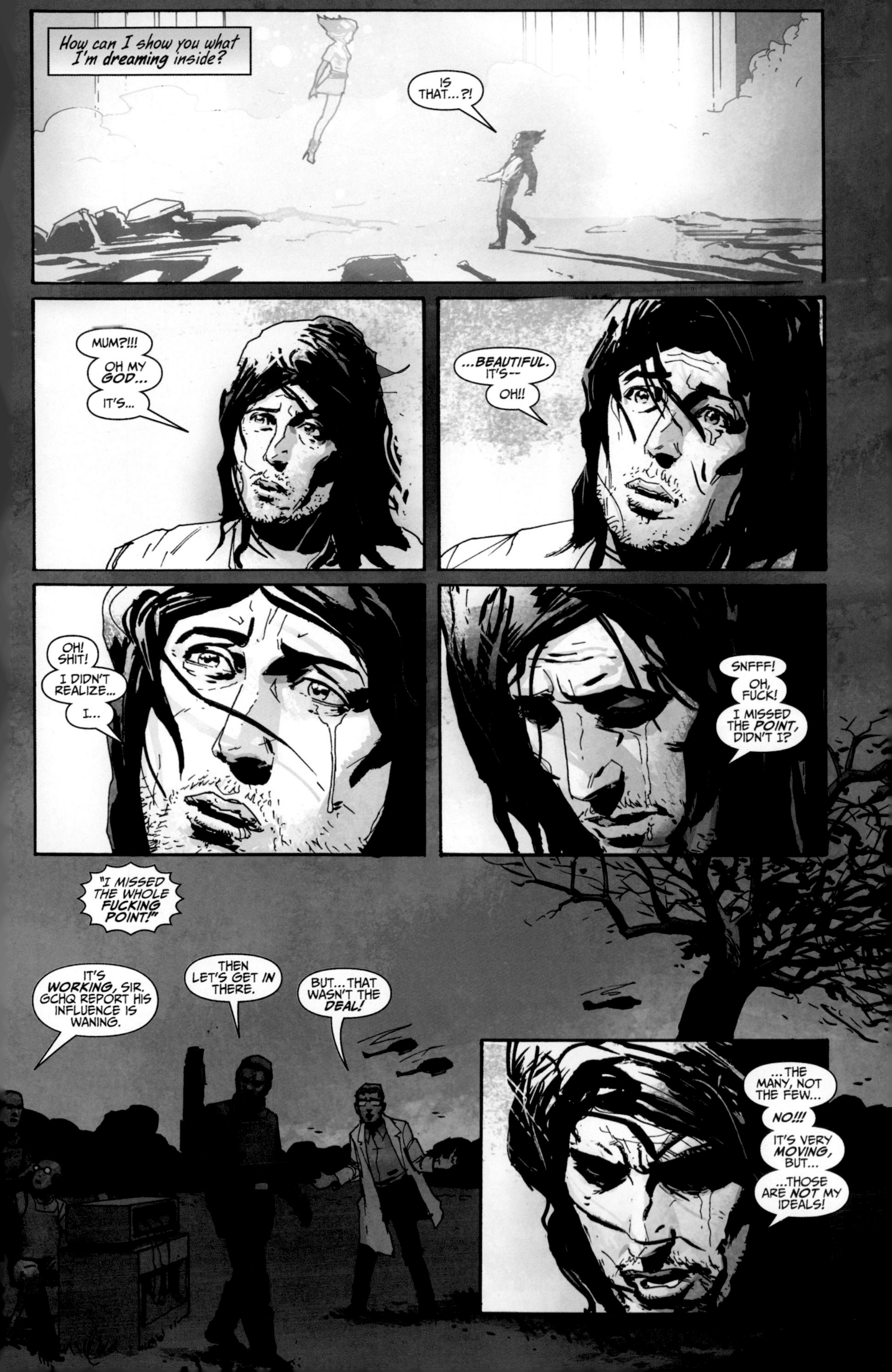
How can I show you what I'm dreaming inside?
IS THAT...?!
MUM?!!!
OH MY GOD...
IT'S...
...BEAUTIFUL.
IT'S--
OH!!
OH! SHIT!
I DIDN'T REALIZE...
I...
SNFFF!
OH, FUCK!
I MISSED THE POINT, DIDN'T I?
"I MISSED THE WHOLE FUCKING POINT!"
IT'S WORKING, SIR. GCHQ REPORT HIS INFLUENCE IS WANING.
THEN LET'S GET IN THERE.
BUT...THAT WASN'T THE DEAL!
...THE MANY, NOT THE FEW...
NO!!!
IT'S VERY MOVING, BUT...
...THOSE ARE NOT MY IDEALS!

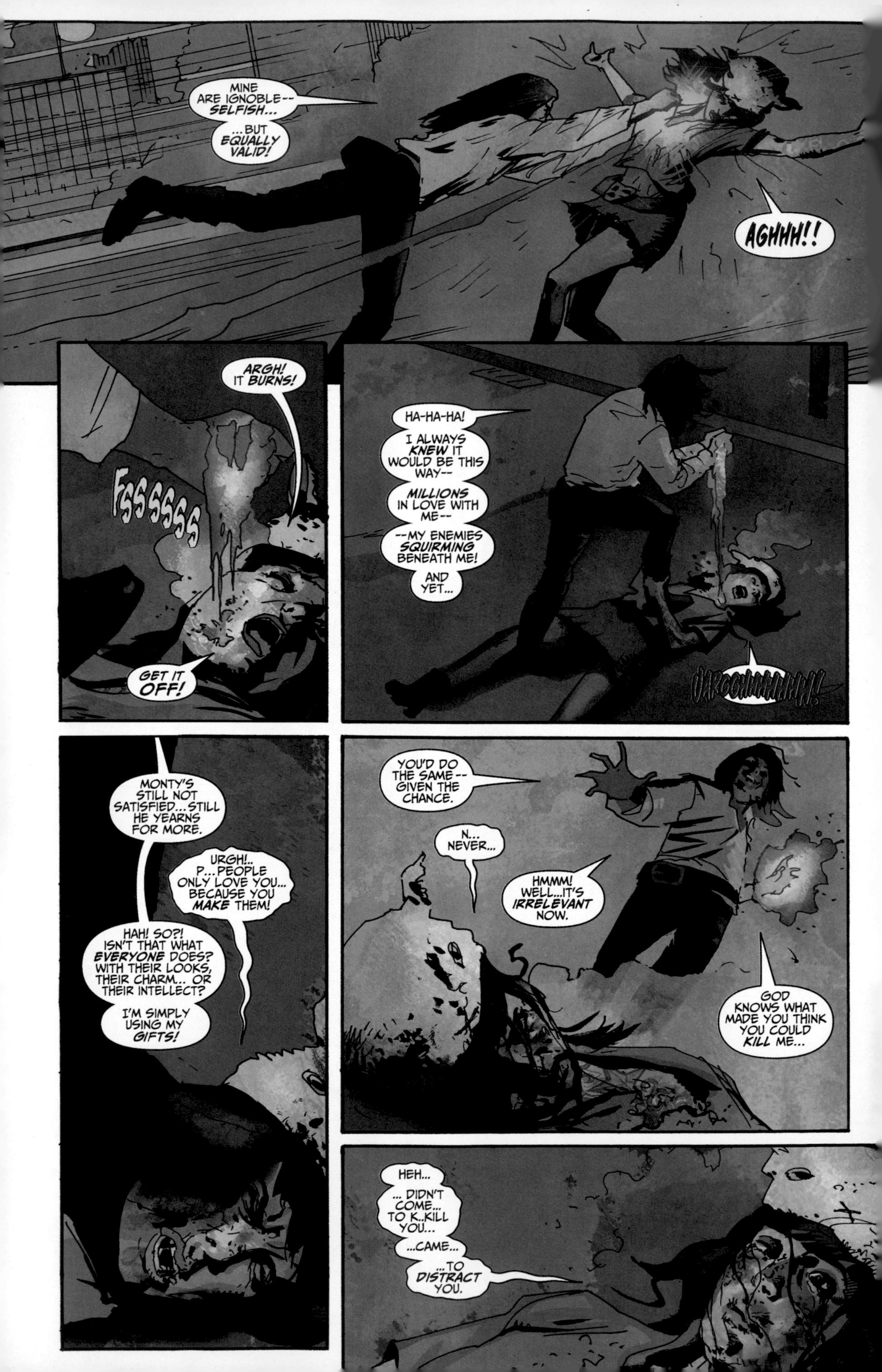

MINE ARE IGNOBLE-- SELFISH...
...BUT EQUALLY VALID!
AGHHH!!
ARGH! IT BURNS!
FSSSSSS
GET IT OFF!
HA-HA-HA!
I ALWAYS KNEW IT WOULD BE THIS WAY--
MILLIONS IN LOVE WITH ME--
--MY ENEMIES SQUIRMING BENEATH ME!
AND YET...
MONTY'S STILL NOT SATISFIED...STILL HE YEARNS FOR MORE.
URGH!.. P...PEOPLE ONLY LOVE YOU... BECAUSE YOU MAKE THEM!
HAH! SO?! ISN'T THAT WHAT EVERYONE DOES? WITH THEIR LOOKS, THEIR CHARM... OR THEIR INTELLECT?
I'M SIMPLY USING MY GIFTS!
YOU'D DO THE SAME-- GIVEN THE CHANCE.
N... NEVER...
HMMM! WELL...IT'S IRRELEVANT NOW.
GOD KNOWS WHAT MADE YOU THINK YOU COULD KILL ME...
HEH...
...DIDN'T COME... TO K..KILL YOU...
...CAME...
...TO DISTRACT YOU.

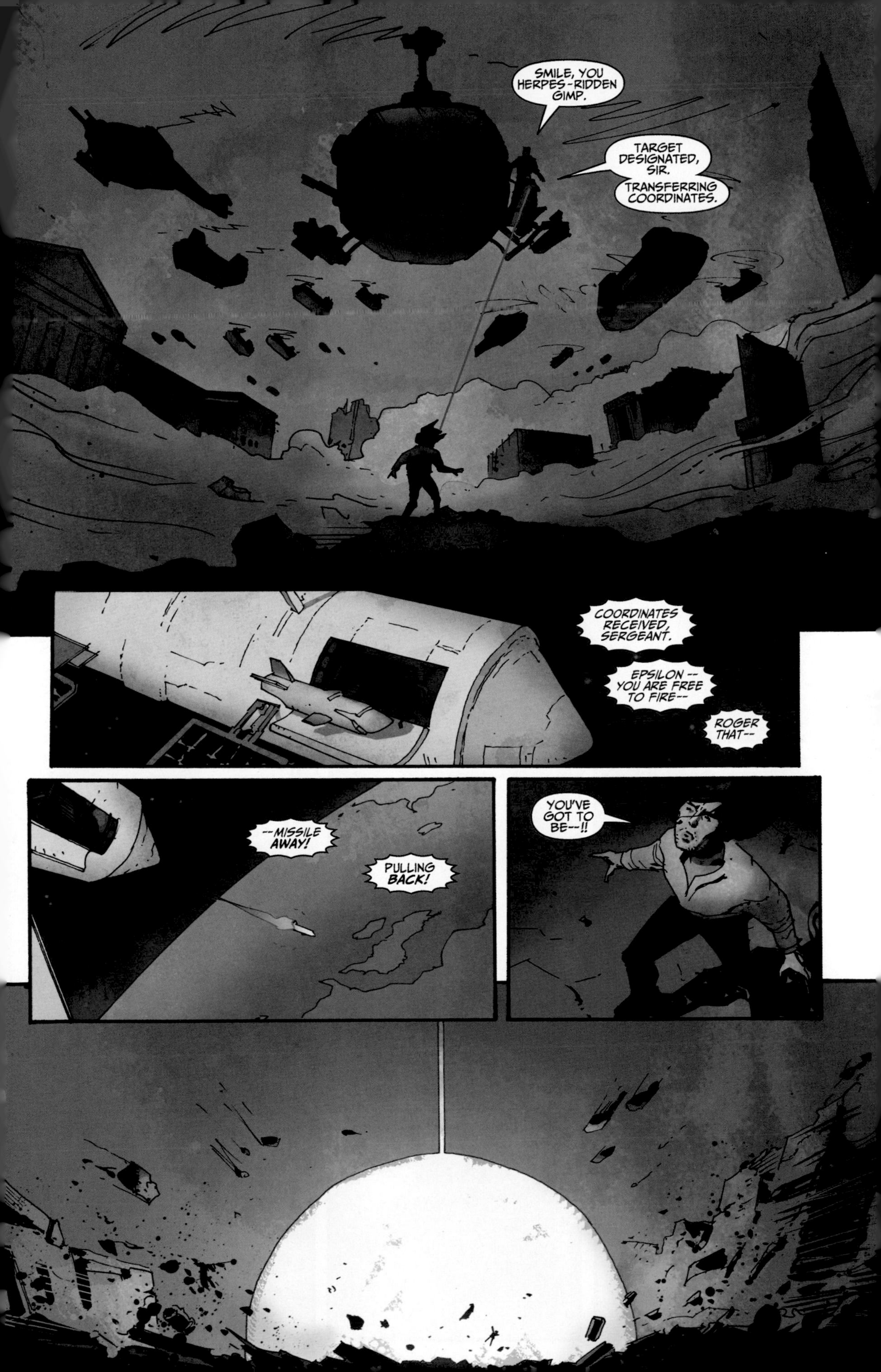
SMILE, YOU HERPES-RIDDEN GIMP.
TARGET DESIGNATED, SIR.
TRANSFERRING COORDINATES.
COORDINATES RECEIVED, SERGEANT.
EPSILON -- YOU ARE FREE TO FIRE--
ROGER THAT--
--MISSILE AWAY!
PULLING BACK!
YOU'VE GOT TO BE--!!

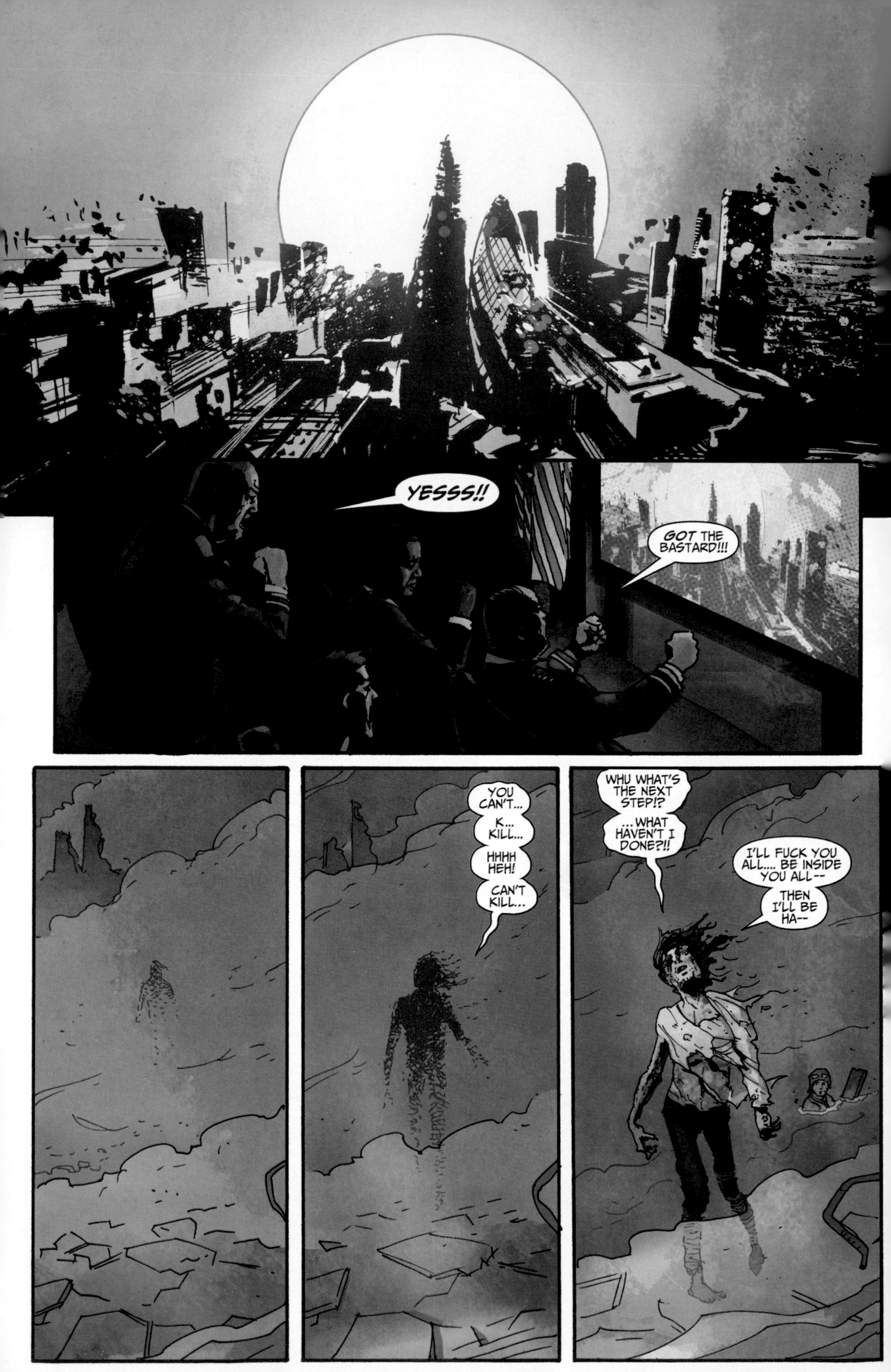
YESSS!!
GOT THE BASTARD!!!
YOU CAN'T...
K... KILL...
HHHH HEH!
CAN'T KILL...
WHU WHAT'S THE NEXT STEP!?
...WHAT HAVEN'T I DONE?!!
I'LL FUCK YOU ALL.... BE INSIDE YOU ALL--
THEN I'LL BE HA--

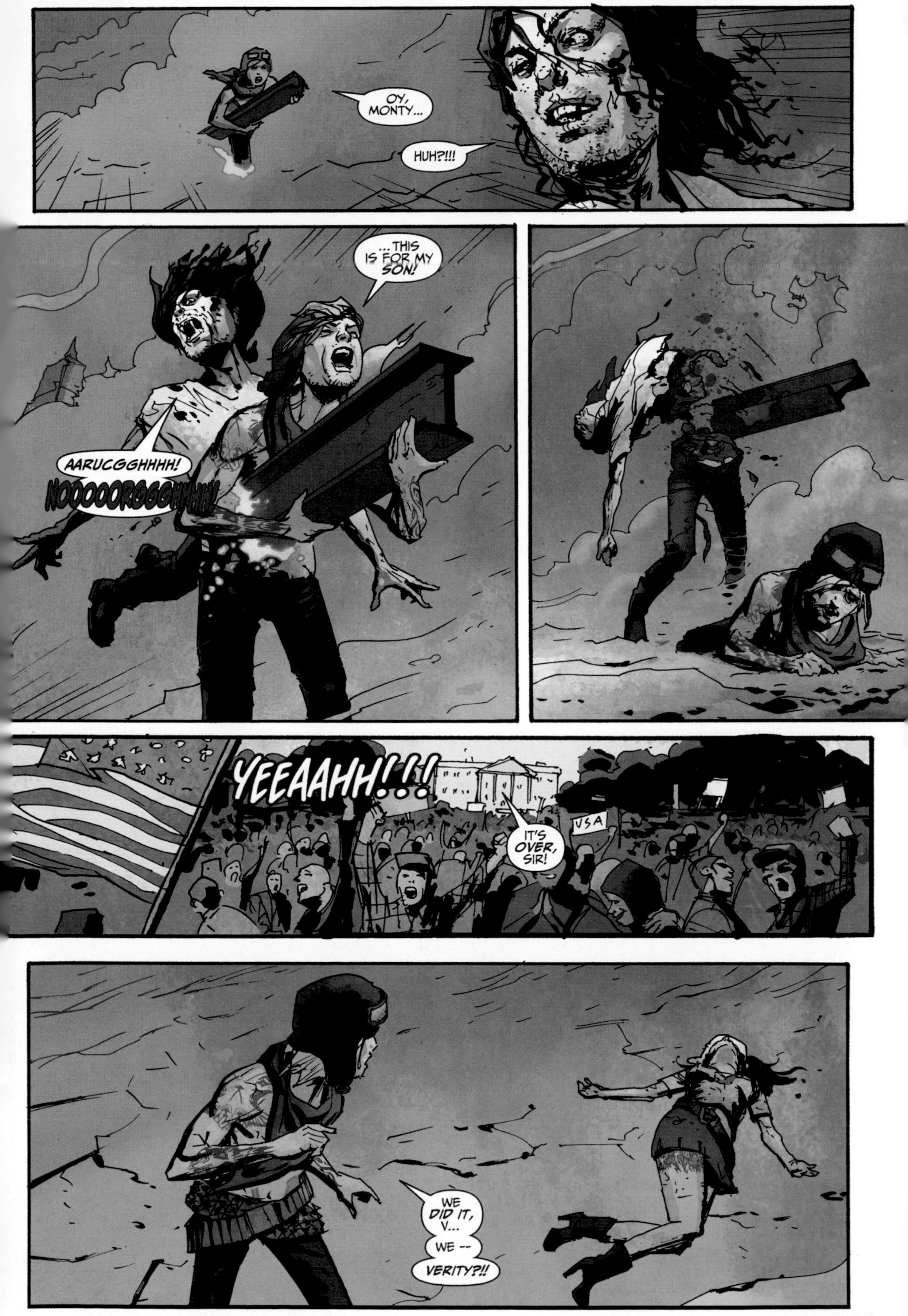
OY, MONTY...
HUH?!!!
...THIS IS FOR MY SON!
AARUCGGHHHH!
YEEAAHH!!!
USA
IT'S OVER, SIR!
WE DID IT, V...
WE --
VERITY?!!

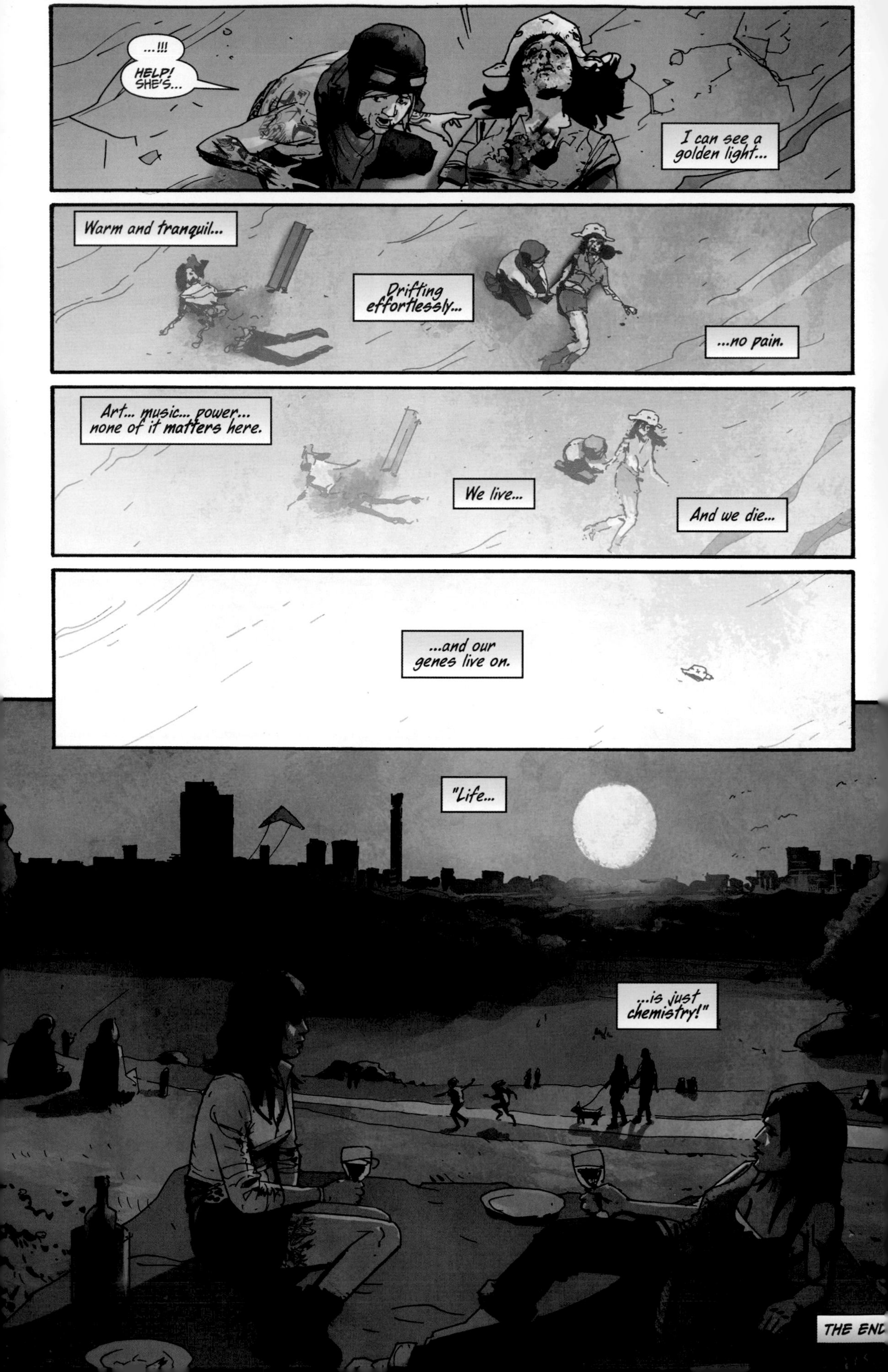
...!!!
HELP! SHE'S...
I can see a golden light...
Warm and tranquil...
Drifting effortlessly...
...no pain.
Art... music... power... none of it matters here.
We live...
And we die...
...and our genes live on.
"Life...
...is just chemistry!"
THE END

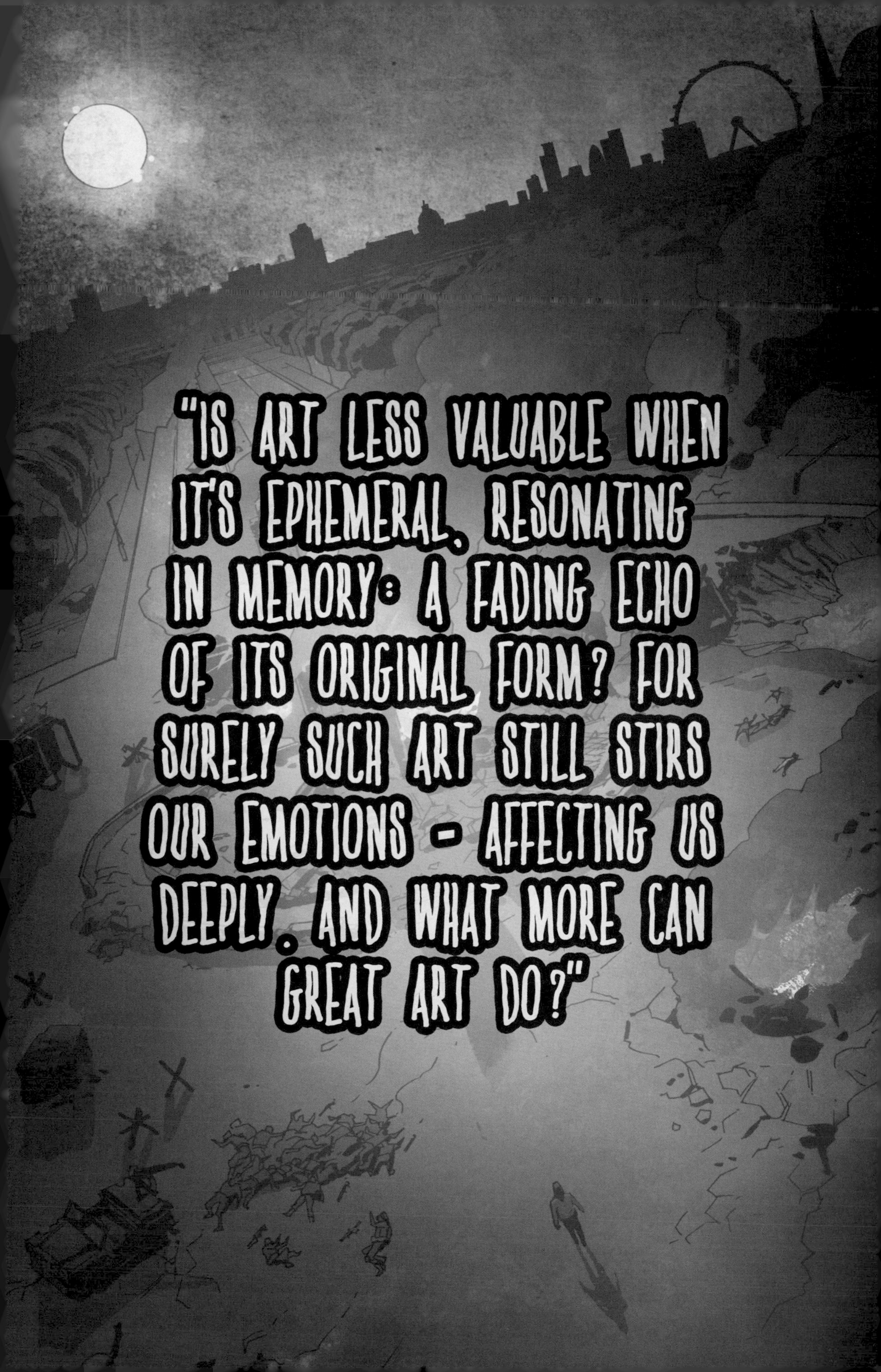
"IS ART LESS VALUABLE WHEN IT'S EPHEMERAL, RESONATING IN MEMORY: A FADING ECHO OF ITS ORIGINAL FORM? FOR SURELY SUCH ART STILL STIRS OUR EMOTIONS – AFFECTING US DEEPLY. AND WHAT MORE CAN GREAT ART DO?"

VARIANT COVERS GALLERY

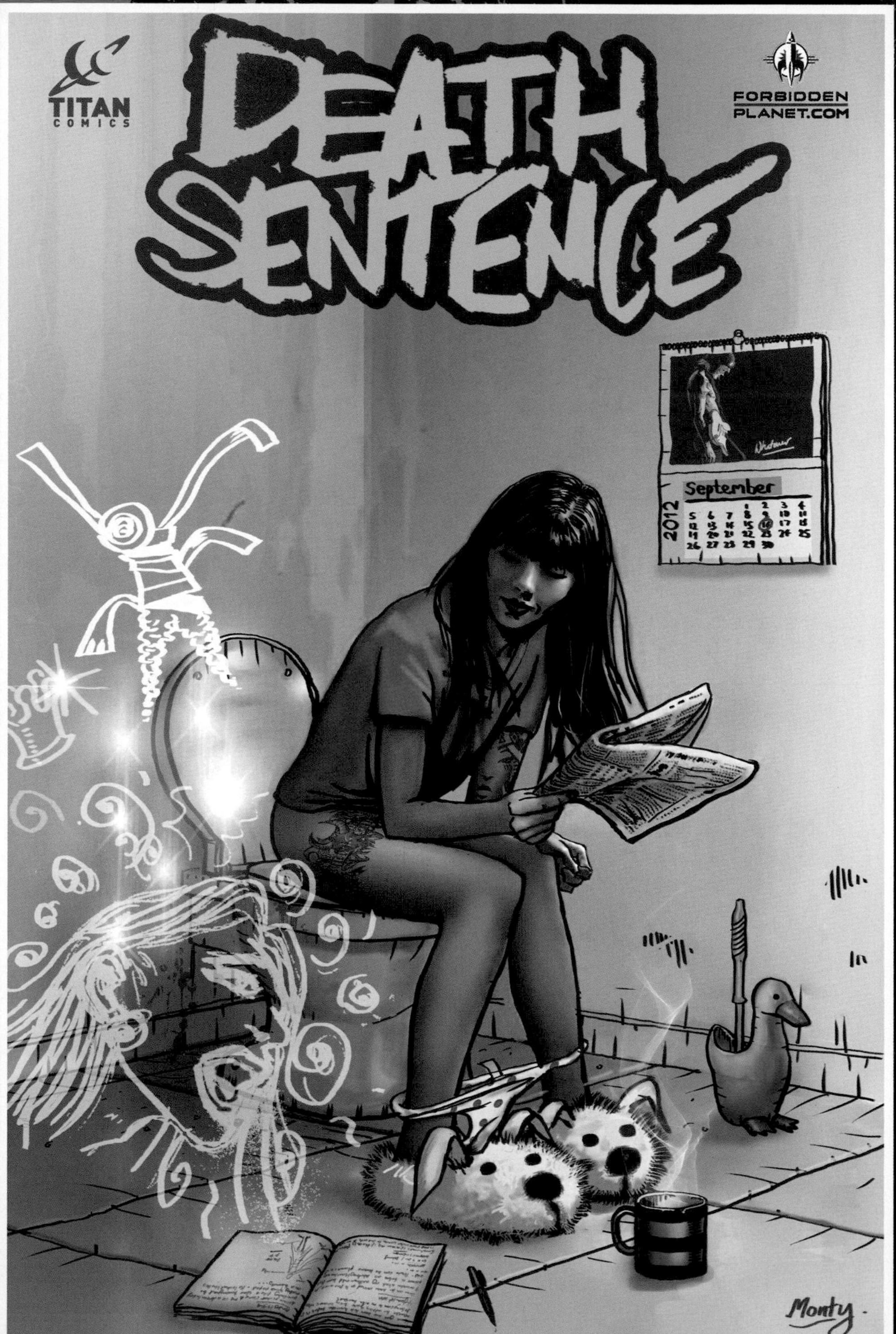
TITAN COMICS
DEATH SENTENCE
FORBIDDEN PLANET.COM
September
2012
Monty

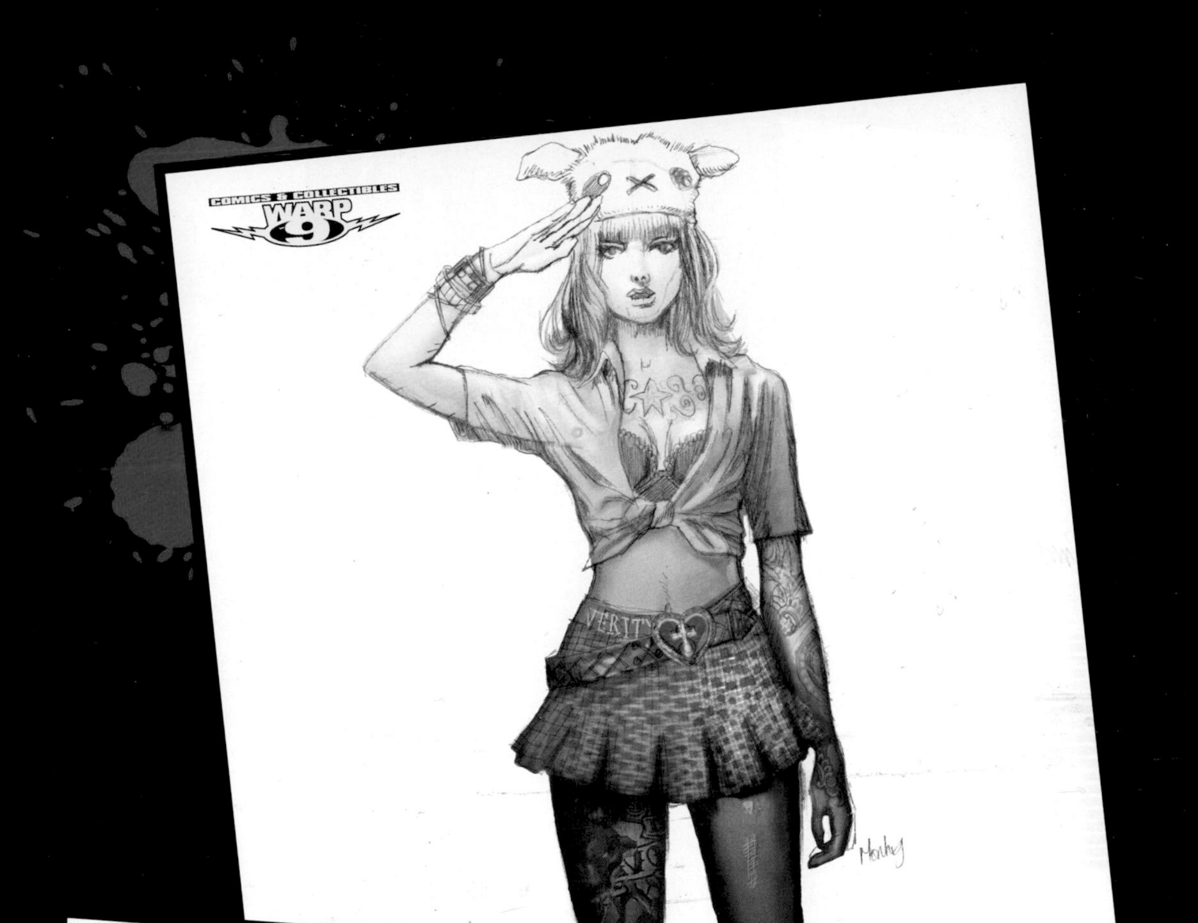
COMICS & COLLECTIBLES
WARP 9
VERITY

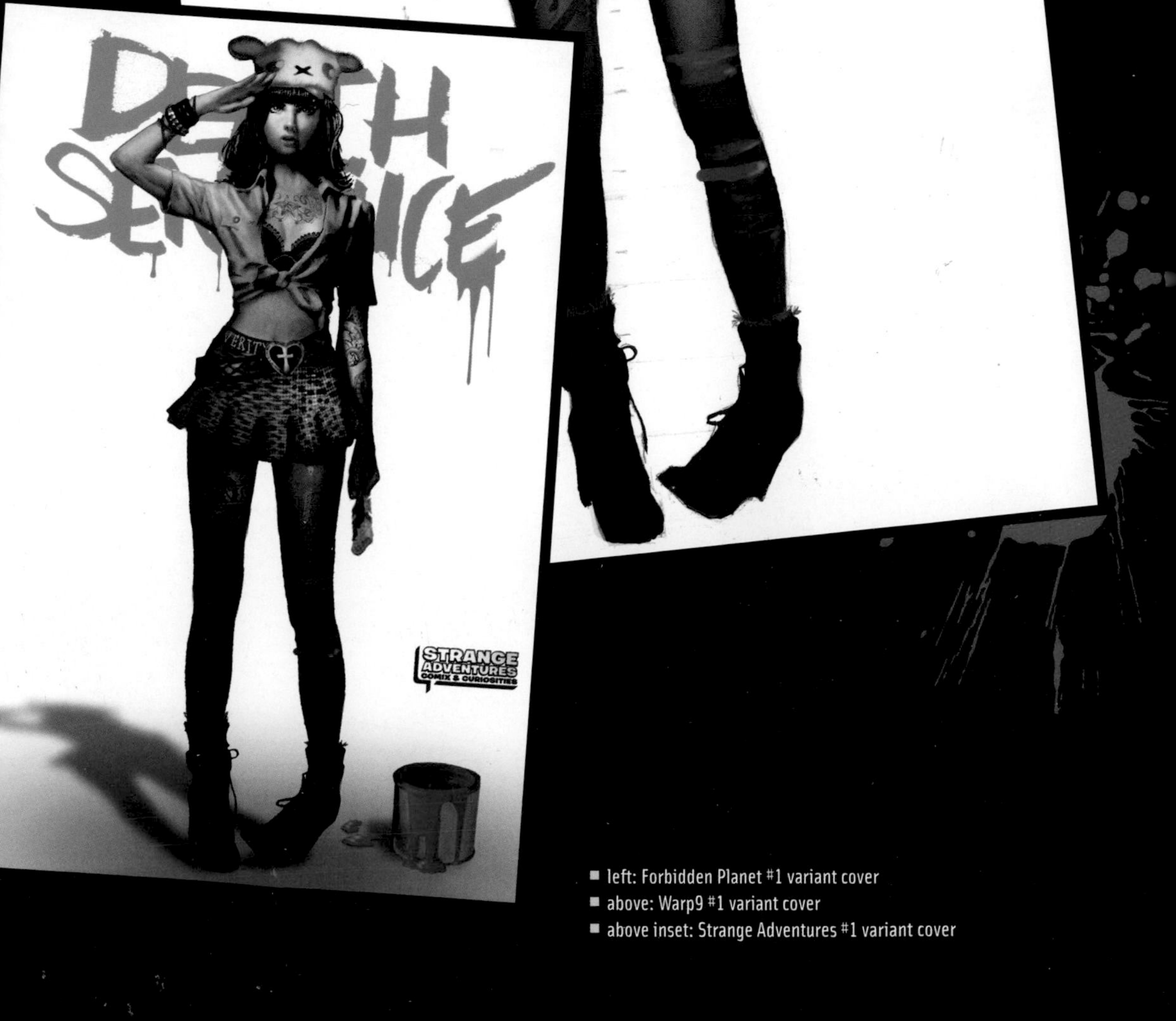
VERITY
STRANGE ADVENTURES
COMIX & CURIOSITIES

- left: Forbidden Planet #1 variant cover
- above: Warp9 #1 variant cover
- above inset: Strange Adventures #1 variant cover

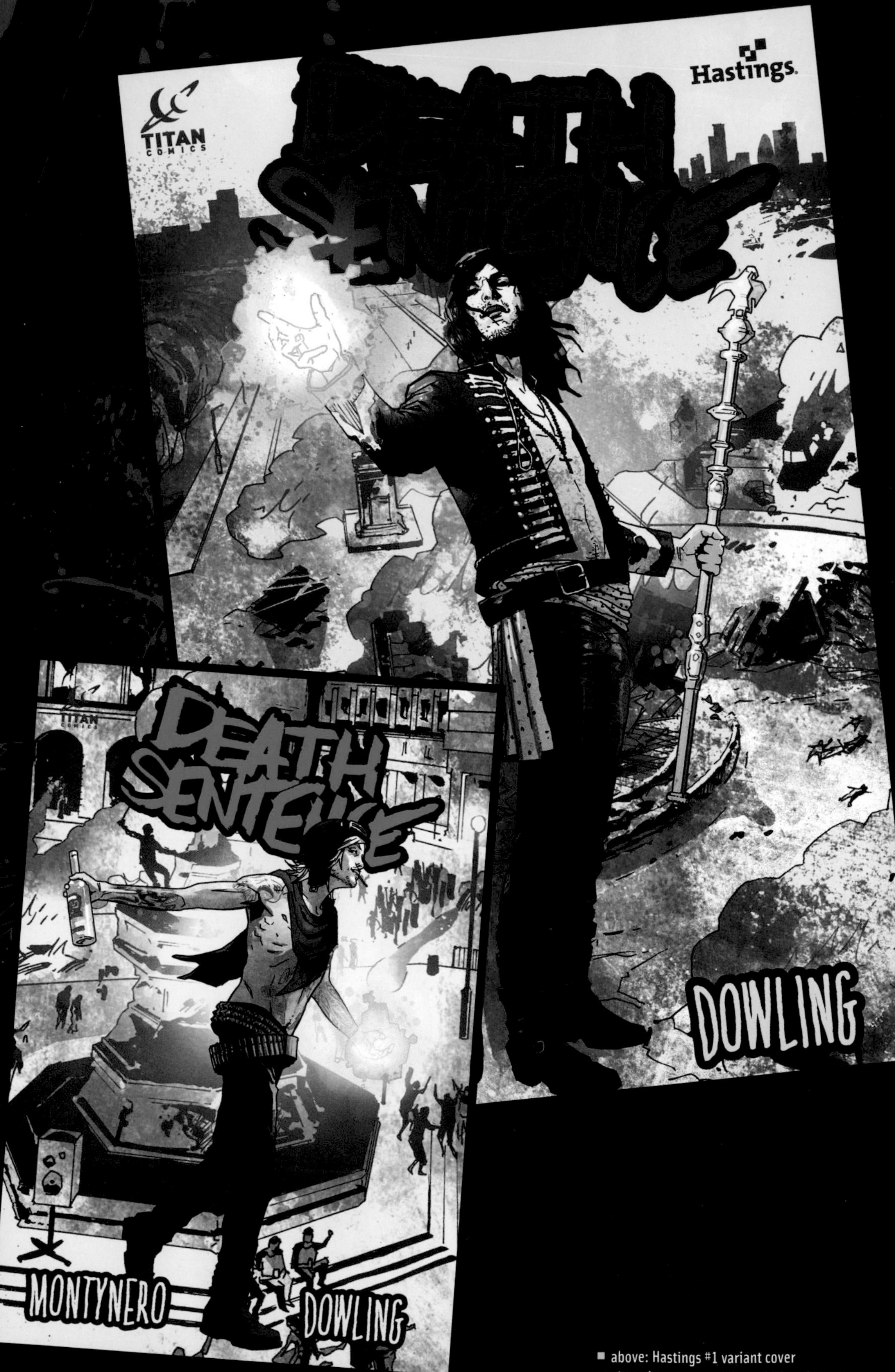
TITAN COMICS
Hastings.
DOWLING
TITAN COMICS
DEATH SENTENCE
MONTYNERO
DOWLING

- above: Hastings #1 variant cover
- above inset: unused Weasel #1 variant cover
- opposite: Second printing #1 variant cover
- opposite inset: Second printing #2 variant cover

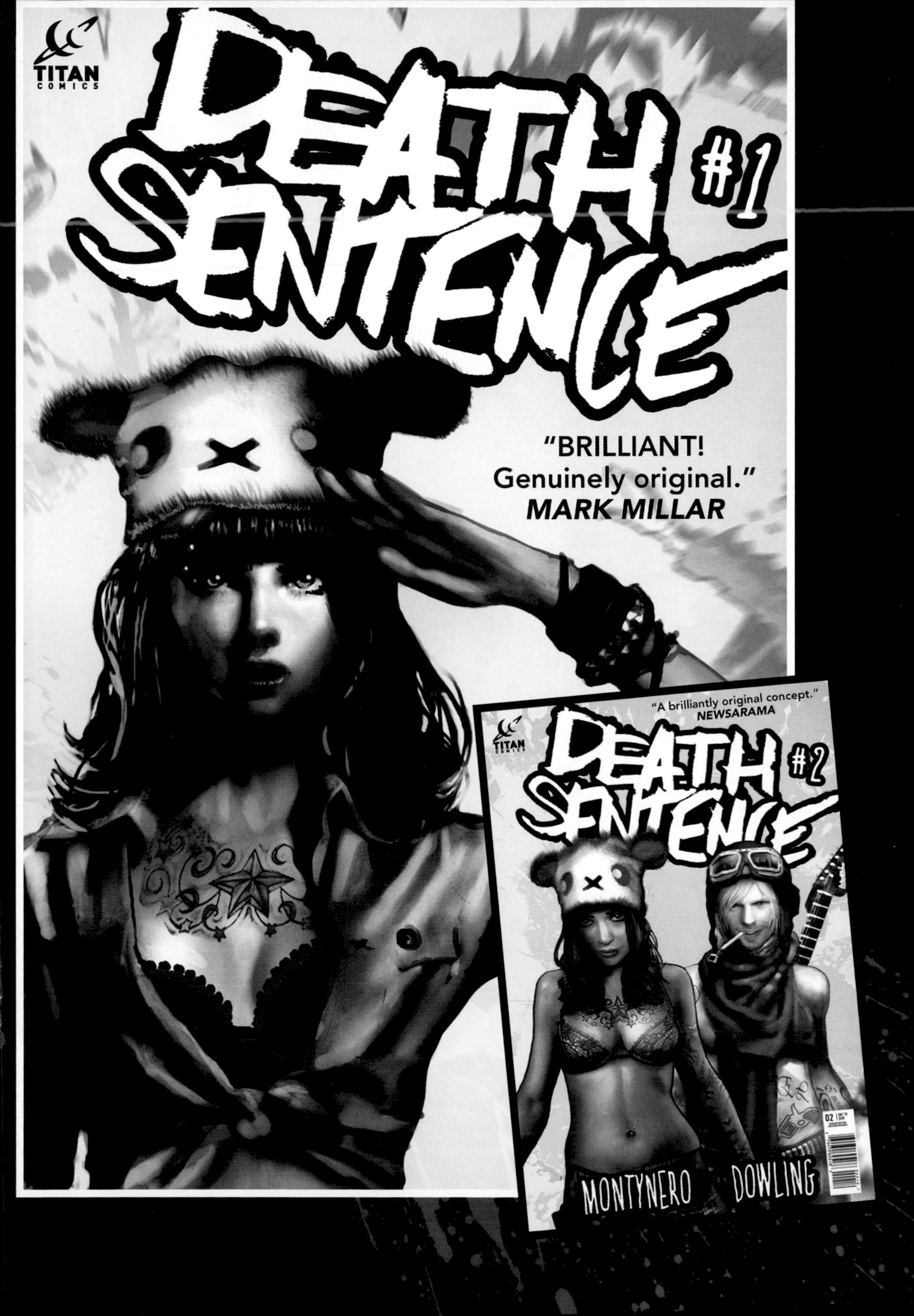
TITAN COMICS
DEATH SENTENCE #1
"BRILLIANT!
Genuinely original."
MARK MILLAR
"A brilliantly original concept."
NEWSARAMA
TITAN COMICS
DEATH SENTENCE #2
MONTYNERO
DOWLING

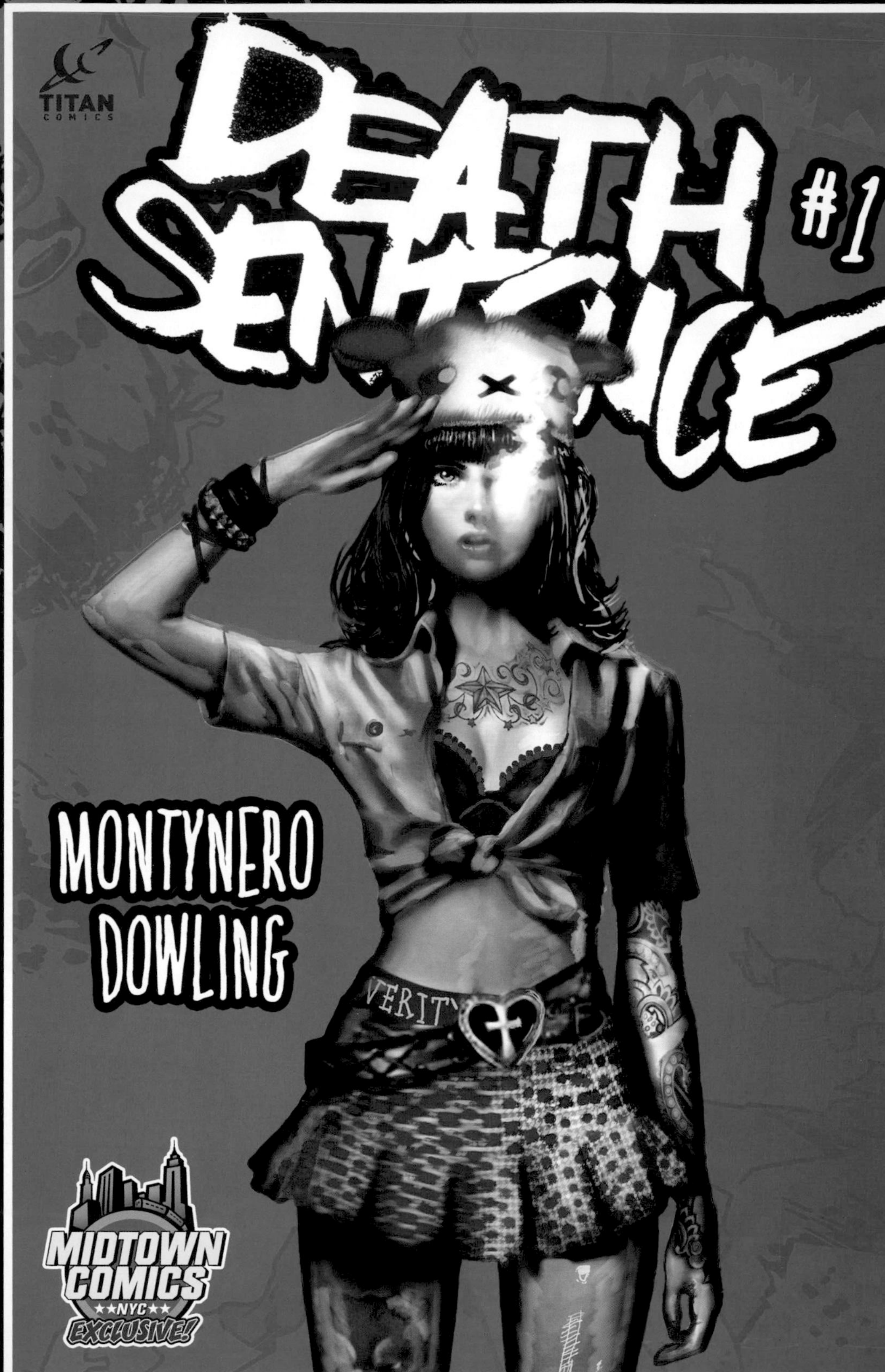
TITAN COMICS
DEATH SENTENCE
#1
MONTYNERO
DOWLING
VERITY
MIDTOWN COMICS
NYC
EXCLUSIVE!

- above: Midtown Comic #1 second printing variant cover
- opposite: Second printing #3 variant cover

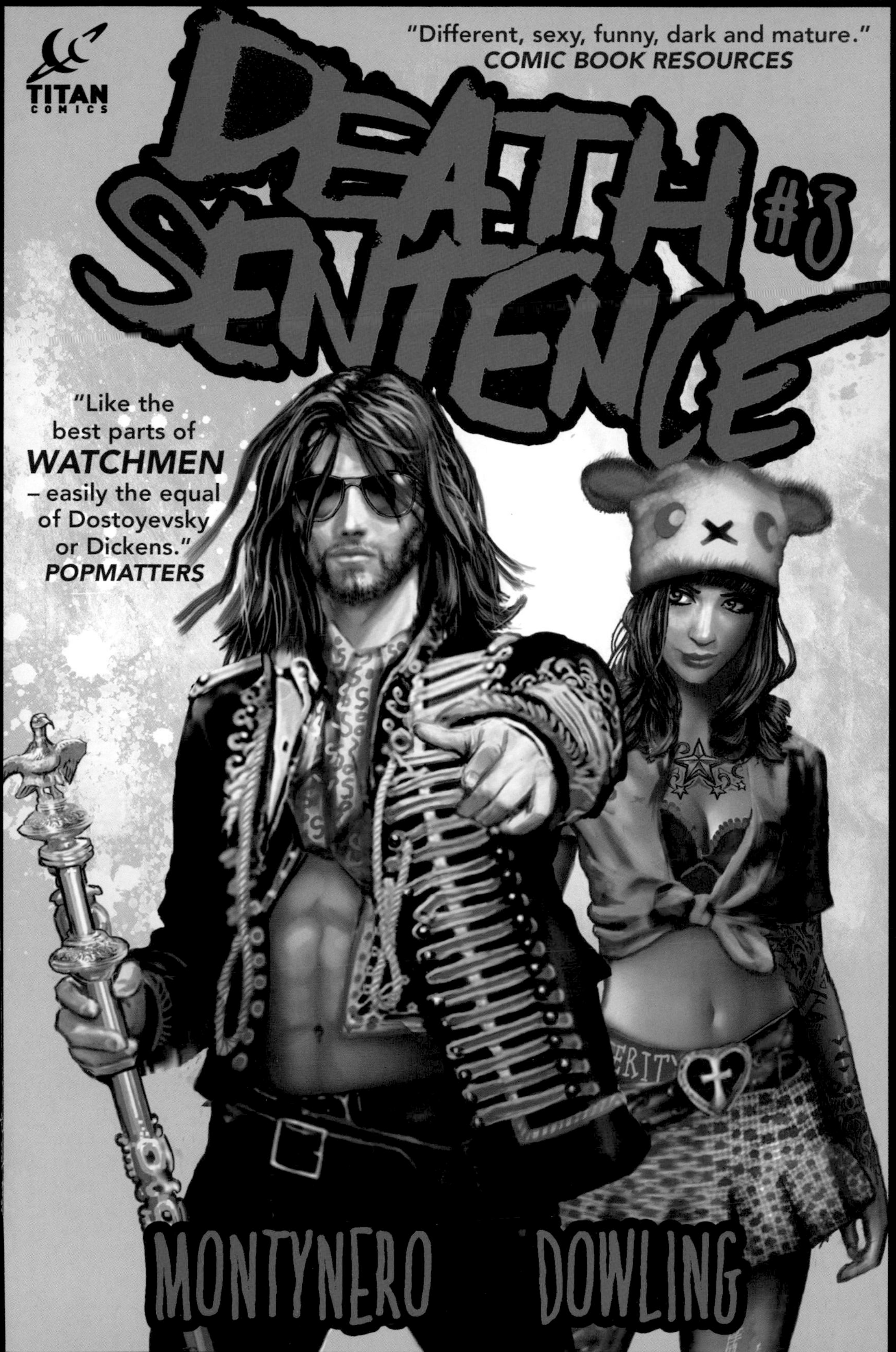
TITAN COMICS
"Different, sexy, funny, dark and mature."
COMIC BOOK RESOURCES
DEATH SENTENCE #3
"Like the best parts of WATCHMEN – easily the equal of Dostoyevsky or Dickens."
POPMATTERS
MONTYNERO
DOWLING

DEATH SENTENCE COMMENTARY

MONTYNERO AND MIKE DOWLING: FEBRUARY 201

When we started making *Death Sentence*, it seemed like a madcap scheme with little chance of success, a road to financial ruin and disappointment – but we had a burning desire to make comics and that trumped everything else. To be honest, we're still a little stunned that we pulled it off. As we emerge blinking into the light, surprised and happy, we thought it might be fun to get together and look back over the pages to try and make sense of it all. This is the transcript of our conversation:

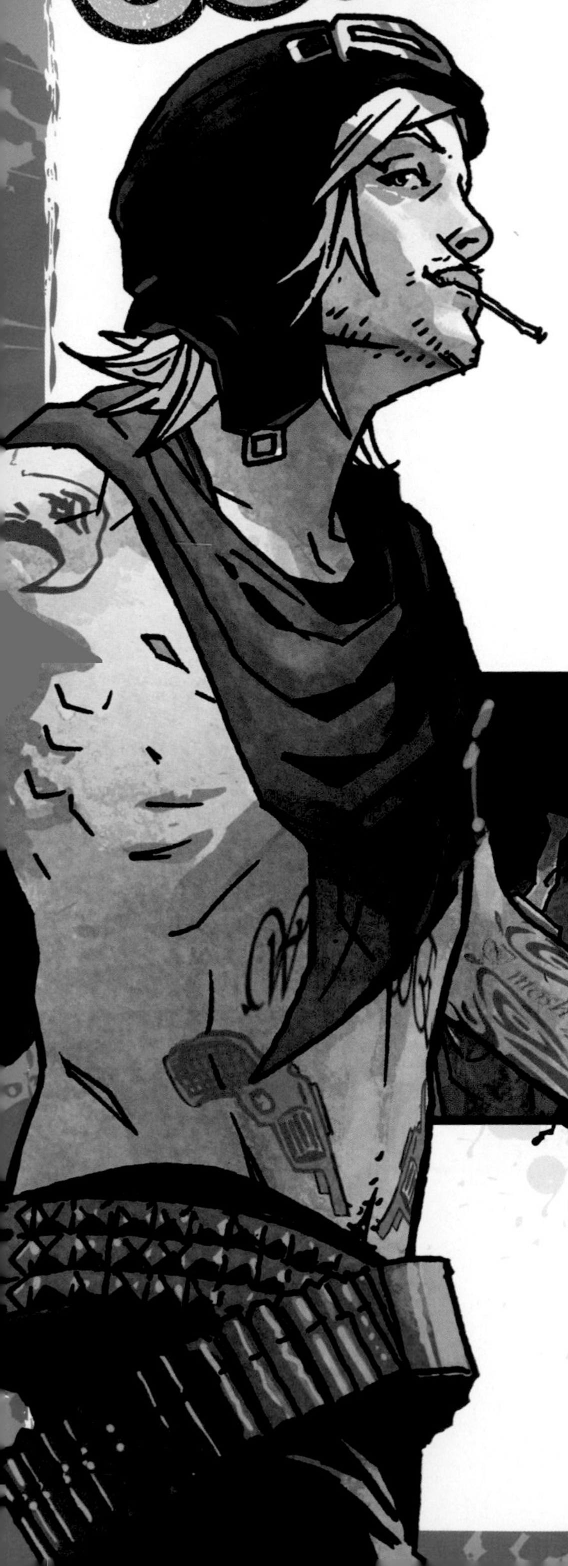

CHAPTER 1

MONTY: I remember we spent a disproportionate amount of time on the first seven pages, didn't we.

MIKE: Yeah, three or four days on some of these pages, going back and forth with the layouts. Trying to figure out the visual language. Making sure the colours and everything worked. It does set the tone: grimy, with flashes of color. I was doing *Rex Royd* and bits of storyboarding, so I was just doing these when time was available initially. Which worked out quite well, because we got to think about it over a long period of time, to make sure we

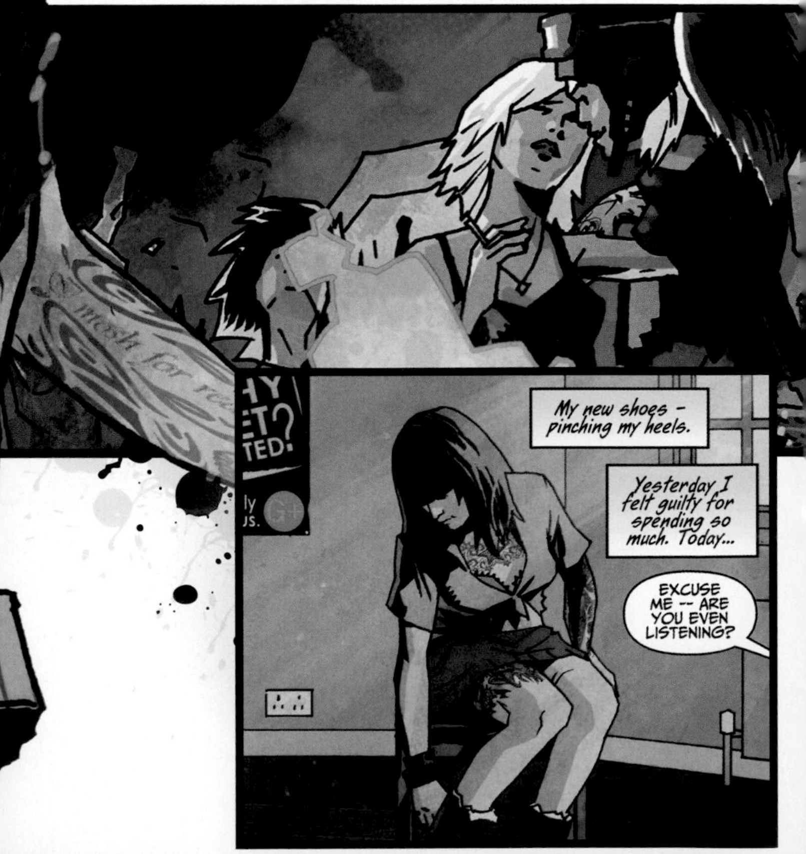
My new shoes - pinching my heels.
Yesterday I felt guilty for spending so much. Today...
EXCUSE ME -- ARE YOU EVEN LISTENING?

really got down the tone of the book and how it would progress. I was pretty tense, a bit nervous with the inking. When you don't have much experience it's quite fraught.

MONTY: Hmmm... It's surprising, because it looks so bold and assured. I guess we were both in the same boat... I was completely unknown as a writer. All the scripts I'd ever sent to publishers had been ignored or rejected. I had no reason to think I could write good comics other than my own delusions. So to eventually get the great feedback on this,

I HAD A TERRIBLE DREAM...

from you initially, and then from Mark Millar and Nick Landau much later, was a real thrill. I think it gave us both lots of confidence to keep on doing what we were doing, and to be more ambitious with the following chapters.

MIKE: We were inspiring each other, I think.

MONTY: We were. The key thing I took from the feedback was that the strength of

the characters, dialogue and storytelling was enough. We didn't need any action or sequential gimmicks. No one ever really notices, because it's very kinetic and punchy, but the first seven pages are simply just a bunch of people you've never met before talking in a room. To make that compelling is quite a challenge.

Page 1: Verity at the doctor's

MONTY: The first page sums up Verity's central predicament, and implies a lot about the wider world we're entering into and how the virus is perceived. You've got the internal monologue: *"The dust motes swirling in sunlight... The burr of the consultant's voice deep and hypnotic... New shoes pinching my heels."* That's what captions are for, as far as I'm concerned – to add texture and depth to the story.

MIKE: It's a really good case of show *and* tell.

MONTY: You've got what Verity sees, hears and feels in that moment. That brings it alive: captions, balloons and images all complimenting each other, all adding something extra. The dialogue gives you the diffidence of the doctor, and Verity's defiance – her inability to cope with this moment. And the empty chair at the end there says more about her emotions than her face ever could. When I saw this page fully lettered, I thought, *"This might actually work!"*

Page 2: Weasel's party

MIKE: This page gave me a clear picture on how Weasel was going to act and how to deal with that. Weasel's a real dick, so I tried to make him as honest and likeable as possible throughout.

MONTY: Yeah, that's integral. The feel of this page, of Weasel's life, was essential to the whole mood I pictured for the comic at the start: this decadent partying – getting wasted. It's fun, and it's a rite of passage. It's just part of growing up. For some people it's a phase, and for others it's the rest of their life – or

the point of their life. Why is that? You did a fantastic job of capturing the mood I wanted.

MIKE: I gave it a go.

MONTY: A lot of the Weasel stuff's inspired by Britpop and characters like Pete Doherty and Brett Anderson. I was living with my sister when she was working for a record company in Camden, so I used to hear all the incredible stories about what really went on. I'd meet her for lunch, and there'd be Graham Coxon or whoever drunk round the table moaning about touring Japan. So these scenes are all informed by that. I remember asking you at the start to get loads of copies of the *NME* to make sure the t-shirts and clothes were all accurate.

MIKE: I just looked at a few pictures of Brett Anderson really. I kept the visual research to a minimum.

MONTY: I guess you've lived the life, so you knew all this stuff anyway.

MIKE: Yeah, I know these people and this part of London. I was living right there.

MONTY: That's why I set the comic in London in the end. Originally it was all set in Edinburgh. But when I met you I thought, with you living right there, it would bring that extra veracity. I remember worrying about all the time passing between each of the five main panels on this page. I wasn't sure they'd work without captions. I thought the close-up you added of Weasel might bugger the rhythm up, but it doesn't. That was a good call on your part, making sure we saw his face close up.

Page 3: Weasel wakes up

MONTY: My favorite element in this page is the two silent panels of Weasel's reaction in the middle, when he sees the test results. It's how I wrote the scene and you did a fantastic job of conveying the sadness and pathos. I remember being thrilled at how well you handled it, because it meant that I could write increasingly nuanced character scenes from then on.

MIKE: This page didn't come together easily, to be honest. I like the central three panels though, Weasel looking down and

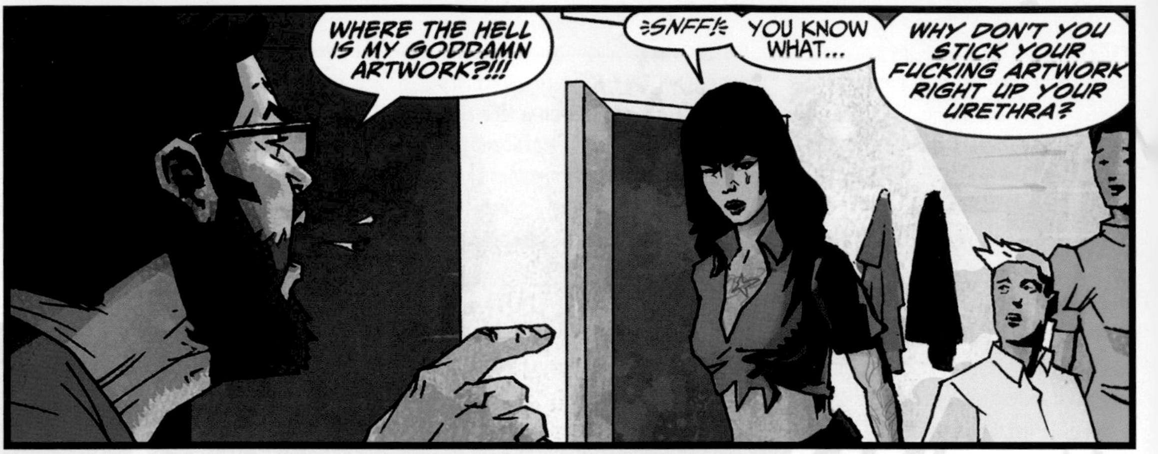
WHERE THE HELL IS MY GODDAMN ARTWORK?!!!
SNFF!
YOU KNOW WHAT...
WHY DON'T YOU STICK YOUR FUCKING ARTWORK RIGHT UP YOUR URETHRA?

considering his mortality. All the other panels I redrew. We had the time back then.

MONTY: Yeah, we enlarged the test results in panel four, too, and flipped it around. Otherwise readers wouldn't know what he was looking at. And I remember you adjusted all the posters on the wall, too – here and in the next scene – to get the right vibe.

Page 4 & 5: Verity quits her job

MONTY: This next page is the only time in the whole comic where a scene doesn't end when a page ends. It's not a big deal, but when I saw it I made a note that I'd rather the scenes ended on a natural page break.

Verity's boss in this scene is based on a guy I used to work for. Sitting on a space hopper at work is an international sign of asshattery – and yet it actually happens. My boss rode a foot scooter round the office too. Sometimes he'd climb under the table and shout 'inspirational' ideas while we were trying to work. He was both good at his job and a certifiable assclown. If he'd been purely one or the other it would have been easier to cope.

MIKE: The guy on the space hopper is wearing a really cool T-shirt, a Panda wearing a Luchadore's wrestling mask. But then I put a shadow across the front. So that's an example of me spending loads of time on something which no one ever sees. Time that was completely wasted! It's a really relatable situation and a great way to introduce Verity. You immediately realize she's willing to go a lot further than most people.

MONTY: Which foreshadows the end of the story.

Verity's dialogue here is all based on the time I used to work as a cleaner at Tesco's supermarket.

My job was to keep the floor shiny, and what I knew, but no-one else did, is the floor basically stayed shiny no matter what. So I used to spend the rest of the time sitting behind rows of clothes reading books, or setting up elaborate booby traps for my co-workers.

Anyway, my supervisor at the time was unremittingly sexually suggestive and highly pedantic. Perhaps she had issues with the amount of work I was doing. So while buffing the floor, I used to entertain these elaborate fantasies about recording a bitter indictment of her character and storming out while it played over the tannoy.

Though when I left I simply shook her by the hand and wished her the best, as you do.

MIKE: I think it's good to have jobs like that for a bit. It's character-building.

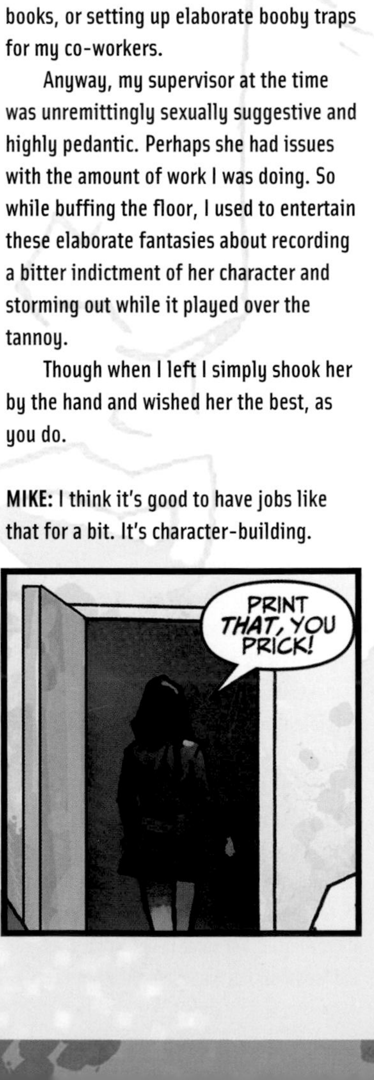
PRINT THAT, YOU PRICK!

Page 6 & 7: Monty's interview

MONTY: Initially I figured on using four characters in the *Death Sentence* story, but it was too crowded. Three works really well though. It lets us tell the story of the virus in a much more interesting way than with one main character.

There's always some resonance between contrasting scenes or panels you can bring out by cutting between the protagonists, or between the dialogue or captions of one character with the visuals of another. That makes for good comics. This sort of scene also allows us to mercilessly satirize celebrity culture. I really enjoy the work of comedians like Monty – but that doesn't excuse them from mockery. Everyone's fair game.

MIKE: I remember spending ages on this page too, the audience and the stage. I'd never drawn anything like that. I barely understood perspective at this point. I was pulling my hair out.

MONTY: We're basically getting into the whole psychosocial mood of the times with these scenes: modern attitudes to sex.

It's completely flipped from when AIDS first hit, and sex was this scary thing that could kill you. Promiscuity was frowned upon. Women were less objectified for a while, as the 'new man' culture had men rejecting the traditional stereotypes of birds, booze and football.

That all started to change in the Nineties, with lad culture. Now you have huge swathes of men and women thinking that being a porn star would be a fantastic life.

They can't see past the gaudy appeal of the surface imagery. There's no emphasis on the spiritual or emotional, it's all about the physical and the visual.

So the fact that there's a deadly disease that can kill you in six months demonstrably isn't going to stop people fucking. And the chance to be 'special', to be famous, that's worth dying for. It's just a satirical exaggeration of what I see around me. It's our job as storytellers to reflect the times.

MIKE: With Monty, you're never entirely sure what the consequences of a freewheeling attitude might be. It's ripe with possibility. Monty's an exemplar of contemporary hedonism.

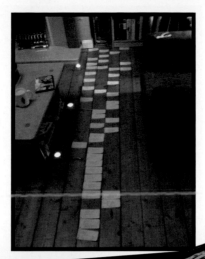

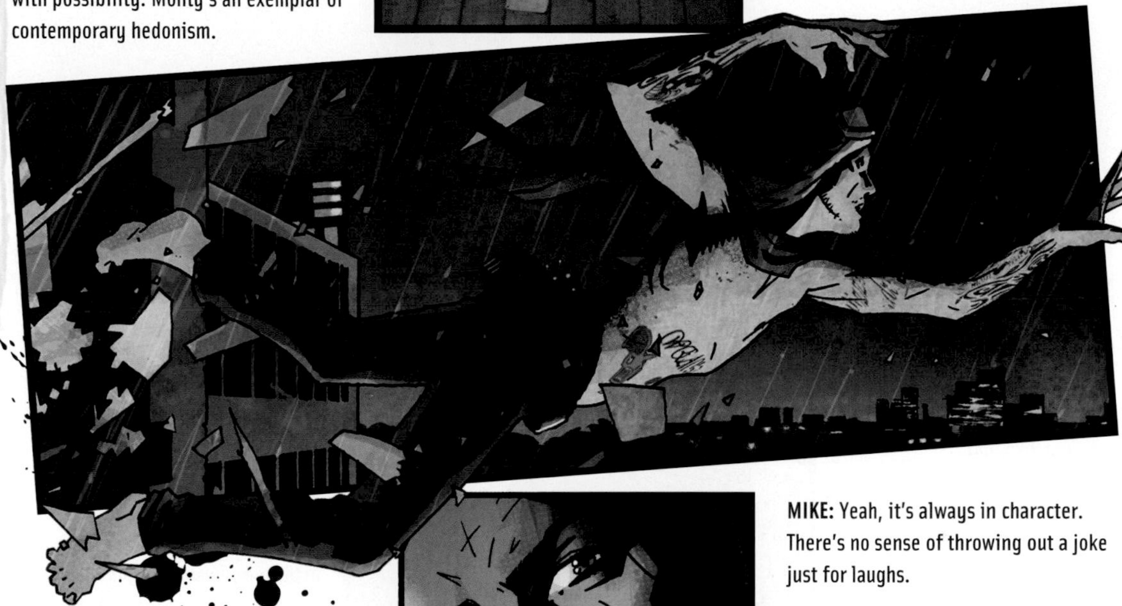

SERIOUSLY...
WHAT'VE I GOT TO LOSE?

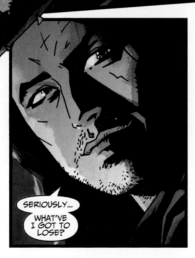

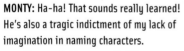

MONTY: Ha-ha! That sounds really learned! He's also a tragic indictment of my lack of imagination in naming characters.

At one point he was called Byron though, which was too awful. I tried on all kinds of names for him, and Monty just seemed to fit the best, unfortunately. I say unfortunately, because people tend to think he's me, and he isn't.

Anyway, by this stage we'd got the first seven pages lettered. So we put them into a preview comic and showed it around at the Kapow! Convention.

MIKE: You took it to Dundee too, I think?

MONTY: Yeah, the Dundee Comics Day. I'd also painted a couple of covers for issues #1 and #2, which were basically just the character designs I sent you at the start, and made a sex health website all about the G-plus virus, and put together a mock-up of a tabloid news story about Weasel's diagnosis.

Those things were important in setting the general tone and the attention to detail I wanted. The idea was to make a credible world that adults could relate to.

The preview got some great feedback and some interest from a couple of publishers. But I think, best of all, it showed us what the other person could do – we knew we could trust each other with more complex stuff. So when we carried on with the rest of the comic, we could both be a lot more ambitious.

Looking back on this time, I was surprised how funny people thought it was. I don't write jokes. I just try to write entertaining scenes and dialogue. The fact that people were laughing out loud comes from the truth of the moment, I think. And shock. I never sit around trying to come up with funny lines or anything like that.

MIKE: Yeah, it's always in character. There's no sense of throwing out a joke just for laughs.

Page 8 to 11: Weasel dives out of the window

MIKE: So at this point, we've introduced all the characters and we're pressing on with the story.

MONTY: Yeah, I guess if everyone who'd seen the preview comic thought it was crap we'd have just stopped on page seven and got on with our lives. We'd seen the art lettered at this point, and that really spurred me on to finish writing issue #1. It was just the full script that needed doing, I had the plot all worked out – I never start writing anything until I know the whole story, and what the ending is.

I use the cards system, which I got from an old screenplay book. The core of that system is simply writing what happens in each scene on a card and shuffling it around and replacing scenes until you have the best possible plot.

A good rule with a story is to always escalate the stakes, whether it's the spiritual, emotional or physical threats. I knew we were going to end with some truly epic action, with the US task force steaming in and missiles dropping all over London...

MIKE: So the sequel's an alien invasion, right?

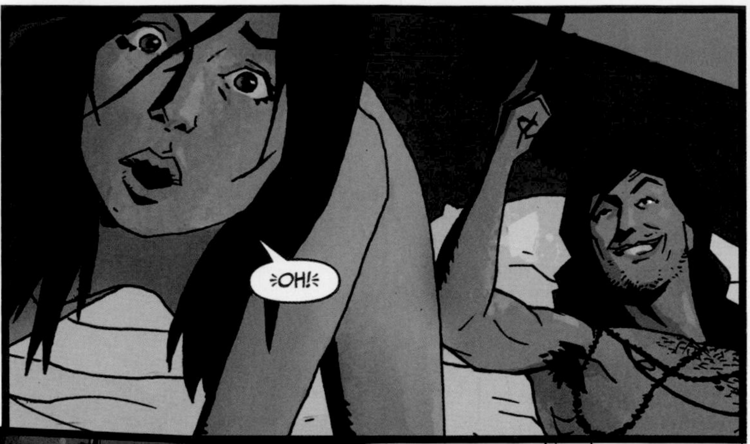
OH!

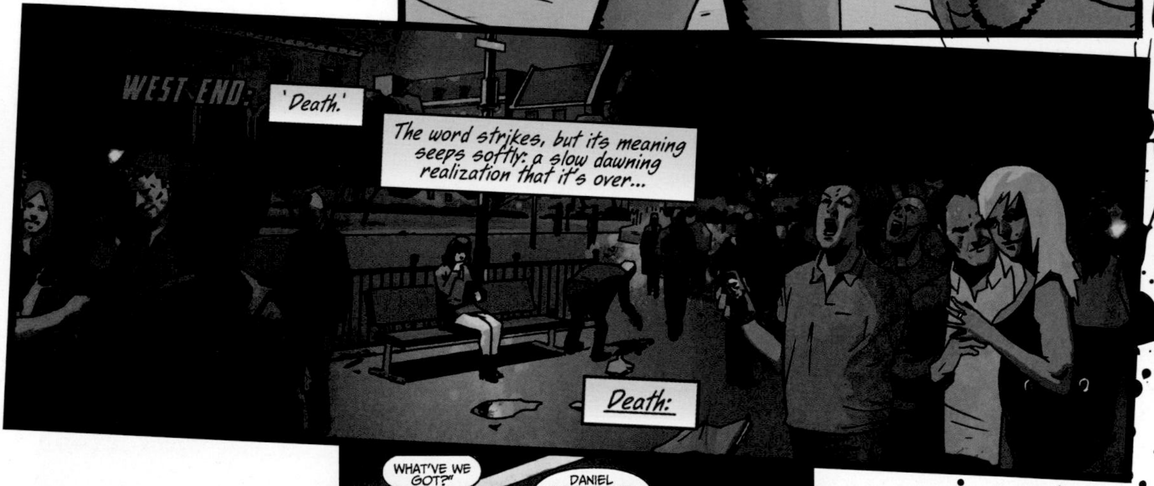
WEST END:
'Death.'
The word strikes, but its meaning seeps softly: a slow dawning realization that it's over...
Death:

MONTY: You joke, but....

MIKE: Transformers and Dinobots combined?

MONTY: Ha-ha! You wish! No, the thing was, it ends so big that you need to start small – with a drug dealer and a knife – to build that sense of progression.

What this scene does is reveal Weasel's admirable refusal to acquiesce to violence, and his private thoughts in the face of death: *"What a fraud I am the tunes I ain't written the first girl I kissed and how nothing really mattered did it!"* That gets to the core.

And it's the first glimpse of anything approaching superpowers. It was pretty late on that I settled on putting any kind of super-powered action in. But as I wrote the script, I found they made fantastic visual metaphors for the kind of issues I wanted to write about.

And they're a lot more fun to do – there's much more scope for imaginative action. We basically approached it from the characters' perspective, with the themes and plot first, and rethought superpowers in a way that felt fresh to us, that added something. So, in that sense, the superpowers are very much secondary.

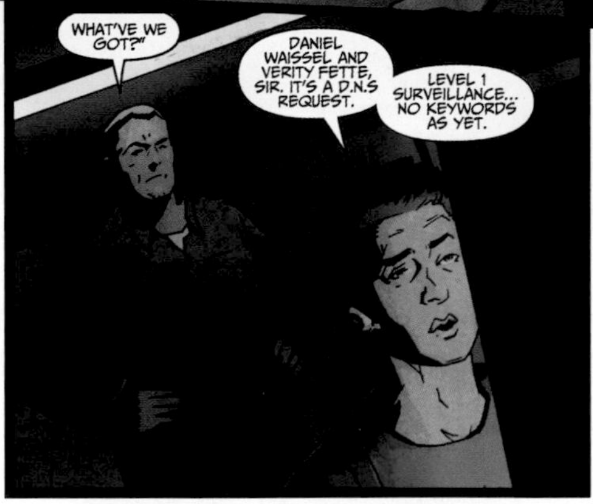
WHAT'VE WE GOT?"
DANIEL WAISSEL AND VERITY FETTE, SIR. IT'S A D.N.S REQUEST.
LEVEL 1 SURVEILLANCE... NO KEYWORDS AS YET.

MIKE: I remember it was tricky figuring out how Weasel slipped the handcuffs. It's almost misdirection in the end, rather than a close up. You're left wondering what's gone on, exactly, for a few pages at least.

MONTY: Yeah, mystery's important. It keeps you interested. That's something I've learned from doing this. As long as everything makes sense, the less you explain the better.

MIKE: In terms of coloring, you can see there's a color key. When you color a comic book it's easy to get lost in the individual panels, in the shades of someone's hair or something, so having these big themes to unify the scenes is really important. I really enjoyed coloring it.

I think it's an underappreciated part of making comic books. When I pick up a comic book I'm always looking at the color, I love seeing what people like Dave Stewart (*Hellboy*) are doing. I felt more confident about the coloring than the drawing. It took me ages to draw that bed for instance, and it's nothing.

There's an emphasis on the blues and greens in that scene - that's there to make the blood and Weasels red scarf stand out. Though I forgot to draw the scarf at first. What's it called?

MONTY: Shemagh. Beloved of Afghans and hipsters everywhere.

MIKE: I can't even pronounce it. I had to add it in later.

MONTY: It definitely took you a while to get your head round it.

MIKE: It's a weird thing to draw. I can't ever say I mastered it. I just discovered a shorthand that partially convinces. A lot of drawing comics is abbreviation.

MONTY: Comic characters don't generally have tattoos and shemaghs and so on. Which is why I designed the characters that way. I wanted an original, contemporary look. I wanted the comic to look different to anything else on the shelves. That's why I gave the covers that magazine feel. No costumes, no cartoon dynamism. I wanted them to appeal to comic fans and non comics fans equally.

But the tattoos are a fucker to draw in every panel – that's why no-one else does it. Your commitment was outstanding.

The other thing I notice looking back at these pages is that everything happens pretty fast. We always try to come into a scene as late as possible and get out as soon as possible, while moving the action forward.

By page 11 I think there's already been as many scenes, amusing lines, and dramatic moments as most full-length comics. I think that's partly why people like the comic; they get a good bang for their buck. I don't know why it came out that way.

MIKE: It's just the British way.

MONTY: Yeah, I guess a lot of it comes from reading *2000AD* growing up, where things happen much faster than in American comics. Partly it comes from knowing what we're doing. And partly it comes from necessity: a manic desire to grab people's attention from page one and never let it go.

Page 12: Monty beds a nun
MONTY: What I like about this page is how the location of the crucifix is entirely suggested – it's all in the reader's mind. You handled it masterfully.

MIKE: The mechanics of the final moment only work from that angle. It's all in the details.

MONTY: It's much more powerful that way, letting the reader do the work. And the shock of that moment misdirects you as to what's really going on with Monty.

Page 13: GCHQ listen in
MONTY: Using someone's iPhone as a de facto listening device is an established bit of spycraft – using the microphone – though it wasn't widely known at the time.

MIKE: You can use *Angry Birds* as a spying device, as it turns out.

MONTY: Yeah, since we made the comic the whole GCHQ and the NSA 'PRISM' thing has brought this center stage, but at the time no one was prominently talking about the privacy issues surrounding the so called 'war on terror'.

MIKE: Another instance of your prescience!

MONTY: Fuck off! I just thought it made a good subtext. Practically, it just seemed the most likely way governments would deal with tracking something like this. Also GCHQ are based in the most fantastic James Bond style building, it was too good to pass up.

MIKE: Even I didn't believe it at first. I just drew a normal looking office block.

MONTY: I had to send over some reference photos of their doughnut HQ. It's one of those times when truth is stranger than fiction.

Page 14 & 15: Verity's diary
MIKE: I don't feel I left enough room for the captions here. If I was doing it now I'd generate more dead space.

But I like the guy bending over next to her in the first panel. In my mind he was farting in her face. It's a real low point for her, everything's going wrong.

MONTY: I love the way you drew it. It genuinely feels like that part of London. And Verity's thoughts here really get to the heart of the book.

I'm really happy with the vibrant tone of *Death Sentence*, and the humor, but the plot concerns people dying in six months, and you have to convey that accurately or the whole premise falls apart.

I spent a long time finding the correct tone, the correct balance between all these elements, and that's what brings the original feel I think.

It all came from the initial painting I did of Weasel, the cover to issue #2. That painting made me feel a certain way, and the challenge was getting the script to

Well, fuck them. Fuck them all.

I'm **not** done yet.

evoke the same emotion. I did loads of research into people who knew they were dying, and that forms the spine of the book with scenes like this.

I've had a fair amount of feedback from cancer survivors who tell me that scenes like this ring true for them. I mean, *Death Sentence* is meant to be entertaining – but it's also about dying and the point of life and the importance of creativity. The *Death Sentence* isn't the virus, it's the short lifespan we all have. The virus is just the lens that brings it all into sharp focus.

Verity's frustrations here also convey my feelings writing the comic: *"All my pretentions and I never amounted to shit. Just another faceless no-mark who fucked and fretted and fizzled out forgotten."* That pretty much sums up how I felt. Most of the essential components of the comic come from personal experience.

Page 16 & 17: Weasel in the studio

MONTY: Like many people I dabbled in bands for a while, but I didn't write the songs – so Weasel's creative frustrations regarding song-writing here are me describing how hard it is to paint.

MIKE: Creativity's a theme of the book. I think a lot of people can relate to that.

MONTY: To me, creativity's an essential part of humanity, something everyone has, and the key reason why we're the dominant species. We can imagine very complex stuff that doesn't exist, and then make it.

Most people have untapped talents, and if their creativity is stifled I've noticed that their desire for fulfilment and validation manifests in other ways. That's explains a lot of the behavior I see around me in the world, and in the comic. I love that bottom panel too. Weasel alone in the darkness.

MIKE: Yeah, I was happy with that one. Weasel might have a lot of cockiness and swagger, but that moment really captures his internal mind-state.

Page 18: The record company pass judgement

MONTY: The music business is often so ridiculous it's unmockable, but that doesn't stop us trying.

MIKE: Probably we haven't gone far enough.

MONTY: It's not hard to spot the Pete Doherty influence in these pages too. Weasel's basically an amalgam of four or five different rock stars and my own imagination. And the guy with the goatee actually looks a bit like the guy who ran the record company I used for inspiration.

MIKE: That's just coincidence. Though the ginger guy is based on Rufus Dayglo, the *Tank Girl* artist.

Page 19 to 21: Verity's appointment

MONTY: So here we're getting to the end of the comic. How do you end a comic? I had no clue, I'd never written one before. Ending with Verity seemed a good plan – she's the main character and we started with her. Bigger panels, to illustrate the shock of these traumatic events, preceded by slowing down the action for greater contrast seemed to work. But when I finished it I thought it lacked something as an ending, so I shortened this scene to add an additional page.

Page 22: How a real team operates

MONTY: This basically serves to take things out on a high, expanding the story to imply a wider scope and much more excitement to come. Tune in next time, kind of thing. I love the old Republic serials, and I love the cliffhanger element of episodic fiction.

MIKE: I remember the mechs had to be designed beforehand; how they worked with the choppers.

It's not always clear how much a drawing comes into play later, when you work on a comic, but you said they'd be integral so we spent some time going back and forth with the design.

MONTY: And with the quote at the end there, the important thing to remember is Grenfell died from a shell wound to the head shortly after writing *'Into Battle'*. That's sadly where his kind of thinking gets you. So the future doesn't look bright for anyone, as we leave the first chapter.

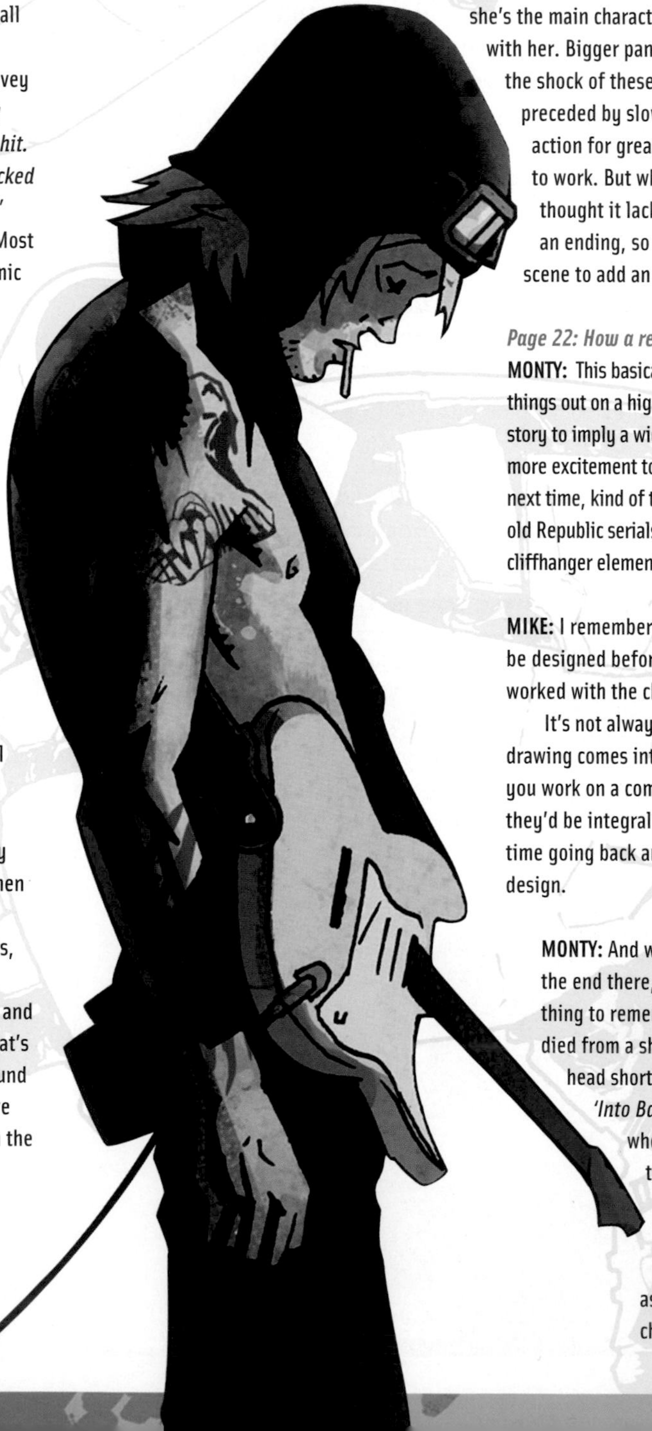

CHAPTER 2

MONTY: One of the main reasons for making the comic was to show what we could do, and to push ourselves and learn new things. That's partly why I didn't want to draw it. Apart from the fact I'm not talented enough, I would have just written easy things to draw instead of what was best for the story.

MIKE: Yeah, similarly, even when I'm doing the layouts I'm just thinking about what the best shot will be, and as I do that, I often realize that I can't draw it. But I still go ahead and do it.

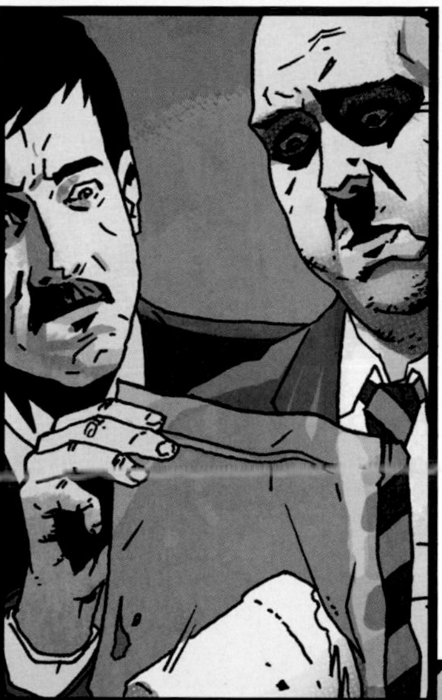

Page 1 and 2: Weasel's impromptu gig:

MONTY: This scene very much encapsulates the mood of the comic that I had in my head from the start. I wanted to capture that whole fucked-up rock star vibe, but in a unique way, not just some clichéd scene in a stadium. I think almost every scene ever set at a gig in any media has been as dull as arsewater. So I dug around and found Pete Doherty had given an impromptu gig to fans from the window of his flat, so that was my inspiration. You can find the footage on YouTube: Kate Moss hanging out the window and so forth.

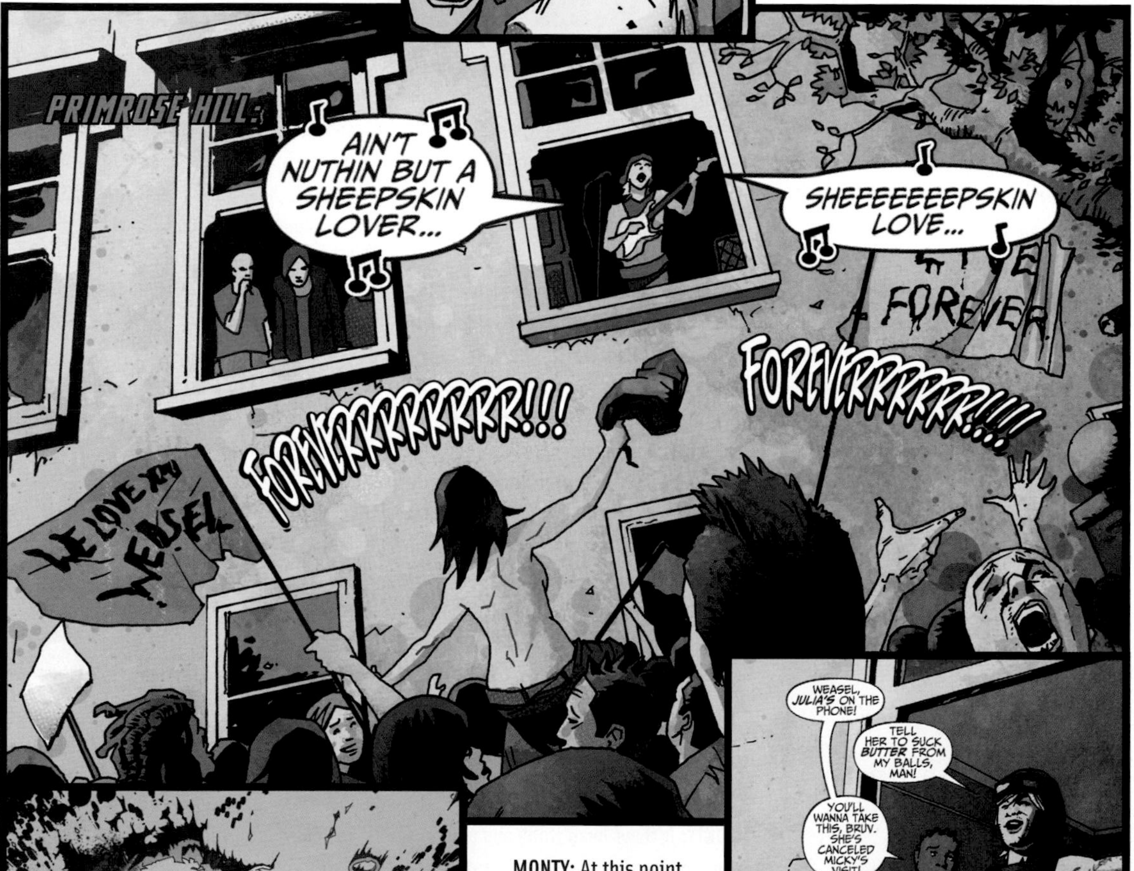
PRIMROSE HILL:
AIN'T NUTHIN BUT A SHEEPSKIN LOVER...
SHEEEEEEEPSKIN LOVE...
FOREVER
FOREVRRRRRRRR!!!
FOREVRRRRRR!!!!
WE LOVE YOU WEASEL
WEASEL, JULIA'S ON THE PHONE!
TELL HER TO SUCK BUTTER FROM MY BALLS, MAN!
YOU'LL WANNA TAKE THIS, BRUV. SHE'S CANCELED MICKY'S VISIT!

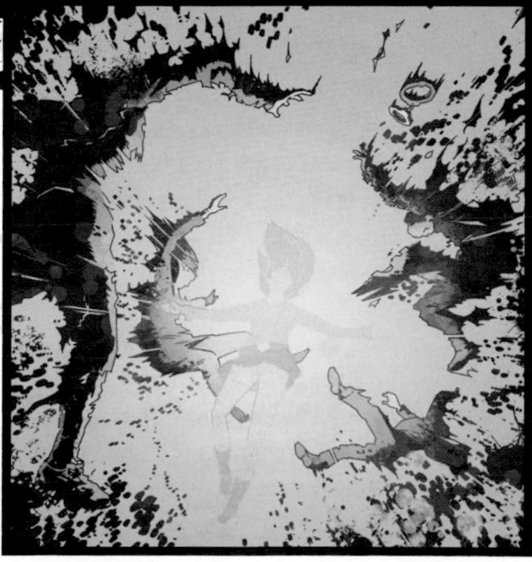

MONTY: At this point, I remember wanting to take the story in unexpected directions, and try some new techniques, without losing what was good about the first issue. So two of the things in my mind were to write some longer scenes, and to write an action scene, but to do it all in an original *Death Sentence* kind of way.

MIKE: It shows what a big star Weasel is, despite his inadequacies, which is important. I do own a Stratocaster, so that made the scene easier. I could smash the guitar around.

MONTY: And it introduces his family and his kid and his problems, which make him more relatable. The ending wouldn't work without all that.

Page 3 & 4: Detectives investigate
MONTY: This is one of my favorite scenes in the comic. I love the timing of the dialogue between the Detectives and Cameron. I like the way it establishes the power and duplicity of The Department of National Security.

The DNS is an invention, but a credible one, I hope. It's one step on from reality. I can see something like this being created to deal with an increase in chronic threats, whether it's terrorists or deadly pandemics.

Page 5 to 11: Verity gets captured
MONTY: This is the big action scene I was talking about. Action scenes aren't why anyone liked the first chapter – because there aren't any – so I was a little nervous about this. But you can only write what you love, and I love a good action scene.

As the soldiers close in we get more of Verity's backstory with Lou, and see some of the weird stuff the virus is doing to her. We spent a long time figuring out how to handle Verity's invisibility.

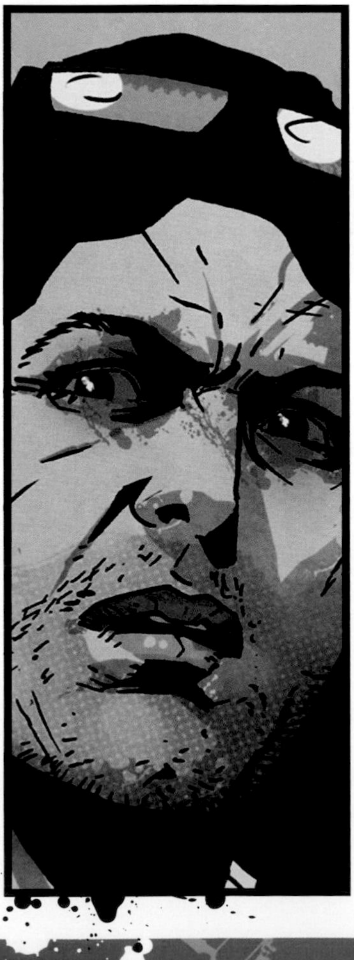

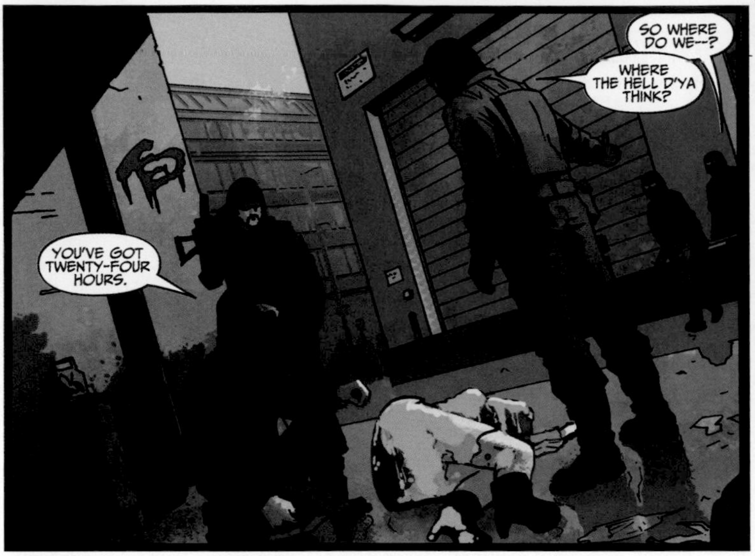
SO WHERE DO WE--?
WHERE THE HELL D'YA THINK?
YOU'VE GOT TWENTY-FOUR HOURS.

There are various options and most are pretty cheesy. I really wanted to do her completely invisible, with just the odd splash of green acid indicating her position. That's easy to write but fucking difficult to draw.

MIKE: It's a question of how invisible to make her, technically, as she dissolves away. And then it's a storytelling challenge. The camera follows her in, and the clue is the acidic discharge. There were more footsteps and so on but we took them out. We spent ages going back and forth on the glow effects too. We wanted the reader to do the work. The café's a real café, too. It's closed now, it was a great place.

MONTY: How did you figure out where she was in each panel, in the end?

MIKE: I think I drew her and then didn't render her, possibly. I can't remember.

MONTY: It flows beautifully and you're never in any doubt where she is or what's occurring, even though she's completely invisible for five pages. It's a great bit of storytelling on your part.

I remember when you were doing the page in the alley you were like, *"This is the best page I've ever done!!"* And then when it was finished you were like, *"Nah... Definitely not."*

MIKE: It often turns out that way. Things that you think are great are not. And things that you think suck turn out great.

Page 12: Weasel get his oats
MONTY: This moves Weasel's story forward and fleshes out his character. I think the facial expressions here are fantastic. With Weasel, the essential challenge is always why would anyone give a shit about him, and acting like this from you just makes establishing that empathy so much easier.

MIKE: I quite like the girl leaning over to kiss him. She gives a nice yin and yang to the composition.

Page 13 to 15: Vainglorious Eruptions, Ltd
MONTY: This introduces us to the real Monty, rather than the glib media presence. There's comedy here, but also consequences.

I remember we spent a lot of time debating whether to make his eyes glow red, or just have his mental influence be implied.

I was worried it was too clichéd, the red eyes, but I knew that with the huge crowd scenes later it'd be a great way to show Monty's influence spreading.

Having decided to do it, I wanted it to be really subtle – almost incidental. But you made it a discreet panel, and in retrospect you were right.

MIKE: It's one of those storytelling things that always come up in comics. Two characters talking to each other, you're looking past one of them at another, but you can't see both of their eyes clearly. So I put in the extra panel to make it clear.

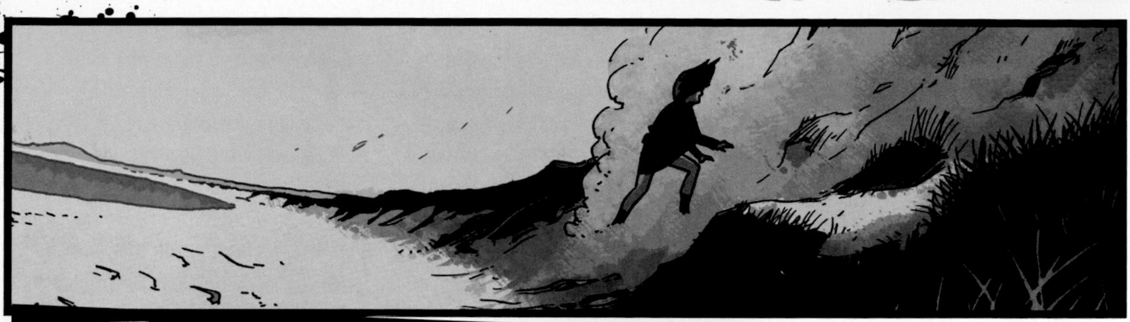

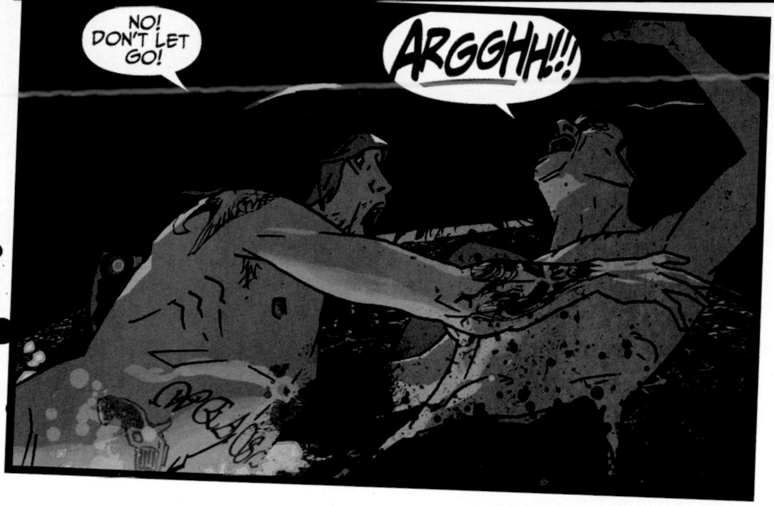

NO! DON'T LET GO!
ARGGHH!!

Page 16: Weasel kills someone

MIKE: This was a tough one.

MONTY: Yeah, I don't want to dwell on the numerous groupies or hangers-on who've died in the company of celebrities, as it's disrespectful.

The point is that the stars involved are making so much money for everyone that there's often a way found for them to wriggle off the hook, and for their career to continue.

When it doesn't, it's more to do with the fact that they're revealed to not be who they said they were, in the public's eyes, rather than because of the death itself. The incredible luster of star power bedazzles the legal system, just as it does the rest of the world. It's disturbing.

We spent ages on how to convey the effect of Weasel sinking into the depths, literally dragging this poor girl down with him. I envisaged it more side on, but you did it from above and I think it works just as well.

Most comics don't have a lead character kill someone innocent like this; it's too risky. But it's a great storytelling challenge, to maintain empathy with Weasel, and we're always pleased by how many people genuinely like him.

To be honest, we're fairly surprised just how much we like him ourselves.

MIKE: I think he probably appeals to the hopeless fuck-up in everyone. That's the secret.

MONTY: You're probably right. And it says something about human nature, I think - the way we assess people on surface characteristics like charm, humour and physical appearance rather than more opaque qualities like their integrity. The former qualities are more obvious and a lot more fun in the pub.

Page 17 to 19: Verity arrives at the Island

MONTY: This is one of my favorite scenes. It's all based on a holiday my wife and I took when she was eight months' pregnant. Naturally, we went to an armed forces live-ammunition zone.

MIKE: Romance isn't dead!

MONTY: Yeah, I really know how to treat a lady! It's one of the least populated areas in Europe, all these uninhabited little islands off the north-west coast of Scotland. The Army, navy and air force get together and bomb the fuck out of rocks and old boats, and do all their combined maneuvers.

I probably do them an injustice, but that's the general gist of it. You can watch from the cliffs, and explore some of the beaches. I sent Mike the photos and he captured the ambience of the beaches and towering sand dunes perfectly. All we did was move it a bit further out to sea.

MIKE: The whole scene's a bit of fresh air, quite literally. It seemed important that it was a nice day, to differentiate it from rainy London. Comics are a visual medium and it's important to let the reader see interesting and contrasting images like this.

MONTY: I like it because no-one was expecting the story to go this way. I love old TV shows like the *Avengers*, the weirdness of it all, and that was very much in my mind. That's why she's not just marched through the door under armed guard, it would be too predictable. I think the wordless reveal of the Island is pretty much the best page in the comic. It's thrilling.

MIKE: It's fun following the planes across, as they fly overhead and you turn with Verity. It really puts you in the moment.

MONTY: There's also something important going on here that no-one's ever noticed, which makes me very happy. We'll pick up on that later.

Page 20 to 22: Weasel goes on the run

MONTY: This argument raises the stakes nicely as the cops close in. There's probably not enough space for the comedy trip as Weasel runs off, but I couldn't resist.

MIKE: Our mission is to entertain. And it's just more entertaining that way.

MONTY: I think you were deep into Moebius at the time. That's why the top two panels at the end are drawn that way.

MIKE: I like the way Moebius was always playing with space and angles, doing this incredible stuff, but then he'd just plop the camera down and go side-on for contrast.

I was reading a lot of European artists at this point. I also remember my normal pen broke down, so I had to use a different one. I got a new pen in the post a few days later, so these are the only pages drawn with the wrong pen.

MONTY: The quote at the end simply highlights that what you want to do with your life is rarely what you're actually doing. That frustration contributes to a lot of the behavior and issues we focus on in *Death Sentence*, as far as I'm concerned.

CHAPTER 3

Page 1 to 3: Monty's backstory

MONTY: At this stage of the story we need to flesh out Monty a bit. We've spent a lot more time with Weasel and Verity, and we've learnt more about their personalities and outlook in every scene. But the end of the comic won't appear credible unless we learn more about Monty's motivations now.

It's the most complex sequence so far, but everything else we'd attempted had worked out well so we were increasingly confident. We had no idea that any of this stuff would work though, back then. There're a lot of shifts in time and juxtapositions between similar compositions, highlighting contrasts and resonances. I spent ages writing it and I was really surprised when it turned out to be only three pages long.

Page 4 to 7: Verity's introduction to the Island.

MONTY: So this scene is basically exposition, though it also establishes the relationship between Dr Lunn's team, Verity, and the Government. I figured I'd spent two chapters teasing and implying things and now it was time to provide a few answers.

MIKE: It's the right time for Verity to be asking questions.

MONTY: She doesn't get all the answers, though – just enough to explain why she sticks around, and to let readers know that there was a thoroughly thought out backstory.

The trick with exposition is to unfold it naturally, so no-one notices. You don't want two people just sitting there telling each other stuff. So I figured a huge tour of the Island would keep things visually interesting, intercut with apposite scenes from Weasel and Monty's narrative. That way no-one really notices it's exposition at all.

It was a really challenging scene for you to draw, and I thought you did a brilliant job. I remember you redrew the elevator scene, to match what you did later. To get a bigger scale and show more people in the facility. It had the epic sweep I was after.

Page 8 to 11: Weasel visits his son

MONTY: As I mentioned earlier, the challenge with Weasel is making anyone give a fuck, so his relationship with his son is really important. It's all part of making him a well-rounded and believable person.

And it's important to establish the close relationship with his son, for the ending to have its emotional impact. People have multiple facets to their personalities - they're never just one-note. Weasel loves his son and wishes he could spend more time with him. That doesn't contradict the other aspects of his character at all.

I remember we had a long discussion about the tree to his window too. You basically said you didn't think it was possible to get to a window in this way, and I did.

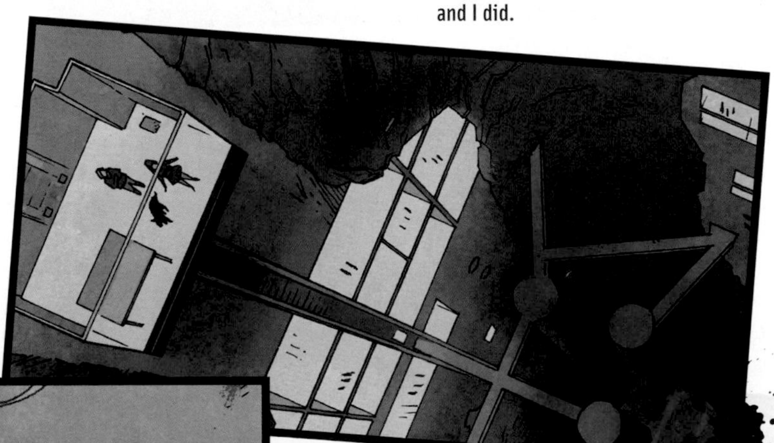

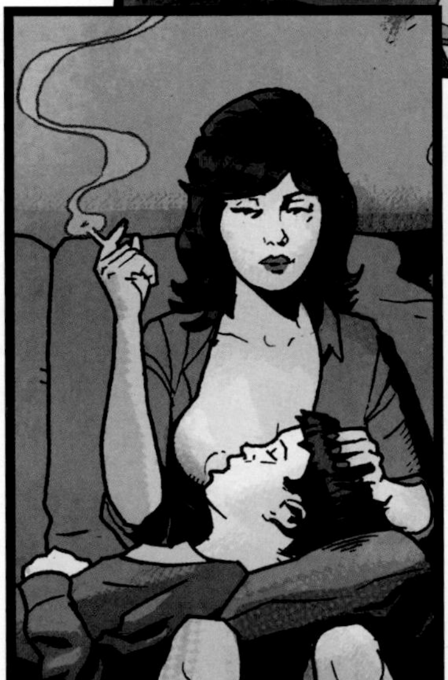

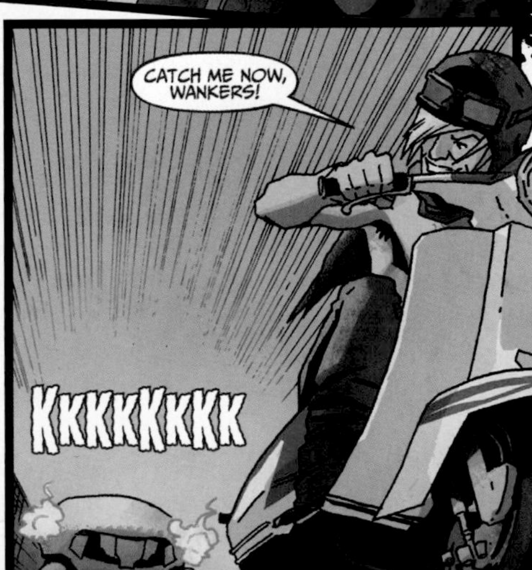
CATCH ME NOW, WANKERS!
KKKKKKKK

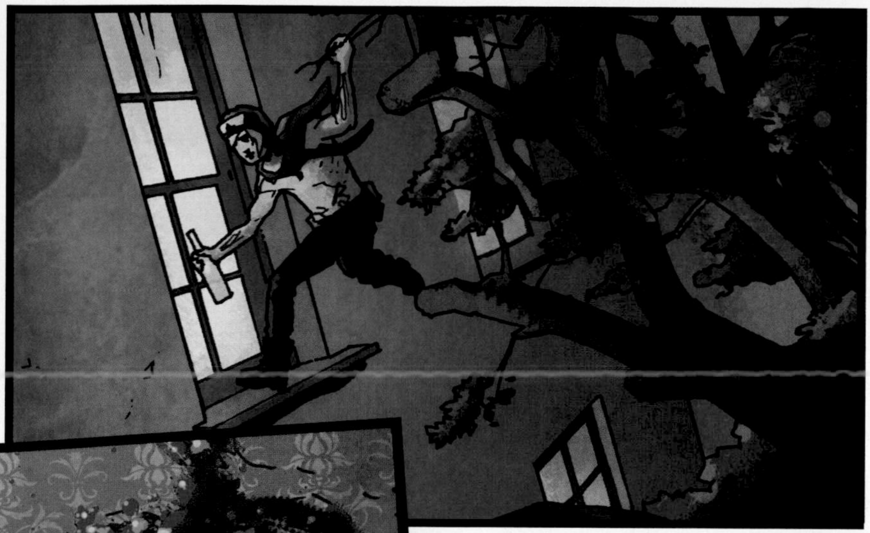

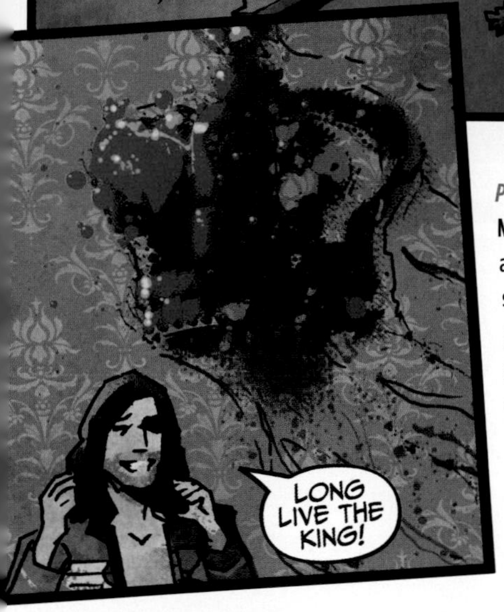
LONG LIVE THE KING!

I was outside when you rang so I started taking scores of tree pictures, anything I could see which could support a man climbing to a window ledge.

Unfortunately my phone can only send one photo at a time, so you rang up shortly after quite annoyed I was spamming you.

MIKE: I didn't want to open them because I thought your email had a virus. And then when I did open them they were full of trees, so I just thought you'd gone mental.

MONTY: Ha-ha! The shredded wheat spew on Weasel's pillow comes from a titanic bender I went on in San Sebastian once. When I woke up I'd thrown up this weirdly-textured puke all over the youth hostel. It was the tapas from twenty or so different bars, and it was everywhere. They were understandably quite pissed off. They found me asleep with a pillow under a running shower – with absolutely no clue what I'd done.

Page 12 to 15: Weasel's scooter chase

MONTY: So this is another in an escalating series of action sequences. As the emotional pressure ramps up, so does the physical pressure: first a guy with a knife, then some soldiers, now mechs.

Much like the scene in Chapter 2, I wanted to make it original, so I figured a mechs vs. scooter sequence was the way to go. I've never seen that before. I got in some nods to The Stone Roses and *Quadrophenia*, which are two of my favourite things. I based it on a real part of London, and you worked out your own map of the area so the chase would make sense.

MIKE: Yeah, I wanted there to be some logic to the layout of the streets and houses. He basically goes round in a loop. Even his brilliant escape is futile and incompetent, going round in circles.

Page 16 to 18: Monty and the Queen

MONTY: This scene arises from thinking of original ways for Monty to take over the capital, in keeping with his character and desires.

We see bad guys take control of the seat of power all the time, and it's usually some tediously militaristic action scene. I think we can safely say no-one's done it this way before. Again, the final moment is entirely suggested, all in the reader's mind, which makes it much more powerful, I hope.

MIKE: You're saying it would look less powerful with a full frontal of Monty shagging the Queen?

MONTY: Um, it would be less credible I think. More cartoonish.

MIKE: Yeah, it's better from outside.

Page 19 to 22: Monty becomes 'King'

MIKE: This scene's difficult, because of the likenesses: do you trace them, or copy photos? Or just do something that's in the spirit? I went with the latter approach. And yet another elaborate rug.

MONTY: You're a master of rugs. What's the story with that?

MIKE: My parents were rugs. It's a tribute to them. Thank you, rugs! Oh, look, I didn't draw the fence round Buckingham Palace for some reason. I have no idea why.

MONTY: The satirical point we're making here is there's apparently nothing a celebrity can do that can't eventually be excused by the right kind of PR advice. The key is simply to pre-empt public condemnation by revealing all your sordid secrets yourself, so you don't appear duplicitous, or engineer ostentatious displays of contrition and 'rehabilitation' to placate the press and public.

MIKE: It gives you free rein to keep acting awfully if you're suitably contrite. You see that with religion, too. Monty knows how to play the game.

MONTY: We've seen this type of nonsense play out so many times in the media, and yet it still works. Though obviously we've exaggerated it all for effect. We also get into the area of why people do the crazy things they do in the first place. Are we masters of our own destiny, or slaves to our physiology? A lot of what we do isn't logical; it's emotional and chemical.

MIKE: In Monty's case, I think he's trying to make up for something lacking in his life.

MONTY: Which isn't logical, it's emotional. The argument here is that among other things, our minds are a survival device looking after our genes, rather than the captain of the ship. A lot of the side-effects of our ability to think are painful and irrelevant to the core benefit, which is to ensure the information within our genes is looked after and passed on. And, on that bomb-shell – we end with the prospect of a huge battle at Buckingham Palace.

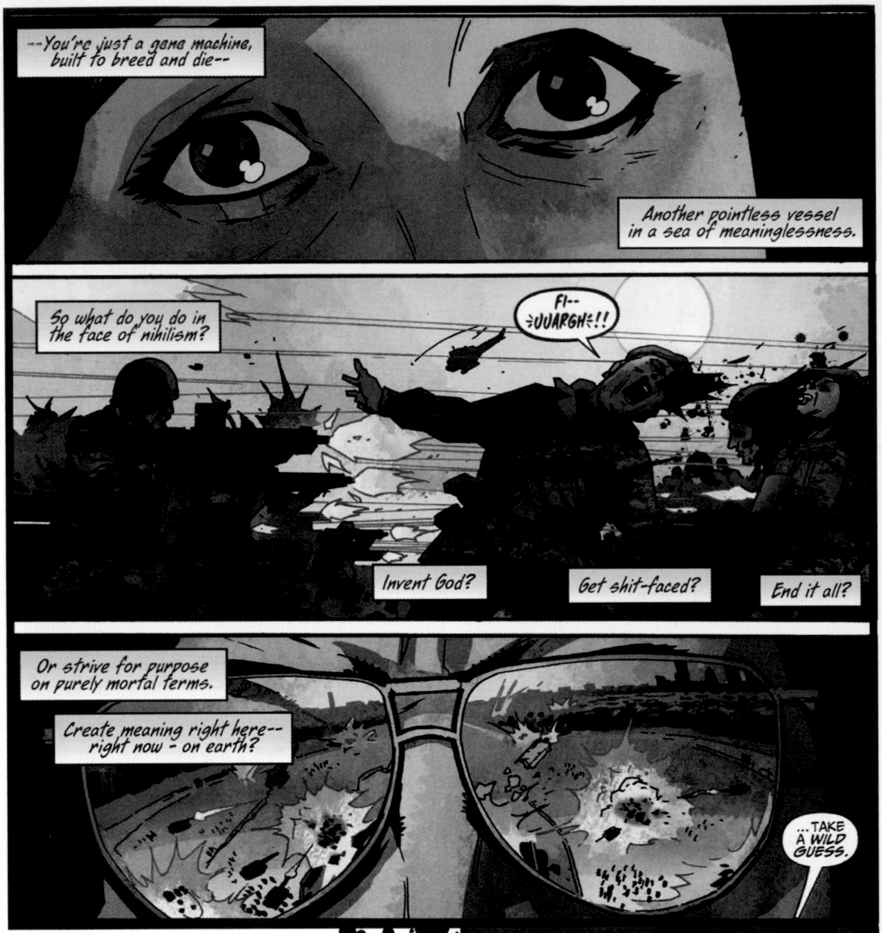
--You're just a gene machine, built to breed and die--
Another pointless vessel in a sea of meaninglessness.
So what do you do in the face of nihilism?
FI-- UUARGH!!
Invent God?
Get shit-faced?
End it all?
Or strive for purpose on purely mortal terms.
Create meaning right here-- right now - on earth?
...TAKE A WILD GUESS.

CHAPTER 4

Page 1 to 3: The Battle for Buckingham Palace

MONTY: The following scenes are the most structurally complex in the whole graphic novel, I think.

We intercut between two or three different narratives and draw various resonances between Verity's predicament and Monty's.

I carried on in this vein for much of Chapter Four, getting more and more complicated and slowly disappearing up my own arse.

MIKE: Yeah. I guess you can only do it for so long.

MONTY: Disappear up my arse? You'd be surprised, I've got a spelunking helmet and sandwiches.

MIKE: No, the juxtapositions! It really works well here: the counterpoint between creativity and destruction. It gives it a dreamlike quality, as she lies in bed there.

MONTY: Eventually I took a dispassionate look at what I'd written and decided it was becoming too self-indulgent.

I don't like it when writers show off how clever they are; it gets between the reader and the story.

So I rewrote all the subsequent scenes and returned to a more conventional approach to telling the story from Chapter Five onwards.

The point about all the different techniques we used through Chapters One to Four is that hopefully no-one really notices them; they're simply the best way to tell the story.

MIKE: There's no point descending into complexity for complexity's sake.

MONTY: We made a conscious effort after Chapter Four to return to the approach that had worked so well in the first three issues, and just finish the story.

We're also expanding on the earlier themes here – Selfish Gene theory, creativity, and how we deal with the aching pointlessness of our existence – foreshadowing the final chapter.

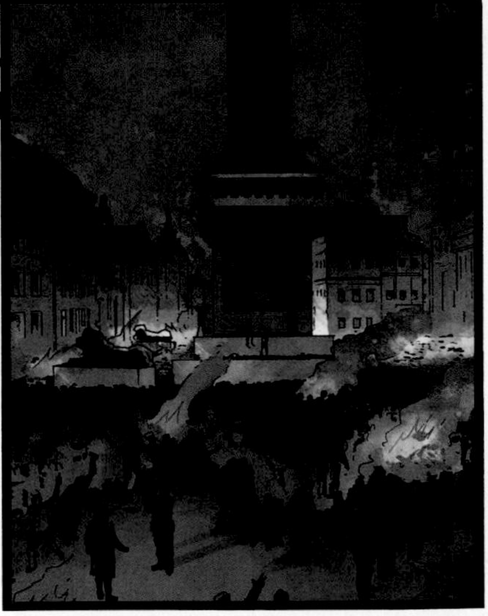

Again, there's a lot of personal stuff about yearning to create a great work of art, failing to be a great painter, and the compromises you make to get by in life. It's much more interesting than just showing Monty defeating the army.

MIKE: It's a bit more relatable than lots of shooting. I've never been in a pitched battle in central London.

Page 4 & 5: Weasel arrives at the Island

MONTY: Another of our one-page scenes, as Weasel eagerly complies with Dr Lunn's program in return for drugs.

It was your idea to take Weasel's helmet and shemagh off, on the grounds it would be ridiculous not to. You were probably right.

MIKE: It drives me mad; the way in cartoons people always wear the same clothes. Like in *Scooby Doo*.

MONTY: Whereas I was very much – *"This is the character's look and I want you to stick with it"*. I guess that comes from my background in character design, and how if an element is missing the whole look and feel of the character changes. So I asked you to put it all back on again as soon as Weasel was practically fit enough to get them from his locker.

MIKE: I guess it's like Indiana Jones' hat, isn't it. It always stays on – even in fight scenes.

MONTY: It's an odd one. Everything else I did was driven by how credible it was, but I was the complete opposite with this.

Maybe I'm just an idiot. Perhaps it's one of those things that no-one really notices unless you draw attention to it. People don't generally worry about how often Batman changed his pants when they're reading a story. Apart from you, obviously, fretting over Shaggy's underkeks.

Page 6 & 7: Monty extends his influence

MONTY: So, again, our principal concern here was to show Monty expanding his influence across London in an original way.

The flashbacks in the briefing room and MTV report do that pretty succinctly I think. It's getting tougher and tougher for you though, with all these crowd scenes.

MIKE: Yeah, crazy.

MONTY: The thing I remember here was agonising for ages over whether it was credible for society to break down in this way, and then as you were drawing it the London riots erupted. It showed how flimsy social order truly really is.

MIKE: It does. I had this on the drawing board while it all kicked off outside. I lived above a shop in Hackney, so I had my back-up hard drive all ready to jump out the back window if it all went up in flames.

MONTY: It was scary because so many shops were being arbitrarily looted and firebombed. I was really worried about you both. I remember you joking you were sleeping with your shoes on.

MIKE: I was ready to go. I don't think anyone was going to break in though. I was living above an organic café.

MONTY: I had visions of you running through the riot-torn streets with a sheet of paper, sketching the scenes around you. I think you started to use a finer line around here though? To convey the distance and scale.

MIKE: I just turned the pen round and drew with the back of the nib. You can do that with a lot of pens. It saves you putting the pen down and picking another one up, which breaks your flow.

Page 8: The DNS respond

MONTY: It's important to show here that Monty hasn't won, that there're still powerful forces arrayed against him.

Without conflict and a sense of peril the story would lose all its impetus. And 'horse tranquilisers' just means ketamine.

MIKE: The guy with the beard is based on Louis CK, the American comedian. I was watching his show, *Louie*, at the time and thought it was the best thing I'd ever seen.

Page 9 & 10 Monty takes down the Prime Minister

MONTY: Again, I just wanted to do this in a way I hadn't seen before, while making it crystal-clear what was going on. And there's always time for a bit of *Top Gun* comedy. It's the type of thing only Monty would do.

My feeling on this kind of humor is you have to choose something everyone's familiar with, and do something fresh with it, rather than worry about being cutting-edge or hip. Because what's hip today might be forgotten tomorrow and no longer make any sense.

MIKE: This scene was strangely enjoyable to draw. I just wish I'd done a better likeness!

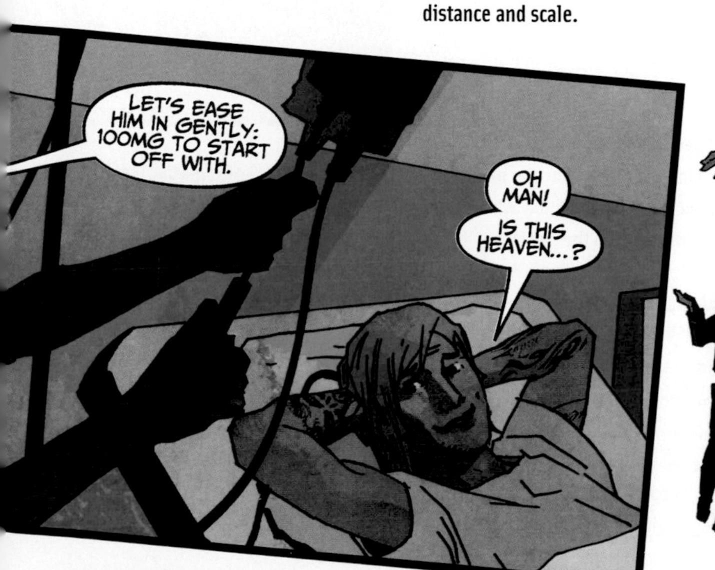
LET'S EASE HIM IN GENTLY: 100MG TO START OFF WITH.
OH MAN! IS THIS HEAVEN...?

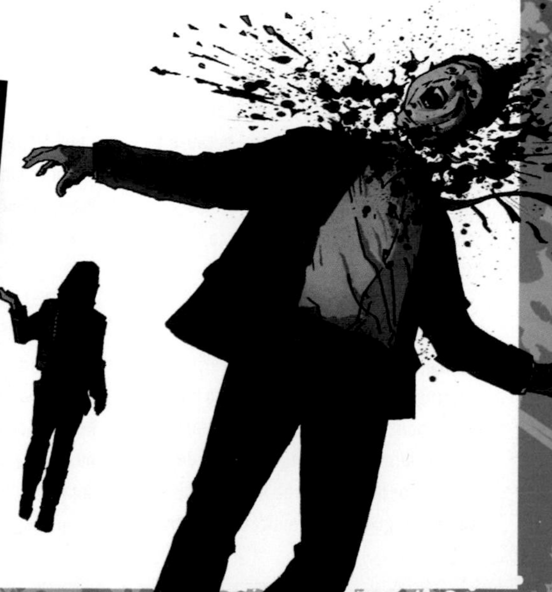

Page 11: Monty sets people 'free'

MONTY: This is the culmination of Monty's machinations, 'setting people free', as he sees it. It's a satirical exaggeration of the notion that the way to be happy is to do whatever the fuck you want while getting off your tits on drugs and alcohol. He's just replacing one form of governance with another, which, like Stalin, is generally more destructive than the original regime.

Page 12 & 13: Dr Lunn reacts to events in London

MONTY: The characters are now in two locations, the Island and London, so you have to keep them linked together. And we also learn more about what they're doing on the Island and the other G-plus patients, some of whom we'll come back to later.

MIKE: It's difficult drawing people round a table. They all have to sit in the order that they're gonna speak, but that order might change from panel to panel. But the order round the table stays the same.

Page 14: Weasel gets creative

MONTY: This scene is based on a certain well-known guitar player in a well-known band, who retained an incredible level of creativity despite being smacked out of his head for twenty years.

Page 15 to 22: Creativity: the key to power

MONTY: This is probably the culmination of our experiments with technique. Every time we'd tried something new so far, it worked, so I thought, why not go for it? Though I did rein back on some of the more experimental stuff here, because I thought it was getting too metaphysical and pretentious. I didn't want to get carried away, so I rewrote it all to be a little simpler.

Basically this sequence shows what Monty's doing with his power, and intercuts that with Weasel and Verity meeting on The Island and finding out more about the virus. What they learn in turn explains how Monty is able to do what he does, because he's the most creatively-successful guy in the comic. Each scene adds to the other.

I also tried a different approach with dialogue, which is basically putting a lot more balloons in each panel in a rat-a-tat kind of way.

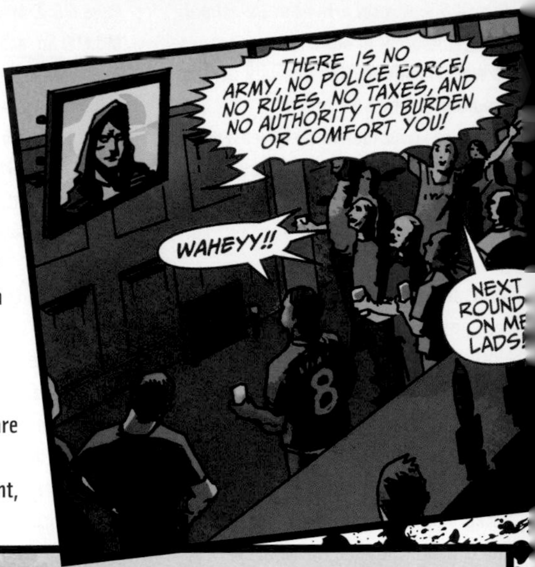
THERE IS NO ARMY, NO POLICE FORCE! NO RULES, NO TAXES, AND NO AUTHORITY TO BURDEN OR COMFORT YOU!
WAHEYY!!
NEXT ROUND ON ME LADS!

It didn't really work for me, so I edited it right down after it was lettered, but it's still the most crowded sequence in the comic in terms of how many people are talking in each panel.

You've got to experiment, because it's the only way to learn.

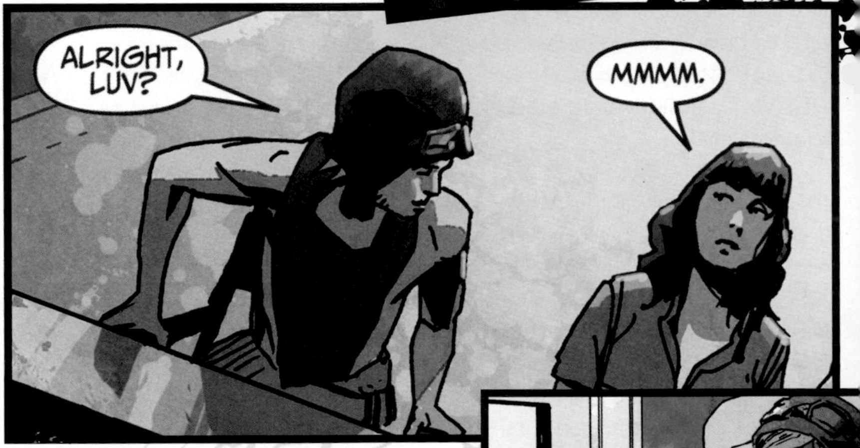
ALRIGHT, LUV?
MMMM.

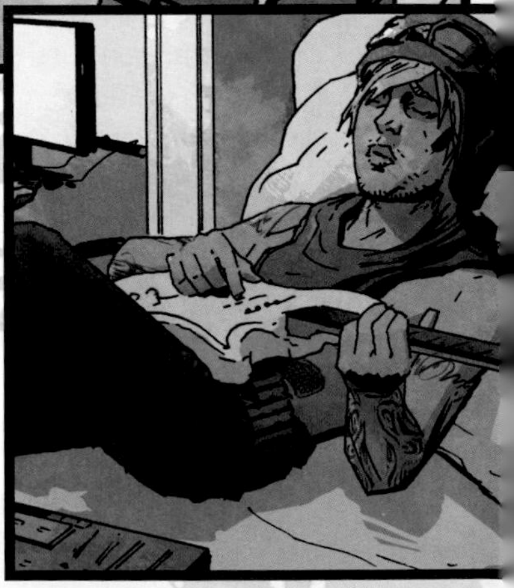

In the end it just solidified my view that the sparse approach to dialogue I'd used in the first few chapters was the right way to go. So there's a lot less talking-per-panel in subsequent chapters. And my favorite panels are generally the ones where no-one talks at all.

MIKE: They're certainly easier for me to draw.
I feel trapped when people are talking about too many emotions in one panel; too many balloons. You don't know what state to hold them in within the panel.

MONTY: I wrote the meeting between Weasel and Verity about five different ways, but in the end I played it cool.

I love the way she looks at him when he sits down. There's some stuff about quantum physics, which is one of the new creative ideas Monty is using to increase his power. It all centers on how ideas are formed, and the role creativity plays.

As a writer, I've a natural interest in generating ideas, so I've researched it all quite deeply: synaptic plasticity, neurotransmission, the biology and science of freeing up different neurons to connect together in unusual ways. That's what happens when you have original thoughts.

The techniques they use on the Island to try and increase their creativity and power are all based on real experiments: Gorges and Beck using magnetic field generators

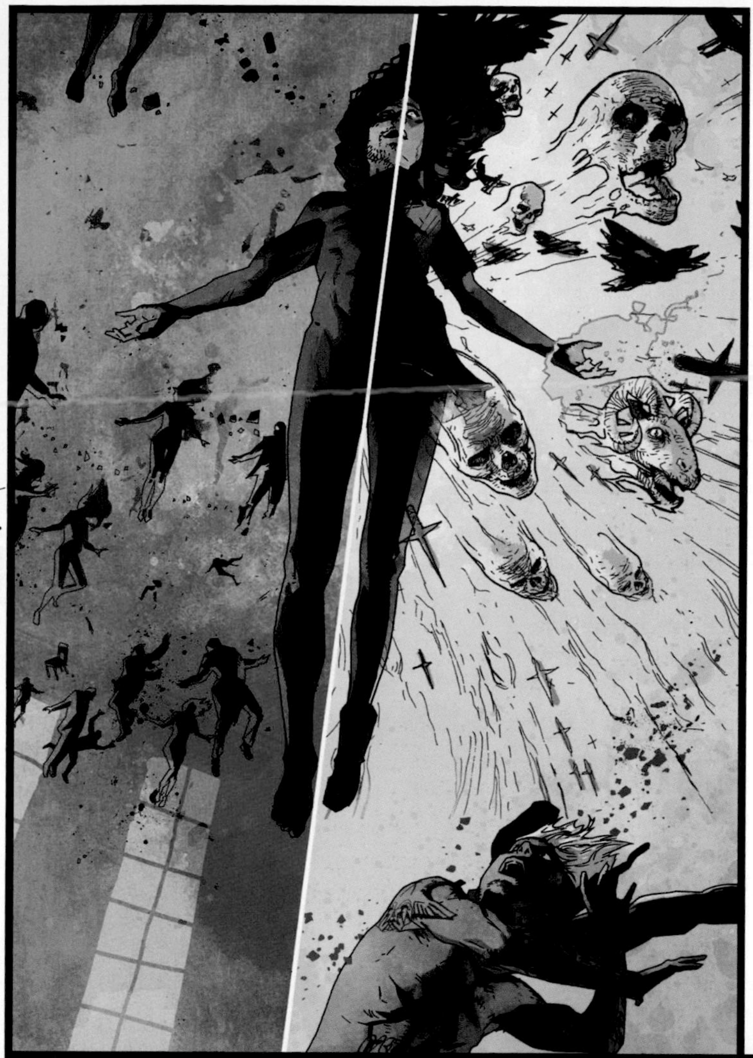

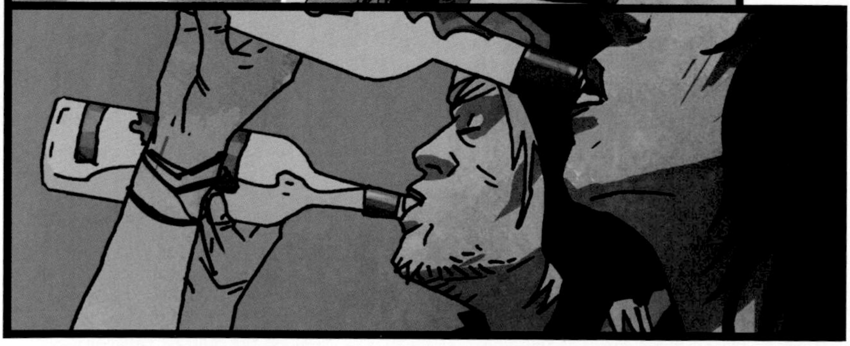

and synchro-energisers to entrain the brain or change states of consciousness, and Oscar Janiger's experiments with artists taking LSD in the Fifties.

Naturally we try to make the information-dump as entertaining as possible. It basically says the more creative you are, the more your abilities will increase, which is a pretty exciting concept for superpowers. You need to understand that for the rest of the comic to work.

MIKE: It was fun to draw that last panel. Using a dip pen to draw all the art manifestations.

MONTY: I'm very lucky to have some of the original art from this scene on my wall. It's a quintessential *Death Sentence* moment.

I'm a big vodka enthusiast, though I only drink it in the right way and at the right time, when it enhances rather than detracts from my creativity, so I had to put that in. And tattoos are the obvious thing Verity and Weasel have in common, so that's how they bond.

Moving tattoos aren't an original notion, but it's where a lot of Verity's creativity is focused, so it seemed a logical extension of how her manipulation of the electomagnetic spectrum would develop. Also, practically, we don't have space for them to start talking about something else before her powers trigger.

Finally, we draw the analogy between Verity and Monty on the final page, though of course Monty achieves his breakthrough without a team of scientists showing him what to do. Verity's not as creative as he is, so she's less powerful.

A lot of Monty's creativity comes from his arrogance, where Verity has more doubts. She more rounded, more realistic. Believing you're brilliant, even when you're not, is a real boon to creativity.

If you don't have the hope and expectation that what you're doing is worthwhile, then it's very difficult to be creative.

Which brings us to the final quote from Charles Sawyer: *"Of all the forces that make for a better world, none is so indispensable, none so powerful, as hope."* That neatly answers Monty's opening question from panel one. Hope is the key to creativity and life, a core tenet of the book.

CHAPTER 5

Page 1 & 2: The US-led task force assembles

MONTY: We're just raising the stakes here. We've seen this kind of thing play out on the news, with Iraq and so forth. I think it's a credible escalation, though lately the US has preferred to go round the UN and not through it.

Technically these two pages mean that everything that follows feels a lot more exciting than it otherwise would.

Page 3 & 4 Weasel hones his skills

MONTY: I love training scenes in films.

MIKE: Training scenes are the best!

MONTY: Like *The Dirty Dozen* or whatever.

MIKE: Or Yoda in *Empire*.

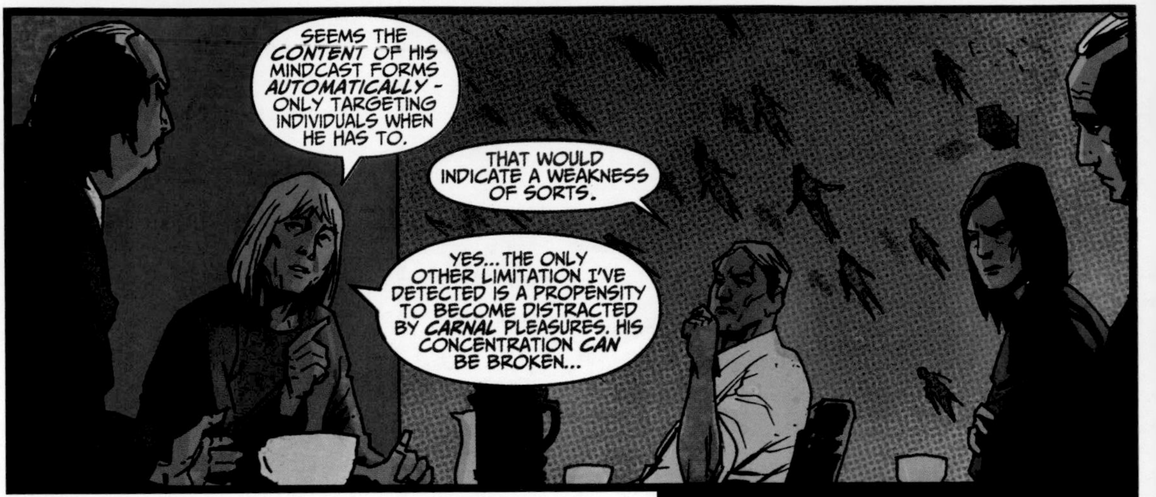
SEEMS THE CONTENT OF HIS MINDCAST FORMS AUTOMATICALLY - ONLY TARGETING INDIVIDUALS WHEN HE HAS TO.
THAT WOULD INDICATE A WEAKNESS OF SORTS.
YES...THE ONLY OTHER LIMITATION I'VE DETECTED IS A PROPENSITY TO BECOME DISTRACTED BY CARNAL PLEASURES. HIS CONCENTRATION CAN BE BROKEN...

MONTY: It's a really cool thing to do, and it also generates a sense of suspense as to what kind of battle's about to go down.

This both celebrates and undercuts the tradition in a humorous way. But it also tells you more about the virus, and the relationship between Weasel and the medical staff on the Island.

I love the wind here, and the moody landscapes and clouds, it totally evokes being in that part of the world.

MIKE: One of my favourite comics is *Lone Wolf and Cub*. It always places the figures in the landscape in a really satisfying way. It's really cool when the landscape and characters convince to make a complete world.

Page 5 & 7: Verity's depressed

MONTY: One reason for this scene is that you can't have the characters be too powerful, because it's boring. That's why all the excitement left the *Matrix* trilogy when the first film ended: Neo became too powerful. And I also felt if the sadness of Verity's imminent demise didn't overwhelm her at some point, she wouldn't be human. And we learn a lot more about her too. I love all her facial expressions – they brilliantly evoke the right mood here.

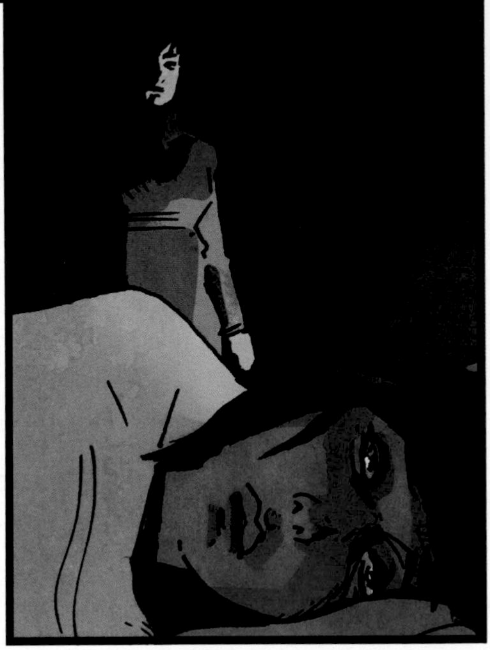

MIKE: I just acted it out. It comes from within. I didn't take photos or look at myself in the mirror or anything.

Page 8: Monty's news conference

MONTY: As we're getting to the end, it's time to provide a few more explicit answers, otherwise readers might lose confidence that this story amounts to anything at all. We have a bit of fun here with Monty teasing the news reader that he's scaring all the nations of the world into giving peace a chance, but that's just a joke. I'm not knocking *Watchmen* in any way. I think in that book, the plot device works brilliantly. But this is a different type of story.

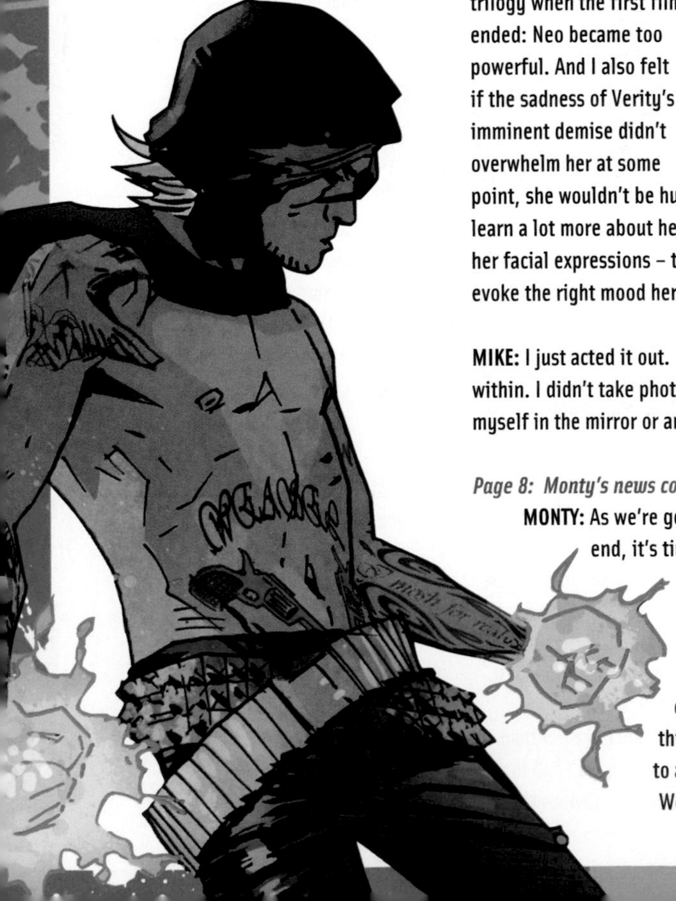

I guess the contrast between Ozymandias's noble goal and Monty's selfish goals speaks to the changes in the zeitgeist since the eighties – and reinforces one of the points we're making about modern society.

MIKE: I just thought it was funny.

MONTY: Yeah, that too.

Page 9 & 11: A plan to take down Monty

MONTY: Here you have the head of the

DNS, Dr. Lunn, the Military, and the government all together for the first time – all figuring out how to take down Monty. As a result, a few juicy details arise about the backstory to all this, and how Monty's powers work.

All these people are from different departments, with different agendas, so I

ARGHH! WAS THAT STRICTLY *NECESSARY*, SIRE?

YES IT *FUCKING WAS!* I'VE NO TIME FOR VIRALLY ENHANCED *AIRHEADS* WITH NO RESPECT FOR MY *PERSONAL SPACE*.

SPLTCHH

felt there'd be a lot of conflict on how to proceed. That's more realistic and punchy than the villains working to a tight plan, which is what you generally see.

This is one of the first scenes I wrote the dialogue for in the whole comic, and it's probably the most rewritten scene in the comic, which is maybe why it's not my favourite scene. It's also really difficult for you to draw a scene like this, much more than people realize, because you have to get everyone in the right place for the dialogue to flow, while maintaining drama and atmosphere

MIKE: Yeah…

MONTY: It's the last scene of its type in the comic, and sets up most of what you need to know for the climax.

Page 12 & 13: Weasel powers up
MONTY: This is simply a continuation of Weasel's training, to create a sense of anticipation, and it also elaborates on how they control his phasing and acid discharge through the drugs they're administering.

MIKE: I changed the lighting again. It's a different time, more portentous. I wanted to spend longer on throwing the acid balls too: eight panels, rather than four.

MONTY: Yeah, we talked about that at the time. I saw your point, but I just felt the quick-fire rhythm to the swearing was funnier.

Page 14 to 16: Monty powers up
MONTY: The main characters are getting ready to throw down, and we show how Monty's powers are developing exponentially, due to his incredible creativity and confidence.

He's not just influencing these people across London; he's drawing strength from the creative ideas in their minds – though the less creative or immature minds are useless to him.

We also see the stark horror of his worldview graphically illustrated, as opposed to the glib sheen he conjures when he wants something.

Monty's story illustrates the logical progression of completely freeing

yourself from any sense of peer review. He considers himself so superior at this point that he loses all regard for other people's opinions or interests.

MIKE: You see that on *Graham Norton* sometimes! You see how people have lost their connection to other people and the real world.

MONTY: Celebrities tend to see themselves as separate, or above it all. Even though it can be annoying at times, our concern for how other people regard us is crucial to our success as a species, in terms of forming societies that function efficiently for the collective good.

Monty has moved beyond that, with catastrophic results. The Big Ben business simply forms a neat bookend.

Page 17: Verity agrees to help
MONTY: In an ideal world, I'd have made this scene a little longer. But it was my first time plotting a comic book series and in my initial blueprint I overestimated how much space there'd be at this point in the story. It works fine, though – it's just not the emotional moment it could've been. There's simply no time.

HATE'S SOMETHING I'VE NEVER GIVEN *INTO* BEFORE. SHOULD SPARK A FEW *FRESH* IDEAS!

FUCK – YEAH! LETS ROLL WITH *HATE*…SEE WHERE THAT *LEADS*…

KRSMSSHH

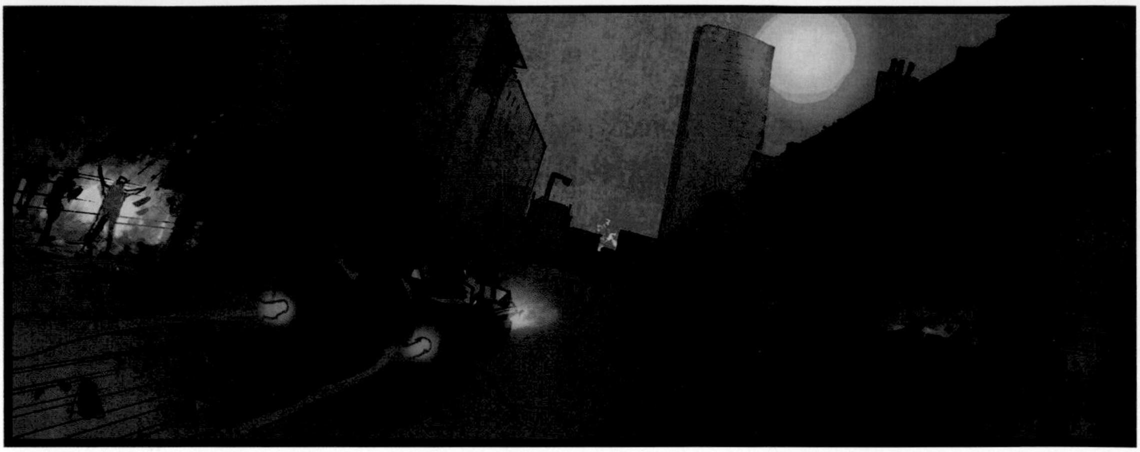

Page 18 to 19: Verity and Weasel fly to London

MONTY: I like the energy of this scene, it's got that core *Death Sentence* vibe, and it also tells you everything else you need to know for the climax. They're experimenting with hate as fuel for creativity here, and they come badly unstuck against Monty as a result. Our argument is that hope is much more powerful than hate, for life and for art.

MIKE: I remember being unsure about the size of the helicopters; how everything would fit.

MONTY: Yeah, I took some stuff out from the interior because of your feedback.

Page 20 to 22: Verity and Weasel drive into London

MONTY: Verity and Weasel are the only people who can resist Monty's mental influence at this point. We get a little foreshadowing of the government's duplicity from the dialogue with the soldiers, and how doomed our heroes are.

I like the way Verity takes the lead throughout; she's the hero. My view is that women are generally a lot more capable than men, who're prone to fuck around with more childish and selfish pursuits in the face of anything emotionally profound occurring. Men tend to prefer binary, practical goals. This is illustrated by Weasel's behavior in the jeep, as the bombs start flying. It's important to know that he hasn't abandoned his musical ambitions, too.

And then Monty looms over them – and it all kicks off!!

CHAPTER 6

MONTY: And so to the finale, which is thirty pages long. Practically and financially, making Chapter Six thirty pages was really problematic, but it was the best thing for the story, so it had to be done.

I didn't want to come this far and fuck up the ending. I had the sequence of the final scenes worked out from before I started writing Chapter One, though of course because I'd never written a comic book before, I could only take my best guess at how much story would fit into each issue.

But I learnt a lot from writing this series, and everything I've written since fits very neatly into a twenty-two page format. In this case, I didn't want to compromise on quality, so we added the extra pages rather than cut or change the crucial elements

MIKE: It was bad luck that I was busy with something else by then. So when you said we'd be adding another eight pages... It was another two or three weeks' work, and I was already scheduled to the max.

MONTY: So how did you do it?

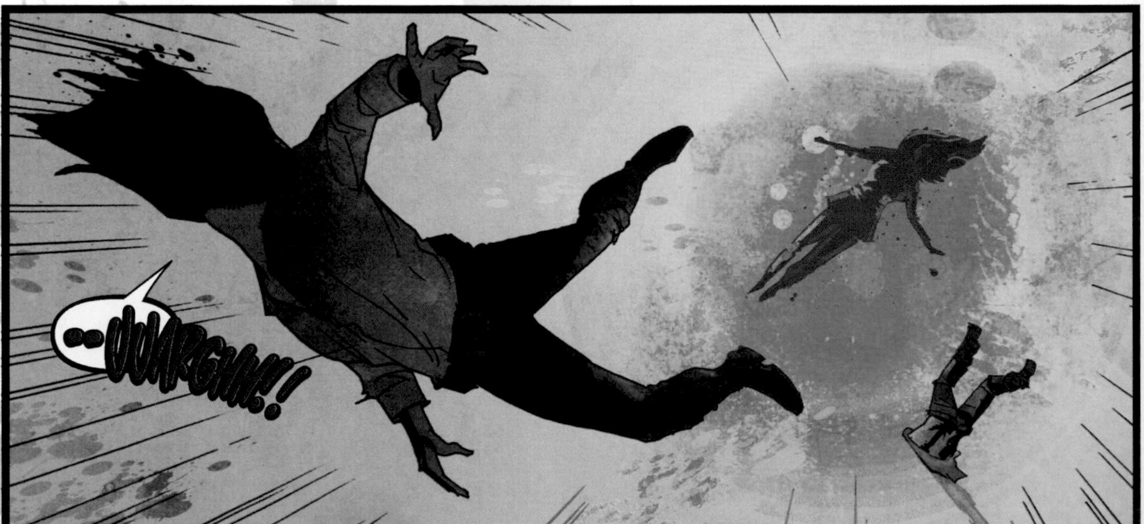
..UUARGHH!!

altruism is a dominant survival trait in terms of evolution, which was in my mind here. Monty embodies the opposite view.

And practically, this scene sets Monty up to take on the US task force. Your art really went up a notch here, I think. I love all the apocalyptic coloring.

MIKE: I just wanted it to look cataclysmic. Basically, from the end of chapter four, the closer you get to Monty, the redder everything gets.

I love the old movie effects where the clouds would start churning: those pre-CGI cloud effects, like in *Ghostbusters*. I think they did them in a petri dish or something.

Page 5 to 10: Weasel and Verity recuperate, as Monty approaches the fleet
MONTY: Combat brings Weasel and Verity closer together, and it has emotional and physical consequences that hopefully make it more exciting than your average fight.

Weasel deliberately appears kind of heroic at some points here. But he's just trying to survive. It seems like he's looking out for Verity, like he's being thoughtful, but he's just hoping to get his end away.

MIKE: He has conflicted impulses. As all addicts do, I suppose

MONTY: The great joy of his character is you never know what he's going to do next, which makes for compelling drama, It's important that Verity starts to rely upon him practically and emotionally. That makes his later betrayal all the more hurtful. When they hole up to lick their wounds, Weasel takes comfort in drugs, and Verity sex.

MIKE: That'll be my secret.

MONTY: Time machine?

MIKE: I just worked every Sunday for three months.

MONTY: 'Just,' he says! Incredible commitment. The artwork doesn't look rushed or tired at all, either.

MIKE: If the story hadn't ended like this it would have been a real anti-climax. I just wanted to draw it all properly, and to do it justice.

Page 1 to 4: Weasel and Verity vs. Monty
MONTY: So the crucial thing I found with the script was the emotional resonance of the ending was much more powerful if they face each other twice.

It's much more dramatic at the end if they all know each other, and Monty's already kicked their arse once. It makes Verity's behavior much more heroic and affecting, to my mind at least.

You see that Monty is completely out of their class in terms of his creativity and power, though it's his narcissistic selfishness that proves his undoing.

Selfish Gene theory explains how

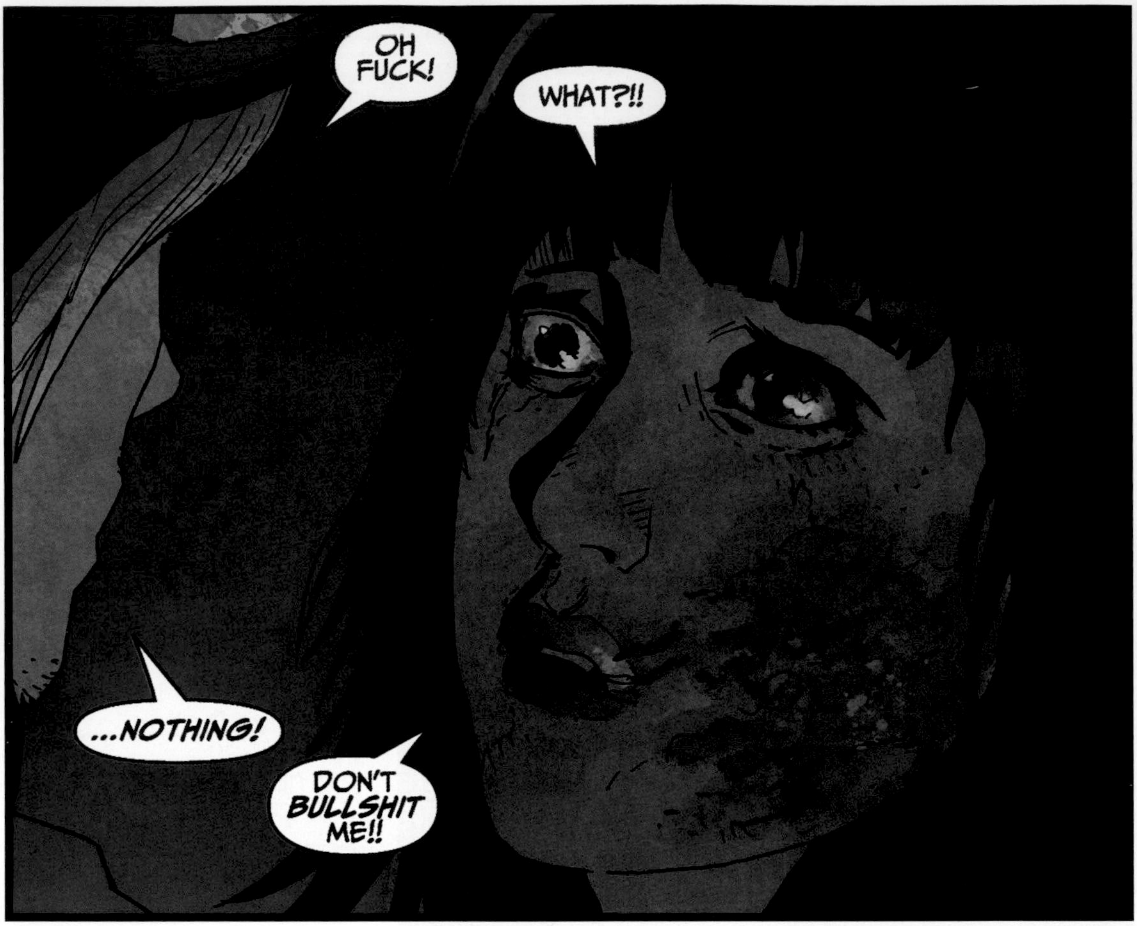
OH FUCK!
WHAT?!!
...NOTHING!
DON'T BULLSHIT ME!!

And during that physical intimacy she has a revelation – a new idea – that makes her more powerful later: the idea that sex is the key to immortality for your genes, but not for you personally; that our genes are the dominant life form on the planet, witlessly engineering this maddening and tortuous dance we call life, purely because

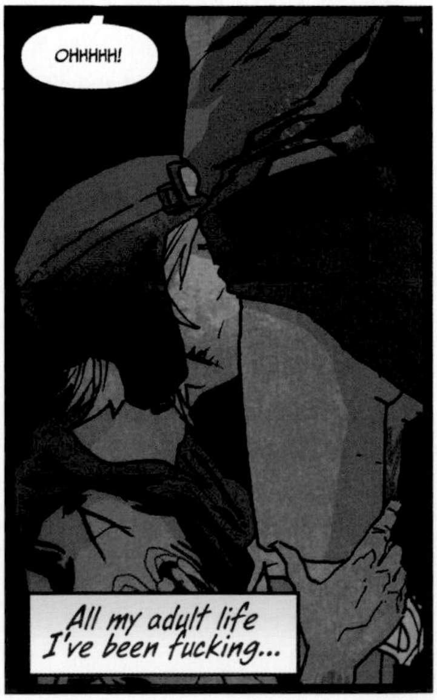
OHHHHH!
All my adult life I've been fucking...

it happens to ensure they pass on the genetic information they carry.

If you look at evolution from the perspective of the gene, rather than the species or human being, it makes a lot more sense. I'm very happy with the physical side of the sex scene too, which could easily be cheesy or naff. Was it fun to draw?

MIKE: Not especially. A sex scene is the same as drawing anything, really.

MONTY: You didn't put on some Barry White and oil yourself up?

MIKE: I do like to get in the mood, emotionally. I lit some candles...

I remember I wanted to crop the panels so the captions existed outside the panels, so the panels would be little held moments for Verity. But the letterer cut the captions into the panels. Not quite what I imagined, but it seems to work. It's easier to do if you sort out the lettering yourself, which is what Frank Miller does.

Page 11 to 13 Weasel backs out

MONTY: This is the ultimate betrayal: just when Verity needs Weasel most, just when they seemed to be close. I love the way you did this scene, and the strength of the punch.

MIKE: It was fun drawing that punch.

MONTY: He really deserves it. She's completely on her own now – which makes everything she does now much more impressive. She's always been the hero of the story, and this just cements that.

You should hate Weasel at this point, just like Verity does. You actually made her look more explicitly heroic than I was expecting, at the end there. I wanted her to look more upset and lost. But she looks really cool and determined. I quite like it though.

Page 14 to 16: Monty attacks the fleet

MONTY: This is one of the first scenes I wrote all the dialogue for.

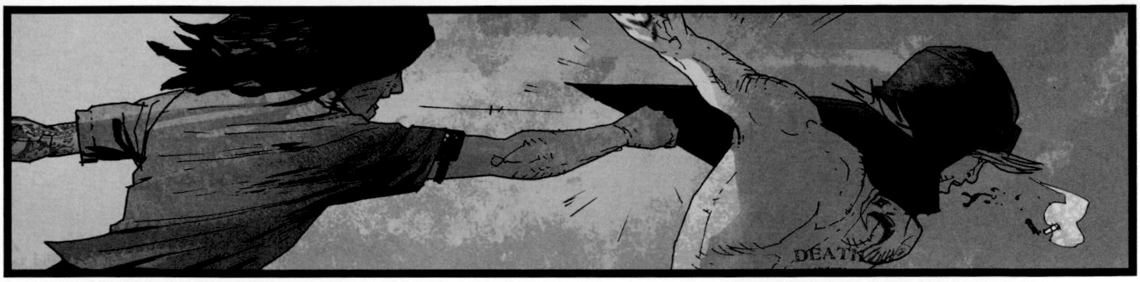
DEATH

MIKE: It was also one of the first scenes I drew in issue six.

MONTY: I've got a mate in the Navy and it was influenced by a few of his stories.

MIKE: There are very few women in the Navy, I notice.

MONTY: I just wanted to do something a bit more entertaining than Monty appearing and blowing stuff up.

Which is why we get the mind control and the giant reveal with the wave, which you drew wonderfully. It's one of those things that are easy to write but hard to draw:

"The giant wave towers over the fleet of battleships." Two seconds to script; two days to render. That's the joy of being a writer.

Page 17 to 18: Obama considers his response

MONTY: So here we foreshadow what really going on with the D-bomb, as America considers their response to their naval defeat.

We started off with a girl facing a doctor in a room, and we've basically been escalating the scale of the physical and spiritual threats with every subsequent scene. Hopefully it creates a sense of mounting excitement.

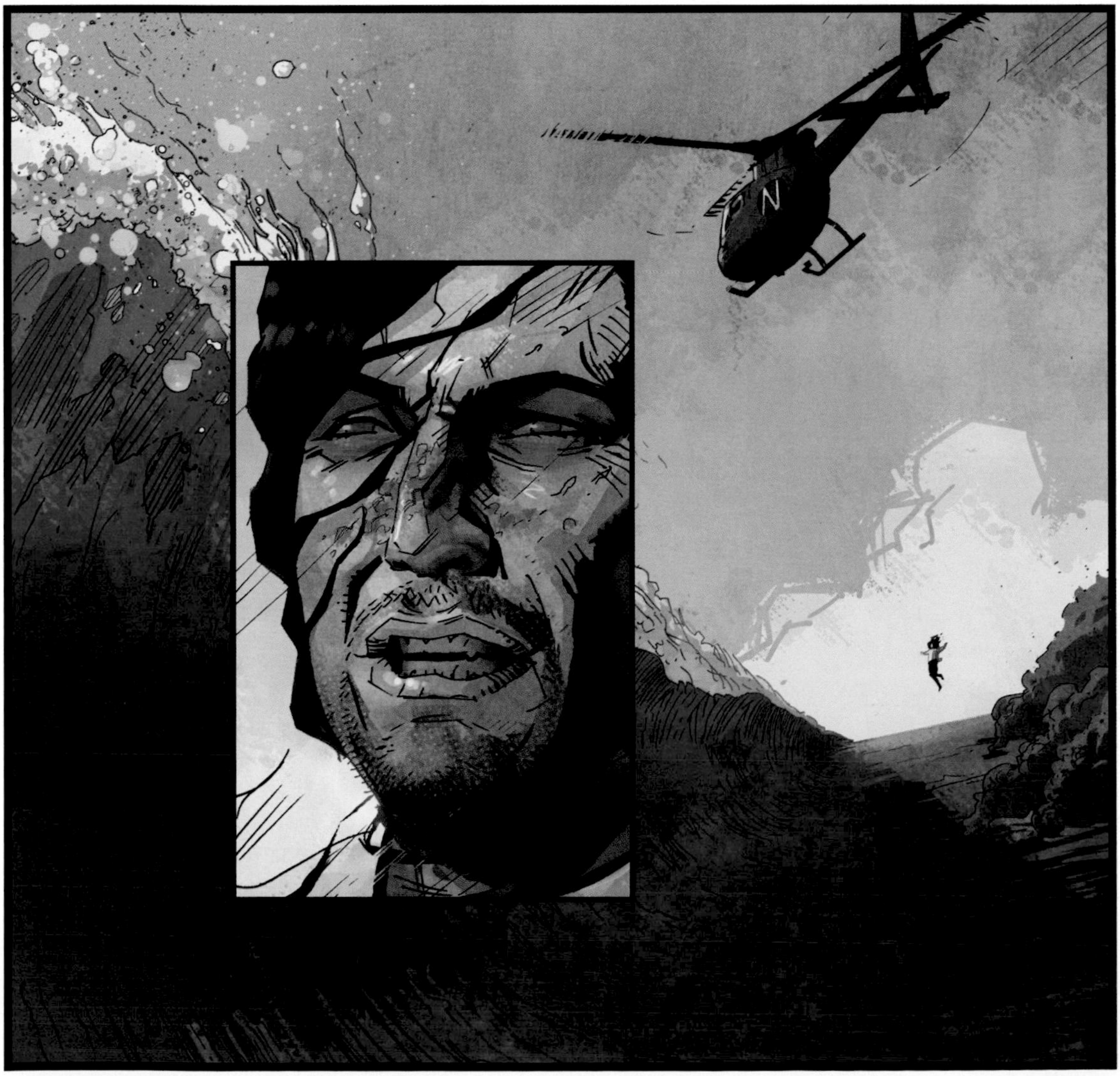
N

Page 19: Verity won't back down

MONTY: It's that escalation that makes this page works so well, for me at least. Verity alone and abandoned, staring into the abyss, refusing to give in, still doing the right thing no matter what. That's heroism. You really rose to the challenge. It's a fantastic page of artwork.

MIKE: Yeah, well – standing on a rooftop always makes you look heroic. That's what free runners are up to. They know the score.

But it's a positive, life-affirming route she's on, that'll probably end in her death. So it's appropriate here.

MONTY: I really did want her to appear very heroic here. She looks awesome!

MIKE: It's the Otomo influence. The way he articulates his character's will through their eyes, these ocular performances. It works very well, in the right context.

MONTY: Ha-ha! True. He overdoes it sometimes though, I think. That's what I'm taking the piss out of in that Verity line: *"Sweating and staring like that just makes you look like a furtive pervert!"*.

Though it's born of affection, teasing something you love. Like the *Watchmen* thing.

Page 20 & 21: Weasel finds his son

MONTY: The concept of someone massacring a million people with their mind is hard to grasp emotionally, but by focusing on one life we hopefully bring

home the full horror of what Monty's done.

Then we pull back to imply the wider picture across the city. It's the only thing that could possibly happen to let you care a jot about Weasel, given what he just did to Verity. And it's the only thing that would credibly convince him to change his priorities. And it's very moving and sad, a powerful moment of tragedy.

But it's a lot more upsetting when it's drawn than when it's an idea in your head. Having a child myself it's very much the worst thing I can think of, emotionally speaking.

MIKE: It's harrowing. But I think we can all relate to Weasel, in that we've all found it hard to do the right thing at times. So we show him at his worst, yet no matter how bad things get, he might still be able to do the right thing, given the opportunity.

MONTY: And we don't make it clear he's had a change of heart. It's just set up so that when he does pop up at the end it's an awesome moment that makes perfect sense.

MIKE: That's it. You don't need to telegraph it.

Page 22 to 30: The End.

MONTY: So: the final scene, the longest scene by far, I think.

MIKE: This was really fun to draw. The scale of it is mental, looking down from space and so on. The rhythm is really fast, too.

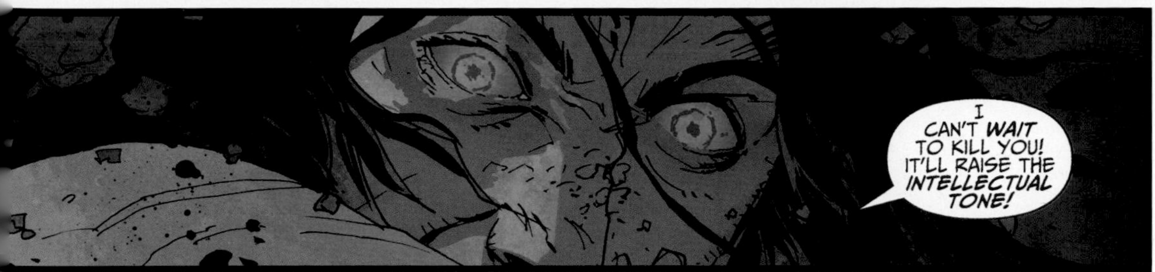
I CAN'T *WAIT* TO KILL YOU! IT'LL RAISE THE *INTELLECTUAL* TONE!

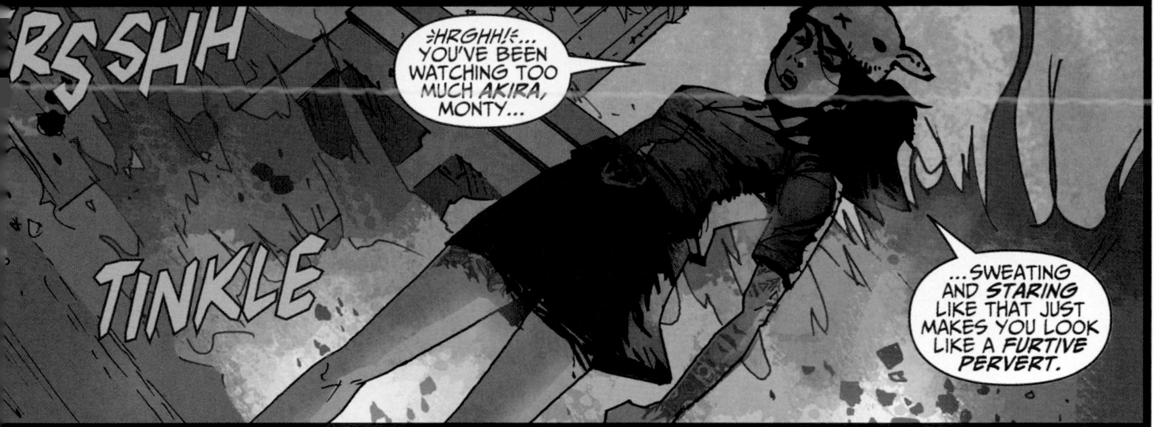
RSSHH
HRGHH!... YOU'VE BEEN WATCHING TOO MUCH *AKIRA,* MONTY...
TINKLE
...SWEATING AND *STARING* LIKE THAT JUST MAKES YOU LOOK LIKE A *FURTIVE PERVERT.*

MONTY: True, but in my mind there's a lot of time passing between some of the panels.

There's a lot of smoke and mirrors, in terms of how it would practically work and how we cut it all together for dramatic purposes.

We don't show the boring things, like the satellite coming down low enough into the atmosphere to fire the missile.

It's like editing a video or something, just showing snapshots of key moments to make it as exciting as possible. It gives it an epic feel, and that seemed to inspire you to do some really incredible artwork. I got tingles when I saw the pages.

MIKE: Yeah, I was excited. *Death Sentence* always moves in a very fast way, but there are also a few more cinematic moments here which were fun to handle.

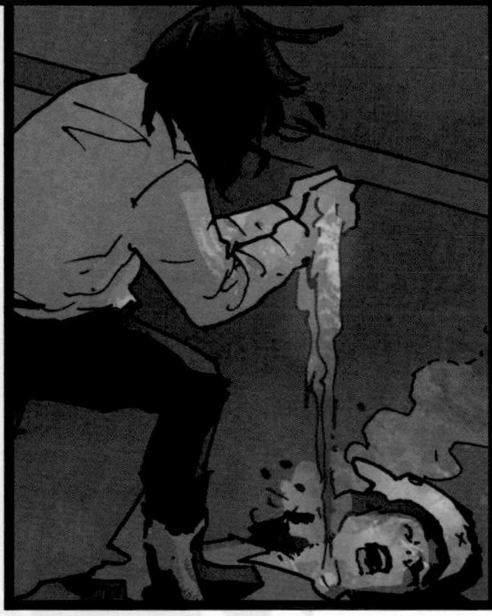

MONTY: I had the core of this scene pretty much written from before I finished Chapter 1, in terms of timing and dialogue. I added bits to it as I went through each script, and rewrote it a few times. At one point I went off in a slightly different direction, but then came back to the original flow we see here.

Nine times out of ten I find my first pass is the best pass. It's generally a matter of keeping the verve and spark from that pass, while filling in all the gaps and panel descriptions.

I added the art manifestations and repeating captions about halfway in, around Chapter Three or Four, I think. In my mind the manifestations were always a radically different style to the comic art, like a Chagall painting or hip hop graffiti over the page, but imagination is one thing and actually making it all work is another.

You did a much better job than I would've done .

MIKE: In some ways the manifestations are a bit underplayed. I dunno.

MONTY: Nah, it's really well handled. It's cohesive. Obviously the captions have a more potent meaning now we've come full circle.

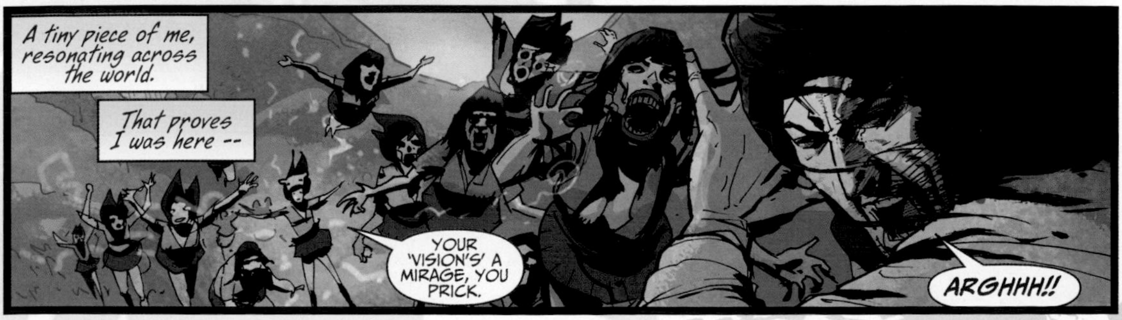
A tiny piece of me, resonating across the world.
That proves I was here --
YOUR 'VISION'S' A MIRAGE, YOU PRICK.
ARGHHH!!

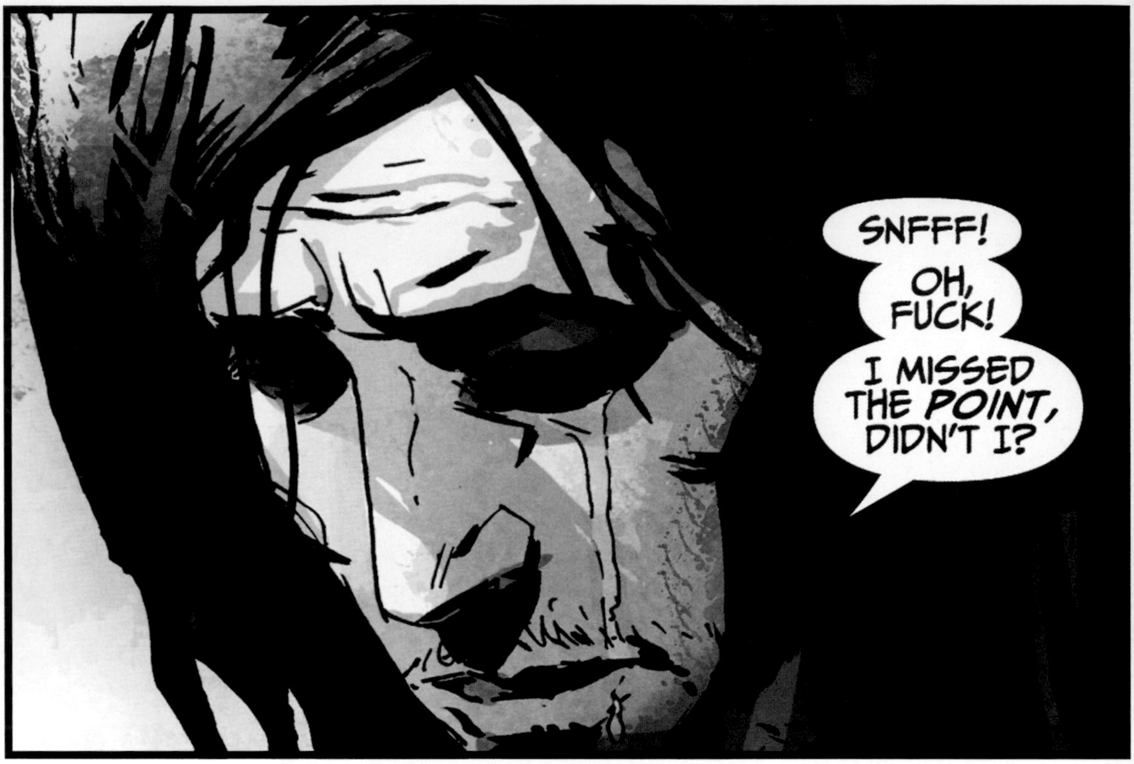
SNFFF!
OH, FUCK!
I MISSED THE *POINT*, DIDN'T I?

I can't talk about everything that's going on here because it has ramifications for the next book.

I'll just say there's a lot you can read in to a number of these panels, and you're probably right.

I'm very happy with the final page, which is the most explicit celebration of Selfish Gene theory thus far. The individual is pretty irrelevant to genes – they're simply useful and very expendable containers for genetic code.

It's not about survival of the species either, it's about the survival of the information within our genes.

That might seem a very depressing thought, until you consider that it frees us to define our own life as we wish!

Art is life, and life can be art.

That's pretty much how to view the statement on the final page. I've always loved books that entertain you, but also say something about the world.

We aspired to do both, though whether we succeeded or not is hard to say.

MIKE: It was fun trying though.

MONTY: It was. It's definitely the thing I'm most proud of, creatively.

I hope people enjoyed it. And I hope we get to do it again!

MONTY & MIKE, 2014 ■

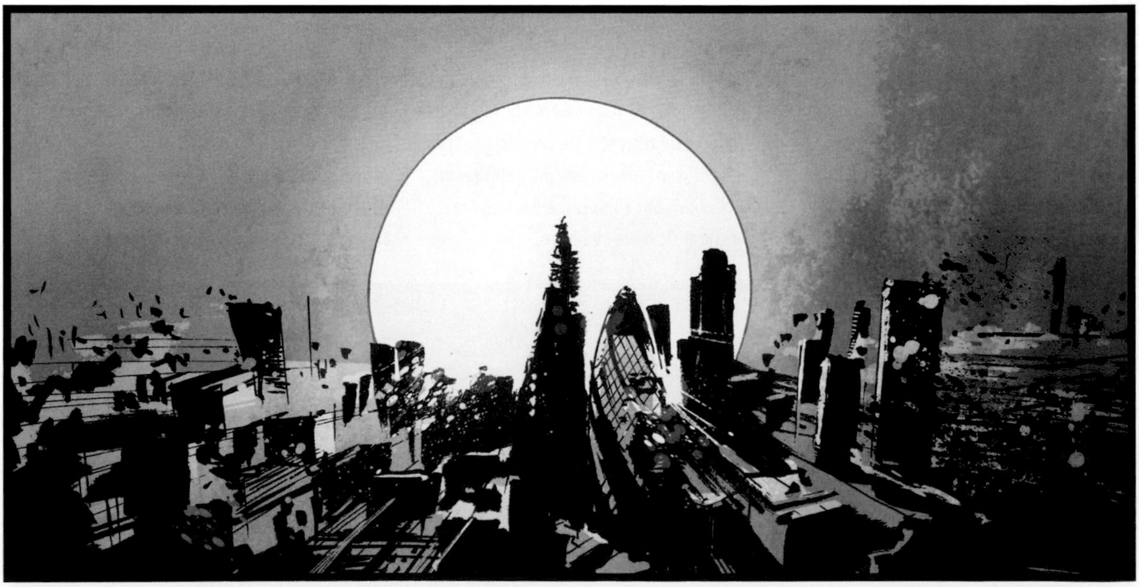

DEATH SENTENCE BIOGRAPHIES

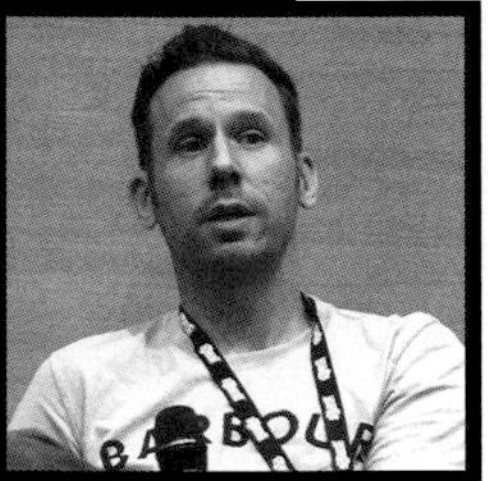

Photo © Jeremy Briggs

MONTY NERO

Monty writes and creates artwork for computer games (*SSX, Need for Speed*) and comics (Titan, Marvel, Vertigo, 2000AD). His agent for written work is James Wills at Watson, Little Ltd. He lives happily in Dundee, Scotland, with his wife and young daughter. You can find him on Twitter @ montynero and at www.montynero.com.

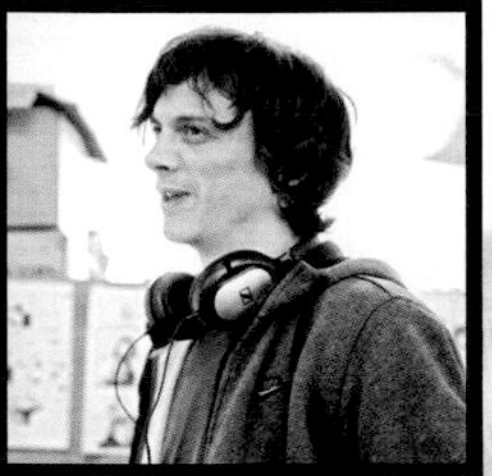

MIKE DOWLING

Mike Dowling lives with his family in Kent. As well as *Death Sentence*, he has worked on stories for 2000AD and Vertigo.

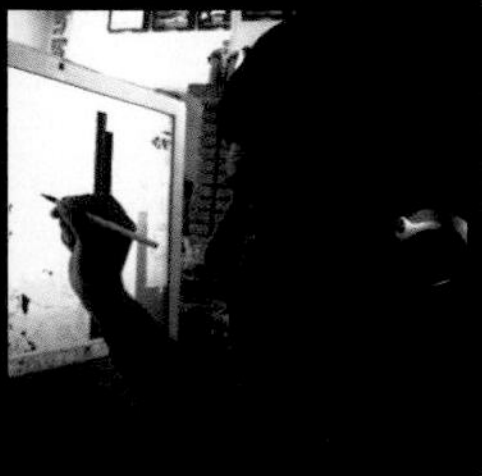

JIMMY BETANCOURT

Jimmy Betancourt has been lettering comics for the award-winning studio Comicraft for 12 years, proudly serving as part of Comicraft founder Richard Starkings' revolutionary army of fontmeisters and designers. When not showing off his skills as 'fastest letterer in the west' or watching the Lakers game, he's enjoying his time with his daughter Delaila in their home sweet home of Los Angeles.

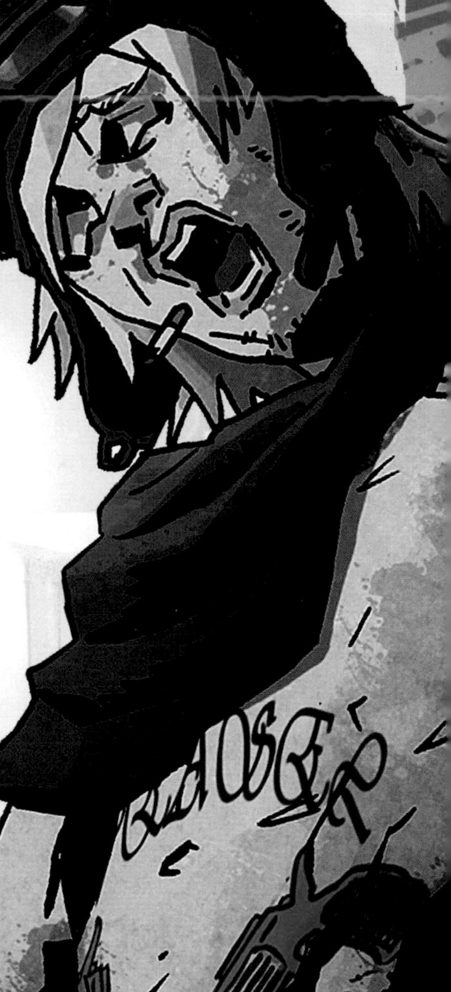

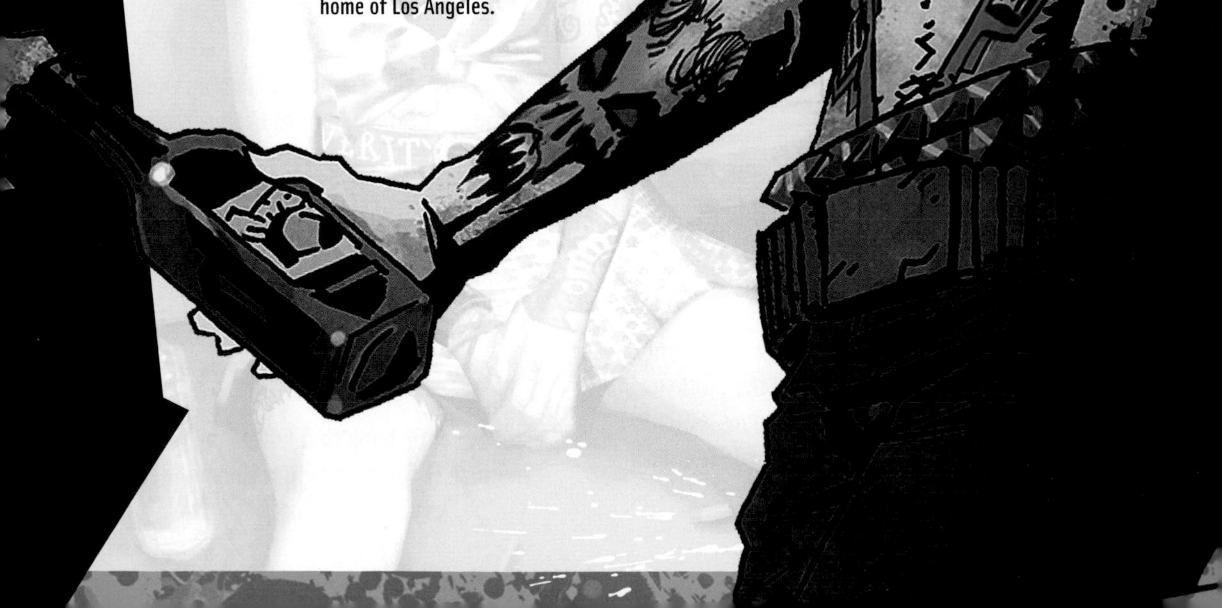

PRAISE FOR

"BRILLIANT. Genuinely original."
Mark Millar (Kick-Ass, Civil War)

"A striking new voice in the superhero genre."
Comic Book Resources

"Like only the best parts of *Watchmen*, like all your favourite episodes of *Doctor Who*—a social analysis that exceeds the medium of comics, easily the equal of Dostoyevsky or Dickens."
PopMatters

"A brilliantly original concept."
Newsarama

"A smart, raw and relevant spin on the superhero genre."
MTV Geek

"It's the AIDS epidemic as an *X-Men* book... and it's brilliant. One of the best damn titles currently being published. If this was a monthly book I don't think I'd ever need to read the *X-Men* again."
Comic Bastards

"Nasty, dirty and oh-so-wonderfully-wrong – and a hell of a lot of fun."
Comics Bulletin

"An edgy, moody feel, with plenty of mystery and fear in the air."
Danica Davidson, CNN, Los Angeles Times

"As over-the-edgy as it gets. This is the stuff I want!"
Broken Frontier

"For those who like high powered superhero action but dislike how 'safe' the plots are, this is a series which offers more realistic characters - warts and all. *Death Sentence* isn't to be ignored."
Examiner.com

"After five 10/10 scores and one 11/10, this run of *Death Sentence* will probably not be bettered. Montynero has managed to get inside my mind and write a comic just for me."
The Cult Den

"One of the massive success stories from the recently launched Titan Comics."
SFX

"Highly original with great dialogue!"
Comic Spectrum

"Unique and deserves your attention."
All-Comic

"Breaking new ground."
Digital Noob

"You've got six months to live, what would you do? I'd say, read this book!"
SciFiPulse

"A realistic, dark and gritty world. 9/10"
Geeks Unleashed

"If all of Titan Comics projects are of this quality, you're looking at a strong contender for publisher of the year."
Graphic Policy

"Go out, buy this comic, and spread the love around... but remember to use protection!"
Following The Nerd

"An awesome book."
Forces of Geek

"I love the premise and ideas."
Major Spoilers

"A stellar comic book that makes my job easy – because it comes highly recommended."
Unleash The Fanboy

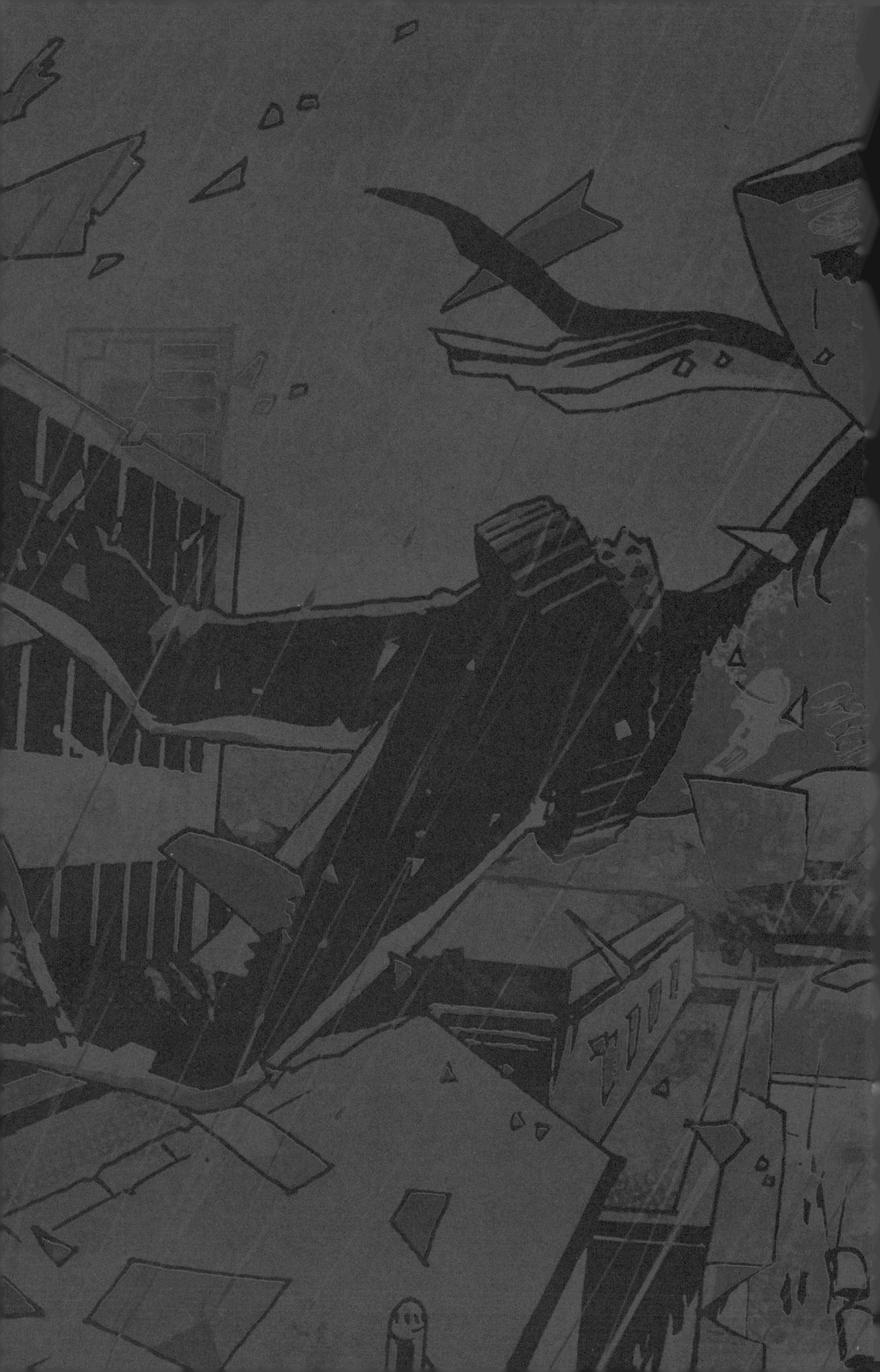